W9-DDJ-113

4. Use a workshop approach. Just as students benefit from varied exercises, they profit from varied approaches to a skill. One way to cover a skill is to work through a chapter page by page, alternating between putting some of the material on the board and explaining or reading some of it aloud. When you get to a practice in a chapter, give students a couple of minutes to do the practice. When a majority of the class has finished the practice, call on someone to read the first question and answer it. If the person is right, say "Good job," and call on someone else to read the next time. If the person is wrong, say something like "Does anyone have a different answer?" This can lead to a discussion where you can see if students are catching on and can provide a way for you to move them in the right direction.

You should feel confident about having students read a sentence or so out loud. Even if they have limited reading skills, a sentence or two will not cause them undue anxiety or embarrassment. On the other hand, reading an entire paragraph may be too much for some students. It is best to call on volunteers for paragraphs, or to read them aloud yourself. Or, if there are time constraints, have students read the paragraph silently and focus on students reading aloud the questions that follow paragraphs.

5. Use a small group approach at times. When you get to a review test, you may want to divide the class into groups of four and ask them to work together to do the answers for the test. Tell them that when they are done and everyone in the group agrees on the answers, a representative from the group should come to the board and write down the group's answers. Say, "Let's see which is the first group to answer all the questions correctly."

Put a grid such as this one on the board:

	1	2	3	4	5
Ralph's Group					
Elena's Group					
Hassan's Group					
Nguyen's Group					

Students will enjoy the competition, and peer pressure will keep everyone attentive and involved. When all of the groups have finished, you have a nice visual where students can see where they agree and where they disagree. You can then focus discussion on answers on which groups disagree.

6. Use a pairs approach at times. Having two students work together on questions is another way to energize students and help them teach one another. When an exercise has been completed by the majority of the class, go over the material by having one student in each pair read a question and the other student read the answer.

7. Use a one-on-one approach at times. If your class is small, have students work on their own on a given chapter, reading the explanations and doing the activities. Call students up to your desk individually to check their answers and to confer on the skill. Make the conference short—five minutes per student is enough time. Students really benefit from the individualized, personal contact.

8. Evaluate frequently. Students have been conditioned to work hard on tests. Take advantage of this conditioning by giving a lot of tests. The mastery tests in Part II of the book will give students a chance to see that they are learning the material and will show them that they are capable of success. The tests are also clear signals to students who are *not* learning the skills. Note that there are over sixty tear-out mastery tests in the book and seventy more tests in the *Instructor's Manual and Test Bank* ready to duplicate.

When you grade a test, try to include some praise or encouragement for each student. A personal comment such as "Good job, Veronica" or "Well done, Tomas" does wonders for students' self-esteem.

9. For variety, make some tests count and some not. When it is time to do a test, have students put their names on it and tell them that you may or not count the test. The fact that you may count the test will ensure that students give their full effort. At times, don't collect the test, but simply go over it in class. Doing so will help to provide immediate feedback to students.

When tests do count, have students exchange papers so they are grading someone else's. The best way to do this is to collect the papers and distribute them to students in other parts of the room. (Some students resist marking an answer as wrong on a paper belonging to the person sitting next to them.) Have class members read and answer the questions. Afterwards, you can give another mastery test that will count as a grade.

10. Require some writing at the end of each class. To help students integrate what they have learned in a given class, have them do a writing assignment in the last ten minutes of the class. One good summarizing activity is to have students write a letter to a missing classmate, telling him or her what was learned in the class. Have them give you the letters before they leave, and tell them you will read them all and then pass them on to the missing student. Another exercise is to have students read one of the reading selections that ends each chapter, then choose a "Writing Activity" that follows each of the reading selections in the book. Many of these activities involve writing a paragraph that serves as a response to the reading selection. Students should turn this in to you before they leave.

These activities will help make your classroom alive and will turn learning into an active process. I think you will find them rewarding, and I encourage you to try them out. Feel free to write me, care of Townsend Press, to tell me how they work, or to suggest other activities.

Bill Broderick

GROUNDWORK FOR COLLEGE READING

SECOND EDITION

BILL BRODERICK

CERRITOS COLLEGE

TOWNSEND PRESS   Marlton, NJ 08053

Books in the Townsend Press Reading Series:

GROUNDWORK FOR COLLEGE READING
KEYS TO BETTER COLLEGE READING
TEN STEPS TO BUILDING COLLEGE READING SKILLS, FORM A
TEN STEPS TO BUILDING COLLEGE READING SKILLS, FORM B
TEN STEPS TO IMPROVING COLLEGE READING SKILLS
IMPROVING READING COMPREHENSION SKILLS
TEN STEPS TO ADVANCING COLLEGE READING SKILLS

Books in the Townsend Press Vocabulary Series:

GROUNDWORK FOR A BETTER VOCABULARY
BUILDING VOCABULARY SKILLS
IMPROVING VOCABULARY SKILLS
ADVANCING VOCABULARY SKILLS
BUILDING VOCABULARY SKILLS, SHORT VERSION
IMPROVING VOCABULARY SKILLS, SHORT VERSION
ADVANCING VOCABULARY SKILLS, SHORT VERSION

Supplements Available for Most Books:

Instructor's Edition
Instructor's Manual, Test Bank and Computer Guide
Set of Computer Disks (IBM or Macintosh)

Copyright © 1996 by Townsend Press, Inc.
Printed in the United States of America
ISBN 0-944210-27-9

All rights reserved. No part of this work may be
reproduced in any form without permission in writing
from the publisher. Send requests to:
Townsend Press, Inc.
Pavilions at Greentree—408
Marlton, New Jersey 08053

Send book orders and requests for desk copies or supplements to:
Townsend Press
1038 Industrial Drive
West Berlin, New Jersey 08091

For even faster service, call us at our toll-free number:
1-800-772-6410

Or FAX your request to:
1-609-753-0649

ISBN 0-944210-27-9

Contents

PART III
Ten Reading Selections   357

Appendixes   451

Note: A reading selection concludes each of the ten chapters in Part I. Here are the titles, authors, and page numbers of these ten selections:

Preface to the Instructor

We all know that many of today's beginning college students do not have the reading skills needed to do effective work in their courses. For any one of a number of reasons, their background in reading is limited. At the same time, their concerns and interests are those of other college-aged students. They need, then, to develop their reading skills through the use of adult-level materials. A related problem, evident even in class discussions, is that they often lack the skills required to think consistently in a clear and analytic way.

The purpose of *Groundwork for College Reading*, Second Edition, is to develop effective reading *and* clear thinking. The book is organized in three main parts. It begins with ten chapters on word and reading skills that are widely recognized as forming the basis for sound comprehension. The first three chapters in Part I present essential word attack skills:

1 Phonics I: Consonants
2 Phonics II: Vowels
3 Phonics III: Syllables

The next two chapters develop two more important word skills:

4 Word Parts
5 Dictionary Use

Literal comprehension, the basic level of understanding, is then taught in the remaining five chapters in Part I:

6 Vocabulary in Context
7 Main Ideas
8 Supporting Details
9 Locations of Main Ideas
10 Transitions

In every chapter in Part I, the key aspects of a skill are explained and illustrated in a clear and simple way. Each skill is followed by a series of practices, and four review tests end each chapter. The last review test centers on a reading selection, so that students can apply the skill just learned to real-life reading material, including newspaper and magazine articles and book excerpts. Each selection is followed by word and comprehension questions that focus on the skill learned in the chapter and on skills from prior chapters. In addition, a *Mapping Activity* provides a visual diagram that helps students think carefully about the basic content of the selection. And two *Discussion Questions* and two *Writing Assignments* provide you with an opportunity to engage students in a variety of reading skills and to deepen their understanding of a selection. Taken together, the ten chapters supply students with the skills needed for a solid understanding of reading materials.

Part II is made up of six mastery tests for each of the ten skills and six combined-skills tests. These tests progress in difficulty, giving students the additional practice they may need for a thorough learning of each skill. The tests allow for easy grading and are designed to ensure that students think carefully before answering each question.

Part III consists of ten additional readings that will help improve both reading and thinking skills. Each reading is followed by a series of *Word Skills Questions* and *Reading Comprehension Questions* that ask students to apply the skills presented in Part I and reinforced in Part II. As with each selection in Part I, a *Mapping Activity*, two *Discussion Questions*, and two *Writing Assignments* are provided. All of the readings have been chosen not only for the clarity of the writing but also for their compelling content.

Important Features of the Book

- **Focus on the basics.** The book seeks to explain in a clear, step-by-step way the essential elements of each skill. Many examples are provided to ensure that students understand each point. In general, the focus is on teaching the skills, not just on explaining them and not just on testing them.

- **Frequent practice and feedback.** In the belief that progress is made largely through abundant practice and careful feedback, this book includes numerous activities. Students can get immediate feedback on the practice exercises in Part I by turning to the answer key in the back. The answers to the review tests in Part I, the mastery tests in Part II, and the readings in Part III are in the *Instructor's Edition* as well as in the *Instructor's Manual and Test Bank*.

    The limited answer key enables students to take an active role in their own learning. And they are likely to use the answer key in an honest and positive way if they know that they may be tested on the many activities and selections for which answers are not provided. (Answers not in the book can be easily copied from the *Instructor's Manual and Test Bank* and handed out at your discretion.)

- **High interest level.** Uninteresting readings and exercises work against learning. The reading selections in this book have been chosen not only for the appropriateness of their reading level but also for the commanding nature of their content. They are meant to appeal to a wide range of developmental students. They also take into account the diverse backgrounds of such students. Teachers and students alike should be able to take pleasure in the selections, and to be genuinely interested in them. This should facilitate the learning process.

- **Ease of use.** The straightforward sequence in each chapter—from explanation to example to practice to review test—helps make the skills easy to teach. The organization of the book into three distinct parts also makes for ease of use. Within a single class, for instance, you can work on a particular skill in Part I, review another skill through the use of a mastery test in Part II, and provide variety by having students read one of the selections in Part III. The limited answer key at the back of the book also makes for versatility: it means that you can assign some chapters for self-teaching. Finally, the review tests in Part I and the mastery and combined-skills tests in Part II— each on its own tear-out page—make it simple for you to test and evaluate student progress.

- **Integration of skills.** Students do more than learn the skills individually in Parts I and II. They also learn to apply the skills together through the reading selections that close the chapters in Part I, through the combined-skills tests in Part II, and through the readings in Part III. Students become effective readers and thinkers through a great deal of practice in applying a combination of skills.

- **Thinking activities.** As indicated above, there are three kinds of thinking activities that follow each reading selection. First is the mapping activity, which will help students see and understand the organizational pattern of each selection. Second are the two discussion questions, designed to encourage different points of view regarding the selection. And third are the two writing activities, which inspire students to further express their opinions on some aspect of the reading. There are also two additional discussion questions and two more writing activities for each selection in the *Instructor's Manual and Test Bank*.

    The book is designed, then, to create activities that truly involve students in the processes of reading and thinking while enabling you to provide feedback. This practice and feedback on interesting, challenging material will help your students to become effective readers and thinkers.

- **Supplementary materials.** The three helpful supplements listed on the next page are available at no charge to instructors using the text. Any or all can be obtained quickly by writing or calling Townsend Press (Pavilions at Greentree—408, Marlton, New Jersey 08053; 1-800-772-6410).

1   An *Instructor's Edition*—chances are you are holding it in your hand—is identical to the student book except that it also provides both of the following: 1) hints for teachers (see the front of the book) and 2) answers to all the practices and tests.

2   A combined *Instructor's Manual, Test Bank, and Computer Guide* consists of the following:

    a   Suggestions for teaching the course, a model syllabus, readability levels, a complete answer key, and two additional discussion questions and writing activities for each reading selection.

    b   Four additional mastery tests for each of the ten skills and four additional combined-skills tests—all on letter-sized sheets so they can be copied easily for use with students.

    c   A computer guide that reproduces the two additional mastery tests for each skill that are on the computer disks available with the book.

3   A set of *computer disks* (in IBM or Macintosh format) contains two additional mastery tests for each of the ten skill chapters in the book. The disks contain a number of other user- and instructor-friendly features: brief explanations of answers, a sound option, frequent mention of the user's first name, a running score at the bottom of the screen, and a record-keeping score file.

    Since the disk tests are reproduced in the *Instructor's Manual, Test Bank, and Computer Guide,* you can readily decide just how to use the materials without having to work through each test on the computer. And if a computer lab is not available, you can copy these tests for use in class as additional mastery tests.

• **One of a sequence of books.** This is the basic text in a series that includes these other books:

    Ten Steps to Building College Reading Skills, Forms A and B, are suited for an early college reading course. These books provide one word skill (dictionary use) and nine comprehension chapters. The two forms of the book allow teachers to easily alternate texts from one semester to the next.

    Ten Steps to Improving College Reading Skills is an intermediate text. It is appropriate for the core developmental reading course offered at most colleges.

    Ten Steps to Advancing College Reading Skills is a slightly higher developmental text than the *Improving* book. It can be used as a sequel to the intermediate book or as a second-semester alternative to it.

    A companion set of vocabulary books, listed on page iv, has been designed to go with each book in the series. Recommended to accompany this book is *Groundwork for a Better Vocabulary* or *Building Vocabulary Skills*.

Together, the books and their full range of supplements form a sequence that should be ideal for any college reading program.

A Note on *Groundwork for College Reading* and *Ten Steps to Building College Reading Skills,* Form B

Some practices and readings in this book overlap with materials in *Ten Steps to Building College Reading Skills,* Form B. Therefore, instructors using *Groundwork for College Reading* in a course should not follow it in a succeeding course with Form B. The recommended sequel is Form A.

Summary and Acknowledgments

To summarize, *Groundwork for College Reading,* Second Edition, presents ten word and reading skills to help developmental college students become independent readers and thinkers. Through an appealing collection of readings and a carefully designed series of activities and tests, students receive considerable guided practice in the skills. The result is an integrated approach to learning that will bring about better readers and stronger thinkers.

Thanks to the exceptional design skills of Janet M. Goldstein, the book enjoys a remarkably clear and "user-friendly" format. I owe appreciation to Janet and to John Langan as well for proofreading and editing help. I value especially the outstanding editorial role played by Carole Mohr, who has worked closely on every page of the book. Finally, I am grateful to my wife, Tari, for her inspiration, her confidence in me, and her patience.

Bill Broderick

How to Become a Better Reader and Thinker

In today's society, the average person watches over *seven hours of television per day!* Watching so much TV leaves little time for reading and is very different from reading. Television watching is passive—all the action is there on the screen and little or no thinking is required for satisfaction. On the other hand, reading is an active undertaking. You have to be attentive if you are to comprehend what you are reading.

• How much television do you watch on an average day? _____

Here are two important points to consider. First, the skilled reader understands that there must be interaction between the reader and the writer. You can't stare at the words on a page and hope that meaning will come to you. You must learn to find the meaning that is intended. This means thinking about what the words and phrases mean and about the message the author is "sending" you.

Second, reading is important for people who want to make something of themselves. People who are successful *make* time to read, even though their responsibilities, including job and family, may make this difficult.

• Do you read on a regular basis (including newspapers, weekly magazines,

and novels)? _____

• When are you most likely to do your reading? _____

The chances are you are not as good a reader as you want to be or as you need to be to succeed at college. This book will help you build a solid foundation in the most important skills you need to become a better reader. In addition, it will help you to strengthen your ability to think clearly and logically. Reading and thinking are closely related skills, and both are vital for your success in college.

To find out just how this book will help you learn these essential skills, read the next several pages and do the brief activities as well. The activities are easily completed and will give you a good sense of how the book is arranged, what it will do for you, and what is expected of you as you interact with the book.

HOW THE BOOK IS ORGANIZED

There are three parts to the book. Each part is described below.

Part I: Ten Steps to College Reading (pages 7–222)

To help you to become a more effective reader and thinker, this book first presents a series of ten key word and reading skills. They are listed in the table of contents on page v. Turn to that page to fill in several skills missing in the list below.

1   Phonics I: Consonants
2   *Phonics II: Vowels* _____
3   Phonics III: Syllables
4   *Word Parts* _____
5   Dictionary Use
6   Vocabulary in Context
7   *Main Ideas* _____
8   Supporting Details
9   Locations of Main Ideas
10   *Transitions* _____

Each chapter is developed in the same way. First of all, clear explanations and examples help you *understand* each skill. A series of practices then give you the hands-on experience needed to *review* the skill.

- How many practices are there in the third chapter, "Phonics III: Syllables" (pages 55–70)? ___*Seven*___

At the end of each chapter are four review tests.

- On which pages are the first three review tests for "Phonics III: Syllables"? ___*63–65*___.

- How many questions are asked in Review Test 2 for the "Phonics III: Syllables" chapter? ___*20*___

The fourth review test for every chapter includes a reading selection that gives you the chance to practice the skill you learned in the chapter and often also to perfect skills you learned in previous chapters.

- What is the title of the reading selection that begins on page 66?

  "Why Johnny Can't Think"

The tests are perforated and can be torn out and given to your instructor. Following the tests are three kinds of activities that will improve your reading and thinking skills. The first is a mapping activity. A map is a visual diagram that will help you think about how the reading selection was organized. Next are discussion questions and writing assignments that your teacher may assign to strengthen your understanding of the selection and to give you a chance to voice your opinion about some aspect of the selection.

- How many *discussion questions* are there on page 70 following "Why Johnny Can't Think"? _____*Two*_____

- How many *writing assignments* are there on page 70 following "Why Johnny Can't Think"? _____*Two*_____

Also, note that there is a "Check Your Performance" box at the end of each chapter so you can track your progress on the four tests and the mapping activity. Your scores can also be entered in the review test section of the "Reading Performance Chart" at the back of the book.

- Exactly where in the book is this chart located? _____*Inside back cover*_____

Part II: Mastery Tests (pages 223–356)

This part of the book provides a series of tests to help you master the ten skills you studied in Part I.

- Look at pages 225–236. How many mastery tests there are for this skill? _____*Six*_____ This is the number of mastery tests provided for each skill.

As with the Review Tests, these tests are perforated and can be torn out and given to your instructor. And there is a scorebox at the top of each test so you can track your progress. Your score can also be entered in the mastery test section of the "Reading Performance Chart" at the back of the book.

Part III: Ten Reading Selections (pages 357–450)

Part III is made up of the ten reading selections followed by questions that will help you to sharpen all of the skills you learned in Part I and practiced in Part II. Turn to page vi in the table of contents and answer the following questions.

• Which two selections may help you in other classes? _____

_____ *"Classroom Notetaking" and "How to Write Clearly"* _____

• Which selection may be about how to live longer? _____

"Friendship and Living Longer"

Each reading selection is organized in the same way. Before the reading actually begins, there are two sections. Look, for example, at "Life Over Death," which starts on page 359. What are the headings of the two sections that come before the reading itself?

• _____ *"Preview"* _____

• _____ *"Words to Watch"* _____

Note that the vocabulary words in "Words to Watch" are followed by the numbers of the paragraphs where the words appear. Now look again at "Life Over Death" (pages 359–361), and explain how each vocabulary word is marked in the reading:

• _____ *It has a small circle after it.* _____

You can check the pronunciation of any word in "Words to Watch" in the "List of Word Pronunciations" beginning on page 453.

Activities Following Each Reading Selection

After each selection there are five kinds of activities that will improve your reading and thinking skills. Look at the activities following "Room with a New View" (pages 393–400). Note that the first activity consists of **word skills questions**. The second consists of (fill in the missing words) _____ *reading comprehension questions* _____. The third is a **mapping activity**. The fourth consists of (fill in the missing words) _____ *discussion questions* _____. And the fifth is **writing assignments**.

Look at the **word skills** questions for "Room with a New View" on pages 395–397. The first five of these questions deal with consonants, vowels, syllables, word parts, and dictionary use. The last five of these questions deal with (fill in the missing words) _____ *vocabulary in context* _____. These questions will help you to improve your understanding of key words presented in the reading.

Now look at the **reading comprehension** questions for "Classroom Note-taking" on pages 407–408. How many questions are there in all? _____ *Ten* _____. The first questions in this and all other selections involve the "Central Point and Main Idea." The next group of questions involves (fill in the missing words) _____ *"Supporting Details"* _____. Finally, the last questions always involve "Transitions."

Look now at the activity titled **Mapping Activity**. A map is simply a diagram of a selection, a visual outline of a reading's organization. It shows at a glance the central point of a selection and the support for that point. Completing the map will help you focus on the most important ideas in each reading. You will sharpen your ability to get to the heart of each selection and to think logically and clearly about what you read.

- How many answers must you fill in for the mapping activity that follows "Cipher in the Snow" on page 374? ___*Six*___ .

Note and write down how many **discussion questions** there are for "Friendship and Living Longer" on page 384: ___*Two*___ . How many **writing assignments** are there? ___*Two*___ . There are the same number of discussion questions and writing assignments for every reading. These questions provide a final chance for you to deepen your understanding of each selection.

At the end of each reading selection is a **chart** where you can enter your scores. Look at the top left of the chart on page 431, and write the chart's name here: _____*Check Your Performance*_____ . This chart helps you keep track of how well you do with the word skills and comprehension questions as well as with the mapping activity. Your scores can then be transferred to the ten reading selections section of the "Reading Progress Chart" at the back of the book.

HELPFUL FEATURES OF THE BOOK

1   The book centers on *what you really need to know* to become a better reader and thinker. It presents ten key comprehension skills, and it explains the most important points about each skill.

2   The book gives you *lots of practice*. We seldom learn a skill only by hearing or reading about it; we make it part of us by repeated practice. There are, then, numerous activities in the text. They are not "busy work," but carefully designed materials that should help you truly learn each skill.

   Notice that after you learn each skill in Part I, you read a selection in Review Test 4 that enables you to apply that skill. And as you move from one skill to the next, you continue to practice and reinforce the ones already learned.

3   The selections throughout the book are *lively and appealing*. Dull and unvaried readings work against learning, so subjects have been carefully chosen for their high interest level. Almost all of the selections here are excellent examples of how what we read can capture our attention. For example, read several paragraphs of "Cipher in the Snow" and then try to *stop* reading.

HOW TO USE THIS BOOK

1   A good way to proceed is to read and reread the explanations and examples in a given chapter in Part I until you feel you understand the ideas presented. Then carefully work through the practices. As you finish each one, check your answers with the "Limited Answer Key" that starts on page 457.

   For your own sake, don't just copy in the answers without trying to do the practices! The only way to learn a skill is to practice it first and *then* use the answer key to give yourself feedback. Also, take whatever time is needed to figure out just why you got some answers wrong. By using the answer key to help teach yourself the skills, you will prepare yourself for the review tests at the end of each chapter as well as for the mastery tests and the reading selection tests in the book. Your instructor can supply you with answers to those tests.

   If you have trouble catching on to a particular skill, stick with it. In time, you will learn each of the ten skills.

2   Read the selections with the intent of simply enjoying them. There will be time afterwards for rereading each selection and using it to develop your comprehension skills.

3   Keep track of your progress. In the "Reading Performance Chart" on the inside back cover, enter your scores for the review tests in Part I and the mastery tests in Part II. In addition, fill in the "Check Your Performance" chart at the end of each reading in Part III. These scores can also be entered on the inside-back-cover chart, giving you a good view of your overall performance as you work through the book.

   In summary, *Groundwork for College Reading,* Second Edition has been designed to interest and benefit you as much as possible. Its format is straightforward, its explanations are clear, its readings are appealing, and its many practices will help you learn through doing. *It is a book that has been created to reward effort*, and if you provide that effort, you will make yourself a better reader and a stronger thinker. I wish you success.

Bill Broderick

Part I

TEN STEPS TO COLLEGE READING

1

Phonics I: Consonants

What do you do when you are reading and come across a word you can't pronounce? Do you ask someone how the word is pronounced? Or do you simply ignore the word, hoping it isn't important? What you should do is look at the word, break it into syllables, sound out each syllable, and put the word back together again. To put it another way, you should use the very helpful method of phonics.

Phonics tells you how to break a word into its parts (syllables) and how to pronounce each part. It is true that English letters don't always sound the way you expect them to. But phonics can help you figure out the sounds of most words. And when phonics isn't enough, then you can use a dictionary (which is the topic of Chapter 5).

This chapter reviews the pronunciation of consonants. The next chapter covers the most important points about vowels. The third chapter will show you how to break words into syllables. In all three chapters, the keys to improvement are practice and patience. By working carefully on each activity, you will sharpen your ability to pronounce words.

But you'll also need to practice using phonics in everyday reading. You'll find it helpful to read the selections that end each chapter, as well as the selections in Part III of this book. And you should also get in the habit of reading every day something that interests you—in magazines, newspapers, and books. Slowly but surely, then, you will improve your reading.

CONSONANTS

Twenty-one of the twenty-six letters in the English alphabet are consonants. (The others are vowels, which will be discussed in the next chapter.) The consonants are shown on the next page.

The Consonants

b	c	d	f	g	h	j
k	l	m	n	p	q	r
s	t	v	w	x	y	z

The sounds of consonants are made when the lips, teeth, or tongue block the breath as you speak. In this chapter, you'll learn about the most common sounds of consonants. These three areas will be covered:

- Single Consonants with Just One Sound
- Single Consonants with More Than One Sound
- Three Types of Consonant Combinations

SINGLE CONSONANTS WITH JUST ONE SOUND

The fifteen consonants listed below generally have just one sound. Each letter is followed by three examples. See if you can add a fourth example of the sound, using the space provided. Note the example.

b	bed	able	crab	*best*
f	fan	gift	grief	*(Answers will vary.)*
h	hog	behave	reheat	_____
j	jab	jaw	banjo	_____
k	kiss	bakery	peek	_____
l	lump	delay	heel	_____
m	mud	dime	ram	_____
n	neck	unit	lemon	_____
p	pat	paper	creep	_____
r	rub	roar	dear	_____
t	tub	note	street	_____
v	vine	river	hive	_____
w	web	award	sewer	_____
y	yell	yawn	mayor	_____
z	zoom	crazy	quiz	_____

SINGLE CONSONANTS WITH MORE THAN ONE SOUND

The following consonants have more than one sound:

c	g	d	q	s	x

Common sounds for each of these letters are explained below.

1 Sounds of *c*

When **c** is followed by an **e, i,** or **y**, it usually has the sound of **s** as in *salt.* This is called the **soft** sound of **c**. Here are some words with the soft sound of **c**:

city	cell	circus
cereal	recipe	bicycle

Whenever **c** is not followed by an **e, i,** or **y**, it sounds like **k**. This is known as the **hard** sound of **c**. Here are some words with the hard sound of **c**:

can	cub	actor
arc	circus	picnic

Compare the two words below. The **c** in the first word has a soft sound; it is followed by an **e**. The **c** in the second word has a hard sound; it is not followed by **e, i,** or **y**.

certain   curtain

➤ *Practice 1*

Show with a check whether the boldfaced **c** in each word has the soft sound (like the **c** in *city*) or the hard sound (like the **c** in *can*). The first one is done for you as an example.

	Soft sound of **c** (sounds like **s**)	Hard sound of **c** (sounds like **k**)
1. **c**igarette	✓	
2. **c**are		✓
3. i**c**e	✓	
4. **c**ustom		✓
5. pea**c**e	✓	

	Soft sound of **c** (sounds like **s**)	Hard sound of **c** (sounds like **k**)
6. postcard		✓
7. decide	✓	
8. record		✓
9. panic		✓
10. decent	✓	

2   Sounds of *g*

The consonant **g** has two common sounds. These sounds follow the same principle as **c**. When **g** is followed by **e**, **i** or **y**, it often has the sound of the letter **j**. This is the **soft** sound of **g**. Here are some words with the soft sound of **g**:

gem	gin	gym
angel	magic	gypsy

(There are exceptions to this rule, including such words as *get*, *girl*, and *gift*.)

When **g** is not followed by **e**, **i** or **y**, it usually has its **hard** sound, as in *gum* and *leg*. Here are some more words with the hard sound of **g**:

game	goal	guess
anger	ago	pig

Compare the two words below. The **g** in the first word has a soft sound; it is followed by an **e**. The **g** in the second word has a hard sound; it is not followed by an **e**, **i** or **y**.

wage	wag

➤ *Practice 2*

Show with a check whether the boldfaced **g** in each word has the soft sound (like the **g** in *gem*) or the hard sound (like the **g** in *game*). The first one is done for you as an example.

	Soft sound of **g** (as in *gem*)	Hard sound of **g** (as in *game*)
1. **g**entle	✓	
2. **g**uest		✓
3. ra**g**e	✓	

	Soft sound of **g** (as in *gem*)	Hard sound of **g** (as in *game*)
4. green		✓
5. pigeon	✓	
6. fog		✓
7. frigid	✓	
8. gesture	✓	
9. legal		✓
10. fragment		✓

Other Consonants with More Than One Sound

The consonants **d**, **q**, **s**, and **x** also have more than one sound. Information about each is listed below.

3   Sounds of *d*

The consonant **d** usually sounds like the **d** in *dot*. Here are some words with the usual sound of **d**:

date   si**d**e   blee**d**

At times **d** sounds like **j**. Here are some words in which **d** sounds like **j**:

e**d**ucate   sche**d**ule   sol**d**ier

There is no sure guideline for knowing when **d** sounds like **j**. But once in a while, you will find that giving a **d** the sound of **j** will be the key to recognizing a word.

4   Sounds of *q* (*qu*)

The consonant **q** is always followed by **u**. **Qu** usually sounds like **kw**. Here are some words in which **qu** sounds like **kw**:

queen   **qu**ilt   re**qu**ire

Sometimes **qu** sounds like **k**. Here are some words in which **qu** sounds like **k**:

anti**qu**e   pla**qu**e   mos**qu**ito

Qu will usually sound like **k** when a word ends in **que**, or when a word such as *mosquito* (from Spanish) or *quiche* (from French) comes to us directly from a foreign language.

5   Sounds of *s*

The consonant **s** usually sounds like the **s** in *salt*. Here are some other words in which **s** has its usual sound:

soup   unsafe   cost

Sometimes **s** sounds like **z**, as in the word *those*. This sound is common in two situations: 1) when **s** comes between two vowels (as in *rose*) and 2) at the end of a word that shows possession or ownership (such as *his*). Here are some words in which **s** sounds like **z**:

nose   reason   hers

6   Sounds of *x*

The consonant **x** usually sounds like **ks**. Here are some words in which **x** sounds like **ks**:

fox   next   toxic

When the combination **ex-** is followed by a vowel, then **x** usually sounds like **gz**. Here are some words in which **x** sounds like **gz**:

exact   exam   exist

Finally, when **x** begins a word (which is rarely), it has the sound of **z**, as in the word *Xerox*.

THREE TYPES OF CONSONANT COMBINATIONS

A **consonant combination** is two or more consonants which work together. There are three kinds of consonant combinations:

- **Consonant Blends**: Combinations that blend the sounds of single consonants
  Examples: **sp**it   fe**lt**   **scr**een

- **Consonant Digraph**s: Consonant pairs that combine to make one sound
  Examples: rou**gh**   wi**sh**   **th**in

- **Silent Consonants**: Consonants that are silent in certain combinations
  Examples: lam**b**   si**ck**   **w**rong

Each of these types of consonant combinations is explained on the following pages.

Consonant Blends

Consonant blends are two or more neighboring consonants that keep their own sounds but are spoken together. The sounds **blend** with each other, or run together. For example, the letters **sm** are a consonant blend. To pronounce this blend, just pronounce the **s** and then glide into the sound of the **m**. This is the sound you say at the beginning of the word *smile*.

Below are some words that begin with consonant blends. Read the words to yourself, and notice that you can hear the sound of each of the boldfaced consonants.

bread	**fl**y	**st**eam

Consonant blends also occur in the middle and at the end of words. Read the following words to yourself, and notice that you can hear the sound of each boldfaced consonant.

mo**nst**er	pi**nk**	sou**nd**

Here are four major types of consonant blends:

1 Blends that begin with **s**
2 Blends that end in **l**
3 Blends that end in **r**
4 Blends in the middle or end of a word

Each type of consonant blend is listed and illustrated below and on the following pages. Read the words given as examples, and note the sounds of their consonant blends.

1 Blends that begin with *s*

sc-	scr-	sk-	sl-	sm-
sn-	sp-	spl-	spr-	squ-
st-	str-	sw-		

The blends in the box are found at the beginnings and in the middles of words. In addition, three of them are also found at the ends of words: **-sk**, **-sp**, and **-st**.

sc	**sc**ore	**sc**ab
scr	**scr**ap	**scr**eam
sk	**sk**ate	a**sk**

sl	slam	asleep
sm	small	smog
sn	snore	unsnap
sp	spank	wasp
spl	splash	split
spr	sprout	respray
squ	squeak	square
st	steel	best
str	street	instruct
sw	swear	sweet

➤ Practice 3

A. Underline the consonant blends beginning with **s**. Remember that several of these blends may occur anywhere in a word.

1. slime

2. sweat

3. stride

4. western

5. masking

6. squeal

7. describe

8. crisp

9. splint

10. unscrew

B. Find the five words with a blend beginning with **s**, and write them in the blank spaces.

My cousin Spencer is the only member of our family who has not given up cigarettes yet. This year we celebrated Thanksgiving at my aunt's house in Springfield. Aunt Mabel hates the odor of cigarettes. Mabel said my cousin could smoke only in the basement, where the dog was. Being both an addict and stubborn, he ate his turkey in the cellar with the dog. He swore his dinner conversation was better than ours.

| *Spencer* | *Springfield* | *smoke* |
| *stubborn* | *swore* | |

2 Blends that end in *l*

bl-	cl-	fl-	gl-	pl-

These consonant blends may be at the beginning or in the middle of a word. Examples are *bless* and *apply*.

bl	**bl**ess	un**bl**ock
cl	**cl**am	de**cl**ine
fl	**fl**ag	re**fl**ect
gl	**gl**ad	re**gl**ue
pl	**pl**ay	ap**pl**y

➤ *Practice 4*

A. Underline the consonant blends ending in l. Remember that they may occur at the beginning or in the middle of a word.

1. <u>fl</u>ick
2. <u>cl</u>ash
3. <u>bl</u>ame
4. im<u>pl</u>y
5. <u>bl</u>eed

6. a<u>bl</u>aze
7. in<u>fl</u>ate
8. <u>gl</u>ass
9. un<u>cl</u>ear
10. <u>pl</u>ug

B. Find the five words with a consonant blend ending with l, and write them in the blank spaces.

The first time I saw a flag fly at half mast was that black day when President Kennedy was killed. Since then, I've seen Old Glory lowered plenty of times. While the sight still saddens me, the feeling has never been the same as with that first shock.

flag	*fly*	*black*
Glory	*plenty*	

3   Blends that end in *r*

br-	**cr-**	**dr-**	**fr-**	**gr-**
pr-	**tr-**			

These consonant blends may be at the beginning or in the middle of a word. Examples are *broke* and *contract*.

br	**br**oke	em**br**ace
cr	**cr**ime	in**cr**ease
dr	**dr**eam	ad**dr**ess
fr	**fr**ee	a**fr**aid
gr	**gr**eed	tele**gr**am
pr	**pr**ay	ex**pr**ess
tr	**tr**ain	con**tr**act

➤ *Practice 5*

A. Underline the consonant blends ending in **r**. Remember that they may occur at the beginning or in the middle of a word.

1. <u>gr</u>ape
2. <u>pr</u>event
3. <u>cr</u>edit
4. ent<u>r</u>ance
5. jaw<u>br</u>eaker

6. <u>dr</u>agon
7. ab<u>r</u>oad
8. <u>fr</u>og
9. un<u>cr</u>oss
10. ung<u>r</u>ateful

B. Find the five words with a blend ending in **r**, and write them in the blank spaces.

Rosario runs between two to four miles a day, in good and bad weather. She prefers to run on grass, but if it rains, she goes to the nearby high school and runs on the indoor track there. People ask her if she is getting ready for a race or wants to break a record, but she says she's afraid of gaining weight and that running keeps her in good shape.

prefers	*grass*	*track*
break	*afraid*	

4 Blends at the end of a syllable or word

-ft	-ld	-lt	-mp	-nd
-nk	-nt			

These consonant blends may be at the end of a word, as in *lift*, or at the end of a syllable (a part of a word), as in *wanting*.

ft	li**ft**	so**ft**ly
ld	chi**ld**	go**ld**en
lt	be**lt**	me**lt**down
mp	la**mp**	du**mp**ster
nd	ha**nd**	wi**nd**bag
nk	i**nk**	ba**nk**book
nt	pa**nt**	wa**nt**ing

➤ *Practice 6*

A. Underline the consonant blend at the end of the syllable or word.

1. sa<u>nk</u>
2. ri<u>ft</u>
3. pu<u>mp</u>
4. mi<u>ld</u>
5. wi<u>nd</u>

6. ha<u>nd</u>cuff
7. ti<u>lt</u>
8. li<u>ft</u>off
9. bu<u>mp</u>
10. pri<u>nt</u>er

B. Complete the passage with the words that contain a consonant blend at the end of a syllable or word.

Miguel and Maria were having a *(tough, difficult)* _____*difficult*_____ time deciding where to take their family for their vacation. Miguel suggested *(staying, camping)* _____*camping*_____ near Las Vegas, where the kids would enjoy the warm weather and he and Maria could enjoy the shows. Maria, however, wanted to go *(rafting, hiking)* _____*rafting*_____ in northern California, even though the weather was *(chillier, colder)* _____*colder*_____. But the kids had the final say, and the family ended up going to *(Hawaii, Disneyland)* _____*Disneyland*_____.

Consonant Digraphs

You have just learned that in consonant blends, each consonant is pronounced. In the blend **nt**, for example, two sounds are heard. However, there are some pairs of consonants with only *one* sound. And that sound is very different from the sound of either of the two letters. These pairs of consonants with only one sound are called **digraphs**.

Three types of digraphs are explained below:

1 Digraphs that sound like **f**
2 Digraphs with new sounds of their own: **sh** and **th**
3 A digraph with three sounds: **ch**

1   Digraphs that sound like *f: gh* and *ph*

The digraphs **gh** and **ph** do not sound like either of the letters they contain. Instead, they each have the sound of a single consonant: **f**.

Following are examples of words in which **gh** sounds like **f**. Note that this digraph appears at the end of a syllable or word.

laughing   enough   tough

Following are examples of words in which **ph** sounds like **f**. Note that this digraph may appear in the beginning, in the middle, or at the end of a word.

phone   dol**ph**in   gra**ph**

2   Digraphs with new sounds of their own: *sh* and *th*

The digraphs **sh** and **th** do not sound like any single letter; instead, they have sounds of their own.

Below are some words that include the digraph **sh**. Pronounce the words to yourself, and note that the **sh** sound is different from either **s** or **h**.

show   wa**sh**er   fi**sh**

The digraph **th** has two of its own sounds that are similar to each other. Say the following two groups of words out loud (not in a whisper), and you will hear the slight difference in the two **th** sounds.

Voiced **th** sound	Unvoiced **th** sound
their	**th**ird
they	**th**in
there	**th**ank
ba**th**e	ba**th**

3   A digraph with three sounds: *ch*

The digraph **ch** has three different sounds. The most common is the sound that you hear at the beginning and end of the word *church*. Here are some other words that contain **ch**. As you pronounce each word, note that the sound of **ch** is a hard, short one.

      chip   a**chi**eve   ran**ch**

      Ch can also sound like another digraph: **sh**. Here are some words in which **ch** sounds like **sh**:

      chef   **chute**   Michelle

These two sounds, **ch** and **sh**, are very different from each other. If you have trouble hearing the difference between the sounds, think of the **ch** as being a short, forceful sound, such as the one you might make if you are sneezing: "Ah-**choo**!" The **sh** is a much more gentle sound, like the sound you would make if you were trying to quiet a young child: "**Shhhh**."

      Finally, **ch** also has the same sound as a single consonant: **k**. Here are some words in which **ch** sounds like **k**:

      chorus   **ch**emist   **ch**aracter
      Christian   **ch**rome   **ch**ronic

Notice that all the words in the second line above begin with **chr**. Whenever **ch** is followed by **r**, **ch** will sound like **k**.

➤ *Practice 7*

Complete each sentence by writing in the word with a consonant digraph.

1. Ms. Vasquez stopped lecturing when a bug flew into her *(eye, nose, mouth)* _____*mouth*_____.

2. The *(Chinese, Swedes, Indians)* _____*Chinese*_____ once trained lions to help them hunt large animals.

3. If you cut off a piece of a *(starfish, lizard)* _____*starfish*_____ the piece will grow into a new animal.

4. Kim's new job didn't leave her much time to *(exercise, shop, gossip)* _____*shop*_____.

5. The catchy *(word, phrase, tune)* _____*phrase*_____ from the ad he heard on the radio stayed with Domingo all day.

6. Bjorn forgot to take the car out of gear, and it kept going until it *(hit, crashed, bumped)* _____*crashed*_____ against the garage wall.

7. Scientists have developed dairy products that are low in *(fat, calories, cholesterol)* ___cholesterol___.

8. The excuse that Nick missed his date with Carol because he was studying sounded *(phony, made-up, false)* ___phony___ to her.

9. If you have a *(bad, hard, rough)* ___rough___ day at work, it may help to come home and take a hot bath.

10. Some ketchup can be so *(thick, heavy, gooey)* ___thick___ that people grow impatient waiting for it to pour from the bottle.

Silent Consonants

In certain letter combinations within syllables, one consonant is silent—in other words, it is not pronounced. Below are some common silent consonants with the combinations in which they are silent. Examples of each combination are also included. Say the words to yourself so you can hear that one letter is silent.

- **b** is silent after **m**:
  comb   limb   climb

- **c** is silent before **k**:
  de**c**k   sti**c**k   pa**c**ker

- **g** is silent before **n**:
  gnaw   **g**narl   sign

- **h** is often silent after **w** when **wh** begins a word:
  w**h**ite   w**h**isper   w**h**ip

- **w** is often silent when a word begins with **who**:
  who   **w**hose   **w**hole

- **k** is silent before **n**:
  know   **k**nee   **k**nick-knack

- **w** is silent before **r**:
  wreck   **w**rite   un**w**rap

- When two of the same consonant are next to each other, one of them is silent:
  bell   add   narrow   fuss

➤ *Practice 8*

Complete each sentence by writing in the word with a silent consonant.

1. I once *(knew, met, dated)* _____*knew*_____ a man who could hum and sing at the same time.

2. Dominick was so hungry that he ate an entire box of *(granola, Cheerios, Wheaties)* _____*Wheaties*_____ .

3. A baby *(goat, pony, lamb)* _____*lamb*_____ at the petting zoo nibbled on my little brother's fingers.

4. A key to making good bread is knowing how to *(bake, prepare, knead)* _____*knead*_____ it.

5. I called to find out where my *(bonus, order, check)* _____*check*_____ was and was told it was in the mail.

6. Many types of birds enjoy the leftover bread *(crumbs, pieces, bits)* _____*crumbs*_____ that people throw their way.

7. Merchandise that is sold at *(discount, retail, wholesale)* _____*wholesale*_____ often attracts people looking for the best bargain.

8. Lewis Carroll, author of *Alice's Adventures in Wonderland*, liked to *(eat, write, sleep)* _____*write*_____ standing up.

9. Andre was glad to get the greeting card until he read its *(contents, poem, message)* _____*message*_____: "Roses are red, violets are blue; because of you, I caught the flu."

10. Canada is a beautiful country, but its short summers are *(hot, humid, muggy)* _____*muggy*_____ and full of insects.

An Important Final Note

You have learned a lot of guidelines in this chapter, and more are coming in the next two chapters. You may wonder if it is possible to remember them all. If so, it may interest you to know that advanced readers don't think about guidelines as they read. In fact, most don't remember what the guidelines are.

That doesn't mean guidelines are not helpful at first. You will make better progress if you review the rules and words in this chapter and the next two chapters often. Even when your instructor is finished with the first three chapters, review the words in them until they are easy for you to read. When you can read those words, you will be able to read many others that are like them. And once you know how to pronounce the words with ease, you won't need to think about the guidelines.

If you feel your progress is too slow, get help from your school's learning resource center or a tutor. But if you have done the work in this chapter carefully, you probably already read better. Progress happens slowly, and you are usually not aware of it. (One way to keep track of your progress is to read a paragraph or two into a tape recorder. Then play the tape back to yourself at the end of this course to see how much your reading has improved.)

Finally, don't forget the one activity that builds good readers best—reading. Read not only school material but as much non-school material as you can—in newspapers, magazines, and books. Read something that especially interests you every day, even if it's only for a few minutes on the bus, on a coffee break, or before you go to sleep. If you do, you will find before long that you can read faster and understand better what you are reading.

➤ *Review Test 1*

To review what you have learned in this chapter, answer each of the following questions. Fill in the blank, or circle the letter of the answer you think is correct.

1. Two consonants that have more than one sound are
   a. **b** and **f**.
   b. **p** and **r**.
   c. **c** and **g**.

2. The consonant **q** (**qu**) usually sounds like
   a. **k**.
   b. **kw**.
   c. **u**.

3. Which of the following is an example of a consonant blend?
   a. **wh**.
   b. **cr**.
   c. **qu**.

4. A consonant digraph is a consonant combination that
   a. blends together.
   b. makes one sound.
   c. always sounds the same.

5. ___T___ TRUE OR FALSE? In the consonant combination **wr**, **w** is silent.

➤ *Review Test 2*

A. Find the five words in which **c** has a *hard* sound (as in *can*) or **g** has a *hard* sound (as in *game*). Write them in the blank spaces.

curse	twice	cut	come	Lucy
cider	hug	page	huge	gun

1. _____*curse*_____   4. _____*hug*_____

2. _____*cut*_____   5. _____*gun*_____

3. _____*come*_____

B. Find and write down the five words that contain consonant blends.

bribe	visit	smile	repair	voice
motion	unplug	heater	found	stain

6. _____*bribe*_____   9. _____*found*_____

7. _____*smile*_____   10. _____*stain*_____

8. _____*unplug*_____

C. Complete each sentence with the word which has a consonant digraph.

11. *(Ketchup, Milk)* _____*Ketchup*_____ was once sold as a medicine.

12. *(Elephants, Ants)* _____*Elephants*_____ need only two hours of sleep a day.

13. A *(blinking, flashing)* _____*flashing*_____ light makes a good fire alarm for the deaf.

14. My aunt says you should sniff oil of wintergreen if you have a bad *(cold, cough)* _____*cough*_____ .

15. "When in doubt," said famous author Mark Twain, "tell the *(truth, facts)* _____*truth*_____ ."

D. Find and write down the five words with silent consonants.

truck	alert	blend	slug	bitten
reign	cheese	wrong	bounce	whole

16. _____*truck*_____   19. _____*wrong*_____

17. _____*bitten*_____   20. _____*whole*_____

18. _____*reign*_____

➤ *Review Test 3*

A. Find the five words in which **c** has a *soft* sound (as in *city*) or **g** has a *soft* sound (as in *gem*). Write them in the blank spaces.

giant	ego	generous	comma	great
cent	rice	tact	cost	germ

1. _____*giant*_____   4. _____*rice*_____

2. _____*generous*_____   5. _____*germ*_____

3. _____*cent*_____

B. Complete each sentence with the word which has a consonant blend.

6. Do you think it is funny when people *(fall, slip)* _____*slip*_____ on a wet pavement?

7. Surprising as it may seem, some Eskimos use refrigerators to keep food from *(mice, freezing)* _____*freezing*_____.

8. My brother can be a *(grouch, pain)* _____*grouch*_____ when he's in a bad mood.

9. After much thought, Ruth decided to buy the *(oval, round)* _____*round*_____ purple earrings.

10. My cousins *(think, feel)* _____*think*_____ that the talk show hosts are their friends.

C. Underline the consonant digraph in each of the following words. Then use each word to complete one of the sentences below. Use each word once.

ne<u>ph</u>ew	<u>sh</u>out	laug<u>h</u>ed	<u>ch</u>imney	<u>th</u>umb

11. Omar _____*laughed*_____ when I told him I loved him.

12. When you use a hammer, be careful not to hit your _____*thumb*_____.

13. Sandy couldn't hear me, so I had to _____*shout*_____.

14. A raccoon family has nested in our _____*chimney*_____.

15. Felix has no children, so he wants his oldest _____*nephew*_____ to run his video store.

D. Find the five words with silent consonants, and write them in the blank spaces.

Last weekend, our family went to a football game between the Chicago Bears and the Green Bay Packers. We didn't know it was going to be as cold as it was. We tried to stay warm by covering ourselves with blankets. When the game ended, my hands and feet were so numb from the cold that I was glad to be going home.

16.	*football*	19.	*when*
17.	*Packers*	20.	*numb*
18.	*know*		

➤ *Review Test 4*

Here is a chance to apply your understanding of consonant sounds to a full-length reading. This selection is about a woman who meets and conquers more obstacles than many of us have experienced. She does not spend a lot of time asking why these things are happening to her. She does what she must to make her life and her family's life better. When you finish reading about Rosa, answer the phonics questions that follow.

Words to Watch

Following are some words in the reading that do not have strong context support. Each word is followed by the number of the paragraph in which it appears and its meaning there. These words are indicated in the article by a small circle (°).

plantation (1): large estate where crops are grown
to no avail (3): without success
trek (3): journey
conveyed (5): communicated
sentiment (5): attitude; thought
halting (6): hesitant
prodded (7): urged
deported (17): forced to leave a country
attained (17): gained
collect myself (20): gain control of myself
immigrants (21): people who come to another country to live
oppressive (21): harsh and cruel

ROSA: A SUCCESS STORY

Edward Patrick

Up until six months before I met her, life for Rosa Perez had been easy. Her father was a wealthy plantation° owner in Nicaragua. Her family owned a large house with all the comforts of the rich. Then came the same type of violent civil war that has torn apart so many Latin American countries.

Rosa's father was identified as a supporter of the rebel cause, and   2
the family's plantation was seized. During the government takeover,
her father was shot and killed. Her mother gathered as much money as
she could and fled with Rosa and her two younger brothers, Adolpho
and Roberto. Their destination was the United States. Rosa's mother
knew a man who knew another man who could get them through
Mexico and across the U.S. border into Texas or California. There was
nothing to worry about, they were told. Rosa believed it.

At first, things went smoothly. Twelve others joined Rosa and her   3
family. The group had no trouble getting into and across Mexico. But
just before they were to cross into California, the guide said he could
go no further. Another man would take them the rest of the way. Rosa's
mother protested, but to no avail°. They were led across by a man they
did not know. He told them to follow his every command. They must
move quickly and silently or risk discovery by the Border Patrol. It was
a difficult trek°. It was dark. It was cold. Coyotes howled in what all
hoped was the distance. Everyone was tired and frightened.

And then came the bright lights. Just as they were about to cross   4
into the United States, the U.S. Border Patrol sighted the group and
turned on the searchlights on their jeeps to track them down. People
scattered. Rosa held on to Adolpho and Roberto. She looked back, but
could not see her mother. "Aqui. Ahora," commanded their guide,
appropriately called a "coyote." Rosa blindly followed him and watched
as the lights of the jeeps sped after the others. They waited quietly for
what seemed like hours. Only when he was convinced that it was safe
did their guide take the five who had managed to follow him the rest of
the way. Eleven were not with them, including Rosa's mother.

I first saw Rosa three months after this nightmare. I arrived at my   5
office early, wanting only to unwind from the freeway drive before my
first class. I was annoyed that someone was standing outside my office
so early in the morning. But I spoke with her, and soon realized that
there was something special about this slender, dark-skinned young
woman with large, expressive brown eyes. I didn't know then what it
was I saw in her. Now I know she revealed an inner strength, conveyed°
an unspoken sentiment° that "You don't know me, but you can believe
in me." It was magnetic. I knew that I would help in any way I could.

Rosa wanted to learn English. She wanted to do more than just get   6
by. Her halting° English told me she could manage that already. She
wanted to be able to read and write the language so that she could
provide for her brothers. My basic reading class had been
recommended to her. She asked what materials she could get to work
on even before the semester started.

Eager students are always easy to work with, and Rosa proved to   7 be one of my most enthusiastic students. She kept me on my toes and constantly challenged me. She prodded° me to provide more information, additional examples, better explanations. If I used a word she didn't understand, she would stop me. She would make me explain it so that she and her classmates could grasp its meaning. If we looked for the main idea in a paragraph and her answer was different from mine, she insisted on giving the reasons why she felt she was right and I was wrong. I could not always convince her that my answer was better. But I always encouraged her to ask questions whenever she was confused or unconvinced. While I looked forward to the class she had enrolled in, I was always exhausted at its conclusion.

Rosa advanced from our basic reading classes to the more difficult study-skills class. Then she moved through the writing classes offered in the department. She enrolled in the Early Childhood Program at the college. This is a program which can lead to certification as a child-care worker. Her progress in her classes was reflected in a steady stream of A's and B's. 8

It took Rosa three years to complete the course work that she needed to graduate. I made plans to attend the graduation ceremonies where she would receive her associate's degree. She insisted that I attend the graduation party her friend Alberto was giving. I said I would be honored to go. 9

The ceremony was typical, with boring speeches made for proud accomplishments. The party was something special. Rosa had come a long way in the three years I had known her. She had made some wonderful friends, had found a decent job at a nearby day-care center, and had provided a good home for her two brothers. 10

Rosa greeted me when I arrived. She wanted for me to meet everyone there, and she hinted at a surprise she had for me. 11

"Dr. P, may I present to you my brothers, Adolpho and Roberto." 12

"Mucho gusto," I began. 13

"Right," said the smaller brother. "Call me Bobby. Nice to meet you, Doc. Say, you don't mind if me and Al 'mingle,' if you know what I mean?" 14

I knew, and encouraged them to meet and greet the others— especially the young ladies—in attendance. 15

I commented on how quickly her brothers had adjusted to life in the States. But Rosa seemed preoccupied. I was puzzled until I saw that we were walking toward an older woman who had the same brown expressive eyes as Rosa. It was her mother. 16

Rosa's mother had been captured by the Border Patrol and deported° to Nicaragua. There, she was jailed. Rosa had been depressed over her mother's lack of the freedom she and her brothers enjoyed. 17

She had located her mother and worked for close to three years to get her released. I don't know all the details of how she did it. Perhaps it is best that I don't. At the moment I met her, I did not care at all about how she had attained° freedom. I was just overjoyed that she was here with her children.

Rosa entered San Diego State University, some ninety miles   18 away. As often happens with students who move on, I saw very little of her. She was working hard toward a degree in early childhood education, I was on leave for a year, and our paths rarely crossed. Sometimes she would come by right before Christmas or at the end of a school year. She stopped by the office again yesterday, with a purpose. She carried two babies in her arms. The six-month-old twins were hers. Their huge, expressive brown eyes told me that before she did.

Rosa proudly told what had happened in the five years since her   19 graduation. I listened enthusiastically as she told me about receiving a Bachelor of Arts degree, marrying Alberto, opening a child-care center with him, and giving birth to their twin sons. "And now," she said, "I want to tell you their names. This is Alberto," she said, nodding toward the larger twin. Then she looked toward the smaller one. Her eyes smiled as much as her mouth. "He is smaller, yes, but obviously more intellectual. That is why we have chosen to name him Eduardo."

I gasped, tried to collect myself°, but did not succeed. Rosa came   20 to the rescue. She calmly explained that Alberto and she decided to name the baby after me because of all the help I had provided when she needed it most. I babbled something about how proud I felt. It was true.

Some people, I know, object to the flow of immigrants° entering   21 our country. They forget that almost all of us came to America from somewhere else. We need every so often to be reminded of success stories like Rosa's. Like many of our ancestors, she fled an oppressive° government and poor economic conditions. She then worked hard to create a new life for herself. Hers is not an uncommon story. Many others like her have come to enrich their lives, and they have enriched our country as well.

Phonics Questions

Use phonics clues you learned from this chapter to answer the following questions. Circle the letter of your choice for each question.

1. The word *nice* in "Nice to meet you, Doc" (paragraph 14) contains a
   a. soft **c** sound.
   b. hard **c** sound.

2. The word *large* in "Her family owned a large ranch with all the comforts of the rich" (paragraph 1) contains a
   a. soft **g** sound.
   b. hard **g** sound.

3. The word *program* in "She enrolled in the Early Childhood Program at the college" (paragraph 8) contains
   a. two consonant blends.
   b. two consonant digraphs.
   c. one consonant blend and one consonant digraph.

4. The word *this* in "I first saw Rosa three months after this nightmare" (paragraph 5) contains a
   a. consonant blend.
   b. consonant digraph.
   c. silent letter combination.

5. The word *knew* in "I knew that I would help in any way I could" (paragraph 5) contains a
   a. consonant blend.
   b. consonant digraph.
   c. silent letter combination.

6. Which word in the sentence below has a soft **c** sound?
   a. *came*
   b. *civil*
   c. *American*

   Then came the same type of violent civil war that has torn apart so many Latin American countries. (Paragraph 1)

7. Which word in the sentence below has a soft **g** sound?
   a. *encouraged*
   b. *greet*
   c. *young*

   I knew, and encouraged them to meet and greet the others — especially the young ladies — in attendance. (Paragraph 15)

8. Which word in the sentence below has a consonant blend?
   a. *another*
   b. *take*
   c. *rest*

   Another man would take them the rest of the way. (Paragraph 3)

9. Which word in the sentence below has a consonant digraph?
   a. *until*
   b. *months*
   c. *life*

   Up until six months before I met her, life for Rosa Perez had been easy.
   (Paragraph 1)

10. Which word in the sentence below has a silent letter combination?
    a. *questions*
    b. *whenever*
    c. *confused*

    But I always encouraged her to ask questions whenever she was confused
    or unconvinced. (Paragraph 7)

Mapping Activity

Many students find it helpful to organize material in a very visual way. They
create a diagram, or **map**, to show the relationship between the main parts of a
selection. A map's shape will be influenced by the information it organizes.

This selection is organized by time: first one thing happened; then another;
after that, another; and so on. Major events of the reading are scrambled in the list
below. Complete the map on the next page by filling in the events in their correct
order.

- Rosa's education toward a bachelor's degree
- Rosa's escape to the U.S.
- Rosa's education toward an associate's degree
- Rosa's visit with the twins
- Rosa's graduation and party

Central point: Many immigrants, like Rosa, come to America to escape oppression and then work hard to become productive citizens.

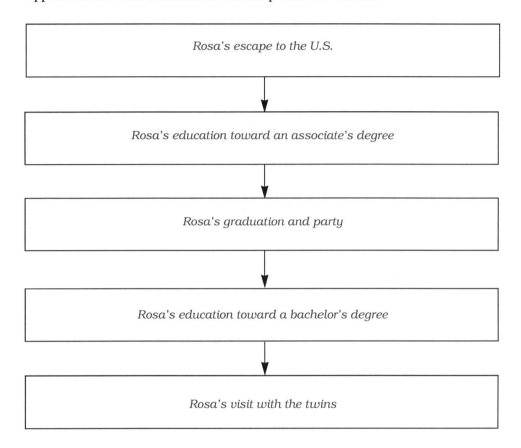

Discussion Questions

1. As Rosa reached the border of the United States, she realized that her mother was not with her. Should she have looked for her mother, or was she right to cross into the U.S. when she did?

2. The author writes that "we need . . . to be reminded of success stories like Rosa's." What are the values of hearing such a story?

Writing Activities

1. Patrick writes that "almost all of us came to America from somewhere else." Where did your family come from, and when? Write a paragraph on the members of your family who first came to America. Include information such as the following: 1) where they came from, 2) the reason they came to America, and 3) what life was like for them at first in America.

2. Rosa's education prepared her for a career. If you want your education to lead to a career, write a paragraph on which one and why you've picked it. Be specific about the types of positions you'd like to hold and why they appeal to you. If you're not sure about the type of career you want, write about one or two that you're considering. Here are two sample topic sentences for this paragraph: 1) "I'm aiming for a career in _____ for two main reasons"; 2) "I'm in the process of weighing the values and drawbacks of a career in _____."

Check Your Performance   **PHONICS I: CONSONANTS**

Activity	Number Right	Points	Total
Review Test 1 (5 items)	_____	x 2 =	_____
Review Test 2 (20 items)	_____	x 1.5 =	_____
Review Test 3 (20 items)	_____	x 1.5 =	_____
Review Test 4 (10 items)	_____	x 2 =	_____
Mapping Activity (5 items)	_____	x 2 =	_____
		TOTAL SCORE =	_____ %

Enter your total score onto the Reading Performance Chart: Review Tests on the inside back cover.

2

Phonics II: Vowels

The sounds of vowels are made with an open mouth, unblocked by teeth, tongue, or lips. Five English letters are vowels:

    a   **e**   **i**   **o**   **u**

In addition, **y** is sometimes a vowel.

In this chapter, you'll learn about the most common sounds of vowels. The areas covered will be:

- Short Vowel Sounds
- Long Vowel Sounds
- Rules for Long Vowel Sounds
- Other Vowel Sounds

SHORT VOWEL SOUNDS

The list below shows how the short vowel sounds are pronounced. Notice that a common symbol for the short sound of a vowel is a cup-shaped curve (˘) over the vowel.

    ă   sounds like the **a** in *pat.*
    ĕ   sounds like the **e** in *pet.*
    ĭ   sounds like the **i** in *pit.*
    ŏ   sounds like the **o** in *pot.*
    ŭ   sounds like the **u** in *cut.*

Remembering these words will help you keep each short vowel sound in mind.

➤ *Practice in the Short* a *Sound*

Say each word below to yourself. Put an **a** with a cup symbol (**ă**) beside each word that contains a short **a** sound, like the a in *pat*. Put an *X* beside each word that does *not* have the short **a** sound. Two are done for you as examples.

1. crack   ă
2. stay   X
3. land   ă
4. tap   ă
5. face   X
6. tame   X
7. jam   ă
8. Spain   X
9. bank   ă
10. pane   X

➤ *Practice in the Short* e *Sound*

Say each word below to yourself. Put an **e** with a cup symbol (**ĕ**) beside each word that contains a short **e** sound, like the e in *pet*. Put an *X* beside each word that does *not* have the short **e** sound. Two are done for you as examples.

1. bent   ĕ
2. feed   X
3. cream   X
4. get   ĕ
5. here   X
6. let   ĕ
7. sea   X
8. speed   X
9. end   ĕ
10. friend   ĕ

➤ *Practice in the Short* i *Sound*

Say each word below to yourself. Put an **i** with a cup symbol (**ĭ**) beside each word that contains a short **i** sound, like the i in *pit*. Put an *X* beside each word that does *not* have the short **i** sound. Two are done for you as examples.

1. wig   ĭ
2. spike   X
3. slim   ĭ
4. lime   X
5. disk   ĭ
6. file   X
7. lint   ĭ
8. ride   X
9. pin   ĭ
10. mice   X

➤ *Practice in the Short* o *Sound*

Say each word below to yourself. Put an **o** with a cup symbol (ŏ) beside each word that contains a short **o** sound, like the **o** in *pot*. Put an *X* beside each word that does *not* have the short **o** sound. Two are done for you as examples.

1. coat	__X__	6. stock	__ŏ__
2. stop	__ŏ__	7. load	__X__
3. cone	__X__	8. rock	__ŏ__
4. soak	__X__	9. grow	__X__
5. fox	__ŏ__	10. bond	__ŏ__

➤ *Practice in the Short* u *Sound*

Say each word below to yourself. Put a **u** with a cup symbol (ŭ) beside each word that contains a short **u** sound, like the **u** in *cut*. Put an *X* beside each word that does *not* have the short **u** sound. Two are done for you as examples.

1. bulb	__ŭ__	6. bump	__ŭ__
2. fuse	__X__	7. prune	__X__
3. rum	__ŭ__	8. blue	__X__
4. tune	__X__	9. uncle	__ŭ__
5. hug	__ŭ__	10. cute	__X__

LONG VOWEL SOUNDS

The list below shows how the long vowel sounds are pronounced. Read them to yourself, and you'll see that each vowel sounds like the letter's name. Also notice the symbol for the long sound, which is a straight line over the letter.

ā	sounds like the **a** in *pay*.
ē	sounds like the **e** in *bee*.
ī	sounds like the **i** in *pie*.
ō	sounds like the **o** in *toe*.
ū	sounds like the **u** in *abuse*.

Note: Some dictionaries show the long **u** sound as **yo͞o** rather than **ū**. But for the activities here, you can simply use the **ū**.

➤ *Practice in the Long Vowel Sounds*

A. Say each of the following words to yourself. Beside each word with a long vowel, write the letter that has that sound. Then put the line above it to show it has the long sound. Put an *X* beside each word that does *not* have a long vowel sound. One is done for you.

1. five _____ $\bar{\imath}$ _____   6. wave _____ $\bar{a}$ _____
2. text _____ X _____   7. brand _____ X _____
3. pole _____ $\bar{o}$ _____   8. slice _____ $\bar{\imath}$ _____
4. miss _____ X _____   9. self _____ X _____
5. sweet _____ $\bar{e}$ _____   10. cube _____ $\bar{u}$ _____

B. Fill in each blank with the word that contains at least one long vowel sound. Remember that a long vowel says its name.

1. You must be patient if you want to train and ride a *(camel, mule, horse)* _____ *mule* _____ .

2. In 1896, the first modern Olympic games were held in *(France, Greece, England)* _____ *Greece* _____ .

3. The entire life of a mayfly lasts only a single *(month, minute, day)* _____ *day* _____ .

4. *(Silver, Copper, Gold)* _____ *Gold* _____ was one of the first metals discovered by humans.

5. Sometimes the *(cost, price, charge)* _____ *price* _____ per ounce is more for a big box of soap than for a small one.

6. The silk of a spider's web is *(three, four, six)* _____ *three* _____ times stronger than iron of the same thickness.

7. Because of the electric light bulb, Americans today *(work, sleep, rest)* _____ *sleep* _____ an hour and a half less each night than Americans in the 1920s.

8. A company recently went broke after an unhappy employee had a computer *(void, cancel, erase)* _____ *erase* _____ all the company's billing records.

9. The famous magician Harry Houdini could free himself from a locked cell by spitting up a *(small, little, tiny)* _____ *tiny* _____ key he had swallowed.

10. The kidnapper wanted a *(big, large, huge)* _____ *huge* _____ ransom for the release of the bank president.

Rules for Long Vowel Sounds

1   The Silent-*e* Rule

Compare the sounds of the words in both columns below. Which column lists words with the long sound of the vowels?

	Column 1	Column 2
a	hat	hate
e	pet	Pete
i	bit	bite
o	rob	robe
u	cut	cute

The second column lists words with the long vowel sound. Notice that while the final **e** makes the vowel before it long, the **e** is not pronounced. Here, then, is the Silent-**e** Rule:

When a word ends in a vowel-consonant-*e*, the vowel before the consonant is long and the final *e* is silent.

Here are some more examples of this rule. The vowel before each final **e** has a long sound. Notice how all the words follow this format: Vowel-Consonant-Final **e**.

	Vowel	Consonant	Final e
n	a	m	e
sc	e	n	e
pr	i	d	e
h	o	p	e
c	u	b	e

➤ *Practice in the Silent-e Rule*

For each sentence below, write in the word that follows the Silent-e Rule.

1. Juan passed me a *(note, book, pen)* _____*note*_____ during English class.

2. When you have time, please change the *(bulb, sheets, fuse)* _____*fuse*_____.

3. Everybody else adores Alice, but I don't *(trust, like, enjoy)* _____*like*_____ her.

4. It's *(dangerous, risky, unsafe)* _____*unsafe*_____ to fall asleep on top of an electric blanket.

5. People believe I'm very *(brave, fearless, bold)* _____*brave*_____. However, the truth is that I'm very shy.

2   The Two-Vowels-Together Rule

Below are some examples of words that are pronounced according to the Two-Vowels-Together Rule. Notice each pair of vowels and how it is pronounced.

seed	plea	play
see	hail	tie
please	road	toe

Did you see any pattern in the way the vowels are pronounced? If you did, you discovered the Two-Vowels-Together Rule:

When two of certain vowels are together in a word, the first one is long and the second is silent.

There are exceptions, but here are vowels that usually follow this rule. Examples are provided as well.

ai	aid	aim	pail
ay	pay	stay	way

Note: In the -**ay** combination, **y** is a vowel.

ea	eat	pea	cream
ee	knee	bee	feet
ie	lie	pie	tied
oa	oat	toad	goat
oe	hoe	goes	woe

➤ *Practice in the Two-Vowels-Together Rule*

The words below follow the Two-Vowels-Together Rule. Write the vowel sound of each word in the blank. One is done for you.

1. road	$\bar{o}$		6. clay	$\bar{a}$
2. tail	$\bar{a}$		7. chain	$\bar{a}$
3. meat	$\bar{e}$		8. soap	$\bar{o}$
4. deep	$\bar{e}$		9. day	$\bar{a}$
5. toe	$\bar{o}$		10. teen	$\bar{e}$

3 Rule for a Final Single Vowel

A single vowel at the end of a word (other than a silent *e*) usually has a long sound.

me	she	hi	no	ago	cry

Remember that **y** is sometimes a vowel, as in *cry*, above. Notice that in *cry*, the y sounds like a long **i**.

➤ *Practice in the Rule for a Final Single Vowel*

Put a check by each word that can be pronounced according to the Rule for a Final Single Vowel. Write an *X* by each word that is *not* pronounced according to this rule.

1. be	✓	6. roam	X
2. rent	X	7. fly	✓
3. pro	✓	8. tack	X
4. robe	X	9. we	✓
5. so	✓	10. crib	X

A NOTE ON VOWEL SOUNDS VERSUS LETTERS

You have already seen that a single vowel sound can be shown by different letters or combinations of letters. For example, read the following words aloud, and note how the boldfaced vowel letters sound.

be	pea	many

In all three words, the boldfaced letter or letters have the same sound—long **e**. In other words, the *sound* of long **e** can be shown by various letters. In one case, *many*, the letter **e** isn't even in the word. Every so often, a word will contain a vowel sound that does not match any of the letters in the word.

Below are several such words. Use them to test your ability to recognize vowel sounds. In the space provided, see if you can give the vowel sound for the boldfaced vowels in each case.

Word	*Vowel Sound Heard*	*Word*	*Vowel Sound Heard*
s**o**n	_____	**a**ny	_____
bur**eau**	_____	w**a**tch	_____
v**ei**l	_____	f**ew**	_____

The boldfaced vowel sounds are as follows: *son*—short **u**, *bureau*—long **o**, *veil*—long **a**, *any*—short **e**, *watch*—short **o**, *few*—long **u**.

The following practice will help you further test your ability to recognize vowel sounds.

➤ *Practice in Identifying Vowel Sounds*

Identify the vowel sound in each of the following words by writing the letter of the sound with either a line (for a long vowel) or a cup (for a short vowel) over the letter. In most cases, the vowel sound differs from the vowel letters in the word. The first has been done for you.

Vowel Sound Heard		*Vowel Sound Heard*	
1. love	ŭ	6. eye	ī
2. **eight**	ā	7. said	ĕ
3. laugh	ă	8. been	ĭ
4. sew	ō	9. wash	ŏ
5. each	ē	10. does	ŭ

OTHER VOWEL SOUNDS

The Vowel *y*

When **y** starts a word (for example, *yell*), it is a consonant. Otherwise, **y** is a vowel and usually has one of the following three vowel sounds:

- In the middle of a word, **y** usually sounds like short **i**, as in *myth*, *gym*, and *syrup*.

- At the end of a one-syllable word, **y** sounds like long **i**, as in *my*, *sty*, and *fry*.

  (*Note:* A **syllable** is a word or part of a word that has one vowel sound. For example, *fry* is a one-syllable word, and *frying* is a two-syllable word. You will learn more about syllables in the next chapter.)

- At the end of a word with more than one syllable, **y** sounds like long **e**, as in *many*, *baby*, and *city*.

➤ *Practice in the Sounds of* y

In the space provided, show whether the **y** in each word below sounds like a short **i** (ĭ), a long **i** (ī), or a long **e** (ē). Three are done for you.

1. stingy	ē	6. lynch	ĭ
2. hymn	ĭ	7. dry	ī
3. try	ī	8. carry	ē
4. sadly	ē	9. fifty	ē
5. by	ī	10. symbol	ĭ

The Sounds of Vowels Followed by an r

The sound of **r** changes the sounds of vowels. When a vowel comes just before an **r**, it is usually neither long nor short, but in between. To see how this works, say the following words to yourself. Notice how the sound of a vowel—and the shape of your mouth—change a bit when the vowel is followed by **r**.

Long vowels	Short vowels	Vowels followed by r
cane	can	car
Steve	set	her
spite	sit	sir
code	cod	cord
fuel	fun	fur

➤ Practice with Long and Short Vowels and Vowels Followed by r

Identify each boldfaced vowel with one of the following:

1) the symbol for a long vowel sound (‾)
2) the symbol for a short vowel sound (ˇ)
3) an **r** if the vowel sound is changed by an **r**

The first three have been done for you.

1. gas	ˇ	8. firm	r
2. hard	r	9. glee	‾
3. page	‾	10. run	ˇ
4. saint	‾	11. loan	‾
5. term	r	12. trick	ˇ
6. purse	r	13. park	r
7. ripe	‾	14. sport	r

Long and Short *oo*

When two o's appear together, they are pronounced in one of two ways. One is called the **long double o sound**, as in *boot*.

Here are some other words with the long sound of **oo**:

spoon   room   shampoo

The other sound is called the **short double o sound**, as in *foot*. Here are some other words with the short sound of **oo**:

stood   good   cook

➤ *Practice in Long and Short* oo

In the space provided, show whether each **oo** vowel sound is long ($\bar{oo}$) or short ($\breve{oo}$). Two are done for you as examples.

1.	choose	$\bar{oo}$		6	foot	$\breve{oo}$
2.	shook	$\breve{oo}$		7.	wool	$\breve{oo}$
3.	loose	$\bar{oo}$		8.	proof	$\bar{oo}$
4.	brook	$\breve{oo}$		9.	zoo	$\bar{oo}$
5.	cartoon	$\bar{oo}$		10.	crook	$\breve{oo}$

➤ *Review Test 1*

To review what you have learned in this chapter, answer each of the following questions. Fill in the blank, or circle the letter of the answer you think is correct.

1. Examples of words with short vowel sounds are
   a. *sat, pet, bit, hot,* and *cut.* *(circled)*
   b. *name, he, like, no,* and *use.*
   c. *care, car, pier,* and *urge.*

2. _T_ TRUE OR FALSE? The silent-e rule states that when a word ends in a vowel-consonant-**e**, the first vowel is long and the **e** is silent.

3. The two-vowels-together rule states that
   a. when two of certain vowels are together in a word, the first is long and the second is short.
   b. when two of certain vowels are together in a word, both vowels are long.
   c. when two of certain vowels are together in a word, the first is long and the second is silent. *(circled)*

4. When **y** is in the middle of a word,
   a. it is a consonant.
   (b.) it usually sounds like short **i**.
   c. it usually sounds like short **e**.

5. ___F___ TRUE OR FALSE? A vowel followed by **r** is usually short.

➤ *Review Test 2*

A. For each item below, write a word from the box with the vowel sound listed. When you are finished, you will have used all the words in the box.

dress	place	cram	file	home
mix	used	nod	dust	green

1. Short **a** sound: _____*cram*_____   6. Long **i** sound: _____*file*_____

2. Long **a** sound: _____*place*_____   7. Short **o** sound: _____*nod*_____

3. Short **e** sound: _____*dress*_____   8. Long **o** sound: _____*home*_____

4. Long **e** sound: _____*green*_____   9. Short **u** sound: _____*dust*_____

5. Short **i** sound: _____*mix*_____   10. Long **u** sound: _____*used*_____

B. Here are the rules for long vowel sounds:

a	When a word ends in a vowel-consonant-**e**, the vowel before the consonant is long and the final **e** is silent.
b	When two of certain vowels are together in a word, the first one is long and the second is silent.
c	A single vowel at the end of a word (other than a silent **e**) usually has a long sound.

Beside each word, write the letter of the rule that applies. Write a short explanation as well. Note the example.

Example

toast ___*b*___ *The "o" is long and the "a" is silent.*

11. face ___*a*___ *The "a" is long and the "e" is silent.*

12. go ___*c*___ *The "o" is long.*

13. road   _b_   *The "o" is long and the "a" is silent.*

14. steal   _b_   *The "e" is long and the "a" is silent.*

15. plane   _a_   *The "a" is long and the "e" is silent.*

C. Here are the rules for **y** as a vowel:

---

a   In the middle of a word, **y** usually sounds like short **i**.

b   At the end of a one-syllable word, **y** sounds like long **i**.

c   At the end of a word with more than one syllable, **y** sounds like long **e**.

Beside each word, identify the **y** sound by writing in one of the following:

    $\breve{\imath}$ (short **i**) $\bar{\imath}$ (long **i**) $\bar{e}$ (long **e**)

Write a short explanation as well. Note the example.

Example

     ready $\bar{e}$ *At the end of a word with more than one syllable*

16. sky $\bar{\imath}$ *At the end of a one-syllable word*

17. party $\bar{e}$ *At the end of a word with more than one syllable*

18. system $\breve{\imath}$ *In the middle of a word*

19. hurry $\bar{e}$ *At the end of a word with more than one syllable*

20. dry $\bar{\imath}$ *At the end of a one-syllable word*

➤ Review Test 3

Answer each question in the space provided.

A. Beside each word, write its vowel sound.

If the vowel is short, write $\breve{a}$, $\breve{e}$, $\breve{\imath}$, $\breve{o}$, or $\breve{u}$.

If the vowel is long, write $\bar{a}$, $\bar{e}$, $\bar{\imath}$, $\bar{o}$, or $\bar{u}$.

If the vowel is followed by **r**, write **r**.

1. seen	$\bar{e}$		6 knock	$\breve{o}$	
2. click	$\breve{\imath}$		7. slang	$\breve{a}$	
3. felt	$\breve{e}$		8. wave	$\bar{a}$	
4. glide	$\bar{\imath}$		9. stove	$\bar{o}$	
5. pump	$\breve{u}$		10. yard	r	

B. Complete each sentence by writing in the word with a *short* vowel. Remember that vowels followed by an **r** are neither long nor short.

11. Makeup couldn't hide the mosquito bite on Nina's *(cheek, chin, nose)*
_____*chin*_____ .

12. Kendrick liked a big breakfast, which always included *(eggs, oatmeal, juice)*
_____*eggs*_____ .

13. Amanpal was the perfect class president—well-informed, intelligent, and
(fair, sincere, warm) _____*sincere*_____ .

14. The FBI can tell the *(model, year, age)* _____*model*_____ of a car
from only a chip of paint left at the scene of an accident.

15. My mother *(clips, saves, keeps)* _____*clips*_____ so many coupons
that most of them expire before she ever uses them.

C. Here are the rules for long vowel sounds:

a	When a word ends in a vowel-consonant-**e**, the vowel before the consonant is long and the final **e** is silent.
b	When two of certain vowels are together in a word, the first one is long and the second is silent.
c	A single vowel at the end of a word (other than a silent **e**) usually has a long sound.

Use the rules to help you place the following words in the right spaces.

be	mean	close	greed	lake

Silent-e Rule	*Two-Vowels-Together Rule*	*Final Vowel Rule*
16. _____*close*_____	18. _____*mean*_____	20. _____*be*_____
17. _____*lake*_____	19. _____*greed*_____	

D. Show with a check whether the **oo** in each word is long or short.

	Long oo	*Short oo*
21. book		✓
22. balloon	✓	
23. food	✓	
24. baboon	✓	
25. hook		✓

➤ *Review Test 4*

Here is a chance to apply your understanding of phonics to a full-length reading. This selection is about a remarkable journey made yearly by an insect most of us probably take for granted: the monarch butterfly. The author describes the butterfly's remarkable annual journey and the problems the monarch is facing. When you finish reading the selection, answer the phonics questions that follow.

Words to Watch

Following are some words in the reading that do not have strong context support. Each word is followed by the number of the paragraph in which it appears and its meaning there. These words are indicated in the article by a small circle (°).

slope (1): steep bank
shimmered (1): sparkled
hordes (2): large groups
roosts (2): resting places
larvae (3): the wingless, wormlike forms of newly-hatched insects
cocoons (4): the silky case spun by the larvae of insects
ancestors (6): parents and grandparents
aerial (6): from the air
hibernation (6): a state similar to sleep that many animals enter during winter
revive (7): become active again
migration (7): seasonal journey
sanctuary (11): a place offering shelter and protection

THE AMAZING MONARCH BUTTERFLY

Peter Sanchez

On a January day in 1975, Ken and Catalina Brugger wandered through an ancient forest in Mexico. The forest sat on a high mountain slope° eighty miles west of Mexico City. The air was damp and cool. The sky was cloudy, so little light reached through the trees. As the Bruggers walked along, they realized they were hearing a quiet, constant noise. It was like rain falling on the fir trees. But there was no rain. They looked around for the source of the sound. Suddenly, sunlight broke through the clouds and lit up the forest. The Bruggers gasped in delight. All around them, the trees shimmered° with the beating of brilliant orange and black wings. The Bruggers were surrounded by millions of monarch butterflies, resting in their winter home.   1

The Bruggers' discovery was important in the world of butterfly study. Butterfly lovers knew that, late every summer, hordes° of monarchs migrate from Canada into Mexico. More than 300 million of the fragile creatures make the 2,500-mile flight. But no one knew what became of the butterflies once they reached Mexico. Within the next few years, twelve more monarch roosts° were discovered. They were all along the same mountain range where the Bruggers had made their find. Now the mystery was solved.   2

The monarchs' stay in Mexico is just one part of an amazing life cycle. Every spring, in Mexico, female monarchs lay enormous numbers of eggs. One female may lay more than four hundred a month. She attaches her eggs to milkweed plants. The milkweed provides a perfect first home for the young monarchs. Because milkweed is poisonous to most creatures, birds and other butterfly enemies avoid it. But monarchs love milkweed. The eggs hatch in three to twelve days, and out come worm-like larvae° which feast on the weed. The poison does not hurt them. But it does have an important effect. It makes the monarch as poisonous as the plant was. A bird that eats a monarch will become very sick—and never eat another one.   3

After living for two weeks as larvae, the monarchs attach themselves to leaves. Then they spin cocoons°. After a week, the cocoons open and the butterflies emerge, soon to begin their 2,500-mile flight northwards. Many of them die as they pass through such southern states as Texas and Louisiana. But first they lay more eggs. After a few weeks, a new generation of monarchs is ready to continue the journey. They—or their children or grandchildren—will finally reach Canada, where they spend the summer.   4

In late August, the monarchs begin the return trip from Canada to   5
Mexico. Flying along southbound breezes, the butterflies travel as fast
as thirty-five miles per hour. Most make the trip in about six weeks.

No one knows how the young butterflies find their way to   6
Mexico. Yet they do. They arrive at the same stands of fir trees their
ancestors° rested in months before. There they crowd onto the trees in
enormous numbers. Their weight sometimes breaks branches. Aerial°
photographs of the monarch roosts show the normally green forest
turned bright orange. The monarchs rest in the Mexican forests for
about seven months. They survive in a state that is similar to
hibernation°. The forests' cool, damp air slows all the butterflies'
bodily functions. The insects rest, using very little energy.

Then in March, responding to some mysterious signal, the   7
butterflies revive°, and the process begins again. They take to the air
again and head north. Again, most of them die while they pass through
southern states. But first they lay their eggs. After a few weeks, a new
generation of monarchs is continuing the migration to Canada through
the U.S.

The monarch butterfly has been making its amazing migration° for   8
perhaps ten million years. Along the way, the beautiful insect has
thrilled countless humans. Sadly, the day of the monarch may be ending.

The actions of human beings are threatening the survival of the   9
monarch butterfly. Cars crush millions of monarchs every year.
Weedkillers destroy milkweed, without which the monarch cannot
survive. The wildflowers that give them nectar are also being wiped
out. Insect poisons contaminate the water that the monarchs drink.
Worst of all, timber companies are threatening the Mexican forests
where the monarchs winter. One sanctuary has already been destroyed,
and others are targeted for large-scale logging.

So far, it is not too late to save the monarch. Environmental   10
groups in Mexico, the U.S., and Canada are trying to stop logging in
the monarch's rest areas. U.S. seed companies have produced a
"monarch mixture" of milkweed and wildflowers for schoolchildren to
plant in meadows. But such efforts must proceed quickly if the
beautiful monarch is to survive.

The Mexican organization Monarca A.C. is one of the groups   11
trying to save the butterfly. Its president, Carlos Gottfried, says that no
effort is too great. "If we lose the monarch," he explains, "we lose a
link with something mysterious and everlasting. When you stand in a
monarch sanctuary°, your soul is shaken and your life is changed."

Phonics Questions

Use phonics clues you learned from this chapter and the previous chapter to answer the following questions. Circle the letter of your choice for each question.

1. The **s** in the word *shimmered* in "All around them, the trees shimmered with the beating of brilliant orange and black wings" (paragraph 1)
    a. sounds like the **s** in *salt.*
    b. sounds like the **s** in *rose.*
    (c.) is part of a consonant digraph.

2. The **kn** in the word *knew* in "Butterfly lovers knew that, late every summer, hordes of monarchs migrate from Canada into Mexico" (paragraph 2) is
    a. a consonant blend.
    b. a consonant digraph.
    (c.) a silent letter combination.

3. The **x** in the word *next* in "Within the next few years, twelve more monarch roosts were discovered" (paragraph 2)
    (a.) sounds like **ks**.
    b. sounds like **gz**.
    c. sounds like **z**.

4. The word *milkweed* in "Because milkweed is poisonous to most creatures, birds and other butterfly enemies avoid it" (paragraph 3) has
    a. two short vowel sounds.
    b. two long vowel sounds.
    (c.) one short vowel sound and one long vowel sound.

5. The word *leaves* in "the monarchs attach themselves to leaves" (paragraph 4) has
    (a.) one long vowel sound.
    b. one short vowel sound.
    c. one long vowel sound and one short vowel sound.

6. The word *while* in "Again, most of them die while they pass through southern states" (paragraph 7) follows which vowel rule?
    a. The two-vowels-together rule
    b. The final single vowel rule
    (c.) The silent-**e** rule

7. The **y** in the word *sadly* in "Sadly, the day of the monarch may be ending" (paragraph 8) sounds like a
    a. short **i**.
    b. short **e**.
    (c.) long **e**.

8. The word *cars* in "Cars crush millions of monarchs every year" (paragraph 9) has a
   a. short vowel.
   b. long vowel.
   (c.) vowel followed by **r**.

9. The word *too* in "So far, it is not too late to save the monarch" (paragraph 10) has a
   a. short vowel sound.
   (b.) long double **o** sound.
   c. short double **o** sound.

10. Which word in the sentence below has two long vowel sounds?
    a. *efforts*
    (b.) *proceed*
    c. *quickly*

    "But such efforts must proceed quickly if the beautiful monarch is to survive." (Paragraph 10)

Mapping Activity

Major events in the life cycle of a monarch butterfly are scrambled below. Write them in the diagram on the next page in their correct order. Two items have been filled in for you.

- The monarchs rest for seven months.
- Larvae hatch from the eggs and feed on milkweed for two weeks.
- Butterflies emerge from the cocoons.
- The monarchs take to the air and head north, they or their children or grandchildren reaching Canada.
- The larvae attach themselves to leaves and spin cocoons.

Central point: The monarch butterfly's amazing life cycle spans many months and many miles.

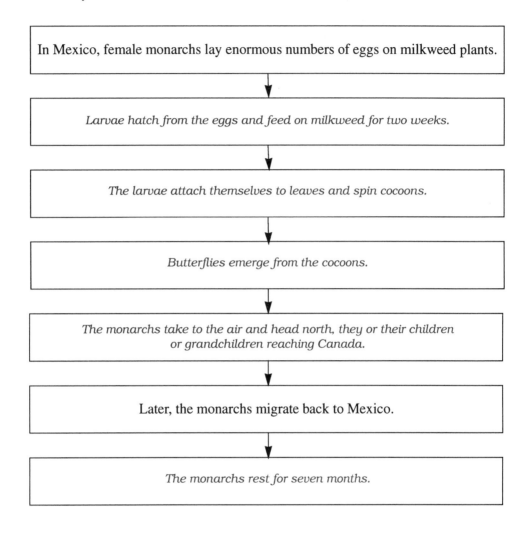

In Mexico, female monarchs lay enormous numbers of eggs on milkweed plants.

↓

Larvae hatch from the eggs and feed on milkweed for two weeks.

↓

The larvae attach themselves to leaves and spin cocoons.

↓

Butterflies emerge from the cocoons.

↓

The monarchs take to the air and head north, they or their children or grandchildren reaching Canada.

↓

Later, the monarchs migrate back to Mexico.

↓

The monarchs rest for seven months.

Discussion Questions

1. The author and some people he mentions in the article believe it is important to save the monarch butterfly. What reasons are given? Do you agree that it is important to save the butterfly? Why or why not?

2. The author mentions two mysteries associated with the monarch butterfly. Which mystery has been solved? Which mystery remains to be solved? What possible answers to that mystery can you think of?

Writing Activities

1. Like the Bruggers, most of us have had dramatic experiences of one sort or another with insects or animals. Write a paper describing one such experience. In addition to telling in detail what happened, explain how the experience made you feel.

2. The president of a Mexican organization trying to save the monarch butterfly implies that a monarch sanctuary is a magical place, one people cannot forget. Write a paragraph about a place that you will never forget. Describe this place, and explain why it is so special to you.

Check Your Performance   **PHONICS II: VOWELS**

Activity	Number Right	Points	Total
Review Test 1 (5 items)	_____	x 2 =	_____
Review Test 2 (20 items)	_____	x 1.5 =	_____
Review Test 3 (25 items)	_____	x 1 =	_____
Review Test 4 (10 items)	_____	x 2.5 =	_____
Mapping Activity (5 items)	_____	x 2 =	_____

TOTAL SCORE = _____%

Enter your total score onto the Reading Performance Chart: Review Tests on the inside back cover.

3

Phonics III: Syllables

Most of the words used in the chapters on consonants and vowels are short ones. But the words that often give you the most trouble are long words. To pronounce such long words, you should first separate them into parts called syllables. You can then focus on pronouncing each syllable and go on to read the entire word.

This chapter first explains what a syllable is. Then it explains five rules that will help you break words into syllables.

SYLLABLES

A **syllable** is a word or part of a word that has one vowel sound. This vowel sound is spoken together with any consonant sounds in the syllable.

For example, the word *rip* has just one vowel sound; thus it has only one syllable. The sounds of **r**, short **i**, and **p** are all spoken together. The word *sunset* has two syllables. It is pronounced in two parts: *sun* and *set*. The vowel sound in the first syllable is short **u**; the vowel sound in the second syllable is short **e**.

Some one-, two-, and three-syllable words are shown below. Say each word to yourself. Notice the single vowel sound in each syllable. Also note any consonant sounds that are spoken with the vowel.

One-syllable words	Two-syllable words	Three-syllable words
go	kindness	happily
I	golden	Superman
fun	moral	professor
pray	confess	humorless
Fred	happy	syllable

Now, in the blank spaces below and under the correct headings, write these words:

brother   lunch   grandparent   market   clock   dishonest

One-syllable words   *Two-syllable words*   *Three-syllable words*

_____   _____   _____

_____   _____   _____

You should have added *lunch* and *clock* to the one-syllable list, *brother* and *market* to the two-syllable list, and *grandparent* and *dishonest* to the three-syllable list.

An Important Reminder

In the three lists on the previous page, each syllable contains just one vowel and one vowel sound. However, remember that some words have *two* vowels but only *one* vowel sound:

1   Words with a silent final *e*

Here are some words in which the final **e** is silent.

same   Eve   write   rose   tune

Each word has two vowels but only one vowel sound. In each case, the final **e** is silent. Since each word has only one vowel sound, each is a one-syllable word.

2   Words with two vowels together in which one vowel is silent

Here are some examples of words with this pattern:

heat   breed   pair   soap   play   toe

Each word has two vowels together but only one vowel sound. In each case, the second vowel is silent. Since each word has only one vowel sound, each is a one-syllable word.

➤ *Practice 1*

Fill in the blank spaces below. The first two items have been done for you.

	Number of vowels	Number of vowel sounds	Number of syllables
1. silent	2	2	2
2. ride	2	1	1
3. boat	2	1	1

	Number of vowels	Number of vowel sounds	Number of syllables
4. doe	2	1	1
5. cane	2	1	1
6. heel	2	1	1
7. among	2	2	2
8. chair	2	1	1
9. however	3	3	3
10. least	2	1	1
11. freezing	3	2	2
12. amuse	3	2	2

FIVE RULES FOR DIVIDING WORDS INTO SYLLABLES

You already know that each syllable has one vowel sound. That knowledge and the following rules will help you divide words into syllables. There are exceptions, but the rules hold true much of the time.

Dividing Between Two Consonants

Rule 1: **When two consonants come between two vowels, divide between the consonants.**

This rule is also known as the VC/CV (vowel-consonant/consonant-vowel) pattern. Here are examples:

hap-pen   don-key   sil-ver

To break each word into syllables, divide between the consonants: between **p** and **p** in *happen*, between **n** and **k** in *donkey*, and between **l** and **v** in *silver.*
According to the VC/CV rule, where would you divide the following words? Draw a line between the syllables.

import   hostage   tunnel

The correct divisions for these words are *im-port, hos-tage, and tun-nel.*

Pronunciation tip: The vowel before a double consonant usually has a short sound. For example, the **i** in *import*, the **o** in *hostage*, and the **u** in *tunnel* are all short vowels.

➤ *Practice 2*

Break the following words into syllables by dividing between double consonants (VC/CV). The first word has been done for you.

1. arrest   *ar-rest*

2. candy   *can-dy*

3. napkin   *nap-kin*

4. harbor   *har-bor*

5. trumpet   *trum-pet*

6. muffin   *muf-fin*

Dividing Between Three Consonants

At times a word will have three consonants in a row. For example:

     monster   surprise   applaud

In such cases, you usually divide between the first consonant and the second two, as shown below:

     mon-ster   sur-prise   ap-plaud

The second and third consonants form a **consonant blend**—two or more consonants that keep their sounds but are spoken together.

➤ *Practice 3*

Break the following words into syllables by dividing between a consonant and a consonant blend. The first word has been done for you.

1. displace   *dis-place*

2. central   *cen-tral*

3. address   *ad-dress*

4. complete   *com-plete*

5. attract   *at-tract*

6. obscure   *ob-scure*

Dividing Before a Single Consonant

Rule 2: **When a single consonant comes between two vowel sounds, divide before the consonant.**

The rule is also known as the V/CV (vowel/consonant-vowel) pattern. Here are examples:

mi-nus   po-ny   e-ven

To break each word into syllables, you divide before the single consonant: between the **i** and **n** in *minus*, between the **o** and **n** in *pony*, and between the **e** and **v** in *even*.

According to the V/CV rule, where would you divide the following words? Draw a line between the syllables.

female   ruby   moment

The correct divisions for these words are *fe-male, ru-by*, and *mo-ment*.

Pronunciation tip: In two-syllable words, the vowel before a single consonant division usually has a long sound. For example, the first **e** in *female*, the **u** in *ruby*, and the **o** in *moment* all are long vowels.

➤ *Practice 4*

Break the following words into syllables by dividing before the single consonants (V/CV). One has been done for you as an example.

1. cater   *ca-ter*
2. bonus   *bo-nus*
3. item   *i-tem*
4. final   *fi-nal*
5. major   *ma-jor*
6. unit   *u-nit*

Dividing Before a Consonant + *le*

> *Rule 3:* **If a word ends in a consonant followed by *le*, the consonant and *le* form the last syllable.**

The words below are divided according to this rule.

        han-dle   ca-ble   sim-ple

> According to the consonant + **le** rule, where would you divide the following words? Draw a line between the syllables.

        circle   middle   ankle

The correct divisions for these words are *cir-cle, mid-dle*, and *an-kle*.

➤ *Practice 5*

> Break the following words into syllables by dividing before the consonant + **le**. One has been done for you as an example.

1. table   _____*ta-ble*_____
2. idle   _____*i-dle*_____
3. ripple   _____*rip-ple*_____
4. purple   _____*pur-ple*_____
5. title   _____*ti-tle*_____
6. gargle   _____*gar-gle*_____

Dividing After Prefixes and Before Suffixes

> *Rule 4:* **Prefixes and suffixes are usually separate syllables.**

Prefixes are word parts that are added to the beginnings of words. Common prefixes include:

com-	**de-**	**dis-**	**ex-**	**in-**
non-	**pre-**	**re-**	**sub-**	**un-**

Suffixes are word parts that are added to the ends of words. Common suffixes include:

-able	**-en**	**-er**	**-ful**	**-ing**
-less	**-ly**	**-ment**	**-ness**	**-tion**

The words below are divided according to this rule.

pre-fix   un-fair   play-er   fall-ing

Divisions occur after the two prefixes (*pre-* and *un-*) and before the two suffixes (*-er* and *-ing*).

According to the rule for prefixes and suffixes, where would you divide the following words? Draw a line between the syllables.

holding   compete   cheapen   dislike

The correct divisions for these words are *hold-ing, com-pete, cheap-en*, and *dislike*.

➤ Practice 6

Break the following words into syllables by dividing after a prefix or before a suffix. The first word has been done for you.

1. preview   _____*pre-view*_____

2. nation   _____*na-tion*_____

3. recall   _____*re-call*_____

4. playful   _____*play-ful*_____

5. jumping   _____*jump-ing*_____

6. export   _____*ex-port*_____

Dividing Between the Words in a Compound Word

Rule 5: Compound words are always divided between the words they contain.

A **compound word** is a combination of two words. When compound words are broken into syllables, they are always divided between the smaller words they contain. Here are examples:

gold-fish   blood-stream   ring-side

According to the rule for compound words, where would you divide the following words? Draw a line between the syllables.

railroad   breakfast   redhead

The correct divisions for these words are *rail-road, break-fast*, and *red-head*.

➤ *Practice 7*

Break the following words into syllables by dividing between smaller words. The first word has been done for you.

1. southeast   _____ *south-east* _____

2. notebook   _____ *note-book* _____

3. raincoat   _____ *rain-coat* _____

4. popcorn   _____ *pop-corn* _____

5. workshop   _____ *work-shop* _____

6. cutback   _____ *cut-back* _____

PRONOUNCING WORDS

To pronounce a word, follow these steps:

1 Use the rules in this chapter to divide the word into syllables. There are exceptions, but the rules hold true much of the time. At the least, they will get you very close to correct word divisions.

2 To pronounce each syllable, apply the phonics principles explained in Chapters 1 and 2. Don't pronounce the entire word at once; just sound out each syllable. Take your time.

3 Then add the accent where it sounds right. (Accents are explained in detail on page 95). The accent, or emphasis, is generally placed on the syllable that will make the word easiest to pronounce.

4 Finally, say the entire word aloud. Repeat it until you are comfortable with your pronunciation of the word.

Note: When you are in doubt about how to pronounce a word, you can turn to the dictionary. In Chapter 5, "Dictionary Use," you will learn how to use dictionary symbols to pronounce words.

➤ Review Test 1

To review what you have learned in this chapter, answer each of the following questions. Fill in the blank, or circle the letter of the answer you think is correct.

1. __F__ TRUE OR FALSE? A syllable is a word or word part that always contains only one vowel.

2. When two consonants come between two vowels, divide
   a. before the two consonants.
   b. between the two consonants.
   c. after the two consonants.

3. When a single consonant comes between two vowel sounds,
   a. divide before the consonant.
   b. divide after the consonant.
   c. both vowel sounds will usually be long.

4. __T__ TRUE OR FALSE? Prefixes and suffixes are usually separate syllables.

5. __T__ TRUE OR FALSE? Compound words are always divided between the words they contain.

➤ Review Test 2

A. Using the rules shown in the box, break the following words into syllables. For each word, also write the number of the rule that applies. The first word has been done for you.

> 1. **Divide between two consonants.**
> 2. **Divide before a single consonant.**

	Syllable Division	Rule Number
1. pencil	pen-cil	1
2. system	sys-tem	1
3. focus	fo-cus	2
4. comment	com-ment	1
5. music	mu-sic	2
6. maintain	main-tain	1
7. lecture	lec-ture	1
8. vacant	va-cant	2

		Syllable Division	*Rule Number*
9.	silent	si-lent	2
10.	immune	im-mune	1

B. Using the rules shown in the box, break the words below into syllables. For each word, also write the number of the rule that applies. The first word has been done for you.

> **3.**   **Divide before a consonant followed by *le*.**
>
> **4.**   **Divide after prefixes and before suffixes.**
>
> **5.**   **Divide between the words in a compound word.**

		Syllable Division	*Rule Number*
11.	footstep	foot-step	5
12.	payment	pay-ment	4
13.	sample	sam-ple	3
14.	pushup	push-up	5
15.	trouble	trou-ble	3
16.	joyful	joy-ful	4
17.	bottle	bot-tle	3
18.	sometimes	some-times	5
19.	toothpaste	tooth-paste	5
20.	unpaid	un-paid	4

➤ *Review Test 3*

A. Using the rules shown in the box, break the following words into syllables. For each syllable break, write the number of the rule that applies. The first word has been done for you.

> **1.**   **Divide between two consonants.**
>
> **2.**   **Divide before a single consonant.**

		Syllable Division	*Rule Numbers*	
1.	festival	fes-ti-val	1	2

	Syllable Division	Rule Numbers	
2. contradict	con-tra-dict	1	2
3. important	im-por-tant	1	1
4. frequency	fre-quen-cy	2	1
5. magnitude	mag-ni-tude	1	2
6. attorney	at-tor-ney	1	1
7. obstinate	ob-sti-nate	1	2
8. dinosaur	di-no-saur	2	2
9. illegal	il-le-gal	1	2
10. privacy	pri-va-cy	2	2

B. Using the rules shown in the box, break the following words into syllables. For each syllable break, write the number of the rule that applies. The first word has been done for you.

> **3.** **Divide before a consonant followed by *le*.**
>
> **4.** **Divide after prefixes and before suffixes.**
>
> **5.** **Divide between the words in a compound word.**

	Syllable Division	Rule Numbers	
11. seasickness	sea-sick-ness	5	4
12. replacement	re-place-ment	4	4
13. disable	dis-a-ble	4	3
14. resettle	re-set-tle	4	3
15. delightful	de-light-ful	4	4
16. breathtaking	breath-tak-ing	5	4
17. unstable	un-sta-ble	4	3
18. invention	in-ven-tion	4	4
19. upbringing	up-bring-ing	5	4
20. prescription	pre-scrip-tion	4	4

➤ *Review Test 4*

Here is a chance to apply your understanding of syllables to a full-length reading. The author of the selection writes, "I don't know if you ever noticed, but it's a lot harder for teachers to fall asleep in class than it is for students." The reason, he suggests, is that the teachers are doing something which the students are not. What is this activity? Could a change in American curriculum encourage students to do it, too? See what you think after you read "Why Johnny Can't Think." When you finish reading the selection, answer the phonics questions that follow.

Words to Watch

Following are some words in the reading that do not have strong context support. Each word is followed by the number of the paragraph in which it appears and its meaning there. These words are indicated in the article by a small circle (°).

occurred (1): came to mind
campaign (1): activities aimed at winning an election
evidence (1): proof
seldom (5): rarely
sound (5): reasonable
sound bite (6): brief bit of TV news
curriculum (7): the courses of study offered at a school

WHY JOHNNY CAN'T THINK

Peter Kugel

It occurred° to me the other day that this year's rather mindless 1
presidential campaign° might be further evidence° of the decline of
American education. Maybe the candidates are giving us such a thin
diet because our schools never taught us how to deal with anything
more substantial.

Look at how we teach people to think. We have teachers stand in 2
front of classrooms and think out loud, while the students listen.

It seems to me that expecting students to learn from such 3
instruction is like expecting people to learn to play football by lying on
a couch and watching it on TV. Schools don't teach football that way;
they teach their students to play football by having them play football.

How come schools don't teach their students how to think by 4
having them think?

Of course, that's what the students are supposed to be doing while 5
the teacher is thinking out loud in front of them, but they seldom° do.

And, even when they do, they can seldom tell whether what they are thinking is sound°.

All they can evaluate is how it makes them feel. That's perfect preparation for the sound bite° on the evening news: you evaluate the candidate by how he makes you feel.   6

Can we do any better? We might consider an idea from an educational movement that started in Great Britain called "writing across the curriculum°." It suggests that one way to make students think about something is to make them write about it.   7

Writing can help you learn. For example, suppose you're learning about the tides. There's five minutes of class time left that the teacher might use to give you more facts.   8

But, instead, the teacher asks you to write a short letter to a ten-year-old explaining what causes tides. You might wonder what you would learn from doing that.   9

Would five more minutes of lecturing by the teacher, who knows the material, be more useful than five minutes of writing by a student who doesn't?   10

Not necessarily. For one thing, listening is passive, while writing is active. It's a lot easier to pay attention when you're being active. I don't know if you ever noticed, but it's a lot harder for teachers to fall asleep in class than it is for students.   11

When students are writing, they're doing something. It not only keeps them awake, but, while they're writing, they're doing a very active form of thinking.   12

We learn to ride a bicycle through the activity of riding a bicycle, and we never forget how to do it. Maybe if we learned to think by writing, we'd forget less of what we had learned.   13

Sure, I know students already do a lot of writing in school. They write essays and term papers. But those who advocate "writing across the curriculum" are suggesting a different kind of writing: writing to learn; writing to develop ideas; writing in all your classes (that's why it's called "writing across the curriculum"); the kind of writing you do when you write notes to yourself on the backs of envelopes; writing to help you think.   14

Suppose that when we were in school we had spent more time writing about what we were thinking and less listening to what others thought? We might have learned to consider whether what the candidates are saying makes sense and whether their ideas fit together.   15

If we were ready to do that, don't you think that the candidates would give us a different kind of campaign? Can you imagine what campaign speeches would be like if, at the end of each one, the entire   16

> audience sat down and tried to write a letter to a ten-year-old, explaining what the candidates had just said?

Phonics Questions

Use phonics clues you learned from chapters 1–3 to answer the following questions. Circle the letter of your choice for each question.

1. The word *teach* in "Look at how we teach people to think" (paragraph 2) contains a
   a. soft **c** sound.
   b. hard **c** sound.
   c. consonant digraph.

2. The word *think* in "How come schools don't teach their students how to think by having them think?" (paragraph 4) contains
   a. a consonant digraph.
   b. a consonant blend.
   c. both a digraph and a blend.

3. The word *feel* in "All they can evaluate is how it makes them feel" (paragraph 6) contains
   a. a short vowel sound.
   b. a long vowel sound.
   c. both a short vowel sound and a long vowel sound.

4. The word *suppose* in "For example, suppose you're learning about the tides" (paragraph 8) contains
   a. two short vowel sounds.
   b. two long vowel sounds.
   c. one short vowel sound and one long vowel sound.

5. The **y** in the word *necessarily* in "Not necessarily" (paragraph 11) sounds like
   a. a long **e**.
   b. a short **i**.
   c. a long **i**.

6. The word *passive* in "For one thing, listening is passive, while writing is active" (paragraph 11) contains
   a. one syllable.
   b. two syllables.
   c. three syllables.

7. The word *bicycle* in "We learn to ride a bicycle through the activity of riding a bicycle, and we never forget how to do it" (paragraph 13) is broken into syllables as follows:
   a. bi-cyc-le.
   (b.) bi-cy-cle.
   c. bic-yc-le.

8. The word *advocate* in "But those who advocate 'writing across the curriculum' are suggesting a different kind of writing" (paragraph 14) is broken into syllables as follows:
   (a.) ad-vo-cate.
   b. ad-voc-ate.
   c. a-dvo-cate.

9. The word *envelopes* in "But those who advocate 'writing across the curriculum' are suggesting a different kind of writing: . . . the kind of writing you do when you write notes to yourself on the backs of envelopes" (paragraph 14) is broken into syllables as follows:
   a. en-vel-opes.
   b. env-el-opes.
   (c.) en-ve-lopes.

10. The word *candidates* in "If we were ready to do that, don't you think that the candidates would give us a different kind of campaign?" (paragraph 16) is broken into syllables as follows:
    (a.) can-di-dates.
    b. cand-i-dates.
    c. can-did-ates.

Mapping Activity

This selection is about a problem and a suggested solution. Both are shown in the list below. Write them in the diagram where they belong.

- Students don't learn to think in school.
- Schools should have students write to think in all their classes.

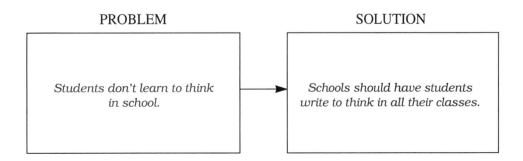

PROBLEM

Students don't learn to think in school.

SOLUTION

Schools should have students write to think in all their classes.

Discussion Questions

1. Kugel says that teachers "stand in front of classrooms and think out loud, while the students listen." What does he mean? Is this what happened in your high school classes?

2. Not all writing is assigned. There is also the type of "writing you do when you write notes to yourself on the backs of envelopes." How much *non-required* writing do you do in a week, both in and out of school? Does it help you think and, if so, how?

Writing Activities

1. Use writing to help you make a decision by describing the advantages and disadvantages of a matter. You might begin with a sentence such as this: "There are advantages and disadvantages to working twenty-five hours a week, rather than fifteen." Your paper would then go on to discuss the most important advantages and disadvantages. Other possible topics include the pluses and minuses of exercising for a half hour every day, getting another car, dropping a course, continuing a certain relationship, or leaving home and getting an apartment.

2. Kugel contrasts feeling and thinking. What is the difference between making a decision according to how you feel and making a decision according to how you think? Write a paragraph contrasting the two methods in some way. If you like, use one of these topic sentences: "When it comes to the foods I eat, my feelings and thinking differ"; "The way I feel about doing homework often contrasts with what I think about doing it."

Check Your Performance   PHONICS III: SYLLABLES

Activity	Number Right	Points	Total
Review Test 1 (5 items)	_____	x 2 =	_____
Review Test 2 (20 items)	_____	x 1.5 =	_____
Review Test 3 (20 items)	_____	x 1.5 =	_____
Review Test 4 (10 items)	_____	x 2 =	_____
Mapping Activity (2 items)	_____	x 5 =	_____
		TOTAL SCORE =	_____%

Enter your total score onto the Reading Performance Chart: Review Tests on the inside back cover.

4

Word Parts

Learning common word parts will help your pronunciation, spelling, and vocabulary. You will be able to pronounce and spell more words because you will recognize common parts used in those words. And because word parts have meanings, knowing them can help you figure out the meaning of a word you don't know.

There are three types of word parts:

1 Prefixes
2 Suffixes
3 Roots

This chapter will help you learn ten of each, thirty common word parts in all.

PREFIXES

A **prefix** is a word part that is added to the beginning of a word. When a prefix is added to a word, it changes its meaning. For example, the prefix *un* means "not." So when *un* is added to the word *known*, a word with the opposite meaning is formed: *unknown*.

Another prefix is *mis*, which can mean *bad* or *badly*. When *mis* is added to *fortune*, the resulting word is *misfortune*, which means "bad fortune." So you can see that knowing the meaning of a prefix helps you figure out the meaning of a word it is in.

The following practice will help you master ten common prefixes. (Alternate forms of prefixes are shown in parentheses.)

➤ *Practice 1*

Carefully read the meanings of each pair of prefixes. Then, in each sentence, complete the partial word (in *italics*) with the prefix that fits. Write the full word in the space provided. The first one is done for you.

1 **ex** — out, from   ***Example:*** exit
2 **in (im)** — within, into; not   ***Examples:*** inside; improbable

   a. The girls at first decided to (*. . . clude*) _____ *exclude* _____ Ginger from their pajama party because they knew she would want to watch television all night.

   b. The girls then voted to (*. . . clude*) _____ *include* _____ Ginger when she said she would bring the popcorn and chips.

   c. Your driver's license (*. . . pired*) _____ *expired* _____, so you'd better not drive until you get it renewed.

   d. When I go to the bank, I'd rather wait in line for a human teller than use an (*. . . personal*) _____ *impersonal* _____ bank machine.

3 **pre** — before   ***Example:*** prepare
4 **post** — after   ***Example:*** postgraduate

   a. Because lightning (*. . . cedes*) _____ *precedes* _____ thunder by a fraction of a second, we see the flash before we hear the boom.

   b. The (*. . . war*) _____ *postwar* _____ economic problems made some people wish for the war to return.

   c. The football field was flooded after the heavy storm, so the school had to (*. . . pone*) _____ *postpone* _____ the season's first game.

   d. Many people skip over the (*. . . face*) _____ *preface* _____ of a book and begin reading at the first chapter.

5 **sub** — below, under   ***Example:*** submarine
6 **super** — over, above, beyond   ***Example:*** superior

   a. The best thing about the (*. . . way*) _____ *subway* _____ is that it's so fast that you don't have to stay on it long.

   b. That movie had one ghost too many; I got bored by all the (*. . . natural*) _____ *supernatural* _____ events.

   c. We told the house painters we would (*. . . tract*) _____ *subtract* _____ from their final bill the cost of the two windows they broke.

d. Alice is a born *(. . . visor)* ___supervisor___ : she loves to watch over other people's work.

---

7 **mis** — bad, badly, wrong   ***Examples:*** misdeed, misunderstand
8 **mono** — one   ***Example:*** monotony

   a. Scott is so afraid of making a *(. . . take)* ___mistake___ that he never raises his hand in class.

   b. My history instructor reads his lectures in a single tone of voice; his *(. . . tone)* ___monotone___ shows he is as bored with his lectures as we are.

   c. *(. . . gamy)* ___Monogamy___ is not limited to humans. Some animals also have only one mate throughout their lives.

   d. That dog is going to *(. . . behave)* ___misbehave___ unless you take him for a walk right now.

---

9 **un** — not   ***Example:*** unwanted
10 **re** — again; back   ***Examples:*** rewrite; respond

   a. "Never *(. . . peat)* ___repeat___ yourself," my English teacher said. "Never, never, never."

   b. As *(. . . likely)* ___unlikely___ as it may seem, the male seahorse gives birth, carrying the eggs inside him until after they hatch.

   c. After working a double shift at the hospital, Ramon was *(. . . able)* ___unable___ to keep his eyes open.

   d. Because our electric blender makes so much noise, I've lent it to a neighbor in the hope that she'll never *(. . . turn)* ___return___ it.

SUFFIXES

A **suffix** is a word part that is added to the end of a word. Like prefixes, suffixes can change the meanings of words. For instance, by adding the suffix *less* (which means "without") to the word *life*, we get a word with the opposite meaning: *lifeless*. Also, suffixes often change a word's part of speech. The suffix *ly*, for instance, can change the adjective *sad* to the adverb *sadly*.

The following practice will help you master ten common suffixes. (Alternate forms of some suffixes are shown in parentheses.)

➤ *Practice 2*

Carefully read the meanings of each pair of suffixes. Then, in each sentence, complete the partial word (in *italics*) with the suffix that fits. Write the full word in the space provided.

11 **able (ible)** — able to be   ***Examples:*** enjoyable, edible
12 **ion** — state of being; act of   ***Examples:*** limitation; celebration

    a. If a job seems too large to handle, just break it down into *(manage . . .)* ___*manageable*___ parts.

    b. The hunter did such a good *(imitat . . .)* ___*imitation*___ of a deer's love-call that another hunter shot him.

    c. My daughter finds it *(comfort . . .)* ___*comfortable*___ reading with her head hanging over the side of the bed and her book on the floor.

    d. Rose saw her high-school boyfriend at her class *(reun . . .)* ___*reunion*___, and now they are dating again.

13 **er (or)** — a person who does   ***Examples:*** dancer, mayor
          something
14 **ist** — a person skilled at   ***Example:*** artist
          something

    a. As a *(visit . . .)* ___*visitor*___ to the rocket base, I had to pass through three security checks before seeing my first rocket.

    b. A *(scient . . .)* ___*scientist*___ lives for the day he or she discovers something that will benefit humanity.

    c. The *(wait . . .)* ___*waiter*___ at Ella's Country Diner was so rude that I complained to the owners.

    d. Liberace was not only an outstanding showman, he was also a talented *(pian . . .)* ___*pianist*___.

15 **ful** — full of   ***Example:*** joyful
16 **less** — without   ***Example:*** homeless

a. On Thanksgiving everyone feels *(thank . . .)* _____*thankful*_____ — except the turkey.

b. Francisco and Susana are both so unpleasant that the world would be *(grate . . .)* _____*grateful*_____ if they married each other.

c. Before he smashed up his car, Amanpal was a very *(care . . . .)* _____*careless*_____ driver. Since then, he drives as cautiously as anyone I know.

d. When I had the flu, I felt (help . . .)_____*helpless*_____—I had trouble moving, thinking, and breathing.

17 **ism** — a practice; a belief or   ***Examples:*** terrorism; communism
      set of principles
18 **ment** — state of being   ***Example:*** engagement

a. I practice *(Catholic . . .)* _____*Catholicism*_____, and my wife practices Judaism.

b. After thirty years of *(imprison . . .)* _____*imprisonment*_____, Eli was not sure he could live in the real world.

c. There was a lot of *(excite . . .)* _____*excitement*_____ at work today; two people angrily told the boss they were quitting.

d. A neighborhood group was formed to deal with the problems of theft and *(vandal . . .)* _____*vandalism*_____.

19 **ish** — similar to   ***Example:*** foolish
20 **ly** — in a certain manner;   ***Examples:*** quickly; hourly
      at a certain time

a. Harry's *(child . . .)* _____*childish*_____ behavior at the party was more like that of a three-year-old, not a thirty-year-old man.

b. Sharks are attracted by soft music such as waltzes, but they leave *(immediate . . .)* _____*immediately*_____ if they hear rock music.

c. Actor Brad Pitt's success is surely due in part to his *(boy . . . .)* _____*boyish*_____ smile.

d. Phone companies look forward to Mother's Day even more *(eager . . .)* _____*eagerly*_____ than mothers do; it's the day on which the most long-distance phone calls are made.

ROOTS

A **root** is a word's basic part and carries its fundamental meaning. Sometimes two roots combine to form a word. The word *telegraph*, for example, is made up of two roots: *tele* (which means "from a distance") and *graph* (which means "write").

Prefixes and suffixes also combine with roots to make words. For instance, the prefix *pre* (meaning "before") and the root *dict* (meaning "say") form the word *predict*. And the root *aud* (meaning "hear") plus the suffix *ible* (meaning "able to be") form *audible*, which means "able to be heard."

The following practice will help you master ten common roots. (Alternate forms of some roots are shown in parentheses.)

➤ *Practice 3*

Carefully read the meanings of each pair of roots. Then, in each sentence, complete the partial word (in *italics*) with the root that fits. Write the full word in the space provided.

21 **bene (bon)** — good, well   ***Examples:*** benediction, bonus
22 **port** — carry   ***Example:*** transport

    a. I have a *(. . . able)* _____*portable*_____ computer that I take into the classroom with me.

    b. Jogging is supposed to be good for the body, but I don't see what's *(. . . ficial)* _____*beneficial*_____ about blisters and muscle cramps.

    c. The mass murderer was known to his neighbors as a very gentle and *(. . . volent)* _____*benevolent*_____ man who fed leftover pizza to the squirrels.

    d. What kind of *(sup . . . ing)* _____*supporting*_____ evidence do you have to back up your idea?

23 **bio** — life   ***Example:*** biochemistry
24 **ven (vent)** — come   ***Examples:*** revenue, invent

    a. *(. . . feedback)* _____*Biofeedback*_____ is a method that teaches people to control some body functions, including blood pressure.

    b. At a recent *(con . . . ion)* _____*convention*_____, hundreds of romance writers and publishers came together.

    c. Why does our English instructor always choose such an *(incon . . . ient)* _____*inconvenient*_____ time for papers to be due?

    d. Reading his *(. . . graphy)* _____*biography*_____, the actor remarked, "Well, I never knew I've had such an exciting life."

25 **man (manu)** — hand   ***Examples:*** manage, manufacture
26 **ped (pod)** — foot   ***Examples:*** pedestal, tripod

    a. The giant organ had so many switches and keys that it required great skill

       to *(. . . ipulate)* _____*manipulate*_____ them all.

    b. Linda was afraid she would forget part of her speech; instead, she tripped

       when she stepped down from the *(. . . ium)* _____*podium*_____.

    c. I keep holding on to my *(. . . al)* _____*manual*_____ typewriter in the
       hope that it will become a valuable antique.

    d. It seems many drivers want to forget that *(. . . estrians)* _____*pedestrians*_____
       have the right of way in a crosswalk.

27 **auto** — self   ***Example:*** automatic
28 **tele** — far, over a distance   ***Example:*** telescope

    a. There is now a *(. . . vision)* _____*television*_____ so small that it's part of
       a wristwatch.

    b. It was Karl Benz of Germany, not Henry Ford, who invented the

       (. . . mobile) _____*automobile*_____; Ford invented the assembly line.

    c. In his *(. . . biography)* _____*autobiography*_____, *Why Me?*, Sammy Davis,
       Jr., describes how he had to fight racism in the early stages of his career.

    d. When my parents blamed me for our high *(. . . phone)* _____*telephone*_____
       bill, I said, "Can I help it if I have so many friends?"

29 **spect** — look   ***Example:*** inspect
30 **audi (audit)** — hear   ***Examples:*** audience, auditorium

    a. In addition to books, libraries now lend various types of *(. . . o-visual)*
       _____*audio-visual*_____ materials, such as language tapes and videocassettes.

    b. So many singers wanted a role in the Broadway musical that over three

       hundred showed up for the *(. . . tion)* _____*audition*_____.

    c. The game lasted so long that most *(. . . ators)* _____*spectators*_____ had
       gone home; only a few dozen people stayed to see the game end.

    d. Benjamin Franklin invented the first *(. . . acles)* _____*spectacles*_____
       with two-part lenses, for seeing both near and far.

➤ *Review Test 1*

To review what you have learned in this chapter, answer each of the following questions. Circle the letter of the answer you think is correct.

1. The prefix *un-* (as in *unlucky*) means
   a. below.
   b. not.
   c. back.

2. When a prefix is added to a word, it changes the word's
   a. ending.
   b. meaning.
   c. part of speech.

3. A suffix can change a word's
   a. part of speech.
   b. meaning.
   c. both *a* and *b*.

4. The suffix *-ist* (as in *violinist*) means a
   a. person skilled at something.
   b. belief or practice.
   c. state of being.

5. The fundamental meaning of a word is carried in its
   a. prefix.
   b. suffix.
   c. root.

➤ *Review Test 2*

Use the word parts in the box to complete the words in the sentences below. Use each word part only once.

bio — life	**ment** — state of being
ex — out, from	**pre** — before
ible — able to be	**spect** — look
in — within, into	**sub** — below, under
ism — a belief or practice	**tele** — far, over a distance

1. A fortuneteller *(. . . dicted)* _____predicted_____ that I'd soon suffer a financial loss; then he charged me fifty dollars.

2. When Judy Garland's personal items were auctioned, they brought in $250,000, *(. . . cluding)* _____including_____ $125 for her false eyelashes.

3. A 14th-century book on table manners warns that "one who blows his nose in the tablecloth" lacks *(refine . . .)* _____refinement_____.

4. Before using the dried mushrooms in a recipe, *(. . . merge)* _____submerge_____ them in water for a while.

5. Certain colors that are *(vis . . .)* _____visible_____ to bees and butterflies cannot be seen by humans.

6. Martin's continued bad behavior finally got him *(. . . pelled)* _____expelled_____ from school.

7. One of nature's most beautiful *(. . . acles)* _____spectacles_____ is thousands of monarch butterflies coming together at their winter home.

8. For my *(. . . logy)* _____biology_____ project, I observed the way mold grows on unwashed dishes.

9. *(Hindu . . .)* _____Hinduism_____ includes the belief that when someone dies, his or her soul begins a new life.

10. Because my camera has a *(. . . photo)* _____telephoto_____ lens, I was able to take a beautiful picture of the distant eagle.

➤ *Review Test 3*

Use the word parts in the box to complete the words in the following passage. Read the passage through one time before trying to complete the words. Use each word part once.

bene — good, well	**ful** — full of
re — again, back	**less** — without
un — not	**or** — person who does something
ven — come	**ion** — state or act of being
man — hand	**ly** — in a certain manner

In the days of the great sailing ships, one narrow channel was known for its rough and rocky waters. Hundreds of ships had been wrecked even when their captains tried to steer through *(cautious . . .)* __cautiously__ .

One day, a dolphin appeared at its entrance. Placing himself at the front of a ship, he guided it safely through. From then on, sailors learned to watch and wait for the dolphin to help them *(. . . age)* __manage__ the trip, rather than travel through the channel *(. . . assisted)* __unassisted__ .

The sailors named the dolphin Jack, and he aided many ships. But when Jack approached a ship called the *Penguin*, he was shot by a drunken *(sail . . .)* __sailor__ . Jack swam away, trailing blood. Now ships had to struggle through the channel without the *(. . . fit)* __benefit__ of Jack's help.

Weeks later, Jack *(. . . appeared)* __reappeared__ , ready to continue guiding ships. There was, however, one *(except . . .)* __exception__ . Whenever the *Penguin* approached, Jack stayed away, *(fear . . .)* __fearful__ of being shot again. Without Jack to guide it safely through the channel, the *Penguin* was *(help . . .)* __helpless__ . *(E . . . tually)* __Eventually__ , it sank.

➤ *Review Test 4*

Here is a chance to apply your understanding of word parts to a full-length reading. This selection is about the obstacles in one man's life, from childhood to adulthood. Juan Angel decided to get past these obstacles, one by one, so that he could make his life better. What enables Juan to keep facing obstacle after obstacle? Think about this as you read "The Struggle Continues." After reading the selection, answer the phonics and word part questions that follow.

Words to Watch

Following are some words in the reading that do not have strong context support. Each word is followed by the number of the paragraph in which it appears and its meaning there. These words are indicated in the reading by a small circle (°).

> *intentions* (2): plans
> *intensely* (5): with great strength
> *deliberation* (7): careful thought
> *acute* (9): sharp

THE STRUGGLE CONTINUES

Juan Angel

My name is Juan Angel. I am thirty years old, and I was born in Mexico.   1

As a child, I was alone for most of the time. My father was an   2
alcoholic, and he abandoned my family and me when I was three years
old. My mother had to struggle to survive by working from place to
place in Mexico. Her good intentions° to support me economically
were not enough because of low salaries, so she eventually ended up
working here in the United States.

I lived with some of my relatives in a little village in Mexico and   3
worked from dawn to sunset and ate sometimes once a day. I felt totally
condemned to die of starvation and hard work. My relatives spent the
money that my mother sent me, claiming that I was just a child and
didn't need it. As a defenseless child, I was innocent, ignorant, and
lacked the courage to stand up against the abuse and the injustice. My
grandmother, who lived in another little village, couldn't do anything
about the oppression I suffered, and she probably didn't even know
what was really happening in my life. My relatives covered everything
up, and the complaints I made were ignored while my suffering

continued to get worse. After five years of being mistreated, humiliated, and abused by my relatives, I decided to put an end to it, and I went to live with my grandmother.

When I moved into my grandmother's house, I started living a   4
new lifestyle. By then, I was eight years old, and I felt for the first time proud of myself because I had made my first big decision in life.

My grandmother had some pigs, so I had to feed them. One day I   5
was feeding them close to a water stream when I saw two boys passing by. They carried some books with them. I saw them every day walking down a grassy road while I fed those pigs. My curiosity grew intensely°, and one day I stopped them on their way back home. I asked them what they were doing, and they told me that they were attending school. I wanted to know if they knew how to read, and immediately they started reading and writing to show me. I simply couldn't believe it. When they left, I scratched my head and nodded for a moment, looking toward the sky. I said, "Going to school! That's exactly the next step I have to work on." After I finished feeding those pigs, I went home. While I was walking home, I thought about how I would convince my grandmother to allow me to to go school. I knew it was going to be hard to convince her because there were around twenty boys in the village, and they were not attending school either, except those two whom I admired.

When I talked to her about my decision on going to school, she   6
got very upset, and she immediately thought about who would care for her pigs. I calmed her down by telling her that I would continue feeding them. She didn't accept my proposal at first, so I looked for the two boys and talked to them about my interest in going to school. They encouraged me to leave the house and forget about the pigs; they would help me to go. I thought it was not a bad idea, but I opposed it because my grandmother and I were living alone. In addition, the closest school was two miles away from the village. For those reasons I hesitated to make such a decision. I had spent two years raising pigs and hesitated about my next step.

Finally, I gave up and left my grandmother alone in the house. My   7
friends helped me find a place to sleep in town where the school was, and they gave me some food every day. They took me to the school, and I explained my situation to the principal; to my surprise, his name was Juan, also. He told me that my age (ten years old) wouldn't match the rules of the school. "You're too old," he said. He questioned me for about five minutes, and then he told me to come back the next day. He met with all the teachers, and after some deliberation°, they approved my enrollment as a new student. I was excited and happy about my

achievement as a ten-year-old boy. On the other hand, I couldn't sleep very well at night because I remembered my grandmother very much. She was desperately looking for me, and she found me after a week. I cried while I explained to her why I had left home. She hugged me very hard, and then she went to talk to the principal about my desire to attend school. I never expected her to talk to the principal, but she did. I have never experienced so much happiness in my life as when I was ten years old.

8   I walked the two miles back and forth to school every day. In addition, I had to feed the pigs early in the morning before I went to school and after I came home from school. I also chopped wood for cooking. I did chores at home as a responsible man in charge of a household. My grandmother and I lived happily for six years while I was in primary school.

9   After I finished my first six years in school, I had to make another tough decision. I had to leave my grandmother completely alone because the secondary school I wished to attend was in another town about three hours away by bus. A few months before I took off, she began to suffer from an acute° pain in her chest. I didn't want to leave her, but I did. I wanted to stay in school as much as I could. I used to visit her every weekend, but sometimes the lack of money made it impossible. When I started my second year in the school, I began to worry about my grandmother's health. Her chest pains were getting worse, and I received a letter in which she said that she missed me very much.

10   A week later a friend of mine was looking for me at the school. He told me that my grandmother was very sick. I immediately went to see her. She was lying down with a blanket on the floor. When she saw me, she hugged me very hard, and then she began to ask how my school was. I could hardly answer her because my tears ran down my cheeks as never before. She asked me not to cry, but I couldn't stop. She told me to continue in school, and I promised her I would. A few minutes later, she died in my arms, and I felt that everything was torn apart inside me. I thought that I could never overcome the painful experience of losing my grandmother forever.

11   My mother, who was here in the United States, got there in time for the funeral. She asked me to come with her, but I refused her offer. She came back to the United States, and I stayed in Mexico for another four years of school. She continued asking me to join her. Finally, I gave in and immigrated to the United States in 1988. I immediately attended an English class at night and worked days. At the end of the year I got here, my English teacher recommended me to a Hispanic program where I could get my GED diploma. When I enrolled in the

program, everything was free, including a room in a dormitory. When I finished the program, I had my GED. I then returned to my mother's house. I was unemployed, and three months later, I started working on an irrigated farm, growing alfalfa. I worked three years, and I quit because I wanted to find a more flexible job which would allow me to go to college.

Now I'm working in a feed department on swing shift, and I'm   12
attending college in the morning. This department where I'm working operates just in the wintertime, so I'm on the verge of being laid off. I'm a part-time student at Blue Mountain Community College, and I would like to continue attending college. I will keep trying to find ways to stay in college.

I have been confronting many obstacles in my life since my   13
childhood. I have challenged those obstacles, and I know by experience how to overcome them. It has not been easy, but I always believe in success through education. Even though I know the struggle is not over yet, I will keep an optimistic smile toward the future.

Phonics Questions

Use the phonics clues you learned from chapters 1–3 to answer the following questions. Circle the letter of your choice for each question.

1. The word *alcoholic* in "My father was an alcoholic, and he abandoned my family and me when I was three years old" (paragraph 2) contains
   a. a soft **c** sound.
   b. a hard **c** sound.
   c. two hard **c** sounds.

2. The word *claiming* in "My relatives spent the money that my mother sent me, claiming that I was just a child and didn't need it" (paragraph 3) contains
   a. two short vowel sounds.
   b. two long vowel sounds.
   c. one short vowel sound and one long vowel sound.

3. The **y** in the word *by* in "I calmed her down by telling her that I would continue feeding them" (paragraph 6) sounds like
   a. a short **i**.
   b. a long **i**.
   c. a long **e**.

4. The word *happiness* in "I have never experienced such happiness in my life as when I was ten years old" (paragraph 7) contains
   a. one syllable.
   b. two syllables.
   c. three syllables.

5. The word *before* in "In addition, I had to feed the pigs early in the morning before I went to school and after I came home from school" (paragraph 8) is broken into syllables as follows:
   a. be-fo-re.
   b. be-fore.
   c. bef-ore.

Word Part Questions

Use the word part clues you learned from chapter 4 to answer the following questions. Circle the letter of your choice for each question.

6. The word *mistreated* in "After five years of being mistreated, humiliated, and abused by my relatives, I decided to put an end to it" (paragraph 3) means
   a. treated badly.
   b. treated again.
   c. treated well.

7. The word *defenseless* in "As a defenseless child, I was innocent, ignorant, and lacked the courage to stand up against the abuse and the injustice" (paragraph 3) means
   a. full of defense.
   b. having defenses again.
   c. without defense.

8. The word *intensely* in "My curiosity grew intensely, and one day I stopped them on their way back home" (paragraph 5) means
   a. in an intense manner.
   b. similar to being intense.
   c. without being intense.

9. The word *enrollment* in "they approved my enrollment as a new student" (paragraph 7) means
   a. belief of being enrolled.
   b. state of being enrolled.
   c. being enrolled again.

10. The word *impossible* in "I used to visit her every weekend, but sometimes the lack of money made it impossible" (paragraph 9) means
    a. possible before.
    b. possible again.
    c. not possible.

Mapping Activity

This selection is organized by time: first one thing happened; then another; after that, another; and so on. Several events that happened in the story are scrambled in the list below. Write them in their correct order in the diagram on the next page.

- Juan moves to town so he can go to school.
- Juan moves to the United States.
- Juan's father abandons his family.
- Juan moves into his grandmother's house.
- Juan's grandmother dies.

Central point: Juan Angel has had to overcome numerous obstacles to get an education.

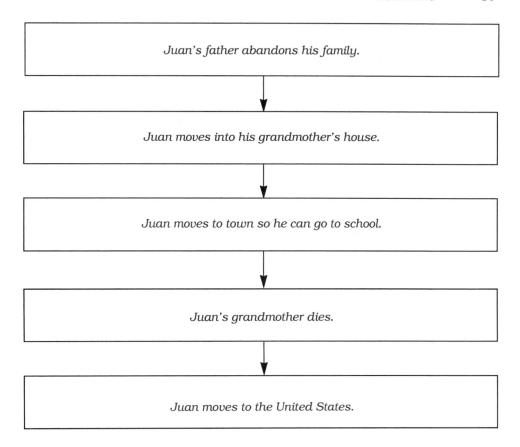

Discussion Questions

1. When Juan's grandmother died, Juan's mother asked him to move to the United States with her, but Juan refused her offer. What reasons might he have had for refusing her?

2. Based on the reading, what personal characteristics can you conclude Juan has? Tell the parts of the story that reveal each characteristic that you mention.

Writing Activities

1. In paragraph 13, Juan says he believes in "success through education." Write about an incident in your life in which your education was helpful to you.

2. Write a letter to Juan telling him what you think about the obstacles that he had to overcome and the successes that he has achieved so far in his life. Share with him some of the obstacles you have had to overcome in your life.

Check Your Performance   **WORD PARTS**

Activity	Number Right	Points		Total
Review Test 1 (5 items)	_____	x 2 =		_____
Review Test 2 (10 items)	_____	x 3 =		_____
Review Test 3 (10 items)	_____	x 3 =		_____
Review Test 4 (10 items)	_____	x 2 =		_____
Mapping Activity (5 items)	_____	x 2 =		_____
		TOTAL SCORE =		_____%

Enter your total score onto the Reading Performance Chart: Review Tests on the inside back cover.

5

Dictionary Use

What do you use a dictionary for? When asked this question, most people reply, "To look up a word." That answer is correct, but not complete. A dictionary can help you do all of the following:

- Spell words
- Break words into syllables
- Pronounce words
- Learn parts of speech and irregular forms of words
- Look up the right meanings of words
- See where words come from
- Find synonyms for words

This chapter will show you how to use a dictionary for all the above purposes.

OWNING YOUR OWN DICTIONARIES

You can benefit greatly by owning two dictionaries. One should be a paperback so that you can carry it with you. Any of the following would be an excellent choice:

The American Heritage Dictionary, Paperback Edition
The Random House Dictionary, Paperback Edition
Webster's New World Dictionary, Paperback Edition

The second dictionary you should own is a desk-sized, hardcover edition, for the room where you study. There are excellent hardcover American Heritage, Webster's and Random House dictionaries, which contain a good deal more information than the paperback editions. While they cost more, they are valuable study aids.

Dictionaries are often updated to reflect changes in the language. New words come into use, and old words take on new meanings. So you should not use a dictionary that has been lying around the house for many years. Instead, invest in a new one. You will find that it is money well spent.

FINDING A WORD IN THE DICTIONARY

Using Guidewords

The two words at the top of each dictionary page are called **guidewords**. Shown below are guidewords from a page in *The American Heritage Dictionary,* Paperback Edition.

---

nonstop / northeast   **568**

speakers or socially disfavored groups.

non•stop (nŏn′stŏp′) *adj.* Made or done without a stop. —**non′stop′** *adv.*

non•suit (nŏn-sōōt′) *n. Law.* 1. A judgment against a plaintiff for failure to prosecute the case or to introduce sufficient evidence.

non•sup•port (nŏn′sə-pôrt′, -pōrt′) *n. Law.* Failure to provide for the maintenance of one's dependents.

non trop•po (nŏn trô′pō, nōn) *adv. & adj. Mus.* In moderation. [Ital., not too much.]

non•un•ion (nŏn-yōōn′yən) *adj.* 1. Not belonging to a labor union. 2. Not recognizing a labor union or employing union members.

non•vi•o•lence (nŏn-vī′ə-ləns) *n.* The doctrine or practice of rejecting violence in favor of peaceful tactics as a means of gaining political objectives. —**non•vi′o•lent** *adj.* —**non•vi′o•lent•ly** *adv.*

noo•dle¹ (nōōd′l) *n.* A narrow ribbonlike strip of dried dough, usu. made of flour, eggs, and water. [Ger. *Nudel.*]

noo•dle² (nōōd′l) *n. Slang.* The human head. [Alteration of *noddle,* back of head.]

nook (nōōk) *n.* 1. A small corner or recess in a room. 2. A hidden or secluded spot. [ME *nok,* prob. of Scand. orig.]

noon (nōōn) *n.* Twelve o'clock in the daytime; midday. See Usage Note at **ante meridiem.** [< OE *nōn,* ninth hour after sunrise < Lat. *nōnus,* ninth.]

norm or standard; typical: *normal room temperature.* 2.a. Of average intelligence or development. b. Free from physical or emotional disorder. —*n.* 1. A norm. 2. The usual state, amount, or degree. —**nor′mal•cy** *n.* —**nor•mal′i•ty** (-măl′ĭ-tē) *n.* —**nor′mal•ly** *adv.*

nor•mal•ize (nôr′mə-līz′) *v.* -**ized,** -**iz•ing.** To make normal or regular. —**nor′mal•i•za′tion** *n.* —**nor′mal•iz′er** *n.*

normal school *n.* A school that trains teachers, chiefly for the elementary grades.

Nor•man (nôr′mən) *n.* 1.a. A member of a Scandinavian people who settled in N France in the 10th cent. b. A member of a people of Norman and French blood who invaded England in 1066. 2. A native or inhabitant of Normandy. —**Nor′man** *adj.*

Nor•man•dy (nôr′mən-dē). A historical region and former province of NW France on the English Channel.

Norman French *n.* The dialect of Old French used in medieval Normandy.

nor•ma•tive (nôr′mə-tĭv) *adj.* Of or prescribing a norm or standard. —**nor′ma•tive•ly** *adv.* —**nor′ma•tive•ness** *n.*

Norse (nôrs) *adj.* 1. Of or relating to medieval Scandinavia. 2. Norwegian. 3. Of or relating to the branch of the Germanic languages that includes Norwegian, Icelandic, and Faeroese. —**Norse** *n.*

Nor•dic (nôr′dĭk) *adj.* 1. Scandinavian. 2. Of a human physical type exemplified by the light-skinned, blond-haired peoples of Scandinavia. [< Fr. *nord,* NORTH.] —**Nor′dic** *n.*

Nor•folk (nôr′fək, -fôk). An independent city of SE VA SE of Richmond. Pop. 261,229.

Nor•gay (nôr′gā), **Tenzing.** 1914–86. Sherpa guide; with Sir Edmund Hillary made the first ascent of Mount Everest (1953).

norm (nôrm) *n.* A standard, model, or pattern regarded as typical. [< Lat. *norma,* carpenter's square.]

nor•mal (nôr′məl) *adj.* 1. Conforming to a

North Car•o•li•na (kăr′ə-lī′nə). A state of the SE U.S. bordering on the Atlantic. Cap. Raleigh. Pop. 6,657,630. —**North Car•o•lin′i•an** (-lĭn′ē-ən) *adj. & n.*

North Dakota. A state of the N-central U.S. bordering on Canada. Cap. Bismarck. Pop. 641,364. —**North Dakotan** *adj. & n.*

north•east (nôrth-ēst′, nôr-ēst′) *n.* 1. The direction halfway between due north and due east. 2. An area or region lying in the northeast. —**north•east′** *adj. & adv.* —**north•east′er•ly** *adj. & adv.* —**north•east′ern** *adj.* —**north•east′ward** *adj. & adv.* —**north•east′ward•ly** *adj. & adv.* —**north•east′wards** *adv.*

In the excerpt above, *nonstop* and *northeast* are guidewords. *Nonstop* is the first word that will be defined on that page, and *northeast* is the last word defined on that page. All the other words on the page fall alphabetically between the first and second guideword.

To see if you understand guidewords, circle the two words below which would appear on the page with *nonstop* and *northeast:*

nomad   noon   nostril   normal

The word *nomad* comes earlier in the alphabet than the guideword *nonstop,* so we know that *nomad* will not appear on the page. And *nostril* comes later in the alphabet than the guideword *northeast,* so we know that *nostril* will not appear on the page. The other two words, *noon* and *normal,* do come alphabetically between *nonstop* and *northeast.* Those are the two words you should have circled.

➤ Practice 1

Below are five pairs of dictionary guidewords. Each pair is followed by a series of other words. Circle the two words in each series which can be found on the page with the guidewords.

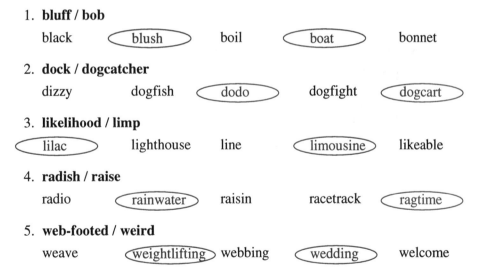

1. **bluff / bob**
   black   blush   boil   boat   bonnet

2. **dock / dogcatcher**
   dizzy   dogfish   dodo   dogfight   dogcart

3. **likelihood / limp**
   lilac   lighthouse   line   limousine   likeable

4. **radish / raise**
   radio   rainwater   raisin   racetrack   ragtime

5. **web-footed / weird**
   weave   weightlifting   webbing   wedding   welcome

Using Hints to Find a Word

Do you know how to find a word in a dictionary if you are unsure of its spelling? What you should do first is to sound out the word. Apply the phonics principles you learned in chapters 1 and 2 to help you do so. Pronouncing the word correctly will help you come closer to spelling it correctly. Then look up the word based on how you think it is spelled. Here are some hints that will help you find the word:

Hints for Finding Words

> *Hint 1:* Look at the consonants in the word. If you used single consonants, try doubling them. If you wrote double consonants, try removing one of them.
>
> *Hint 2:* Remember that vowels often sound the same. Try an **i** in place of an **a**, an **i** in place of an **e**, and so on. For example, if you can't find a word you think starts with **hi**, try looking under **hy**.
>
> *Hint 3:* Below are groups of letters or letter combinations that often sound alike. If you can't find the word as you think it is spelled, try substituting a letter or group of letters from the pairs below. For example, if a word isn't spelled with a **c**, it may be spelled with a **k**; if it isn't spelled with an **f**, try **v** or **ph**.
>
> | | | | | | |
> |---|---|---|---|---|---|
> | c / k | c / s | f / v / ph | g / j | qu / kw / k | s / c / z |
> | sch / sc / sk | sh / ch | shun / tion / sion | | w / wh | able / ible |
> | ai / ay | al / el / le | ancy / ency | ate / ite | au / aw | ea / ee |
> | er / or | ie / ei | ou / ow | oo / u | y / i / e | |

➤ *Practice 2*

Use your dictionary and the spelling hints above for this practice. Apply your knowledge of spelling hints and guidewords to help you find the correct spelling of each of the following words. Write the correct spelling in the answer space.

1. revize _revise_
2. kiddnap _kidnap_
3. karry _carry_
4. jiant _giant_
5. realy _really_
6. skoolteecher _schoolteacher_
7. pleeze _please_
8. comming _coming_
9. beleive _believe_
10. tunnal _tunnel_

LEARNING FROM DICTIONARY ENTRIES

Each word that is defined in the dictionary is called an **entry word**. Entry words are in **boldfaced** print. Look at the entry word below.

Sample Dictionary Entry

> **in•spire** (ĭn-spīr′) *v.* **-spired, -spiring. 1.** To fill with noble or reverent emotion; exalt. **2.** To stimulate to creativity or action. **3.** To elicit or create in another. **4.** To inhale. [< Lat. *īnspīrāre.*] —**in•spir′er** *n.*

All or most of the following information is provided in a dictionary entry:

1 Spelling and Syllables
2 Pronunciation Symbols and Accent Marks
3 Parts of Speech
4 Irregular Forms of Words
5 Definitions and Usage Labels
6 Word Origins
7 Synonyms

The rest of the chapter will look at each kind of information. The entry words used are taken from *The American Heritage Dictionary,* Paperback Edition (abbreviated in this book as *AHD*).

1 SPELLING AND SYLLABLES

An entry word give you the spelling and syllable breakdown of the word. Dots separate the word into syllables. As Chapter 3 taught you, each syllable is a separate sound that includes one vowel sound and any connected consonant sounds. The following entry word, *detachment,* has three vowel sounds, and therefore it has three syllables.

de•tach•ment (dĭ-tăch′mənt) *n.*

How many syllables are in these entry words?

ru•mor   **ex•plic•it**   **stim•u•late**   **launch**

The dots tell you that *rumor* has two syllables and that *explicit* and *stimulate* have three syllables each. *Launch,* on the other hand, has no dots and only one syllable.

➤ *Practice 3*

Use your dictionary to separate the following words into syllables. Insert dots between syllables. Then write the number of syllables in each word. An example is provided.

Example: c o n•f o r•m i•t y   ___4___ syllables

1. h i c c u p   *hic•cup, 2* syllables

2. m i n i m a l   *min•i•mal, 3* syllables

3. d i s p o s a l   *dis•pos•al, 3* syllables

4. i n s e n s i t i v e   *in•sen•si•tive, 4* syllables

5. c o m m u n i c a t i o n   *com•mu•ni•ca•tion, 5* syllables

2   PRONUNCIATION SYMBOLS AND ACCENT MARKS

After the entry word is information in parentheses, as you see in the following entry for *colorblind*.

col•or•blind (kŭl′ər-blīnd′) *adj.* **1.** Partially or totally unable to distinguish certain colors. **2.** Not subject to racial prejudices.

This information in parentheses shows you how to pronounce the word. It includes two kinds of symbols: pronunciation symbols and accent marks. They are explained below and on the pages that follow.

Pronunciation Symbols

Pronunciation symbols tell you how the letters within the word should be pronounced. The sounds of the consonants and vowels are shown in a Pronunciation Key. Such a key typically appears at the front of a dictionary or at the bottom of every other page of the dictionary. Here is a pronunciation key (drawn from the *AHD*'s) for the vowels and a few other sounds that often confuse dictionary users.

Pronunciation Key

ă pat	ā pay	â care	ä father	ĕ pet	ē bee	ĭ pit
ī pie, by	î pier	ŏ pot	ō toe	ô paw, for		oi noise
o͝o took	o͞o boot	ou out	th thin	*th* this		ŭ cut
û urge	yo͞o abuse	zh vision	ə about, item, edible, gallop, circus			

To use the above key, match each symbol (ă, ā, and so on) with the pronunciation of the letter or letters in bold print in the word that follows the symbol. For instance, ă sounds like the **a** in *pat*. You can pronounce the first **o** in *colorblind* by first finding the matching symbol within parentheses in the entry (ŭ). Then look for that symbol in the key, which shows you that ŭ has the sound of **u** in the word *cut*. The key also shows you that the **i** in *colorblind* (ī) is pronounced like the **i** in the word *pie* (and the **y** in *by*).

The second vowel sound in *colorblind* is indicated in the entry by the symbol ə. That symbol, which looks like an upside-down **e**, is called the **schwa**. The key tells you that the schwa has a short, unstressed sound that sounds much like "uh" (as in *about, gallop* and *circus*) or "ih" (as in *item* and *edible*).

➤ *Practice 4*

Use your dictionary to answer the following questions.

1. In the word *contest*, the **o** is pronounced like the **o** in what common word?

   _____ *pot* _____

2. In the word *finger*, the **i** is pronounced like the **i** in what common word?

   _____ *pit* _____

3. In the word *trust*, the **u** is pronounced like the **u** in what common word?

   _____ *cut* _____

4. In the word *rapid*, the **a** is pronounced like the **a** in what common word?

   _____ *pat* _____

5. In the word *shelf*, the **e** is pronounced like the **e** in what common word?

   _____ *pet* _____

Accent Marks

The mark ′ which comes after the first syllable in the word *colorblind* (kŭl′ər-blīnd′) is called an **accent mark**. It tells you that you should put more force, or accent, on the first syllable of *colorblind*.

Words of one syllable have no accent mark. Longer words may have more than one accent mark since they sometimes have emphasis on more than one syllable. When there is more than one accent mark, the darker mark shows which syllable gets the stronger accent. For example, in the word *colorblind*, the first syllable has a darker accent mark, so it receives more stress than the accent on the last syllable.

➤ *Practice 5*

Use your dictionary to separate the following words into syllables. Put dots between the syllables. Then show how the word is pronounced by writing out the pronunciation symbols and the accent mark or marks. Note the example.

Example j u m•b l e	*jŭm′bəl*	
1. m a g n e t	*mag•net*	măg′nĭt
2. j a n i t o r	*jan•i•tor*	jăn′ĭ-tər
3. e n c o u r a g e	*en•cour•age*	ĕn-kûr′ĭj

4. s p e c u l a t e   *spec•u•late*   spĕk′yə-lāt′

5. t r o u b l e m a k e r   *trou•ble•mak•er*   trŭb′əl-mā′kər

3   PARTS OF SPEECH

Every word has at least one part of speech (noun, verb, and so on). The parts of speech are indicated in an entry by abbreviations in *italicized* print. Look at the italicized abbreviations in the entry below.

> **pil•low** (pĭl′ō)   *n.* **1.** A cloth case stuffed with soft material and used to cushion the head, esp. during sleep. **2.** A decorative cushion. — *v.* To serve as a pillow for. [< Lat. *pulvīnus.*] — **pil′low•y** *adj.*

The first abbreviation is *n.* It stands for *noun* and shows that the first set of definitions is for the noun form of *pillow*. The second part-of-speech abbreviation is *v.*, which stands for *verb*. It introduces the definition of the verb form of *pillow*. At the end of the entry is the abbreviation *adj.* It refers to the added form of the entry word, *pillowy*.

The parts of speech are abbreviated in the *AHD* as follows:

n. — noun	*v.* — verb
pron. — pronoun	*conj.* — conjunction
adj. — adjective	*prep.* — preposition
adv. — adverb	*interj.* — interjection

➤ *Practice 6*

Each of the following words has more than one part of speech. For each, list the parts of speech given in the dictionary.

Parts of speech:

1. go   *verb, noun*

2. inside   *noun, adverb, preposition*

3. just   *adjective, adverb*

4. plus   *conjunction, adjective, noun*

5. quiet   *adjective, noun, verb*

4   IRREGULAR FORMS OF WORDS

After the part of speech, the dictionary shows any irregular forms, difficult spellings, and comparison words.

First of all, the dictionary shows any irregular plurals and irregular verb parts. For example, if we followed normal rules with *goose*, the plural would be *gooses*. But, as shown below, the dictionary tells us that the normal rule does not apply in this case. The plural of *goose* is *geese*. And if we followed normal rules with *draw*, the past tense, for instance, would be *drawed*. *Draw*, however, is an irregular verb, so the dictionary shows us its verb forms, including its past tense, *drew*.

> **goose** (go͞os) *n., pl.* **geese** (gēs).
>
> **draw** (drô) *v.* **drew** (dro͞o), **drawn** (drôn), **draw•ing**.

Also shown after the part of speech are plurals and verb forms that may present spelling problems to writers. Some writers, for example, may not know how to write the plural of a noun ending in **y** or the past tense and **-ing** form of verbs ending in **e**. As the entry beginnings below show, the dictionary provides that spelling information.

> **bun•ny** (bŭn′ē) *n., pl.* **-nies**.
>
> **dare** (dār) *v.* **dared**, **dar•ing**.

Finally, comparative forms of adjectives and adverbs are also given at this point in an entry, both irregular forms (as for *good*) and regular forms (as for *high*).

> **good** (good) *adj.* **bet•ter** (bĕt′ər), **best** (bĕst).
>
> **high** (hī) *adj.* **-er**, **-est**.

➤ *Practice 7*

Each of the following words has at least one irregular form. Using your dictionary, write the irregular form(s) for each word listed. Note the example.

Example: hero	*heroes*
1. hide	*hid, hidden* or *hid, hiding*
2. one-up	*one-upped, one-upping*
3. skinny	*skinnier, skinniest*
4. bad	*worse, worst*
5. party	*parties*

5   DEFINITIONS AND USAGE LABELS

Words often have more than one meaning. When they do, their definitions may be numbered in the dictionary. These meanings are divided according to part of speech. For example, in the entry below, *sport* has six meanings as a noun, three as a verb, and one as an adjective.

> **sport** (spôrt) *n.* **1.** An activity usu. involving physical exertion and having a set form and body of rules; game. **2.** An active pastime; diversion. **3.** Light mockery. **4.** One known for the manner of one's acceptance or defeat or criticism: *a bad sport.* **5.** *Informal.* One who lives a jolly, extravagant life. **6.** *Biol.* A mutation. —*v.* **1.** To play or frolic. **2.** To joke or trifle. **3.** To display or show off. —*adj.* Also **sports.** Of or appropriate for sport: *sport fishing.* [<OFr. *desport*, pleasure.] —**sport'i-ness** *n.* —**sport'y** *adj.*

You can tell which meaning of a word fits a given sentence by the meaning of the sentence. For example, which definition of *sport* fits the sentence below?

> Gail *sported* a new outfit when we went to the dance last night.

The answer is the third verb definition for *sport*: Gail showed off a new outfit at the dance.

In addition to listing definitions, a dictionary provides **usage labels** that tell you if a meaning is considered something other than "Standard English." That is the type of English most widely considered acceptable in speech and writing by educated speakers in both formal and informal situations. For example, words that are considered acceptable only for informal use are labeled *Informal* in the dictionary. The fifth noun meaning for *sport* has that label. Following are several common labels:

- *Informal.* Considered acceptable only for informal speech or writing.
- *Slang.* A type of casual, playful language in which terms usually have short lives. Considered improper for formal speech or writing.
- *Nonstandard.* Considered unacceptable usage, either formally or informally.
- *Offensive.* A word or expression considered insulting.

Words may also have **field labels**. These labels tell if a word has a special meaning within a certain field. An example is the sixth definition of *sport*, which is labeled *Biol.* This means that the definition which follows applies only to the field of biology.

➤ *Practice 8*

Below are three words and some of their definitions. A sentence using each word is also given. Write in the number of the definition that best fits each sentence.

1. **conceive**   **1.** To become pregnant (with).
                    2. To think; imagine.

Which definition of *conceive* fits the following sentence? _____2_____

It's hard to *conceive* of being five stories tall, but if you look out a fifth-floor window, you'll be able to imagine how some dinosaurs viewed the world.

2. **prominent**   1. Projecting outward or upward.
  2. Immediately noticeable; conspicuous.
  3. Widely known; eminent.

Which definition of *prominent* fits the following sentence? _____3_____

Carmen's father is *prominent* in local and state politics.

3. **retain**   1. To keep or hold in a particular place, condition or position.
  2. To keep in mind; remember.
  3. To keep in one's service or pay.

Which definition of *retain* fits the following sentence? _____2_____

To *retain* more of what you study, review the material before going to sleep.

6   WORD ORIGINS

Most dictionaries will give you an idea about where a word comes from and what the word meant when it was created. In the *AHD*, this information is given in brackets at or near the end of the entry. For instance, look at the following entry for *gorgeous*:

> **gor•geous** (gôr′jəs) *adj.* **1.** Dazzlingly brilliant or magnificent: *a gorgeous gown.* **2.** *Informal.* Wonderful; delightful. [< OFr. *gorrias,* elegant.]
> — **gor′geous ly** *adv.* — **gor′geous ness** *n.*

A list of abbreviations near the front of the dictionary explains that *OFr.* stands for "Old French." The information in brackets tells us that *gorgeous* came from the Old French word *gorrias,* which meant "elegant."

➤ *Practice 9*

Use your dictionary to tell what language each of the following words came from and what the word originally meant in that language.

Word	Language	Original Meaning
1. season	*Latin*	*act of sowing*
2. hurt	*Possibly Old French*	*bang into*
3. magazine	*Arabic*	*storehouse*

7 SYNONYMS

A **synonym** is a word whose meaning is similar to that of another word. For instance, two synonyms for the word *fast* are *quick* and *speedy*.

Dictionary entries sometimes end with synonyms. Notice that the entry below ends with a list of synonyms for the verb form of the entry word, *slant*.

> **slant** (slănt) *v.* **1.** To slope or cause to slope. **2.** To present in a way that conforms with a particular bias. — *n.* **1.** A sloping plane, direction, or course. **2.** A particular bias. [< ME *slenten*.] — **slant′ing ly** *adv.* — **slant′-wise′** *adv. & adj.*
> *Syns: slant, incline, lean, slope, tilt, tip v.*

If you want information on how synonyms might differ in meaning, look the words up in the dictionary.

Still more information on synonyms and **antonyms** (words with opposite meanings) can be found in a **thesaurus**, which is a collection of synonyms and some antonyms. A thesaurus can improve your writing by helping you find the precise word you need to express your point. A thesaurus works much like a dictionary. You look up a word, and instead of definitions provided by a dictionary, you get a list of synonyms for the word. Here are three good thesauruses:

The New American Roget's College Thesaurus in Dictionary Form
The Random House Thesaurus
Webster's Collegiate Thesaurus

➤ Practice 10

Each word below has synonyms listed in the dictionary. Write the synonyms for each word in the blank space.

1. benefit   *capitalize, profit*

2. cold   *arctic, chilly, cool, frigid, frosty, gelid, glacial, icy*

3. decision   *conclusion, determination*

➤ *Review Test 1*

To review what you've learned in this chapter, answer each of the following questions by circling the letter of the answer you think is correct.

1. Guidewords can help you
   a. pronounce a word in the dictionary.
   b. find a word in a dictionary.
   c. define a word in a dictionary.

2. You can learn to pronounce a word by using the pronunciation symbols and the
   a. part of speech.
   b. special labels.
   c. pronunciation key.

3. A bold accent mark shows
   a. which syllable has the strongest stress.
   b. which syllable has the weakest stress.
   c. that the word has only one syllable.

4. A label such as *Biol.* or *Math.* means the definition that follows
   a. is informal.
   b. applies only to the indicated field.
   c. no longer is used for the entry word.

5. A thesaurus lists
   a. definitions.
   b. synonyms.
   c. word origins.

➤ *Review Test 2*

A. Below are five pairs of dictionary guidewords. Each pair is followed by a series of other words. Circle the two words in each series which would be found on the page with the guidewords.

1-2. **featherweight / feet**

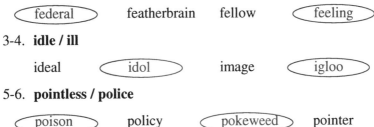

federal   featherbrain   fellow   feeling

3-4. **idle / ill**

ideal   idol   image   igloo

5-6. **pointless / police**

poison   policy   pokeweed   pointer

7-8. **subway / suffer**

suburb   (suede)   (sudden)   suffix

9-10. **yore / yummy**

(yourself)   yuppie   (Yule)   yogurt

B. Use your dictionary and the spelling hints on page 92 to find the correct spelling of the following words.

11. toppic   _____*topic*_____   14. bycicle   _____*bicycle*_____

12. kwiz   _____*quiz*_____   15. writting   _____*writing*_____

13. sirprise   _____*surprise*_____   16. vizitor   _____*visitor*_____

C. Use the pronunciation key on page 94 to answer the following questions.

17. In **fumble** (fŭm′bəl), the **u** is pronounced like the **u** in what common word?

_____*cut*_____

18. In **cable** (kā′bəl), the **a** is pronounced like the **a** in what common word?

_____*pay*_____

19. In **reside** (rĭ-zīd′), the first **e** is pronounced like the **i** in what common word?

_____*pit*_____

20. In **reside** (rĭ-zīd′), the **i** is pronounced like the **i** in what common word?

_____*pie*_____

➤ *Review Test 3*

Use your dictionary to do all of the following.

A. Place dots between the syllables in each of the following words. Then write out the word with the correct pronunciation symbols, including the accent mark or marks.

1. p r i o r   _____*pri•or*_____   *prī′ər*

2. i n s u r e   _____*in•sure*_____   *ĭn-shŏŏr′*

3. e n g a g e   _____*en•gage*_____   *ĕn-gāj′*

4. l e g i b l e   _____*leg•i•ble*_____   *lĕj′ə-bəl*

5. s o c i a l i z e   _____*so•cial•ize*_____   *sō′shə-līz′*

B. List the parts of speech for the following words.

    6. glow   *Parts of speech:* _____*verb, noun*_____

    7. major   *Parts of speech:* ____*adjective, noun, verb*____

C. Write the irregular plural spelling of the following word.

    8. factory   *Irregular spelling:* _____*factories*_____

D. Write in the dictionary definition of *lemon* that fits the following sentence.

    Don't sell me the car if you know it's a lemon.

    9. *Definition of* lemon *that fits:* _____

            One that is unsatisfactory or defective

E. Write five synonyms given by the dictionary for the following word.

    10. field   *Synonyms:* *Any five of the following would*

                     be acceptable: bailiwick, domain,

                     province, realm, sphere, territory.

➤ Review Test 4

Here is a chance to apply your understanding of dictionary use to a full-length selection. This is a true story about Malcolm X, an African American civil rights leader in the 1950s and 1960s. In this excerpt from his autobiography, Malcolm X (with his co-author, Alex Haley) explains how he used his time in jail to become "truly free." Read the selection and then answer the dictionary questions that follow.

Words to Watch

Following are some of the more difficult words that appear in the reading. Each word is followed by the number of the paragraph in which it appears and its meaning there. These words are indicated in the reading by a small circle (°).

    acquire (1): get
    painstaking (5): very careful
    ragged (5): uneven

burrowing (6): digging
succeeding (7): following
word-base (8): vocabulary
bunk (8): bed
wedge (8): a tool shaped like a triangle, used to separate two objects

---

DISCOVERING WORDS

Malcolm X with Alex Haley

It was because of my letters [which Malcolm X wrote to people   1
outside while he was in jail] that I happened to stumble upon starting to
acquire° some kind of a homemade education.

I became increasingly frustrated at not being able to express what   2
I wanted to convey in letters that I wrote. . . . And every book I picked
up had few sentences which didn't contain anywhere from one to
nearly all the words that might as well have been in Chinese. When I
skipped those words, of course, I really ended up with little idea of
what the book said. . . .

I saw that the best thing I could do was get hold of a dictionary—   3
to study, to learn some words. I requested a dictionary along with some
tablets and pencils from the Norfolk Prison Colony school.

I spent two days just riffling uncertainly through the dictionary's   4
pages. I'd never realized so many words existed! I didn't know *which*
words I needed to learn. Finally, just to start some kind of action, I
began copying.

In my slow, painstaking°, ragged° handwriting, I copied into my   5
tablet everything printed on that first page, down to the punctuation
marks. I believe it took me a day. Then, aloud, I read back to myself
everything I'd written on the tablet. Over and over, aloud, to myself, I
read my own handwriting.

I woke up the next morning, thinking about those words—   6
immensely proud to realize that not only had I written so much at one
time, but I'd written words that I never knew were in the world.
Moreover, with a little effort, I also could remember what many of
these words meant. I reviewed the words whose meanings I didn't
remember. Funny thing, from the dictionary's first page right now, that
aardvark springs to my mind. The dictionary had a picture of it, a long-
tailed, long-eared, burrowing° African mammal, which lives off
termites caught by sticking out its tongue as an anteater does for ants.

I was so fascinated that I went on—I copied the dictionary's next   7
page. And the same experience came when I studied that. With every
succeeding° page, I also learned of people and places and events from
history. Actually, the dictionary is like a miniature encyclopedia.
Finally, the dictionary's A section had filled a whole tablet—and I went
on into the B's. That was the way I started copying what eventually
became the entire dictionary. It went a lot faster after so much practice
helped me to pick up handwriting speed.

I suppose it was inevitable that as my word-base° broadened, I   8
could for the first time pick up a book and read and now begin to
understand what the book was saying. Anyone who has read a great
deal can imagine the new world that opened. Let me tell you
something: from then until I left the prison, in every free moment I had,
if I was not reading in the library, I was reading on my bunk°. You
couldn't have gotten me out of books with a wedge°. Months passed
without my even thinking about being imprisoned. In fact, up to then, I
never had been so truly free in my life.

Dictionary Questions

Answer the questions that follow the two dictionary entries, both for words taken
from the selection. The pronunciation key on page 94 will help you answer the
pronunciation questions.

stum•ble (stŭm′bəl) *v.* **-bled, -bling. 1. a.** To trip and almost fall. **b.** To proceed
unsteadily; flounder. See Syns at **blunder. c.** To act or speak falteringly or
clumsily. **2.** To make a mistake. **3.** To come upon accidentally. [< ME *stumblen.*]
—stum′ble *n.*

1. *Stumble* would be found on the dictionary page with which guidewords?
   a. strongbox / study
   b. sulk / sunburst
   (c.) stuff / suave
   d. Stockton / store

2. How many syllables are in the word *stumble*?
   a. One
   (b.) Two
   c. Three
   d. Four

3. The **u** in *stumble* sounds like the **u** in
   a. *cut.*
   b. *urge.*
   c. *abuse.*
   d *circus.*

4. The part of speech of *stumble* is
   a. adjective.
   b. adverb.
   c. pronoun.
   d. verb.

5. Which definition of *stumble* fits the sentence below?
   a. Definition 1a
   b. Definition 2
   c. Definition 3

> It was because of my letters that I happened to stumble upon starting to acquire some kind of a homemade education. (Paragraph 1)

con•vey (kən-vā′) *v.* **1.** To carry; transport. **2.** To transmit. **3.** To communicate; impart. **4.** *Law.* To transfer ownership of or title to. [< Med. Lat. *conviare,* to escort.] — **con•vey′a•ble** *adj.* — **con•vey′er, con•vey′or** *n.*

6. *Convey* would be found on the dictionary page with which guidewords?
   a. controlled substance / convey
   b. contort / control
   c. coordination / cord
   d. cordage / corner

7. How many syllables are in the word *convey*?
   a. One
   b. Two
   c. Three
   d. Four

8. The **o** in *convey* sounds like
   a. the **o** in *pot.*
   b. the **o** in *toe.*
   c. the **o** in *for.*
   d. the schwa in *gallop.*

9. The part of speech of *convey* is
   a. adjective.
   b. adverb.
   c. noun.
   d. verb.

10. Which definition of *convey* fits the sentence below?
    a. Definition 1
    b. Definition 2
    c. Definition 3

    I became increasingly frustrated at not being able to express what I wanted to convey in letters that I wrote. (Paragraph 2)

Mapping Activity

This selection is organized by time: first one thing happened; then another; after that, another; and so on. The major events are scrambled in the list below. Write them in the diagram in their correct order.

- His education gives him freedom in jail through reading.
- He is frustrated with his weak language skills.
- He builds his vocabulary and knowledge through the dictionary.

Central point: By studying the dictionary, Malcolm X finds intellectual freedom in prison.

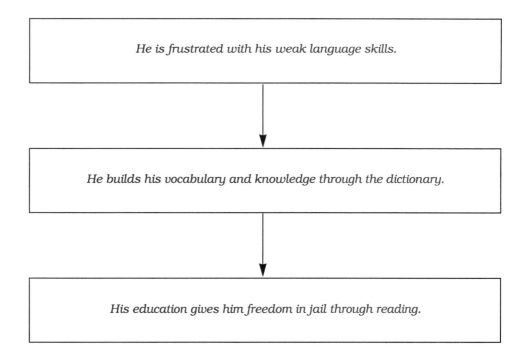

He is frustrated with his weak language skills.

He builds his vocabulary and knowledge through the dictionary.

His education gives him freedom in jail through reading.

Discussion Questions

1. At the end of the selection, Malcolm X says that even though he was still in jail, he "never had been so truly free" in his life. What does he mean by that? What is it that makes you feel free?

2. Malcolm X decided to improve his vocabulary in order to express himself better in letters. What was it that made you decide to continue your education? What do you hope to do with the knowledge you are gaining?

Writing Activities

1. Write about a significant discovery in your life. Explain the discovery in detail, including when and where it occurred and its meaning for you.

2. Malcolm X tells us that he felt free. What does the word *freedom* mean to you? Write a paragraph on your definition of *freedom*, giving specific examples to show what you mean. Your first sentence will begin "Freedom is. . . ."

Check Your Performance   **DICTIONARY USE**

Activity	Number Right	Points	Total
Review Test 1 (5 items)	_____	x 2 =	_____
Review Test 2 (20 items)	_____	x 2 =	_____
Review Test 3 (10 items)	_____	x 2 =	_____
Review Test 4 (10 items)	_____	x 2 =	_____
Mapping Activity (3 items)	_____	x 3⅓ =	_____
		TOTAL SCORE =	_____ %

Enter your total score onto the Reading Performance Chart: Review Tests on the inside back cover.

6

Vocabulary in Context

Do you know the meaning of the word *queries*? How about the words *tedious* and *transmit*?

You may be having trouble thinking of the definitions of these words. However, you will be more likely to know what they mean when you see them in the following sentences:

> Dan was nervous about answering Detective Miller's *queries*. Why was he asking so many questions, anyway?

> Most of my history teacher's lectures were *tedious*, but the one about what really happened on Paul Revere's famous ride was very interesting.

> Mosquitoes *transmit* sleeping sickness through biting.

Now, see if you can choose the meaning of each word based on the way it is used above. Circle the letter of the meaning you think is correct.

Queries are

a. statements of fact.   b. questions.   c. charges.

Tedious means

a. interesting.   b. long.   c. boring.

Transmit means to

a. spread.   b. enjoy.   c. cure.

To help you decide on the right meanings, you used **context clues**. These are clues provided by the **context**, the surrounding words. With the help of context clues, you could probably tell that *queries* means "questions," that *tedious* means "boring," and that *transmit* means to "spread."

Context clues, then, can help you figure out what new words mean. In general, using these clues will help you in three ways:

1 It will save you time since you won't have to stop and look up every important new word you read. (However, you should still keep a dictionary handy. Sometimes there will be no context clues.)

2 It will improve your understanding of what you read since you will know more of the words.

3 It will improve your vocabulary because you will be learning the meanings of many new words. As you continue to run into these words, they will become a part of your working vocabulary.

TYPES OF CONTEXT CLUES

Here are four common types of context clues:

1 Examples

2 Synonyms

3 Antonyms

4 General Sense of the Sentence or Passage

You will learn about each of these clues in the rest of the chapter. Examples will help you understand how each type of clue works. In addition, practice exercises will help you to recognize and use context clues and to add new words to your vocabulary.

1   Examples

An unknown word may be followed by examples that reveal what the word means. The examples often follow signal words such as *for example, including, for instance, such as, like,* or *e.g.* (which means "for example").

To see how this type of clue works, read the sentences below. The examples, which are **boldfaced**, serve as context clues and should help you figure out the meanings of the words in *italics*. Circle the letter of the definition of each word in italics.

1. *Assets* such as **good health, a loving family,** and **an enjoyable job** make life rewarding.

   Assets are

   a. things of value.   b. rewards on the job.   c. helpful people.

2. John F. Kennedy, Jr., gets so much attention because of such *conspicuous* features as **a muscular build, good looks,** and **a height of 6′ 3″**.

   Conspicuous means

   a. large.   b. noticeable.   c. famous.

3. The car had *defects* such as **a dented fender** and **torn seats**. But I didn't care. I had wanted a Corvette sports car for years, and I was going to buy it.

   Defects are

   a. faults.   b. out-of-date features.   c. foreign qualities.

Answers:

In each sentence, the examples probably helped you to figure out the meanings of the words in italics:

1. a   The *assets* listed are "things of value."
2. b   The *conspicuous* features mentioned are "noticeable."
3. a   The *defects* described are "faults."

➤ *Practice 1*

Read each item below, and then do two things:

   1) Underline the examples given for the word in italics.
   2) Circle the letter of the definition of the word in italics.

1. There is much to see at Hearst Castle. It even has an indoor swimming pool whose *dimensions* are <u>a length of 100′</u>, <u>a width of 15′</u>, and <u>a depth of 10′</u>.

   Dimensions are

   a. costs.   b. benefits.   ⓒ measurements.

2. The *notables* at the charity event included <u>actor Tom Cruise, tennis star Steffi Graf,</u> and <u>film critics Siskel and Ebert</u>.

   Notables means

   a. average people.   ⓑ people worthy of notice.   c. movie stars.

3. The San Diego Zoo has not only such common animals as lions and tigers, but also *exotic* ones, like <u>snow leopards</u> and <u>koala bears</u>.

   Exotic means

   ⓐ unusual.   b. dangerous.   c. ordinary.

4. *Fictitious* television investigators such as <u>Columbo</u> and <u>Jessica Fletcher</u> make detective work seem much more glamorous than it really is.

   Fictitious means

   a. true-life.   b. unknown.   ⓒ imaginary.

5. We communicate much through *gestures*, like <u>the thumbs-up sign</u> and <u>a shrug of the shoulders</u>.

   Gestures are

   a. hand signals.   b. good feelings.   ⓒ motions of the body.

2   Synonyms

Synonyms are words that mean the same or almost the same as another word. For example, the words *watch, look, see,* and *observe* are synonyms—they all mean about the same thing. Synonyms serve as context clues by providing the meaning of an unknown word that is nearby.

The sentences below illustrate this type of context clue. Underline the synonym for each word in italics.

1. Jack was a *mediocre* student, but he was a better-than-average baseball player.

2. It is hard to believe my millionaire cousin was once *indigent*, so poor that he walked the streets without knowing where his next meal would come from.

3. My company has a *regulation* allowing new mothers three months off from work. There should be a rule allowing fathers the same time off.

Answers:

The synonym in each sentence provides the meaning of the word in italics.

1. Someone who is *mediocre* at something is "average."
2. Someone who is *indigent* is "poor."
3. A *regulation* is a "rule."

➤ Practice 2

In each item, underline the synonym for the word in italics.

1. Rodolfo is one of the best *patrons* of Jackie's Diner. He's a <u>steady customer,</u> not because he likes the food there, but because he likes Jackie.

2. While your *vocation* is important, most experts advise that you treat it for what it is—a <u>job,</u> not your entire life.

3. Calcium <u>strengthens</u> teeth, and it also *fortifies* bones.

4. Your *absurd* idea that people from outer space live among us is as <u>ridiculous</u> as the belief that the Earth is flat.

5. Judges are supposed to be *impartial*, but the judge in Harold's trial was not very <u>fair</u>.

3 Antonyms

Antonyms are words with opposite meanings. For example, *summer* is the opposite of *winter*, and *soft* is the opposite of *hard*. Antonyms are often signaled by words such as *unlike, but, however, instead, in contrast,* or *on the other hand.* Antonyms serve as context clues by providing the opposite meaning of an unknown word.

The examples below should help you to understand how this type of clue works. Each item has an antonym as a context clue. Read each item, and do two things:

1) Underline the antonym for the word in italics.
2) Circle the letter of the meaning of the word in italics.

1. The *adverse* weather conditions forced us to stay inside for most of our vacation. The day the weather finally turned nice, we had to leave.

   Adverse means

   a. nice.   b. bad.   c. summer.

2. Some experiences are only *fleeting*, but their memories are long-lived.

   Fleeting means

   a. lasting a short time.   b. easy to forget.   c. lasting forever.

3. After years of *defying* my parents, I decided life might be better if I instead tried agreeing with them once in a while.

   Defying means

   a. avoiding.   b. obeying.   c. opposing.

Answers:

The antonyms are clues to the meanings of the words in italics:

1. b   *Adverse* weather conditions are the opposite of "nice" ones.
2. a   *Fleeting* is the opposite of "long-lived."
3. c   *Defying* one's parents is the opposite of "agreeing with them."

➤ *Practice 3*

Antonyms provide context clues in the sentences below. Read each item, and do two things:

1) Underline the antonym for the word in italics.
2) Circle the letter of the meaning of the word in italics.

1. Your science project is much more *elaborate* than mine. In fact, mine looks downright simple compared with yours.

   Elaborate means

   a. plain. b. large. (c.) complicated.

2. Gordon would not remain an *obscure* author all his life. He knew that someday he would be famous.

   Obscure means

   (a.) unknown. b. well known. c. good.

3. The attorney introduced facts she felt were *relevant* to the case. However, the judge said the facts were unrelated to this trial.

   Relevant means

   a. legal. (b.) related. c. known.

4. The patient's pains were *acute* yesterday, but today they are rather mild.

   Acute means

   a. weak. (b.) sharp. c. noted.

5. The bank president assigned *trivial* problems to new employees. He gave the serious problems to experienced workers.

   Trivial means

   a. important. b. customer. (c.) unimportant.

4   General Sense of the Sentence or Passage

Often, the context of a new word contains no examples, synonyms, or antonyms. How, then, can you understand the word? You can use the general sense of the sentence or passage. Careful reading and your own experience will often give you the meaning of a word.

In each sentence on the next page, look for general clues to the meaning of the word in italics. Then circle the letter of your choice.

1. Leilani lived in Hawaii for fifteen years, so it is hard for me to *conceive of* why she decided to move to Minnesota.

   Conceive of means to

   a. plan.   b. remember.   c. imagine.

2. At the animal shelter, Rita fell in love with a poodle, and Dan could not resist a collie. So they felt there was no *alternative* but to adopt both animals.

   An *alternative* is a

   a. choice.   b. reason.   c. confusion.

3. As a *consequence* of his bad report card, my brother could not watch TV until his teachers said he was improving.

   A *consequence* is a

   a. right.   b. result.   c. chance.

Answers:

Each sentence provides context clues that become clear if you read carefully.

1. c   To *conceive of* something means to "imagine" something. The speaker could not imagine why his friend Leilani would move from Hawaii to Minnesota.

2. a   An *alternative* is a "choice." Rita and Dan felt they had no choice but to take both dogs home.

3. b   A *consequence* is a "result." The result of the brother's bad report card was not being able to watch TV until teachers reported that he had improved.

➤ Practice 4

Use your experience and general understanding to figure out the meaning of each word in italics. Think about the context in which the word is used, and then circle the letter of the word's meaning.

1. Jesse was surprised when his speech *elicited* laughs from the audience. He was perfectly serious about his topic.

   Elicited means

   a. brought out.   b. hid.   c. included.

2. Elena was glad she had *ample* time to collect her thoughts for the afternoon's mid-term. Then she discovered her watch was incorrect—she was actually late for the test!

   Ample means

   a. no.   (b.) plenty of.   c. little.

3. My brother felt it would be *futile* to try to make the basketball team. The other players were at least eight inches taller than he.

   Futile means

   a. helpful.   (b.) useless.   c. easy.

4. The *impact* of the crash was so great that you couldn't tell the make of either car. Each was totally destroyed.

   Impact means

   (a.) force.   b. time.   c. place.

5. The young eagle was clearly a *novice* at flying. As he tried to land, he got himself all tangled up in a thornbush.

   A *novice* is a

   a. bird.   b. success.   (c.) beginner.

A Note and Study Hint

You don't always have to use context clues or the dictionary to find definitions. Textbook authors usually give formal definitions and explanations of important terms. Often one or more examples are also given, as shown with the excerpts on the next page.

Below are three short excerpts from college texts. In each case, a term to be defined is set off in **boldface** or *italic* type, and the definition is nearby. In one case, an example is also included. Which one of the three textbook excerpts includes both a definition and an example? In the margin of that excerpt, write a "DEF" beside the definition and an "EX" beside the example. You will find it helpful to mark off definitions and examples in the same way when you are reading a textbook chapter.

Excerpt from a psychology textbook:

The *case study* method is used mainly by clinical psychologists working with troubled persons. A case study is an in-depth examination of one individual. The purpose is to learn as much as possible about the person's problems. The technique is expensive and takes several sessions to complete.

Excerpt from a business textbook:

Short-range plans tend to be specific. One part of a short-range plan, **procedures**, tells employees exactly what steps to take in a given situation. A factory's procedures, for instance, may require moving raw materials from the receiving platform to the beginning of the assembly line.

Excerpt from a sociology textbook:

Some religious practices can be classified as **rituals,** or standardized sets of actions used in ceremonies or on other occasions. Rituals rely on symbols to communicate their meaning to participants.

The second textbook excerpt above includes both a definition and an example. The word being defined is *procedures*—the "part of a short-range plan" that "tells employees exactly what steps to take in a given situation." The words *for instance* signal that the author is also illustrating the new word. In this case, the author gives an example of a factory's procedures.

By using italic or boldface type, textbook authors show which terms are important to learn. Indeed, one early step you should take to understand a textbook chapter is to mark definitions and examples in the text. Then write down each definition and, if available, an example that makes the definition clear. Identifying definitions and examples will help as you reread a chapter for increased understanding.

CHAPTER OVERVIEW

In this chapter, you learned that you can often figure out word meanings by being alert to four types of context clues:

- **Examples** of a new word. The examples may be introduced by such signals as *for example, including, for instance, such as, like,* or *e.g.*
- A **synonym** of a new word. Two or three words that mean the same as the new word may also reveal its meaning.
- An **antonym** of a new word. Antonyms may be signaled by words such as *unlike, but, however, instead, in contrast,* or *on the other hand.*
- A **general sense of the sentence or passage**. Often the general context of a new word reveals the word's meaning.

You also learned that textbook authors provide definitions for important new terms. Learning those definitions is an important part of studying a chapter.

➤ *Review Test 1*

To review what you have learned in this chapter, answer each of the following questions. Circle the letter of the answer you think is correct, or fill in the blank.

1. The context of a word is
   a. its meaning.   b. its opposite.   (c.) the words around it.

2. Which type of context clue is introduced by such signal words as *however* and *on the other hand*?
   a. example   b. synonym   (c.) antonym

3. In the sentence below, which type of context clue is used for the word in italics?

   a. example   (b.) synonym   c. antonym

   Since I was brought up in a city environment, I am comfortable with *urban* life.

4. In the sentence below, which type of context clue is used for the word in italics?

   a. example   b. synonym   (c.) antonym

   Don't allow *despair* to get you down. Keep hope uppermost in your mind.

5. When textbook authors introduce an important term, they usually provide you with its _____*definition*_____ and often also with an example.

➤ *Review Test 2*

Using context clues for help, circle the letter of the best meaning for each word or phrase in italics.

1. I have found that if I *adhere to* a schedule, I accomplish more. When I don't follow a set routine, I get little done.

   Adhere to means to
   (a.) follow.   b. avoid.   c. buy.

2. After standing empty for fifteen years, the old mansion had *deteriorated*. The wood was decaying, the plaster was peeling, and most of the windows had broken.

   Deteriorate means to
   a. become older.   (b.) become worse.   c. become empty.

3. When Yoko asked Alex whether he wanted to go camping or visit her brother, he said he was *indifferent*—it didn't matter to him where they went on their vacation.

   Indifferent means

   a. not the same.   b. unable to decide.   c. having no preference.

4. Your version of the accident *distorts* the events, while mine tells it just as it happened.

   Distort means to

   a. explain.   b. misrepresent.   c. forget.

5. It was hard for Leon to *refrain* from hitting Michael. Michael had pushed him and knocked his books down.

   Refrain means to

   a. learn.   b. hold back.   c. think.

6. Although the teacher rarely complimented anyone in class, he *commended* Maria on her outstanding work.

   Commended means

   a. blamed.   b. graded.   c. praised.

7. Lucy is so *gullible* that she'll believe almost anything you make up. She believed me the other day when I told her milk has lots of caffeine.

   Gullible means

   a. clever.   b. easy to fool.   c. willing to learn.

8. You can't *equate* winning the Super Bowl with beating me in a game of basketball. The two are just not the same.

   Equate means to

   a. treat as equal.   b. treat as normal.   c. cover up.

9. Some of my friends love mountain climbing, but I find it too *treacherous*. I prefer less dangerous activities, like floating in a swimming pool.

   Treacherous means

   a. athletic.   b. safe.   c. dangerous.

10. I have never met anyone as *obstinate* as my father. Once he makes up his mind, he won't change it for anything.

    Obstinate means

    a. stubborn.   b. agreeable.   c. serious.

➤ *Review Test 3*

Using context clues for help, write the definition of each word in italics. Choose from the definitions in the box below. Each will be used once.

alone	stingy	false show
matching	witty reply	safe place
get smaller	remove	very great enthusiasm
given to		

1. Cheryl felt that the honor *bestowed on* her for work with the homeless could have been given to many others who had worked hard as well.

   Bestowed on means _____ *given to* _____

2. Juan looked forward to being *isolated* at his mountain cabin. He had been in the crowded city too long.

   Isolated means _____ *alone* _____

3. I had to *delete* a lot of information from my report on zoos because it was longer than my teacher wanted it to be.

   Delete means _____ *remove* _____

4. Roland was so *miserly* that he refused to give his sons spending money. Also, to save electricity, he insisted they study by the light of one lamp.

   Miserly means_____ *stingy* _____

5. The Wildlife Animal *Refuge* is home to injured animals who have been rescued by concerned people.

   A *refuge* is a _____ *safe place* _____

6. Olga always comes up with quick *retorts* to people's comments, but I can never think of clever answers until it's too late.

   A *retort* is a_____ *witty reply* _____

7. Experts say exercise makes the appetite *diminish.* So being on a diet provides another good reason to exercise.

   Diminish means _____ *get smaller* _____

8. Antonio made a *pretense* of writing the answers to the essay test, but he was just scribbling. He hadn't studied for the test at all.

   Pretense means a _____ *false show* _____

9. My roommate has a *mania* for stuffed animals. She has dozens all over the place.

   A *mania* is a _____ *very great enthusiasm* _____

10. Twins separated early in life often lead *parallel* lives. For instance, many get jobs in the same field and marry similar people.

    Parallel means _____ *matching* _____

➤ *Review Test 4*

Here is a chance to apply the skill of understanding vocabulary in context to a full-length selection. How much of a difference do you think reading can make in your life? Consider this story written by a woman who grew up in Brazil and read everything she could get her hands on. She tells why she reads so much and describes the impact reading has had on her life. When you finish the selection, answer the vocabulary questions that follow.

Words to Watch

Following are some words in the reading that do not have strong context support. Each word is followed by the number of the paragraph in which it appears and its meaning there. These words are indicated in the story by a small circle (°).

enchanted (1): fascinating
devoured (5): took in with great enthusiasm
intriguing (6): interesting
illicit (9): not permitted
sadistic (9): cruel
exult (9): rejoice
horizon (12): view of the world
seduces (13): attracts
abyss (13): bottomless hole
precision (13): exactness
subversive (15): turning people against something

A LOVE AFFAIR WITH BOOKS

Bernadete Piassa

When I was young, I thought that reading was like a drug which I   1
was allowed to take only a teaspoon at a time, but which, nevertheless,
had the effect of carrying me away to an enchanted° world where I

experienced strange and forbidden emotions. As time went by and I took that drug again and again, I became addicted to it. I could no longer live without reading. Books became an intrinsic part of my life. They became my friends, my guides, my lovers. My most faithful lovers.

I didn't know I would fall in love with books when I was young and started to read. I don't even recall when I started to read and how. I just remember that my mother didn't like me to read. In spite of this, every time I had an opportunity I would sneak somewhere with a book and read one page, two pages, three, if I were lucky enough, always feeling my heart beating fast, always hoping that my mother wouldn't find me, wouldn't shout as always: "Bernadete, don't you have anything to do?" For her, books were nothing. For me, they were everything.

In my childhood I didn't have a big choice of books. I lived in a small town in Brazil, surrounded by swamp and farms. It was impossible to get out of town by car; there weren't roads. By train it took eight hours to reach the next village. There were airplanes, small airplanes, only twice a week. Books couldn't get to my town very easily. There wasn't a library there, either. However, I was lucky: My uncle was a pilot.

My uncle, who owned a big farm and also worked flying people from place to place in his small airplane, had learned to fly, in addition, with his imagination. At home, he loved to sit in his hammock on his patio and travel away in his fantasy with all kinds of books. If he happened to read a bestseller or a romance, when he was done he would give it to my mother, who also liked to read although she didn't like me to. But I would get to read the precious book anyway, even if I needed to do this in a hiding place, little by little.

I remember very well one series of small books. Each had a green cover with a drawing of a couple kissing on it. I think the series had been given to my mother when she was a teenager because all the pages were already yellow and almost worn-out. But although the books were old, for me they seemed alive, and for a long time I devoured° them, one by one, pretending that I was the heroine and my lover would soon come to rescue me. He didn't come, of course. And I was the one who left my town to study and live in Rio de Janeiro, taking only my clothes with me. But inside myself I was taking my passion for books that would never abandon me.

I had been sent to study in a boarding school, and I was soon appalled to discover that the expensive all-girls school had even fewer books than my house. In my class there was a bookshelf with maybe fifty books, and almost all of them were about the lives of saints and the miracles of Christ. I had almost given up the hope of finding something to read when I spotted, tucked away at the very end of the shelf, a small book already covered by dust. It didn't seem to be about religion because it had a more intriguing° title, *The Old Man and the Sea*. It was written by an author that I had never heard of before: Ernest Hemingway. Curious, I started to read the book and a few minutes later was already fascinated by Santiago, the fisherman.

I loved that book so much that when I went to my aunt's house to 7 spend the weekend, I asked her if she had any books by the man who had written it. She lent me *For Whom the Bell Tolls*, and I read it every Sunday I could get out of school, only a little bit at a time, only one teaspoon at a time. I started to wait anxiously for those Sundays. At the age of thirteen I was deeply in love with Ernest Hemingway.

When I finished with all his books I could find, I discovered 8 Herman Hesse, Graham Greene, Aldous Huxley, Edgar Allan Poe. I could read them only on Sundays, so, during the week, I would dream or think about the world I had discovered in their books.

At that time I thought that my relationship with books was kind of 9 odd, something that set me apart from the world. Only when I read the short story "Illicit° Happiness," by Clarice Lispector, a Brazilian author, did I discover that other people could enjoy books as much as I did. The story is about an ugly and fat girl who still manages to torture one of the beautiful girls in her town only because her father is the owner of a bookstore, and she can have all the books she wants. With sadistic° refinement, day after day she promises to give to the beautiful girl the book the girl dearly wants, but never fulfills her promise. When her mother finds out what is going on and gives the book to the beautiful girl, the girl runs through the streets hugging it and, at home, pretends to have lost it only to find it again, showing an ardor for books that made me exult°. For the first time I wasn't alone. I knew that someone else also loved books as much as I did.

My passion for books continued through my life, and it had to 10 surmount another big challenge when, at the age of thirty-one, I moved to New York. Because I had almost no money, I was forced to leave all my books in Brazil. Besides, I didn't know enough English to read in this language. For some years I was condemned again to the darkness; condemned to live without books, my friends, my guides, my lovers.

But my love for books was so strong that I overcame even this 11 obstacle. I learned to read in English and was finally able to enjoy my favorite authors again.

Although books have always been part of my life, they still hold a 12 mystery for me, and every time I open a new one, I ask myself which pleasures I am about to discover, which routes I am about to travel, which emotions I am about to sink in. Will this new book touch me as a woman, as a foreigner, as a romantic soul, as a curious person? Which horizon° is it about to unfold to me, which string of my soul is it bound to touch, which secret is it about to unveil for me?

Sometimes, the book seduces° me not only for the story it tells, but also because of the words the author uses in it. Reading Gabriel Garcia Marquez's short story "The Handsomest Drowned Man in the World," I feel dazzled when he writes that it took "the fraction of centuries for the body to fall into the abyss°." The fraction of centuries! I read those words again and again, infatuated by them, by their precision°, by their hidden meaning. I try to keep them in my mind, even knowing that they are already part of my soul.   13

After reading so many books that touch me deeply, each one in its special way, I understand now that my mother had a point when she tried to keep me away from books in my childhood. She wanted me to stay in my little town, to marry a rich and tiresome man, to keep up with the traditions. But the books carried me away; they gave me wings to fly, to discover new places. They made me dare to live another kind of life. They made me wish for more, and when I couldn't have all I wished for, they were still there to comfort me, to show me new options.   14

Yes, my mother was right. Books are dangerous; books are subversive°. Because of them I left a predictable future for an unforeseeable one. However, if I had to choose again, I would always choose the books instead of the lackluster life I could have had. After all, what joy would I find in my heart without my books, my most faithful lovers?   15

Vocabulary Questions

Use context clues in the reading to help you decide on the best meaning for the italicized words. Then circle the letter of your choice.

1. The word *intrinsic* in "I could no longer live without reading. Books became an intrinsic part of my life" (paragraph 1) means
   a. rare.
   b. efficient.
   c. essential.
   d. unpleasant.

2. The word *abandon* in "inside myself I was taking my passion for books that would never abandon me" (paragraph 5) means
   a. please.
   b. strengthen.
   c. leave.
   d. join.

3. The word *appalled* in "I was soon appalled to discover that the expensive all-girls school had even fewer books than my house" (paragraph 6) means
   a. shocked.
   b. unwilling.
   c. pleased.
   d. proud.

4. The word *anxiously* in "She lent me *For Whom the Bell Tolls*, and I read it every Sunday I could get out of school. . . . I started to wait anxiously for those Sundays" (paragraph 7) means
   a. fearfully.
   b. eagerly.
   c. very patiently.
   d. with much worry.

5. The word *dearly* in "day after day she promises to give to the beautiful girl the book the girl dearly wants" (paragraph 9) means
   a. foolishly.
   b. with great humor.
   c. rudely.
   d. sincerely.

6. The word *ardor* in "the girl . . . pretends to have lost it only to find it again, showing an ardor for books. . . . I knew that someone else also loved books as much as I did" (paragraph 9) means
   a. passion.
   b. doubt.
   c. kindness.
   d. improvement.

7. The word *surmount* in "My passion for books continued through my life, and it had to surmount another big challenge when . . . I moved to New York" (paragraph 10) means
   a. remain.
   b. select.
   c. overcome.
   d. search for.

8. The word *condemned* in "I didn't know enough English to read in this language. For some years I was condemned again to the darkness; condemned to live without books" (paragraph 10) means
   a. rescued.
   b. doomed.
   c. captured.
   d. attracted.

9. The word *infatuated* in "I read these words again and again, infatuated by them, by their precision, by their hidden meaning" (paragraph 13) means
   a. disturbed.
   b. protected.
   c. worried.
   d. fascinated.

10. The word *lackluster* in "She wanted me to stay in my little town, to marry a rich and tiresome man. . . . However, . . . I would always choose the books instead of the lackluster life I could have had" (paragraphs 14 and 15) means
    a. exciting.
    b. dull.
    c. famous.
    d. sickly.

Mapping Activity

The selection is organized according to time, describing events in Piassa's life in the order in which they happened. The major events that happened to Piassa are scrambled below. Write them in the diagram in their correct order.

- She goes to boarding school in Rio de Janeiro.
- Piassa lives in a small town in Brazil.
- She learns to read in English.
- Piassa moves to New York.

Central point: Reading books has greatly enriched Piassa's life and has led her to give up a traditional life for a more adventuresome one.

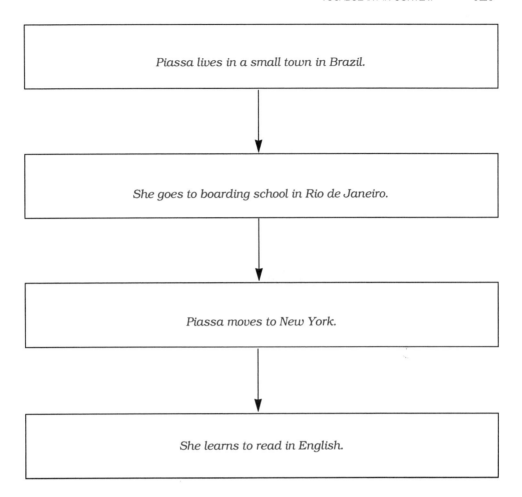

Piassa lives in a small town in Brazil.

⬇

She goes to boarding school in Rio de Janeiro.

⬇

Piassa moves to New York.

⬇

She learns to read in English.

Discussion Questions

1. The author's mother discouraged her from reading. What was the attitude of the adults in your family to reading? Were you encouraged or discouraged to read? Explain.

2. What was reading like for you in school? Explain why it was a positive or a negative experience.

Writing Activities

1. Write a paper that begins with one of the following sentences:

   • My family encouraged me to read when I was growing up.
   • My family environment discouraged me from reading when I was growing up.
   • Reading in school was a positive experience for me.
   • Reading in school was a negative experience for me.

   Develop your paper with convincing, colorful details, as Piassa has done in her story. Feel free to draw upon the details you mentioned in response to the discussion questions above.

2. Piassa shows us that reading was an important activity in her life. Write a paper about an activity that has been very important in your life. Explain several ways in which that activity has been important to you.

Check Your Performance		VOCABULARY IN CONTEXT		
Activity	*Number Right*	*Points*		*Total*
Review Test 1 (5 items)	_____	x 2 =		_____
Review Test 2 (10 items)	_____	x 3 =		_____
Review Test 3 (10 items)	_____	x 3 =		_____
Review Test 4 (10 items)	_____	x 2 =		_____
Mapping Activity (4 items)	_____	x 2.5 =		_____
		TOTAL SCORE =		_____ %

Enter your total score onto the Reading Performance Chart: Review Tests on the inside back cover.

7

Main Ideas

The most helpful reading skill is the ability to find an author's main idea. This chapter and chapter 9 will increase your understanding of main ideas and help you develop your skill in locating them.

UNDERSTANDING THE MAIN IDEA

The **main idea** is a general idea. It states the chief point of a paragraph. Very often, the main idea appears in a sentence called the **topic sentence**. The rest of the paragraph consists of specific ideas and details that support and explain the main idea.

Think of the main idea as an "umbrella" statement. Under the main idea fits all the other material of the paragraph. The other material is specific ideas in the form of examples, reasons, facts, and other supporting evidence. The diagram below shows the relationship:

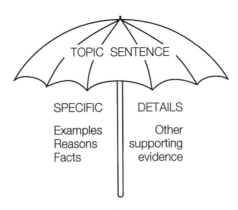

Look now at the paragraph that follows, and see if you can find its topic sentence. The topic sentence will state the main idea: a general idea that includes, or covers, all or most of the other material in the paragraph.

¹Americans love to send greeting cards. ²For instance, over 4 million birthday cards are sent out in this country every day. ³During Valentine's Day last year, over 900 million cards were mailed. ⁴And close to 3 billion holiday greeting cards were sent out over the Christmas season.

Which sentence states the main idea of the paragraph? In the space provided below, write the number of the topic sentence. Then read the explanation that follows.

Topic sentence: _____

Explanation:

Sentence 1: The idea that Americans love to send greeting cards is the most general idea in the paragraph. "Greeting cards" is broad enough to include the three specific types of cards named in the paragraph—birthday, Valentine's Day, and Christmas cards. Sentence 1 is therefore the topic sentence, the sentence that states the main idea.

Sentence 2: The number of birthday cards sent by Americans is just one specific detail in the paragraph. Sentence 2 is not general enough to cover the details on other types of greeting cards.

Sentence 3: The idea that Americans sent millions of Valentine's Day cards is another specific detail. It is too narrow to include the other types of greeting cards.

Sentence 4: The number of Christmas cards sent is a final specific detail. Sentence 4 is also too narrow to include the other types of greeting cards.

In summary, the main idea of the paragraph on greeting cards is stated in sentence 1. The other sentences support the main idea. They give specific examples of the idea that Americans love to send greeting cards. Here is the umbrella diagram again. This time it shows the relationship between the ideas in the paragraph about greeting cards.

AMERICANS LOVE TO
SEND GREETING CARDS

4 million for birthdays every day
900 million on Valentine's Day
3 billion over Christmas

Remember, then, that the main idea is a general idea that includes most or all of the other information in a paragraph. That general idea is often stated in one sentence called the topic sentence. The other information is made up of specific details that support or explain the main idea.

GENERAL VERSUS SPECIFIC IDEAS

You have learned that the main idea in a paragraph is a *general idea*. In contrast, the supporting information in a paragraph is made up of *specific* ideas. To improve your skill at finding main ideas, then, it will be helpful for you to practice separating general from specific ideas.

We often separate general and specific ideas in our lives. For example, you may do so in choosing your school classes. You may think, "I need credits in science. Should I take biology or chemistry?" In this case, *science* is the general idea, and *biology* and *chemistry* are the specific ideas. A general idea (science) includes specific ideas (biology and chemistry).

Or you may go home from school or work and think, "I'll get some fish for dinner." You may consider flounder, salmon, and tuna. In this example, *fish* is the general idea; *flounder, salmon* and *tuna* are the specific ideas.

In other words, **general ideas** are broad, and **specific ideas** are narrower. *Countries* is a broad term that includes *Brazil*, which is more narrow. *Rodent* is a broad term that includes specific terms such as *mouse* and *rat*, which are more narrow.

The practice that follows will give you experience in recognizing general and specific ideas.

➤ *Practice 1*

A. Each group of words below consists of one general idea and four specific ideas. The general idea includes all the specific ideas. Underline the general idea in each group. Before beginning, look at the two examples and explanations:

Example   anger   love   fear   <u>emotion</u>   envy

Emotion is the general idea; *anger, love, fear,* and *envy* are specific kinds of emotions.

Example   booth   table   <u>diner</u>   cash register   menus

Diner is the general idea; specific parts of the diner include a booth, table, cash register, and the menus.

1. parrot   kitten   goldfish   hamster   <u>pet</u>

2. square   circle   triangle   <u>shape</u>   diamond

3. up   down   sideways   <u>direction</u>   north

4. soda	beer	orange juice	<u>beverage</u>	water
5. tires	meter	seats	<u>taxi</u>	doors
6. sleeping bag	sheet	pillow	blanket	<u>bedding</u>
7. "hello"	<u>greeting</u>	a wave	"hi"	open arms
8. screech	<u>noise</u>	crash	off-key music	sirens
9. jump	<u>command</u>	stop	move	hurry
10. jail	hanging	suspension	fine	<u>punishment</u>

B. In each pair below, one idea is general and the other is specific. The general idea includes the specific one. Do two things:

    1) Underline the general idea in each pair of words.
    2) Write in one more specific idea that is covered by the general idea. Look first at the example and explanation.

Example   purple   <u>color</u>   _red_

Color is the general idea; _purple_ is a specific color; another specific color is _red_.

11. <u>bird</u>	eagle	_sparrow_
12. <u>furniture</u>	table	_chair_
13. bus	<u>vehicle</u>	_car_
14. sunshine	<u>weather</u>	_cloudy_
15. pretzels	<u>snack</u>	_potato chips_
16. <u>planet</u>	Earth	_Venus_
17. tango	<u>dance</u>	_polka_
18. <u>insect</u>	bee	_grasshopper_
19. lipstick	<u>cosmetics</u>	_eye shadow_
20. <u>job</u>	salesclerk	_waiter_

(Other answers are possible.)

Moving from General to Specific

It can be helpful to arrange groups of ideas in order of how general or specific they are. For instance, which of the words below is most general, which is less general, and which is most specific?

    medicine   profession   surgery

Profession is more general than *medicine*. Why? Because medicine is one kind of profession. Likewise, *medicine* is more general than *surgery* because surgery is one type of medicine.

Try arranging the following three ideas in order of how specific they are. Put a *1* in front of the most general idea, a *2* in front of the less general idea, and a *3* in front of the most specific idea. Then read the explanation that follows.

_____ aspirin   _____ pain reliever   _____ medication

Explanation:

The most general of the three ideas is *medication*. *Pain reliever* is less general than *medication* because it is a type of medicine. Finally, *aspirin* is the most specific idea because it is a kind of pain reliever. So the correct answers are: *3* aspirin, *2* pain reliever, *1* medication.

➤ Practice 2

Put a *1* by the most general idea in each group, a *2* by the less general idea, and a *3* by the most specific idea.

1. __1__ machine   __3__ copy machine   __2__ office machine

2. __2__ candy   __1__ sweets   __3__ chocolate kisses

3. __2__ kitchen appliance __1__ electric appliance __3__ toaster oven

4. __3__ bow tie   __1__ menswear   __2__ ties

5. __3__ banana   __2__ tropical fruit   __1__ fruit

6. __2__ uncle   __1__ man   __3__ Uncle George

7. __1__ liquid   __3__ coffee   __2__ beverage

8. __2__ national holiday __1__ holiday   __3__ Thanksgiving

9. __3__ ice cream sandwich __2__ frozen dessert __1__ frozen food

10. __3__ Washington, D.C. __1__ city   __2__ capital city

TOPICS

Finding the topic of a paragraph can help you find the main idea. The **topic** of a paragraph is the subject that it's about. To find the topic, ask yourself this simple question:

In general, who or what is this paragraph about?

Your answer to this question will be the paragraph's topic. For example, read the paragraph below. As you do so, ask yourself, "In general, who or what is this paragraph about?"

> Several remedies for too much sun can be made right in your kitchen. For instance, you can soothe a case of sunburn by spreading plain yogurt over the burnt area for ten minutes. Or you can sit in cool bath water to which you have added a cup of vinegar or baking soda. If your eyes have been irritated by the sun, cover them for five minutes with chilled tea bags or cotton soaked in milk.

Now circle the letter of the item that you think is the topic. Your answer should not be too broad or too narrow. Then read the explanation that follows.

a. Using yogurt to soothe sunburn
b. Remedies for too much sun
c. Remedies

Explanation:

The topic of the paragraph is "Remedies for too much sun"; this subject is general enough to include all of the other ideas in the paragraph. "Using yogurt to soothe sunburn" is too narrow to be the topic of the paragraph. It does not cover the other remedies, such as the one with tea bags. "Remedies" is too broad—it includes remedies other than those for getting too much sun.

Now try finding the topic of the paragraph below. One of the subjects shown is too broad—it is too general to be the topic. That is, it covers much more than what the paragraph is about. Another subject is too narrow—it is too specific to be the topic. In other words, it covers only a part of what's in the paragraph. Put a *T* by the subject that is the topic of the paragraph. Also, put a *B* by the subject that is too broad and an *N* by the topic that is too narrow. Then read and complete the explanation that follows.

> It's well known that trees provide shade, beauty, and wind protection. However, there are also two lesser-known benefits of trees. First, trees clean the air. Their leaves actually filter out pollution in the air. One large sugar maple, for example, can remove as much pollution as is put in the air by cars burning a thousand gallons of gas. The second lesser-known benefit of trees is that they reduce stress. Experiments show that people relax more when shown scenes with trees than when shown city scenes without natural greenery.

_____ Nature

_____ Lesser-known benefits of trees

_____ Anti-stress benefits of trees

Explanation:

"Lesser-known benefits of trees" is general enough to _____ all that is said about trees in the paragraph, so it is the topic *(T)*. "Nature" is too broad *(B)* to be the topic. It includes many types of natural objects other than just trees. "Anti-stress benefit of trees" is too narrow *(N)*. It covers only one of the two lesser-known _____ mentioned in the paragraph. It does not cover the other benefit, which is that trees _____ .

In summary, to decide if a particular subject is the topic of a passage, ask yourself these questions:

1 Does this subject include much more than what the passage is about? If so, the subject is too broad to be the topic.

2 Is there important information in the passage that isn't covered by this subject? If so, the subject is too narrow to be the topic.

➤ Practice 3

After each paragraph are three subjects. One is the topic, another is too broad to be the topic, and a third is too narrow to be the topic. Label each subject with one of the following:

> *T*—for the topic of each paragraph
> *B*—for the subject that is too broad
> *N*—for the subject that is too narrow

Then write the missing words in the explanation that follows each paragraph.

1. People who are addicted to shopping have a high need for excitement and a low self-esteem. There seem to be two types of addicted shoppers. One is the daily shopper, who cannot miss a single day at the stores. The other is the binge buyer, who goes shopping weekly to buy huge numbers of things.

    __*B*__ Addicts

    __*T*__ Shopping addicts

    __*N*__ The binge buyer

The topic of this paragraph is "Shopping addicts." "Addicts" is too broad because it includes all kinds of ____*addicts*____, but the paragraph discusses only shopping addicts. "The binge buyer" is too narrow; it isn't general enough to _____*cover*_____ the other information about shopping addicts.

2. There are two main causes of headaches. Research shows that most headaches result from muscle tension. And the most common reason for that muscle tension is continuing stress. Headaches can also be caused by changes in the supply of blood to the head. Such changes are often reactions to pollen and food chemicals.

   _T_   Headaches

   _B_   Pain

   _N_   Muscle tension as a cause of headaches

"Pain" is too broad to be the topic of this paragraph. A paragraph with that topic would include information about pain other than ___*headaches*___. But this paragraph discusses only "headaches," which is therefore its topic. "Muscle tension as a cause of headaches" is too narrow. It doesn't _____*include*_____ the information about changes in the supply of blood to the head.

3. Researchers who do surveys depend on what people tell them. People, however, sometimes lie to surveyors. In one survey, for instance, people were asked if they used seat belts. Later, researchers checked to see how many people really did use their seat belts. It turned out that almost 40 percent of those who said they buckled up did not. Also, researchers once asked people about their smoking habits. Then they tested the people's saliva to find a chemical that is found in the mouths of smokers. The tests showed that 6 percent of the women and 8 percent of the men had lied about smoking.

   _T_   People who are surveyed

   _N_   People who are surveyed about smoking

   _B_   Research studies

The topic of this paragraph is "People who are surveyed." "People who are surveyed about smoking" is too narrow. It doesn't include the other example in the paragraph about people who were surveyed about ___*seat belts*___ _____. "Research studies" is too broad; it covers all types of research, not just _____*surveys*_____.

➤ *Practice 4*

After each paragraph are three subjects. One is the topic, another is too broad, and a third is too narrow. Label each subject as follows:

T—for the topic of the paragraph
B—for the subject that is too broad
N—for the subject that is too narrow

1. Every human body has electricity. However, Pauline Shaw of England has so much electricity in her body that she is destructive. She has destroyed irons, toasters, radios, and other appliances. She has also ruined over two hundred light bulbs. One scientist at Oxford University says that Shaw can produce an electric charge as high as eighty thousand volts. He believes that a rare allergy to some foods is at fault. Shaw's system breaks down these foods in a way that affects her body's electricity.

    __N__   Pauline Shaw's effect on light bulbs

    __B__   Pauline Shaw's life

    __T__   The electricity in Pauline Shaw's body

2. Your visit to the hospital can be a helpful experience for a patient. Comfort a patient who is ill and afraid with a warm pat or by holding his or her hand. People often wonder what they should say to patients, but it is good to remember that patients often need someone to listen to them. So be a caring listener. And remember not to stay too long—people who are seriously ill tire easily.

    __T__   Your visit to a patient in the hospital

    __B__   Your visit to people

    __N__   Listening to a hospital patient you visit

3. The crocodile and a small bird called the plover have a surprisingly friendly relationship. A crocodile's jaws are strong, and its teeth are razor sharp. Yet the plover dares to step inside the croc's mouth. You see, after eating, the crocodile opens his mouth. This allows his "living toothbrush" to step in and clean uneaten food from his teeth. In return for his service, the plover gets a free meal.

    __B__   The crocodile's habits

    __T__   The crocodile and the plover

    __N__   Cleaning the crocodile's teeth

TOPIC SENTENCES

Finding the topic of a paragraph prepares you to find the main idea of the paragraph. Once you have found the topic, ask yourself this question:

What is the author's main point about the topic?

The answer will be the main idea. Authors often state that main idea in a sentence called a **topic sentence**. For instance, the paragraph on remedies for too much sun on page 134 contains a topic sentence:

> [1]Several remedies for too much sun can be made right in your kitchen. [2]For instance, you can soothe a case of sunburn by spreading plain yogurt over the burnt area for ten minutes. [3]Or you can sit in cool bath water to which you have added a cup of vinegar or baking soda. [4]If your eyes have been irritated by the sun, cover them for five minutes with chilled tea bags or cotton soaked in milk.

As we already know, the topic of this paragraph is "remedies for too much sun." To find the topic sentence, we must ask, "What is the author's main point about remedies for too much sun?" Sentences 2–4 give specific remedies. But sentence 1 is more general—it states that several remedies for too much sun can be made in the kitchen. All the details support this idea, describing a series of remedies that can be made in the kitchen. Sentence 1 is thus the topic sentence—the umbrella statement. The other sentences support the main idea by providing specific examples.

To become skilled at finding main ideas, you need to distinguish between a paragraph's topic, main idea, and supporting details. Below is a group of four items. One is the topic, one is the main idea, and two are details that support the main idea. Label each item with one of the following:

> *T* —for the topic
> *MI*—for the main idea
> *SD*—for the supporting details

The topic will be the subject the items are about. The main idea will be the author's main point about the topic. And the supporting details will be specific ideas that help explain and clarify the main idea. After labeling each item, read the explanation.

_____ a. Countless children have learned letters and numbers from *Sesame Street*.

_____ b. For twenty years, *Sesame Street* has taught American children a great deal.

_____ c. *Sesame Street*, the children's TV show.

_____ d. The show has also covered such important topics as love, death, and marriage.

Explanation:

All of the items are about *Sesame Street,* the children's TV show. Thus the topic *(T)* is item *c.* The main idea *(MI)* is item *b*—it gives the author's main point about the topic of *Sesame Street.* Items *a* and *d* are supporting details *(SD)*; each supports the main idea by providing specific details to explain the main idea that *Sesame Street* has taught American children a great deal.

➤ *Practice 5*

Each group of items below includes one topic, one main idea (topic sentence), and two supporting details. In the space provided, label each item with one of the following:

> *T* —for the topic
> *MI*—for the main idea
> *SD*—for the supporting details

In addition, complete the explanation that follows the first group.

Group 1

_MI_   a. TV has begun to deal with sex in a more realistic way.

_SD_   b. Couples on TV now openly discuss topics such as birth control.

_SD_   c. Bedroom scenes are now being shown in detail on some TV shows.

_T_   d. TV's treatment of sex.

> Each item is about how television handles _____sex_____. So we can conclude that item *d* is the topic *(T).* Item *a* tells us the author's main point about that topic; thus *a* is the main idea *(MI).* Items *b* and *c* give *(general or specific?)* _____specific_____ ideas that are examples of the main idea. Thus *b* and *c* are supporting details *(SD).*

Group 2

_SD_   a. If you stop carrying matches or a lighter, you can cut down on impulse smoking.

_T_   b. Quitting smoking.

_MI_   c. You can behave in ways that help you quit smoking.

_SD_   d. By keeping a record of when and where you smoke, you can avoid the most tempting situations.

Group 3

_SD_   a. New technology will allow people to live longer and healthier lives in the twenty-first century.

_MI_   b. Specialists predict that the world will be a very different place in the twenty-first century.

_T_   c. The twenty-first century.

_SD_   d. In the twenty-first century, new means of transportation will make our jets look old-fashioned.

➤ Practice 6

Now that you've sharpened your skills at finding a topic and the main idea about that topic, use those skills on the following full paragraphs.

First, circle the letter of the correct topic of each paragraph. Then find the sentence in which the author states the main idea about that topic, and circle the letter of that topic sentence. In addition, complete the explanations after the first paragraph.

A.   [1]Work-sharing can benefit both employees and employers. [2]In work-sharing, full-time jobs are divided into part-time jobs shared by two or more workers. [3]Working mothers, students, and those just returning to work find these positions very appealing. [4]Employers like work-sharing too. [5]In a two-year work-sharing project, workers had a mere 13 percent turnover rate; the usual turnover rate is 40 percent. [6]In addition, worker productivity was greater than expected.

   1. The topic is
     a. work.
     (b.) work-sharing.
     c. students using work-sharing.

The subject of work is too *(broad or narrow?)* _____broad_____—it covers a great deal more than just the subject of sharing work. The subject of

students using work-sharing is too *(broad or narrow?)* _____narrow_____; it does not cover the other specific details in the paragraph. Two such specific details, for example, are that mothers use work-sharing and that work-sharing workers have a low turnover rate. Thus the topic is

_____work-sharing_____, which is general enough to cover all the other material in the paragraph.

2. The main idea is in sentence
  (a.) 1.
  b. 3.
  c. 6.

What is the author's main point *about* the topic of work-sharing? The general point is that work-sharing has _____*benefits*_____ for both _____*employees*_____ and _____*employers*_____.

B. [1]As you speak with someone, you can gather clues as to whether he or she understands you. [2]Then you can adjust what you say accordingly. [3]But when you write, you must try to foresee the reader's reactions without such clues. [4]You also have to give stronger evidence in writing than in conversation. [5]A friend may accept an unsupported statement such as "He's a lousy boss." [6]But in most writing, the reader would expect you to back up such a statement with proof. [7]Obviously, effective writing requires more attention to detail than everyday conversation.

3. The topic is
  a. speaking.
  b. conversation.
  (c.) effective writing.

4. The main idea is in sentence
  a. 1.
  b. 5.
  (c.) 7.

C. [1]Male and female children are often treated and viewed differently from birth on. [2]First, boys get a blue blanket and girls get pink. [3]Also, although more male than female babies fall ill, studies say parents are more likely to consider a baby strong if it is male. [4]Similarly, parents urge boys to take part in rough-and-tumble play. [5]But parents prefer that girls watch and talk rather than be physically active. [6]When questioned, most parents say they want their sons to be successful and independent, and they want their daughters to be loving and well behaved.

5. The topic is
  a. males and females.
  (b.) male and female children.
  c. childhood illness.

6. The main idea is in sentence
  (a.) 1.
  b. 2.
  c. 6.

THE CENTRAL POINT

In selections made up of many paragraphs, such as articles and chapters, the overall main idea is called the **central point**. From now on, when you read longer selections in this text, you will be given practice in finding the central point, as well as in finding the main ideas of paragraphs within the reading.

CHAPTER OVERVIEW

In this chapter, you did the following:

- First, you worked on recognizing the difference between general and specific ideas.

- Second, you practiced distinguishing the topic of a paragraph from subjects that are too broad or too narrow.

- The first two activities prepared you for the third and the main activity of this chapter—recognizing the main idea of a paragraph as expressed in its topic sentence.

The next chapter will sharpen your understanding of how specific details support and develop main ideas.

➤ *Review Test 1*

To review what you've learned in this chapter, answer each of the following questions by filling in the blank or circling the letter of the answer you think is correct.

1. The supporting details are always more *(general* or *specific?)*
   _____*specific*_____ than the main idea.

2. The umbrella statement that covers all of the material in a paragraph is the
   a. topic.   (b.) topic sentence.   c. central point.

3. ___*T*___ TRUE OR FALSE? To find the main idea of a paragraph, you may find it helpful to look first for the topic.

4. When the main idea is stated in one sentence of a paragraph, that sentence is called the
   a. topic.   (b.) topic sentence.   c. central point.

5. For selections made up of many paragraphs, the author's overall main point is called the
   a. central topic.   (b.) central point.   c. topic sentence.

➤ Review Test 2

A. Each group of words below consists of one general idea and four specific ideas. The general idea includes all the specific ideas. Underline the general idea in each group.

1. uncle	grandmother	<u>relative</u>	cousin	sister
2. vanilla	<u>flavor</u>	chocolate	strawberry	butterscotch
3. poker	hide and seek	baseball	Monopoly	<u>game</u>
4. paper plates	potato salad	ants	<u>picnic</u>	lemonade
5. sandals	boots	sneakers	<u>footwear</u>	high heels
6. ghost story	armed robbery	final exam	<u>scary experience</u>	horror movie
7. fingerprints	hairs	<u>clues</u>	bloodstains	ransom notes

B. In each pair below, one idea is general and the other is specific. The general idea includes the specific one. Do two things:

   1) Underline the idea in each pair that you think is more general.
   2) Write in one more specific idea that is covered by the general idea.

8. sneezing	<u>cold symptom</u>	*coughing*
9. tongue	<u>mouth</u>	*teeth*
10. <u>magazine</u>	*Time*	*People*
11. infancy	<u>life stage</u>	*adulthood*
12. <u>length</u>	inch	*foot*
13. <u>payment</u>	personal check	*money order*
14. taking a hot bath	<u>relaxing activity</u>	*watching TV*

(Other answers are possible.)

C. Each group of three items below contains three levels of ideas. Write a *1* by the most general idea in each group, a *2* by the less general idea, and a *3* by the most specific idea.

15. _2_ flower	_1_ plant	_3_ lily
16. _2_ winter clothing	_3_ wool scarf	_1_ clothing
17. _1_ fruit	_2_ dried fruit	_3_ raisin
18. _3_ *Reading Rainbow*	_1_ TV show	_2_ children's TV show
19. _1_ songs	_3_ "Silent Night"	_2_ Christmas carols
20. _2_ jokes	_1_ humor	_3_ knock-knock jokes

➤ *Review Test 3*

A. After each paragraph are three subjects. Label each subject with one of the following:

> *T*—for the topic of each paragraph
> *B*—for the subject that is too broad
> *N*—for the subject that is too narrow

1-3. Riding a bicycle through busy city streets isn't dangerous if riders follow a few guidelines. One is to wear a helmet to prevent head injury in case the rider falls. Another precaution is to stay off the sidewalk. Also, riders should obey traffic rules, including respecting one-way signs.

___*B*___   Transportation safety

___*N*___   Wearing a biker's helmet

___*T*___   Bicycle riding in busy city streets

4-6. Despite all the criticism it gets, television has its good points. First of all, it is educational. From *Mister Rogers' Neighborhood* to nature programs, it teaches in a colorful and interesting way. TV is also relaxing and entertaining. After a stressful day, it's restful just to put your feet up and enjoy a favorite program or a good movie.

___*T*___   Television

___*B*___   The media

___*N*___   The educational side of TV

B. (7-18.) Each group of four items includes one topic, one main idea (topic sentence), and two supporting ideas. Label each item with one of the following:

> *T* —for the topic
> *MI*—for the main idea
> *SD*—for the two supporting details

Group 1

___*T*___   a. Eye movements.

___*SD*___   b. We blink often when we are stressed, angry, or bored.

___*MI*___   c. Our eye movements reveal our state of mind.

___*SD*___   d. When we are concentrating or very interested, we blink less.

Group 2

_SD_   a. An older woman has useful experiences to share.

_MI_   b. There are advantages to marrying an older woman.

_SD_   c. An older woman will be more settled in her career.

_T_   d. Marrying an older woman.

Group 3

_SD_   a. We could reduce our garbage by starting more home composting programs.

_T_   b. Our garbage crisis.

_SD_   c. Laws could encourage manufacturers to make products that are more recyclable.

_MI_   d. We must address our garbage crisis by developing more ways to reduce garbage.

C. (19-20.) Circle the letter of the correct topic of the following paragraph. Then find the sentence in which the author states the main idea about that topic and circle the letter of that topic sentence.

> ¹Speech experts recommend various tactics for dealing with children who stutter. ²First, say the experts, speak to children slowly. ³This will allow them time to process what they are hearing. ⁴Second, don't talk so much. ⁵Too much talk may actually overstimulate children so that their mouths can't keep up with their brains. ⁶Third, allow a couple of seconds between the time the child speaks and the time you begin your response. ⁷Finally, don't ask a stuttering child to recite or read a long story out loud. ⁸Anxiety can increase stuttering.

1. The topic is
   a. speech.
   (b.) dealing with children who stutter.
   c. speaking slowly to stuttering children.

2. The main idea is in sentence
   (a.) 1.
   b. 2.
   c. 6.

➤ *Review Test 4*

Here is a chance to apply your understanding of main ideas to a full-length selection. First, read the following piece by a Vietnamese immigrant, Andrew Lam. Lam is associate editor for the Pacific News Service. In this article, he compares some American and Vietnamese views on life and death. After reading the selection, answer the questions that follow on topics, main ideas, and the central point. There are also vocabulary questions to help you continue working on vocabulary in context.

Words to Watch

Following are some words in the reading that do not have strong context support. Each word is followed by the number of the paragraph in which it appears and its meaning there. These words are indicated in the story by a small circle (°).

Tet (1): the Vietnamese lunar New Year festival
shield (2): cover up
reassuring (2): comforting
quips (2): jokes
disjointed (4): disconnected
pang (6): deeply felt pain
filial (6): due from a son or daughter
piety (6): devotion to and honor of family
evading (9): avoiding
feeble (9): weak
embellished (10): exaggerated
satirized (10): made fun of
monsoon rain (13): seasonal heavy rains in Asia

THEY SHUT MY GRANDMOTHER'S DOOR

Andrew Lam

When someone died in the convalescent home where my   1
grandmother lives, the nurses rush to close all the patients' doors.
Though as a policy death is not to be seen at the home, she can always
tell when it visits. The series of doors being slammed shut remind her
of the firecrackers during Tet°.

The nurses' efforts to shield° death are more comical to my   2
grandmother than reassuring°. "Those old ladies die so often," she
quips° in Vietnamese, "every day's like new year."

Still, it is lonely to die in such a place. I imagine some wasted old   3
body under a white sheet being carted silently through the empty
corridor on its way to the morgue. While in America a person may be
born surrounded by loved ones, in old age one is often left to take the
last leg of life's journey alone.

Perhaps that is why my grandmother talks now mainly of her   4
hometown, Bac-Lieu, and its river and green, rich rice fields. Having
lost everything during the war, she can now offer me only her distant
memories: Life was not disjointed° back home; one lived in a gentle
rhythm with the land; people died in their homes surrounded by
neighbors and relatives. And no one shut your door.

So it goes. The once gentle, connected world of the past is but the   5
language of dreams. In this fast-paced society of disjointed lives, we
are swept along and have little time left for spiritual comfort. Instead of
relying on neighbors and relatives, on the river and land, we deal with
the language of materialism: overtime, stress, down payment, credit
cards, tax shelter. Instead of going to the temple to pray for good health
we pay life and health insurance religiously.

My grandmother's children and grandchildren share a certain   6
pang° of guilt. After a stroke which paralyzed her, we could no longer
keep her at home. And although we visit her regularly, we are not
living up to the filial° piety° standard expected of us in the old country.
My father silently grieves and my mother suffers from headaches.
(Does she see herself in such a home in a decade or two?)

Once, a long time ago, living in Vietnam we used to stare death in   7
the face. The war in many ways had heightened our sensibilities toward
living and dying. I can still hear the wails of widows and grieving
mothers. Though the fear of death and dying is a universal one, the
Vietnamese did not hide from it. Instead, we dwelt in its tragedy. Death
pervaded our poems, novels, fairy tales and songs.

But if agony and pain are part of Vietnamese culture, pleasure is   8
at the center of America's culture. While Vietnamese holidays are
based on death anniversaries, birthdays are celebrated here. American
popular culture translates death with something like nauseating humor.
People laugh and scream at blood and guts movies. The wealthy freeze
their dead relatives in liquid nitrogen. Cemeteries are places of big
business, complete with colorful brochures. I hear there are even drive-
by funerals where you don't have to get out of your own car to pay
your respects to the deceased.

That America relies upon the pleasure principle and happy endings   9
in its entertainments does not, however, assist us in evading° suffering.
The reality of the suffering of old age is apparent in the convalescent

home. There is an old man, once an accomplished concert pianist, now rendered helpless by arthritis. Every morning he sits staring at the piano. One feeble° woman who outlived her children keeps repeating, "My son will take me home." Then there are those mindless, bedridden bodies kept alive through a series of tubes and pulsating machines.

But despair is not newsworthy. Death itself must be embellished° or satirized° or deep-frozen in order to catch the public's attention. 10

Last week on her eighty-second birthday I went to see my grandmother. She smiled her sweet sad smile. 11

"Where will you end up in your old age?" she asked me, her mind as sharp as ever. 12

The memories of monsoon rain° and tropical sun and relatives and friends came to mind. Not here, not here, I wanted to tell her. But the soft moaning of a patient next door and the smell of alcohol wafting from the sterile corridor brought me back to reality. 13

"Anywhere is fine," I told her instead, trying to keep up with her courageous spirit. "All I am asking for is that they don't shut my door." 14

Reading Comprehension Questions

Vocabulary in Context

1. The word *wails* in "I can still hear the wails of widows and grieving mothers" (paragraph 7) means
   a. joking.
   b. cries.
   c. delays.
   d. suggestions.

2. The word *pervaded* in "Though the fear of death and dying is a universal one, the Vietnamese did not hide from it. . . . Death pervaded our poems, novels, fairy tales, and songs" (paragraph 7) means
   a. filled.
   b. ignored.
   c. stopped.
   d. escaped.

3. The word *rendered* in "There is an old man, once an accomplished concert pianist, now rendered helpless by arthritis" (paragraph 9) means
   a. happy to be.
   b. no longer.
   c. made.
   d. willing to be.

4. The word *wafting* in "the soft moaning of a patient next door and the smell of alcohol wafting from the sterile corridor brought me back to reality" (paragraph 13) means
   a. absent.
   b. smelling pleasant.
   c. causing illness.
   (d.) drifting through the air.

Central Point

5. Which of the following is the topic of the entire selection?
   a. Life in Vietnam.
   (b.) The Vietnamese and American views of death.
   c. Escaping the suffering of old age.
   d. War's influence on a people's view of death.

6. Which sentence best expresses the central point of the selection?
   a. Dying in a convalescent home can be lonely.
   b. In Vietnam, life and death were connected.
   c. The war made the Vietnamese more aware of death and dying.
   (d.) While death is an accepted part of life in Vietnam, in America death is hidden or altered.

Main Ideas

7. The topic of paragraph 6 is
   (a.) the guilt felt by the grandmother's children and grandchildren.
   b. the reason the grandmother is in a home.
   c. the number of visits made to the home.
   d. the health of the author's family.

8. The main idea of paragraph 6 is expressed in its
   (a.) first sentence.
   b. second sentence.
   c. next-to-last sentence.
   d. last sentence.

9. The topic of paragraph 9 is
   a. American entertainment.
   b. America's escape from suffering.
   (c.) the pleasure principle and suffering in America.
   d. keeping people alive longer.

10. The main idea of paragraph 9 is expressed in its
    (a.) first sentence.
    b. third sentence.
    c. fourth sentence.
    d. last sentence.

Mapping Activity

The author compares the way Americans and Vietnamese view and deal with death. On the left are his main comments on death in Vietnam. On the right, fill in the two missing contrasting comments on death in America.

Central point: Americans treat death very differently than the Vietnamese.

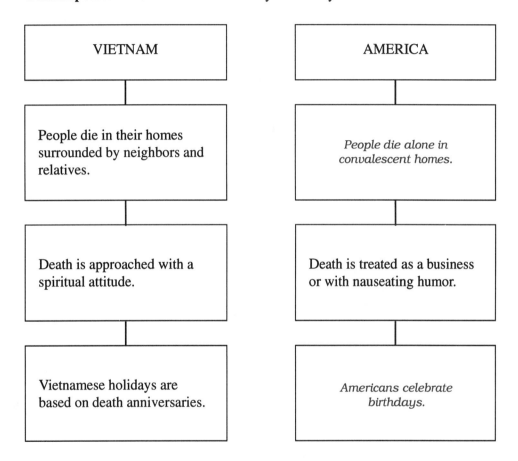

VIETNAM	AMERICA
People die in their homes surrounded by neighbors and relatives.	*People die alone in convalescent homes.*
Death is approached with a spiritual attitude.	Death is treated as a business or with nauseating humor.
Vietnamese holidays are based on death anniversaries.	*Americans celebrate birthdays.*

Discussion Questions

1. Do you agree that Americans try to hide death and often deal with it "with something like nauseating humor"? How has death been handled in your family?

2. Lam says that his grandmother's children and grandchildren feel guilty about putting her in a home. Should they feel guilty? What other options might there be for caring for an elderly family member?

Writing Activities

1. Lam writes that the rhythm of life in Vietnam was gentle and that people there felt connected to their neighbors and relatives. In contrast, he states, Americans live a less connected, fast-paced life. How connected do you feel to your neighbors, friends, and relatives? How fast-paced is your life? Write a paper explaining how your life does or does not fit in with Lam's observations about America. Use detailed examples throughout.

2. What would you say to the author or to his grandmother if you had the chance? Write a letter to either, explaining your thoughts and feelings about some points in the reading. Use whatever tone you feel—anger, sympathy, pity, admiration, and so on.

Check Your Performance   **MAIN IDEAS**

Activity	*Number Right*	*Points*	*Total*
Review Test 1 (5 items)	_____	x 2 =	_____
Review Test 2 (20 items)	_____	x 1.5 =	_____
Review Test 3 (20 items)	_____	x 1.5 =	_____
Review Test 4 (10 items)	_____	x 2 =	_____
Mapping Activity (2 items)	_____	x 5 =	_____

TOTAL SCORE   =   _____%

Enter your total score onto the Reading Performance Chart: Review Tests on the inside back cover.

8

Supporting Details

The last chapter introduced you to the most important reading skill—finding the main idea. To master this skill, you must understand another key reading skill—locating supporting details. These details provide the added information that is needed for you to make sense of a main idea. In this chapter you will learn what supporting details are and how to identify them.

WHAT ARE SUPPORTING DETAILS?

Supporting details are reasons, examples, facts, steps, or other kinds of evidence that develop and support a main idea. The information that details give helps us understand main ideas. For example, look at this main idea from the previous chapter:

> Americans love to send greeting cards.

To explain this statement, the author went on to provide evidence—details that support the main idea. Here, again, is the full paragraph:

> [1]Americans love to send greeting cards. [2]For instance, over 4 million birthday cards are sent out in this country every day. [3]During Valentine's Day last year, over 900 million cards were mailed. [4]And close to 3 billion holiday greeting cards were sent out over the Christmas season.

Sentences 2–4 give facts to show that the main idea is true. Those facts are the supporting details of the paragraph.

MAJOR AND MINOR SUPPORTING DETAILS

There are two types of supporting details, major and minor. To illustrate, let's look at another paragraph you've already seen. Below is the main idea of the paragraph.

Main Idea:

There are two main causes of headaches.

How much do we learn from that general sentence? Not much. If the author named the two causes, we would have a better understanding of the general idea. Those two causes would then be the major supporting details of the paragraph. **Major details** are the separate, chief points that support the main idea. Below is the same main idea with two major details.

Main Idea with Major Details:

There are two main causes of headaches. Research shows that most headaches result from muscle tension. Headaches can also be caused by changes in the supply of blood to the head.

Now there is some meat on the bare bones of the main idea. The author has provided major details (the two main causes of headaches) to support the main idea. Together, the main idea and the major supporting details form the basic framework of paragraphs.

These major details are often more fully explained, and that's where minor supporting details come in. Major details provide added information about the main idea. In the same way, **minor details** provide added information about the major details.

The paragraph on headaches can be filled out even more with some minor details. The result might be the paragraph below.

Main Idea with Major and Minor Details:

There are two main causes of headaches. Research shows that most headaches result from muscle tension. The most common reason for that muscle tension is continuing stress. Headaches can also be caused by changes in the supply of blood to the head. Such changes are often reactions to pollen and food chemicals.

Just as the major details expanded on the main idea, the minor details have further explained the major details. Now the main idea has even more meaning for us.

On the next page is an umbrella design like the ones in the chapter on the main idea. It shows the main idea and the major and minor supporting details that fit under the main idea.

THERE ARE TWO MAIN
CAUSES OF HEADACHES

(MAJOR DETAIL 1)
MUSCLE TENSION

(Minor Detail 1)
Caused by stress

(MAJOR DETAIL 2)
CHANGES IN BLOOD
SUPPLY TO BRAIN

(Minor Detail 2)
Caused by pollen
and food chemicals

Sometimes paragraphs contain only major details, as in the paragraph on greeting cards. Reread that paragraph (on p. 153), and you will see that each sentence presents one major detail, one fact to support the main idea. More often, however, paragraphs include both major and minor details. When this happens, you should be able to distinguish between the major details and the minor details that support them. The following exercises will give you practice in separating major and minor details.

➤ Practice 1

Major and minor supporting details are mixed together in the lists that follow. Separate the major, more general details from the minor ones by filling in the outlines.

List 1

- Snakes
- Dogs
- Unusual pets
- Spiders
- Rats
- Traditional pets
- Birds
- Cats

Main idea: People enjoy different kinds of pets.

Major detail: 1. <u>Unusual pets</u>

Minor details: a. <u>Snakes</u>

b. <u>Spiders</u>

c. <u>Rats</u>

Major detail: 2. <u>Traditional pets</u>

Minor details: a. <u>Dogs</u>

b. <u>Birds</u>

c. <u>Cats</u>

List 2

- Junk food
- Apples
- Doughnuts
- Healthful food
- Carrot sticks
- Potato chips
- Candy
- Raisins

Main idea: Snacks can be divided into two types.

Major detail: 1. *Junk food*

Minor details: a. *Doughnuts*

b. *Potato chips*

c. *Candy*

Major detail: 2. *Healthful food*

Minor details: a. *Apples*

b. *Carrot sticks*

c. *Raisins*

TWO HELPFUL WAYS TO LOCATE MAJOR DETAILS

Two common ways in which authors alert you to the major details of a passage are by using two types of signals:

1 An opening phrase

2 Addition words, such as *first, second,* and *next*

An opening phrase often tells you that a particular series of details is coming. And addition words often introduce each of the details. You can use each of these clues to help you find the major details of a passage. Often a paragraph contains both an opening phrase and one or more addition words. Following is a look at each type of signal.

Opening Phrases

Paragraphs often contain a main idea and a list of supporting details—a list of reasons, examples, steps, and so on. Opening phrases often signal what type of detail to watch for. Here are some typical opening phrases:

Opening Phrases

several kinds of	a few causes of	two advantages
a few reasons	several characteristics	four steps
various factors	three types	a number of ways

When you see phrases like those above, you can expect a list of major supporting details to follow.

Note that each of the opening phrases in the box on the previous page includes a word that ends in the letter *s*. The words ending in *s* are plurals that refer to the kinds of details that will be listed, such as kinds, characteristics, reasons, steps, and factors. These plurals will help you identify the major details that are listed. At times, you will even know how many major details to expect. For example, opening phrases may "tell" you to look for two advantages, three types, or four steps.

Opening phrases are often part of the topic sentence. Following, for example, are two typical topic sentences:

1. There are four main causes of heart disease.

   (The opening phrase *four main causes of heart disease* suggests that the author will list the four causes.)

2. Five magazines have a circulation of over ten million a month.

   (The opening phrase *five magazines* suggests that the author is going to list these magazines.)

To better understand opening phrases, read the paragraph below. Then complete the outline: First write down the opening phrase that is used as a heading. Be sure to include the word that ends in *s*. Next, list the three major details. Then read the explanation that follows the outline.

Psychologists have suggested three methods for helping people overcome test anxiety. One method is to write out answers when you are completely relaxed. As you write, imagine that you are taking a test. The second suggestion is to overlearn. Even when you think you know the information completely, keep studying. This will increase your confidence. It will also help you remember answers better when anxiety does strike. The third technique is to put yourself into a relaxed state before entering the test room. Think of something soothing, perhaps the sounds of waves splashing on the shore. This method is useful for people who tend to be very anxious.

Heading: _____s for helping people
           overcome test anxiety

List of major details:

1. _____

   _____

2. _____

3. _____

   _____

Explanation:

The topic sentence of the paragraph is the first one: "Psychologists have suggested three methods for helping people overcome test anxiety." The opening phrase that describes the type of detail being listed is "three methods for helping people overcome test anxiety." Those methods are the three major details:

1. Imagining you are in a test situation as you write out answers while relaxed
2. Overlearning
3. Putting yourself in a relaxed state before entering the test room

Writing out main ideas and supporting details in this manner is often a good way to take textbook notes.

Addition Words

Addition words are words used to introduce new ideas or points. The addition word *first*, for example, often introduces the first idea in a list of major details. Below are some addition words commonly used to introduce major details:

Addition Words

first	third	next	finally
first of all	also	in addition	last
one	another	additionally	last of all
second	moreover	furthermore	

In the paragraph above on overcoming test anxiety, all three major details are introduced with addition words. The first major detail is introduced with the addition word *one* (" One method is to write out answers when you are completely relaxed.") The second major detail is introduced with the addition word *second* ("The second suggestion is to overlearn.") The third major detail is introduced with the addition word *third* ("The third technique is to put yourself into a relaxed state before entering the test room").

To check your understanding, read the paragraph below. Underline the opening phrase that tells you a list is coming. Next, complete the outline that follows by filling in the major details. Then read the explanation.

¹In our busy lives, there are several ways we manage to save time. ²First, we use modern inventions that help us do more in less time. ³We use a microwave oven, for instance, to cook a baked potato at least ten times faster than once possible. ⁴We also save time by doing more than one thing at once. ⁵For example, a student may finish writing a paper, eat breakfast, and put on his or her shoes all at the same time. ⁶Finally, of course, we may simply rush. ⁷We may save time by gulping a meal or running to catch a bus.

Main idea: There are several ways we manage to save time.

Major supporting details:

1. _____

2. _____

3. _____

Explanation:

The main idea of this paragraph is in the first sentence. It includes the opening phrase "several ways." We learn right away that the paragraph will list several ways we save time.

In sentence 2, the addition word *first* introduces the first major detail: "we use modern inventions that help us do more in less time." Sentence 3 gives a minor detail, in the form of an example about the microwave oven. (Remember, minor details do not introduce new points; minor details make major details more clear.)

In sentence 4, the addition word *also* signals the second major detail: "We also save time by doing more than one thing at once." Sentence 5 gives a minor detail—an example of saving time by doing two or more things at once.

In sentence 6, the addition word *finally* introduces the third and last major detail: "we may simply rush." Sentence 7 gives examples, the minor details about gulping food and rushing for a bus.

The opening phrase and the addition words have helped us identify the major details. Here is an outline showing the main idea and major details:

Main idea: There are several ways we manage to save time.

1. We use modern inventions that help us do more in less time.
2. We save time by doing more than one thing at once.
3. We may simply rush.

Be on the lookout, then, for opening phrases. They signal the topic sentence, and they suggest what kind of major detail to look for in a paragraph. Also look for addition words, which often indicate that major details will follow.

➤ *Practice 2*

In the spaces provided, write the major supporting details for each paragraph. Note that in each paragraph, the topic sentence is **boldfaced**, and the addition words are set off in *italic type*.

A. **In any high school, almost every student belongs to one of three subcultures.** *One* subculture is the delinquent group, the least popular of the subcultures. Members of this group hate school, the faculty, and any other authority figures. The *next* step up the ladder of popularity is the academic subculture. Hard-working students who value their education belong to this group. The *third* subculture is the most popular—the fun subculture. Looks, clothes, cars, dates and social status are what interest members of this group.

Three Subcultures in Any High School

1. *The delinquent group*
2. *The academic subculture*
3. *The fun subculture*

B. **Various types of remedies have been developed for snoring.** The *first* common type of remedy tries to keep people from sleeping on their backs, the usual position for snoring. Such remedies include gadgets like the "snore ball whistle," a rubber ball clipped to the seat of the snorer's pajamas. The ball whistles when the snorer rolls onto his or her back. There are *also* various anti-snoring chin straps. They are based on the fact that people can't snore if they don't open their mouths. *Another* remedy is surgery. That works only in the rare cases where the snoring is caused by growths of tissue in the sinus area.

Types of Remedies for Snoring

1. *Remedies that keep people from sleeping on their backs*
2. *Anti-snoring chin straps*
3. *Surgery*

➤ *Practice 3*

In the spaces provided, write the major supporting details for each paragraph. Note that the topic sentence has been highlighted but *not* the addition words.

A. **Although smoking cigarettes is never healthy, there are three ways you can reduce the risk involved.** First of all, switch to a low-tar and low-nicotine brand. Some cigarettes have twice as much of these dangerous ingredients as others. Secondly, allow less smoke to enter your lungs. Instead of inhaling deeply, take short, shallow puffs of the cigarette. And finally, put out the cigarette when it's half gone. The last half of each cigarette contains 60 percent of its tar and nicotine.

Ways to Reduce the Risks of Smoking

1. _Switch to a low-tar, low-nicotine brand._

2. _Allow less smoke to enter your lungs._

3. _Put out the cigarette when it's half gone._

B. **You will do better on tests if you follow a few simple suggestions.** First, study experts say that slow and steady preparation for exams is best. Cramming the night before is less effective and more stressful. Another helpful method is to arrive early for a test. It's calming to have a few minutes to sit down in the classroom, collect one's thoughts, and find a pen. Third, once the test begins, answer the easier questions first. Then go back and tackle the hard ones. Finally, you will do better on essay questions if you make a brief outline before beginning to write.

Suggestions for Doing Better on Tests

1. _Prepare slowly and steadily._

2. _Arrive early for a test._

3. _Answer the easier questions first._

4. _Make a brief outline before beginning to write essay questions._

READING CAREFULLY

As you have seen, the major details support the main idea, and the minor details expand on the major ones. Keeping these relationships in mind will make you a more careful reader.

Now practice using your knowledge of main ideas and supporting details. First read the paragraph below. (Note that the topic sentence is set off in boldface.) Then answer the questions that follow. Finally, read the explanation that comes after the questions.

There are two relaxation methods you can use in just a few minutes. One method involves slowly inhaling and exhaling. As you inhale, mentally check the muscle groups in your body: face, neck, shoulders, arms, belly, legs, and feet. As you exhale, relax some muscles that are tense. Another short method uses images. First, close your eyes. Then imagine a lovely, relaxing scene, such as a beach. Spend a few minutes noticing every detail of the scene. If you are imagining a beach, for instance, see the water, hear the waves, and feel the warm sun.

1. As the topic sentence suggests, the major details of this paragraph are
   a. breathing methods.
   b. muscle groups.
   c. relaxation methods.

2. The paragraph lists
   a. one major detail.
   b. two major details.
   c. three major details.

3. What are the brief relaxation methods for a busy day? (The answer will be the major supporting details of the paragraph.)
   a. 1) inhaling, 2) exhaling, and 3) images
   b. 1) inhaling and exhaling and 2) using images
   c. 1) closing your eyes and 2) imagining a relaxing scene

4. When doing the inhaling/exhaling method, what should be done when exhaling? (The answer will be a minor detail.)
   a. Mentally check muscle groups.
   b. Relax tense muscles.
   c. Imagine a relaxing scene.

5. *Fill in the blank to complete a minor detail:* When using images, the first step is to _____.

Explanation:

The answer to question 1 is *c*; the paragraph lists relaxation methods. The answer to question 2 is *b*; two relaxation methods are listed. The answer to question 3 is *b*; the two methods listed are the inhaling/exhaling method and using imagery. The answer to question 4 is *b*; when exhaling, one should relax tense muscles. And the answer to question 5 is *close your eyes*.

If you missed any of these questions, reread the paragraph and try to see why you chose the wrong answer. Then go on to the following practice.

➤ Practice 4

Answer the questions that follow each paragraph. The topic sentence of each paragraph is boldfaced.

A. Science fiction writer Arthur C. Clarke correctly predicted when a rocket would first go to the moon. **Clarke has also made many interesting predictions that have yet to come true.** One of these predictions is that we'll have cars without wheels. He feels cars will be made that can float on air instead of rolling on the ground. He has also predicted that there will be settlements on the moon. They will exist in air-conditioned areas under domes, where food will be grown. Materials for the buildings in these settlements will be mined from the moon itself, he says.

1. The topic sentence suggests that this paragraph will list certain
   a. writings.
   b. times.
   c. predictions.

2. The major details of this paragraph are
   a. 1) predictions, 2) cars, and 3) settlements on the moon.
   b. 1) cars without wheels and 2) settlements on the moon.
   c. 1) food grown under domes and 2) building materials mined on the moon.

3. *Fill in the blank:* The first major detail is introduced with the addition word _____ *one* _____ .

4. *Fill in the blank:* Clarke feels cars will one day move by _____
   _____ *floating on air* _____ .

5. *Fill in the blank:* Clarke predicts that people will live on the moon under
   _____ *air-conditioned domes* _____ .

B. [1]Prescription drugs can be just as dangerous as illegal drugs if used carelessly. [2]**To avoid the dangers of prescribed drugs, consumers should follow several guidelines.** [3]One is to become aware of a drug's possible side effects. [4]Unexpected side effects, such as dizziness, can be frightening and even dangerous. [5]The patient should also find out if it is safe to take the medicine along with other drugs he or she is using. [6]Some combinations of drugs can be deadly. [7]Finally, medicine should always be stored in its own labeled bottle. [8]Accidental mix-ups of drugs can have tragic results.

6. The opening phrase that signals the list of major details is
   a. *to avoid.*
   b. *prescribed drugs.*
   c. *several guidelines.*

7. As the topic sentence suggests, this paragraph lists
   a. prescription drugs.
   b. guidelines for avoiding the dangers of prescription drugs.
   c. side effects of prescription drugs.

8. Fill in the missing major detail: The major details of the paragraph are 1) know a drug's side effects, 2) know if a drug can be taken with one's other medicines, and 3) _____
   _____ *medicine should always be stored in its own labeled bottle.* _____ .

9. *Fill in the blank:* Drugs can be deadly if combined with certain
   _____ *other drugs the patient is using.* _____ .

10. The last major detail is introduced by the transition
    a. *one.*
    b. *also.*
    c. *finally.*

➤ *Review Test 1*

To review what you've learned in this chapter, answer each of the following questions. Fill in the blank, or circle the letter of the answer you think is correct.

1. __*T*__ TRUE OR FALSE? Major supporting details are more general than minor supporting details.

2. Opening phrases can tell us
   a. that a list of some type will follow.
   b. how many major details will follow.
   c. both of the above.

3. An addition word can tell us
   a. how many major details to expect.
   b. that a new major detail is being introduced.
   c. both of the above.

4-5. Fill in each blank with an addition word or phrase:
   _____ *Answers will vary.* _____

6-10. Label each part of the outline form below with one of the following:

   • Main idea
   • Major supporting detail
   • Minor supporting detail

   Main idea _____
   1. *Major supporting detail* _____
      a. *Minor supporting detail* _____
      b. *Minor supporting detail* _____
   2. *Major supporting detail* _____

➤ *Review Test 2*

A. (1–8.) Major and minor supporting details are mixed together in the list below. The details of this list support the main idea shown. Separate the major, more general details from the minor ones by filling in the outline. Some of the details have been filled in for you.

- Comedy shows
- *60 Minutes*
- *Friends*
- Game shows
- *Jeopardy*
- News shows
- *Frasier*
- *20/20*
- *Nightline*
- *Home Improvement*
- *Wheel of Fortune*
- *The Price Is Right*

Main idea: TV shows can be classified according to type.

Major detail: 1. _Comedy shows_

Minor details: a. _Friends_

b. _Frasier_

c. _Home Improvement_

Major detail: 2. _Game shows_

Minor details: a. _Jeopardy_

b. _Wheel of Fortune_

c. _The Price Is Right_

Major detail: 3. _News shows_

Minor details: a. _60 Minutes_

b. _20/20_

c. _Nightline_

B. (9–14.) Major and minor supporting details are mixed together in the list that follows. The details of this list support the main idea shown. Separate the major, more general details from the minor ones by filling in the outline. Some of the details have been filled in for you.

- Manufactured materials
- Straw
- Marble
- Glass
- Natural materials
- Wood
- Plastic
- Concrete

Main idea: Building materials can be classified in two groups.

Major detail: 1. _Natural materials_

Minor details: a. _Straw_

b. _Marble_

c. _Wood_

Major detail: 2. _Manufactured materials_

Minor details: a. _Glass_

b. _Plastic_

c. _Concrete_

C. (15–20.) Write the numbers *1, 2* and *3* before the major details in each paragraph. (Remember that words like *first, also,* and *next* can help you identify supporting details.) Then write the major details in the spaces provided.

To help you focus on the details, topic sentences have been set off in boldface, and headings have been provided.

1. **There are certain kinds of employee behavior that bosses dislike, says a recent survey.**[1]First is dishonesty. If a boss thinks an employee cannot be trusted, nothing else about that worker will matter.[2]The second thing bosses dislike is irresponsibility. They hate when workers waste time or do personal business during the workday.[3]Bosses also dislike many absences and lateness. One employer said, "It doesn't matter when we start—9 a.m. or 10 a.m. Some people will still be fifteen minutes late."

    Kinds of Employee Behavior That Bosses Dislike

    1. _Dishonesty_

    2. _Irresponsibility_

    3. _Many absences and lateness_

2. **Good speakers talk with their bodies in several ways.**[1]First, they use eye contact. Eye contact helps speakers build a warm bond with the audience. It also tells them whether or not they are keeping the audience's interest.[2]Facial expressions are another way speakers use their bodies. Good speakers use facial expressions to stress their words.[3]Last are hand movements, which good speakers also use to accent what is being said.

Several Ways That Good Speakers Talk with Their Bodies

1. _Eye contact_
2. _Facial expressions_
3. _Hand movements_

➤ Review Test 3

Answer the questions that follow the paragraphs. The topic sentence of each paragraph is set off in boldface.

A. **In addition to fresh vegetables, gardening offers several health benefits.** One study found that gardeners have fewer heart attacks than others. The reasons seem to be that being around plants lowers blood pressure and helps people better resist stress. Another benefit of gardening is harder bones. For women, who are more likely to be at risk of weak bones, this benefit is especially important. Experts feel that work such as pushing a wheelbarrow or lugging bags of manure slows bone loss. A third benefit of gardening is that it provides safe exercise.

1. As the topic sentence suggests, the major details of the paragraph are
   a. fresh vegetables.
   b. health benefits of gardening.
   c. reasons that gardeners have fewer heart attacks.

2. Specifically, the major details of this paragraph are
   a. 1) blood pressure and 2) resistance to stress.
   b. 1) the pleasures of fresh vegetables and 2) health benefits.
   c. 1) fewer heart attacks, 2) harder bones, and 3) safe exercise.

3-4. According to some researchers, what are the two reasons that being among plants may lower the number of heart attacks? _____
   Blood pressure is lowered. People resist stress better.

5. Experts feel that bones benefit from
   a. fewer heart attacks.
   b. low blood pressure.
   c. certain work.

B.   [1]**The word** *spinster* **has had different meanings throughout history.** [2]In the 1600s, this word referred to any female. [3]Spinning thread or yarn for cloth was something every woman did at home. [4]By 1700, *spinster* had become a legal term for an unmarried woman. [5]Such women had to work to survive, and spinning was their most common job. [6]Before long, however, spinning was done in factories. [7]*Spinster* then suggested someone who was "left over" or "dried up," just as the job of home spinning had dried up for women. [8]Today, with so many women working, most single women consider the word *spinster* an insult.

6. In general, the major supporting details in this paragraph are
   a. important events in the history of women's work.
   b. events in the history of spinning thread and yarn.
   (c.) different meanings of the word *spinster* throughout history.

7. Fill in the blank: In the 1600s, the word *spinster* referred to _____
   _____ *any female.* _____

8. The answer to question 7 can be found in sentence
   a. 1.
   (b.) 2.
   c. 4.

9. By 1700, single women were called spinsters because
   a. spinning was done by all women.
   (b.) most single women made their livings by spinning.
   c. spinning was no longer done at home.

10. When spinning was done in factories, *spinster* came to mean
    a. any woman.
    b. a woman who spins.
    (c.) a "left over" or "dried up" woman.

➤ *Review Test 4*

Here is a chance to apply your understanding of supporting details to a full-length reading. First, read the following selection by a college student who has had a tough time figuring out her life. She has had to move between countries and adjust to their cultures, and she has had a difficult time making friends. Yet she is determined to succeed. After reading the selection, answer the supporting detail questions that follow. There are also other comprehension questions to help you continue practicing the skills you learned in earlier chapters.

Words to Watch

Following are some words in the reading that do not have strong context support. Each word is followed by the number of the paragraph in which it appears and its meaning there. These words are indicated in the story by a small circle (°).

shuttled (1): sent back and forth
detested (5): hated
prescribed (5): required
perennial (5): continual
ironic (5): opposite to what might be expected
arrogant (6): conceited
snobbish (6): self-satisfied and superior
expectant (12): looking forward

MY OWN TWO FEET

Irina Marjan

Sometimes in my life, I have felt like the world's orphan. I have been shuttled° between two countries, yet I don't fully belong to either one. I speak their languages, but I sound "foreign" to the native speakers of both. I have had two sets of parents, yet neither set has really wanted or accepted me. I turned 18, and I just started attending college. Even if neither of my two sets of parents has truly helped me, I am finding that I have my own two feet, and I'm beginning to stand on them.

In the beginning, I didn't know who my parents were or where I belonged. I was born in Queens, New York, and shipped off at nine months to Belgrade, Yugoslavia. My parents had their own problems and couldn't take proper care of me.

I lived with my grandparents and aunt and uncle in Lokve, 3
Yugoslavia. For a long time, I thought that my aunt and uncle were my
parents, so when my mother came to see me, I ran away from her
because I didn't know who she was. My foster parents had never told
me that they were not my parents, much less who my parents were.
They didn't like my mother, so they didn't say a word to help me to
understand who this strange visitor was. My mother was upset because
I didn't want to talk to her. One day, she caught me by my hair and
made me listen. "You listen," said the woman, "I'm your mother."
After that, she brought me back to the U.S., where I stayed with my
parents for a year but was sent back to Yugoslavia because they still
didn't get along, and I wasn't welcome any more.

At the age of five, when it was time to start school in Yugoslavia, 4
the children in kindergarten were rude. I only had one friend, and we
used to cry together because no one liked us. We would run out the
door as soon as the teacher went on her break. I would run home, and
my grandfather would bring me back to school. It was the "highlight"
of every school day. My schoolmates reminded me about this till I was
in seventh grade.

If this was not enough, then there was the obstacle of learning to 5
speak Serbian. The Serbian language was the official language of
Yugoslavia even though there were many other languages spoken
regionally. For example, the school I attended was the school for the
children of Romanian-speaking people living in the area. All of my
classes were in Romanian except for my Serbian language class. At that
school, the only foreign language offered was French. I had to make a
decision whether to stay in that school and learn French or transfer to a
Serbian school which had more foreign languages, including English,
which I wanted to learn. If I'd transferred, then I'd have had to take all
my classes in Serbian, which I hated. What I already detested° in my
Serbian language class were the prescribed° essays that I had to write,
in particular the perennial° favorite "Moja domovina"—"My country."
This was ironic° because it wasn't even my country!

There was a Serbian school nearby, but the Serbians who attended 6
it were arrogant° and had snobbish° attitudes toward non-Serbians who
wanted to go to their school. Therefore, I decided to stay and learn
French. I never did learn English.

In the summer of 1988, at 14, I came to the U.S. to visit my 7
parents. At that point, there was nothing for me to go back to in
Yugoslavia because I had gotten to be too much of a responsibility for
my aunt and uncle since I'd entered puberty. But ultimately I didn't
want to go back because I knew I would have to attend a high school
where classes were taught entirely in Serbian.

At that moment, I decided that I ought to remain in the U.S. My father still wanted to send me back, but that's when I started taking charge of my life. I told him that I wanted to stay in the U.S. and make something out of my life. I decided that I would go to school here and reach high. I would graduate with a master's degree in business some day. And I would speak and write perfect English. 8

A dream and the realization of a dream may be separated by many years and many hurdles. One hurdle for me was graduating from high school. High school was hard. I had to learn English. I had to make new friends. I had to work to make money. In English my biggest problem was my accent. I will never forget my first oral report. It was a health class, and we had to do a report on drugs and alcohol. I listened to everyone's report, but no one listened to mine. The whole class was laughing instead of listening. I had a strong accent, and I was reading very fast because I was nervous. It was funny for my classmates, but for me it was one of the worst experiences in my life. I had to talk to people who didn't care what I had to say about drugs and alcohol. Also, these rude people were the very people that I had to become friends with. I cried every day because I was lonely and had no one to call a friend. I had an accent, and I was different than everyone else. Therefore, it was hard for them to accept me. As my English improved, they began to accept me. I could feel that my life was getting better. I did better in my classes and became friends with many people. Still, I was working from 4 to 8 p.m. I had to stay up till 2 a.m. to finish my school work; I had to learn English and do well in my classes in order to graduate. 9

Although my life was getting better, little things had a way of making me stumble. The silly matter of my hair almost held me back from going to college this fall. I had damaged my hair badly with chemical processes, and I couldn't do anything to fix it because it was far too damaged. It was mixed gray, yellow straw, and brown. I was scared because I lost a lot of hair when I brushed it. Handfuls of the tangled colors came out. I didn't know how I could start college with so little and such hair. Finally, I cut it all to the roots and bravely started college with a boy's crew cut. I was not going to let anything push me aside in my path to a degree. 10

Now that I'm here in an English-speaking college on this side of the Atlantic at last, I foresee a rough road financially, but at 18 and with my sense that I can grapple with hardship and come out on my feet, I think I can do it. I work twenty-five hours a week for five dollars an hour and have scheduled a full college load. I don't play around with perms or hair color, but I do keep my eyes on the prize. I'm beginning to feel as American as my passport declares, and I'm told by my teachers that I'm a real student. 11

> I guess I had to learn who I was, where I came from, where I   12
> belonged, what I wanted to do with my life, and where I would want to
> live it before I could start taking charge of it. Now at 18, I've started
> taking charge of my life, and I'm trying to make the best of it. I can
> look back and see the long road from the tears in my first grade class to
> the hopeful and expectant° attitude I bring to college, and to the rest of
> my life.

Reading Comprehension Questions

Vocabulary in Context

1. The word *foresee* in "Now that I'm here in an English-speaking college on this side of the Atlantic at last, I foresee a rough road financially" (paragraph 11) means
   a. forget.
   (b.) predict.
   c. appreciate.
   d. want.

2. The word *grapple* in "I can grapple with hardship and come out on my feet" (paragraph 11) means
   a. avoid dealing.
   b. write.
   (c.) struggle.
   d. speak.

Central Point and Main Ideas

3. Which sentence best expresses the central point of the selection?
   a. Sometimes Marjan felt like "the world's orphan."
   b. Marjan did not want to go back to Yugoslavia because she knew she would have to attend a high school there where classes were taught entirely in Serbian.
   (c.) From her childhood on, Marjan overcame many obstacles to eventually take charge of her life and aim for success.
   d. It was during her high school years that Marjan had to learn English, make new friends, and work hard to earn money.

4. Which sentence best expresses the implied main idea of paragraphs 4–6?
   a. The author found her school life in Yugoslavia to be pleasant.
   b. The author had big social problems.
   c. The author's grandfather was her best friend.
   (d.) The author had great challenges to deal with in Yugoslavian schools.

5. The main idea of paragraph 10 is expressed in its
   a. first sentence.
   b. fourth sentence.
   c. fifth sentence.
   d. next-to-the-last sentence.

Supporting Details

6. ___F___ TRUE OR FALSE? The author never found out who her parents were.

7. ___T___ TRUE OR FALSE? At age 14, the author did not want to return to Yugoslavia because the classes at the school she would attend were taught in Serbian.

8. Marjan feels she began taking charge of her life when she
   a. lived in Yugoslavia.
   b. decided not to attend the Serbian school.
   c. decided at age 14 to stay in the U.S.
   d. bravely started college with a boy's crew cut.

9. The major details of paragraphs 4–6 are
   a. the author's Yugoslavian friends and family.
   b. the languages the author knew as a child.
   c. the author's schoolmates and neighbors in Yugoslavia.
   d. the challenges of dealing with rude classmates and the Serbian language in school.

10. A central point is supported by major details, just as main ideas are. The major details of the entire selection are
    a. obstacles the author faced in Yugoslavia.
    b. the author's family problems.
    c. challenges the author has met on the way to taking charge of her life.
    d. obstacles the author has faced in all of her school work.

Mapping Activity

This selection follows Marjan's life in two countries. The major events described by the author are written below. Underline the name of the country she was in when each incident occurred.

Central point: Marjan has faced and dealt with many problems and has created a promising life for herself.

- Marjan is born in (Yugoslavia; ___United States___).
- At nine months, Marjan is sent to (Yugoslavia; the United States).
- Marjan starts kindergarten in (Yugoslavia; the United States).
- At age 14, Marjan visits her parents in (Yugoslavia; the United States).
- Marjan graduates from high school in (Yugoslavia; the United States).

Discussion Questions

1. Marjan states that she had trouble making friends in high school because, she says, "I had an accent, and I was different than everyone else." What can schools do to make life easier for foreign students like Marjan? What can other students do?

2. Marjan's self-esteem must have suffered when her parents sent her back to Yugoslavia, when her classmates in high school laughed at her, and when she had to begin college with a crew cut. How strong do you think her self-esteem is now? What experiences and attitudes do you think influenced her self-esteem? Point out parts of the reading that you think support your answers.

Writing Activities

1. We might conclude from the reading that one of Marjan's struggles was to build her self-esteem. Write a paragraph telling what steps people can take to strengthen their self-esteem. Your topic sentence might be "There are a few things people can do to build up their own self-esteem." Use examples to illustrate your points.

2. In paragraph 9, Marjan discusses the difficulties she had to face in high school. Write a paper describing the difficulties you had to face in high school. If you eventually overcame them, explain how. To illustrate the points you make, include detailed descriptions of incidents.

    Alternatively, write a paper about the challenges you had to face as a young child or as an elementary school student.

Check Your Performance			SUPPORTING DETAILS	
Activity	*Number Right*	*Points*		*Total*
Review Test 1 (10 items)	_____	x 1 =		_____
Review Test 2 (20 items)	_____	x 2 =		_____
Review Test 3 (10 items)	_____	x 2 =		_____
Review Test 4 (10 items)	_____	x 2 =		_____
Mapping Activity (5 items)	_____	x 2 =		_____
		TOTAL SCORE =		_____ %

Enter your total score onto the Reading Performance Chart: Review Tests on the inside back cover.

9

Locations of Main Ideas

Most of the topic sentences you have seen so far have been located in the first sentence of a paragraph. But the topic sentence may appear elsewhere within a paragraph. This chapter first describes common locations of topic sentences. It then provides practice in finding the topic sentence in a series of paragraphs. By the end of the chapter, you should have a solid sense of how to locate topic sentences.

Note: As you work through the practices, keep in mind that a topic sentence is a statement of the main idea. It will always be a general statement that covers most or all of the material in a paragraph.

TOPIC SENTENCE AT THE START OF A PARAGRAPH

```
┌─────────────────────────────┐
│       Topic Sentence        │
├─────────────────────────────┤
│      Supporting Detail      │
│      Supporting Detail      │
│      Supporting Detail      │
│      Supporting Detail      │
└─────────────────────────────┘
```

Authors often begin a paragraph with the main idea. The rest of the paragraph then supports the main idea with details. Here is an example:

My desk is well organized. I keep pencils and pens in the top left drawer. Typing and writing paper are in the middle left drawer. The bottom left side has all the other supplies I might need, from paper clips to staples. The top of the desk is clear, except for a study light and a clock. The right side of the desk has two drawers. The bottom one is a file drawer, where I keep my notes for each class. And in the top drawer? That's where I keep nuts, raisins, and M&M's to snack on while I work.

Explanation:

> This paragraph follows a very common pattern: The first sentence is a general statement. The rest of the paragraph supports the general statement. The main idea—that the writer's desk is well organized—is in the first sentence. The rest of the sentences provide specific supporting details. They show us just how well organized the desk is.

TOPIC SENTENCE WITHIN A PARAGRAPH

> Introductory Details
> **Topic Sentence**
> Supporting Detail
> Supporting Detail
> Supporting Detail

When the topic sentence is *within* a paragraph, it often follows one or more introductory sentences. Those sentences lead up in some way to the main idea. They may introduce the topic of the paragraph, catch the reader's interest, relate the main idea to a previous paragraph, give background for the main idea, or ask a question. Below is an example of a paragraph with a topic sentence that is not first or last. See if you can find it. Write its number in the blank space.

> ^{1}Do you know what to do if you have trouble sleeping? ^{2}In many cases, sleep problems can be avoided by following a few simple guidelines. ^{3}First, don't drink alcoholic beverages or drinks with caffeine close to bedtime. ^{4}Next, do not exercise within three hours of bedtime. ^{5}Finally, plan a sleep routine. ^{6}Go to bed at the same time and get up at the same time.

> *Topic sentence:* _____

Explanation:

> The first sentence introduces the topic of sleep problems by asking a question. A question can *never* be a topic sentence. It is only asking something—it is not making a statement. The second sentence states the author's main idea about that topic—that sleep problems can often be avoided by following a few simple guidelines. The rest of the paragraph lists the specific guidelines referred to only generally in the topic sentence.

Topic sentences within paragraphs are often second sentences, as in the example above. But they may come even later than the second sentence. See if you can find the topic sentence in the following paragraph. Then write its number in the space provided.

¹Today we take world-wide communications for granted. ²Through TV and radio, we learn almost instantly what happens throughout the world. ³In Roman times, however, military leaders relied on a much slower, less technical method to send important messages back to headquarters—pigeons. ⁴Homing pigeons have a strong instinct to return home from just about anywhere. ⁵The birds were kept in cages at the military camps. ⁶When a message had to be sent, a soldier strapped it to the bird's leg. ⁷The bird was then released, and it flew home, delivering the message.

Topic sentence: _____

Explanation:

At first, we might think that sentence 1 states the main idea since sentence 2 gives examples of the world-wide communications. But notice what happens in sentence 3. This sentence, also a general idea, takes the reader in a different direction (as signaled by the contrast word *however*). This sentence is then supported by details in sentences 4–7. Now it becomes clear that the first two sentences are leading up to the true main idea of the paragraph, stated in sentence 3. This is clear because sentences 4–6 all give information that explains in detail the general statement in sentence 3.

TOPIC SENTENCE AT THE END OF A PARAGRAPH

When the topic sentence *ends* a paragraph, the previous sentences build up to the main idea. Here is an example of a paragraph in which the topic sentence comes last:

¹A museum in London has a fur-covered trout on display. ²It also has a letter written by Jesus Christ and a painting by Rembrandt. ³In addition, the crown jewels of England are displayed there. ⁴These items have one thing in common. ⁵They are all frauds. ⁶The London museum, you see, exhibits only jewelry, coins, letters, and artwork that have been proven to be fakes or forgeries.

Explanation:

When a topic sentence ends a paragraph, it often acts as a summary of the points made in the paragraph, or as a conclusion, with all the details leading up to a final, general point. In the paragraph above, sentences 1–5 introduce and then discuss specific items on display at a museum. The last sentence is a general one that connects all the specific details that come before it.

TWO TOPIC SENTENCES: AT THE BEGINNING AND END OF A PARAGRAPH

Topic Sentence
Supporting Detail
Supporting Detail
Supporting Detail
Topic Sentence

An author will sometimes introduce a main idea at or near the *beginning* of a paragraph and then restate the idea, or make a similar general statement, at the *end* of the paragraph. The following paragraph is an example. Read it and the explanation that follows.

¹There are a number of ways to get young people involved in cutting down on the family food bill. ²First, have your children go through newspapers to clip coupons. ³They can also sort them into different categories and note expiration dates. ⁴Next, have them help you compare generic products and brand-name products. ⁵Buy each, and have a taste-testing contest. ⁶If kids can't taste a difference, point out the savings there will be by buying the generic product. ⁷Finally, give kids the responsibility to load the shopping cart and calculate the savings their work has produced. ⁸In these ways, children can feel the pride of making an impact on their family's food budget.

Explanation:

The first sentence introduces a general idea, and sentences 2–7 provide several specific examples. Sentence 8 states a general idea similar to the one in sentence 1. Sentences 1 and 8 each cover all the details of the passage. Thus the paragraph has two topic sentences—one at the beginning and one at the end.

➤ Practice 1

The topic sentence is in different places in the following five paragraphs. Identify each topic sentence by filling in the correct number in the blank space. For the one paragraph that has a topic sentence at the beginning *and* at the end, write in both numbers.

To find each topic sentence, do the following:

  a Identify the *topic* of the paragraph by asking yourself, "Who or what is the paragraph about?"

 b Find the *general statement* that tells you what the author's main point is about the topic.

 c Test your answer by asking yourself, "Is this general statement supported by all or most of the material in the paragraph?"

1. [1]Have you ever come across someone whose name seemed to fit his or her work? [2]There are, in fact, many people whose names match their jobs. [3]For instance, Ivan Doctor is an eye doctor, and Patience Scales is a piano teacher. [4]Then there are Sergeant Vice, a police officer, and James Judge, a superior court judge. [5]There's even a dentist named Toothaker.

 Topic sentence(s): ___2___

2. [1]They may seem to be peaceful vegetarians, but squirrels (including chipmunks) do prey on other animals. [2]Tree squirrels are the main enemies of young snowshoe hares in British Columbia. [3]Ground squirrels sometimes feed on moles and gophers. [4]U.S. chipmunks eat lizards and eggs. [5]And Mexican chipmunks living along coastal areas eat crabs.

 Topic sentence(s): ___1___

3. [1]A recent study found that over 80 percent of mountain bikers reported being injured at least once. [2]Twenty-five percent needed to see a doctor. [3]In contrast, 50 percent of on-road, or street, bikers reported an injury, with 33 percent needing medical attention. [4]The study concluded that while mountain bikers have more injuries, street bikers have more severe injuries.

 Topic sentence(s): ___4___

4. [1]The Council on Physical Education for Children has some suggestions on exercise for children. [2]First, have children play games in which everyone is involved. [3]For example, play soccer, not baseball. [4]Next, make sure equipment is the right size. [5]Smaller, lighter equipment helps young children develop skills. [6]Finally, avoid boring exercises such as jumping jacks. [7]Following the Council's suggestions should result in better-developed skills and more fun for children.

 Topic sentence(s): ___1, 7___

5. [1]Some shoppers enjoy running from sale to sale, looking for the lowest possible prices on their sheets, towels, and microwaves. [2]But more shoppers today prefer stores that offer everyday low prices—not just occasional sale prices. [3]These shoppers dislike waiting for a sale on an item they need. [4]When they decide they want or need an item, they want to get it right away. [5]Also, they hate buying something and seeing it go on sale the next week.

 Topic sentence(s): ___2___

A NOTE ON PARAGRAPHS WITHOUT TOPIC SENTENCES

Sometimes a paragraph does not have a topic sentence. In such cases, the author has decided to let the supporting details suggest the main idea. The main idea is **unstated**, or implied, and you must figure it out by deciding upon the point of the supporting details.

Asking two questions will help you figure out the author's main idea:

1 What is the topic, or subject, of the paragraph? In other words, what is the whole paragraph about?

2 What is the main point being made about the topic?

The next exercise will introduce you to the skill of finding an implied main idea. You will have another chance to apply this skill when answering some of the main idea questions that follow the reading selections in the book.

➤ *Practice 2*

In each paragraph that follows, the main idea is unstated—there is no topic sentence. Apply the two questions shown above to help you find the answer that best states each main idea. Circle the letter of that answer.

1. Why do some people avoid crossing the path of a black cat? The reason is centuries old. People in the Middle Ages believed that witches were very dangerous creatures who could change themselves into black cats. Witches were also thought to be easily irritated. So if you wanted to avoid trouble, the safest thing to do was simply to avoid all black cats.

    The unstated main idea is:
    a. Some people avoid crossing the path of a black cat.
    b. Superstitions have interesting historical backgrounds.
    c. The fear of crossing the path of a black cat stems from beliefs about witches in the Middle Ages.
    d. During the Middle Ages, people believed that witches were dangerous and could change themselves into black cats.

2. I recently took a long hike into the woods. I was stung by a hornet, and I scratched my arm when I fell into a thorn bush while trying to get away from the hornet. Then I got lost during the hike and had to walk an extra four miles to find the trail again. At one point I walked into a patch of shrubs with three leaves on each stem, and I realized they were poison ivy. Finally, I was drenched by a sudden shower before I got back to my car. I don't think I'll go hiking again for a while.

The unstated main idea is:

a. The woods are not a good place for an inexperienced hiker.

b. Never go hiking in the woods alone.

c. The author's hike through the woods was filled with great dangers to his life.

(d.) The author's hike in the woods was troublesome and discouraging.

3. Two workers on the twenty-third floor of a building saw a bird banging its head against a window of their office. They rescued the bird and took it to a nearby animal hospital. The vet explained that what happened was not unusual. The bird had eaten berries which had been on the vine long enough to ferment—the sugar had partially turned to alcohol. The bird, in other words, was drunk. The vet gave it time to sober up and then released it.

    The unstated main idea is:

    (a.) Two office workers learned that birds get drunk.

    b. Workers in skyscrapers often rescue birds.

    c. Birds often bang their heads on windows.

    d. A bird was taken by office workers to an animal hospital.

4. First it was racquetball, then jogging, and then aerobic exercises. What will the next exercise craze be? Would you believe walking? One reason for more people to walk for exercise is that the body is better suited for it than for running or jumping. Also, walking can give the same benefits to the heart that any exercise can. And just about anyone can walk, regardless of age or location. In addition, walking will burn off the same number of calories as aerobics or running. But perhaps the main advantage of walking is that it is almost completely injury-free.

    The unstated main idea is:

    a. People keep changing the exercises they do.

    b. There are several good reasons for exercising.

    (c.) There are good reasons for walking to become the next exercise craze.

    d. Walking benefits the heart and uses up the same number of calories as running.

FINDING TOPIC SENTENCES ON FOUR LEVELS OF DIFFICULTY

As has already been said, finding the main idea is the most important of all reading skills. To give you practice in finding the main idea, the rest of this chapter presents a series of paragraphs. They are grouped into four levels of increasing difficulty, with the topic sentences appearing at varying places. Don't skip any levels. Doing the easier ones will prepare you for the more difficult ones. Finally, remember these guidelines for finding the topic sentence:

   a Identify the *topic* of the paragraph by asking yourself, "Who or what is the paragraph about?"

   b Find the *general statement* that tells you what the author's main point is about the topic.

   c Test your answer by asking yourself, "Is this general statement supported by all or most of the material in the paragraph?"

➤ *Practice: Level 1*

Write the number of each topic sentence in the space provided.

1.   ¹People who are overweight simply eat too much, right? ²Wrong. ³There are other causes for gaining weight besides eating more. ⁴One is eating the wrong kinds of food, such as fatty and sugary foods. ⁵Another may be eating at the wrong times, like just before going to bed. ⁶And a third cause of gaining weight not related to overeating is getting too little exercise.

   Topic sentence: ___3___

2.   ¹The types of animals considered endangered or threatened are increasing. ²In 1985, there were 329 species listed by the U.S. Fish and Wildlife Service as being endangered or threatened. ³This year, there are 402 species listed. ⁴In addition, there are over 3,000 other species that officials have not had time to study. ⁵Some of these may also qualify for the list.

   Topic sentence: ___1___

3.   ¹Hannibal Hamlin was one. ²So were George Dallas and John Breckinridge. ³And you can add the names of Schuyler Colfax, Henry Wilson, and John Garner. ⁴What do all of these men have in common? ⁵Although few people know them by name, each of these men has been a vice president of the United States.

   Topic sentence: ___5___

4.   ¹Child abuse has many tragic results. ²A child who is abused often believes he is unworthy. ³This low self-esteem can lead to alcoholism, drug addiction or even suicide. ⁴Of course in many cases, the abuse is physically harmful and even fatal. ⁵In addition, most abused children grow up to become abusers of their own children.

   Topic sentence: ___1___

5.   ¹There is much that people can do for their pets. ²But the opposite is also true—many studies have shown that owning a pet can improve a person's mental and physical well-being. ³A pet that a person feels attached to improves the owner's frame of mind. ⁴A pet gives a feeling of being needed to the person who takes care of it. ⁵Pets also give an unconditional love that

makes coming home after a rotten day more bearable. ⁶Even being in the same room as a pet can lower one's blood pressure and heart rate.

Topic sentence: ___2___

➤ Practice: Level 2

Write the number of each topic sentence in the space provided. For the one case in which there are two topic sentences, write in both numbers.

1.   ¹If asked, you might say that ceramics are for pottery and plastic is for toys. ²That may be true today. ³In the near future, however, ceramics and plastics will be put to some very different uses. ⁴New methods have produced ceramics sturdy enough to be made into scissors and knives that never rust. ⁵The new ceramics can also be made into engines that don't need cooling. ⁶The new plastics can be molded into bridges, fuel tanks, and high-fidelity loudspeakers.

Topic sentence(s): ___3___

2.   ¹There are various types of personalized license plates. ²Some show a person's name or, as in the case of TOOTH DR, a driver's occupation. ³Sports enthusiasts show their love of a sport, as with license LV2GOLF, or a team: GO PHILS. ⁴Others display greetings such as GDAYM8 and GR8T DAY. ⁵Some license plates reveal the driver's status, as with NO MO 925, apparently about a retired person, or the vehicle's status, as with 4 RNR, seen on a recreational vehicle.

Topic sentence(s): ___1___

3.   ¹Survey statistics are convincing food makers to pay more attention to children. ²Children influence $132 billion in annual purchases. ³In addition, 62 percent of children visit supermarkets each week, and 50 percent participate in the choice of food or brand. ⁴Fifty percent of children also say that they prefer a different salad dressing than their mothers. ⁵And a full 78 percent of them claim to influence their family's choice of cold cereal. ⁶Such statistics tell food makers that appealing to children's taste can be profitable.

Topic sentence(s): ___1, 6___

4.   ¹Parents have shown concern about the quality and safety of baby food. ²As a result of parental concern, the leading baby-food companies have started a strict set of safety checks. ³First, representatives of the companies visit the farms where the produce is grown. ⁴The representatives make sure that levels of pesticides are the lowest possible. ⁵Next, they check every piece of incoming produce for chemicals and other impurities. ⁶Finally, spot checks are done before the baby food is shipped to stores.

Topic sentence(s): ___2___

5.   ¹Today there are summer camps for a wide variety of specialized activities, from adventure to law. ²For instance, a ranch in Texas offers a camp where children can learn to care for exotic animals. ³Another in Pennsylvania lets kids work on community service projects. ⁴A camp in Minnesota is divided into small villages where children can learn the language and culture of China, Russia, and other countries. ⁵There is even a camp in Florida where kids can learn what it is like to be a lawyer.

Topic sentence(s): __1__

➤ *Practice: Level 3*

Write the number of each topic sentence in the space provided. For the one case in which there are two topic sentences, write in both numbers.

1.   ¹The time-honored tradition of flirting is in no danger of falling into disuse. ²However, because women and men flirt for different reasons, flirting can lead to mixed messages. ³Women often flirt just to be friendly or to meet someone new. ⁴They do not necessarily expect or want further involvement. ⁵Men, on the other hand, view flirting as a means to action. ⁶They hope it will lead to something more than conversation.

Topic sentence(s): __2__

2.   ¹According to the National Education Association, there are six major problems that students bring into the high-school classroom. ²First, about a quarter of all students smoke marijuana regularly, and more than two-thirds use alcohol. ³Forty percent of today's 14-year-old girls will get pregnant in their teens, and 80 percent of these will drop out of high school. ⁴Also, 30 percent of all students now in high school will drop out. ⁵One out of three girls and one out of eight boys under 18 years old have reported being sexually abused. ⁶Fifth, 15 percent of girls will suffer an eating disorder during part or all of their teenage years. ⁷Finally, suicide is the second most common cause of death among 15- through 19-year-olds.

Topic sentence(s): __1__

3.   ¹Because turnips were often eaten by the poor, people often turned up their noses at them. ²Carrots grew wild in ancient times and were used then for medicinal purposes. ³But they weren't considered fit for the table in Europe until the thirteenth century. ⁴In the early seventeenth and eighteenth centuries, some Europeans considered potatoes fit only for animals. ⁵They were thought to cause leprosy in humans. ⁶Obviously, though root vegetables are delicious and easily grown, their virtues haven't always been appreciated.

Topic sentence(s): __6__

4.   [1]European men do it. [2]Gay men do it. [3]Some celebrities do it. [4]"It" is hugging and kissing between men, and it's something the majority of males in our society are not comfortable doing. [5]Some are afraid of being labeled as homosexual. [6]Others come from ethnic backgrounds that frown on displays of affection. [7]And for others, being affectionate toward a friend makes them feel vulnerable, something they've learned a "real man" should not be.

Topic sentence(s):   4

5.   [1]A medical journal offers some important guidelines for having your ears pierced. [2]First, let a professional who uses sterile instruments perform the task. [3]Second, do not pierce an ear if you have a serious medical condition, such as heart disease or diabetes. [4]Also, for six weeks, do not wear earrings that contain nickel or a gold alloy or that are gold-plated. [5]Next, avoid the risk of infection by washing the earlobe twice a day with cotton dipped in rubbing alcohol. [6]Finally, if a lobe becomes red, swollen, or sore, see a doctor immediately. [7]Following this advice should result in a successful ear piercing.

Topic sentence(s):   1, 7

➤ *Practice: Level 4*

Write the number of each topic sentence in the space provided. For the one case in which there are two topic sentences, write in both numbers.

1.   [1]Being a judge may be a lofty job, but judges often face the down-to-earth problem of fighting off sleepiness during a long trial. [2]One reason is that arguments made by attorneys are usually routine. [3]They are also often long and boring. [4]A second reason is that judges are seated for the entire trial. [5]Sitting in one position can slow the body down, especially after lunch. [6]Also, courtrooms are usually stuffy. [7]Air circulation is poor, and there are no windows. [8]Lighting is dim. [9]These factors all make staying awake during trials a challenging task for judges.

Topic sentence(s):   1, 9

2.   [1]Marta is 14 and lives in a village in San Salvador. [2]As in most peasant families there, every day the women prepare tortillas, thin round pancakes made from mashed corn. [3]In San Salvador, the tortillas are made in the same way they were made hundreds of years ago. [4]Marta collects the corn and puts it in a pot of water to soak. [5]The next day, she puts the wet corn through a hand grinder. [6]Her mother then puts the ground corn on a block of stone and mashes it back and forth many times until it is a pasty dough. [7]This dough is then patted into tortillas, which are cooked on a flat griddle over an open fire. [8]They are eaten with salt and a portion of beans.

Topic sentence(s):   3

3. ¹Half of all Americans live within fifty miles of an ocean beach. ²No wonder there's hardly room for a beach towel—124 million people visit the seashore annually, and the number is growing as development booms. ³Unfortunately, all twenty-three coastal states lose two to four feet of beach a year to the ocean. ⁴More people and less beach should make for some very crowded seashores in the coming years.

    Topic sentence(s): ___4___

4. ¹People complain about their doctors. ²"He rushes me through." ³"She doesn't explain what she's doing." ⁴Rather than just complain, patients need to become better managers of their own health care by asking questions and demanding answers. ⁵When patients visit a doctor, they should be prepared to describe their health problems fully and precisely. ⁶They should question the doctor when they don't understand what he or she is doing. ⁷They should make a habit of asking why certain procedures are recommended. ⁸They should ask exactly how, when, and why they should take any medication. ⁹If a doctor reacts badly to a patient's questions, it may be time to find a new doctor.

    Topic sentence(s): ___4___

5. ¹Daylight-saving time usually ends on the last weekend of October. ²This can be confusing as not all states are on daylight-saving time. ³But it is unlikely that any place has a harder time coping with time changes than Tuba City, Arizona. ⁴The state of Arizona does not observe daylight-saving time. ⁵But Tuba City is on a Navajo reservation, and the Navajo Nation does observe daylight-saving. ⁶The local school board, however, voted to return to standard time in *early* October. ⁷Yet the school's maintenance staff has a contract that states it must follow the usual daylight-saving schedule. ⁸Further, the Navajo Community College, next to the school, goes to standard time in early October. ⁹The continuing education department, in the same building, stays on the usual daylight-saving schedule.

    Topic sentence(s): ___3___

➤ Review Test 1

To review what you've learned in this chapter, answer each of the following questions. Fill in the blank or circle the letter of the answer you think is correct.

1. The topic sentence of a paragraph states the
    a. supporting details.   b. introductory material.   ⓒ main idea.

2. ___T___ TRUE OR FALSE? To find the topic sentence of a paragraph, look for a general statement.

3. ___F___ TRUE OR FALSE? The supporting details of a paragraph are more general than the main idea.

4. The topic sentence can appear in a paragraph
   a. once. ⓑ more than once. c. either *a* or *b*.

5. When the main idea is stated in the last sentence of a paragraph, it is likely to be
   a. a summary. b. a conclusion. ⓒ either *a* or *b*.

➤ *Review Test 2*

The five paragraphs below are on the first and second levels of difficulty. Write the number of each topic sentence in the space provided. For the one case in which there are two topic sentences, write in both numbers.

1. ¹Is there a lot of stress in your life? ²Deep breathing—a simple exercise—can help you relax. ³Begin by standing or sitting up straight. ⁴Then inhale fully, until the belly is pushed out. ⁵Finally, exhale slowly, pulling the belly in and up until the lungs are empty.

   Topic sentence(s): __2__

2. ¹We Americans have a love affair with chocolate. ²In one day, we eat six million pounds of chocolate candy—enough to make a candy bar the size of a football field and two feet thick. ³The Hershey's Chocolate company turns out a quarter million pounds of Hershey's kisses per day. ⁴That's enough to fill up the cabs of sixty full-size pickup trucks.

   Topic sentence(s): __1__

3. ¹There will probably be more use of home computers in the next century. ²People will use them to vote, to file taxes, and to take college exams. ³Also, there may be much more leisure time then. ⁴Experts say the work week will shrink to thirty-two hours or less. ⁵In addition, robots will take over routine service jobs and dangerous cleanups. ⁶As these expert forecasts suggest, the next century is likely to be very different from this one.

   Topic sentence(s): __6__

4. ¹You can attract wildlife to your garden by following a few guidelines. ²First, plant shrubs around your garden. ³Shrubs provide protection for animals and resting and nesting spots for birds. ⁴Also, plant vegetation that the birds and animals like to eat. ⁵A local nursery can help you select the right vegetation. ⁶Third, leave some water for the wildlife to drink. ⁷Finally, keep dogs and cats away. ⁸Their presence will discourage wildlife from coming around. ⁹These procedures should tempt wildlife into any garden.

   Topic sentence(s): __1, 9__

5. ¹The American home can be a violent place. ²Consider, first, that some parents punch and kick their children and even use weapons on them. ³Evidence suggests that almost four million children are abused by their parents each year. ⁴Second, husbands and wives hit, shoot and stab each other. ⁵Almost two million people are abused by their spouses. ⁶Finally, some adults beat, tie up, and neglect the elderly. ⁷There may be over two million old people abused by their children and other caretakers.

    Topic sentence(s):   1

➤ Review Test 3

The five paragraphs below are on the third and fourth levels of difficulty. Write the number of each topic sentence in the space provided. For the one case in which there are two topic sentences, write in both numbers.

1. ¹Have you ever thought that a week in bed would do you good? ²Well, think again. ³Several days of bed rest can actually do harm. ⁴First, just as moving around keeps bones strong, lying in bed weakens them. ⁵Also, when someone is in bed for several days, blood gathers in the upper body. ⁶This causes the heart to function less well and leads to more risk of blood clots. ⁷Lying down also changes the position of the lungs, making breathing more difficult.

    Topic sentence(s):   3

2. ¹On an island in the Indian Ocean, people honor the dead by treating them as if they were still alive. ²Dead bodies are often removed from their tombs and dressed in new clothes. ³Then, before being reburied, the bodies may be danced with, sung to, and given tours of their old neighborhoods. ⁴Recently, a dead soccer player was treated to three games of soccer before being placed in the family tomb.

    Topic sentence(s):   1

3. ¹Some say victimless crimes should not be illegal. ²However, the argument that some crimes have no victims is weak. ³First, whoever commits a so-called victimless crime can do himself harm. ⁴For example, a drug user may overdose. ⁵In addition, family members can be hurt. ⁶Drug addicts may be unable to care properly for their children. ⁷Finally, society can be harmed. ⁸For instance, drug addicts often need costly treatment, paid for with our tax dollars.

    Topic sentence(s):   2

4. [1]Scientists check and recheck evidence before coming to conclusions. [2]But careful research hasn't stopped scientists from making big mistakes. [3]In 1903, for example, n-rays were supposedly discovered. [4]Many papers were published on such subjects as how bricks absorb n-rays and how loud noises interfere with n-rays. [5]Several years later, scientists agreed no such ray exists. [6]In the 1970s, scientists believed a new water called polywater had been invented. [7]They feared that if any escaped a lab, all water would turn into polywater, ending life on Earth. [8]That danger passed when polywater was proved to be ordinary water with impurities.

Topic sentence(s): _2_

5. [1]Our lives have been enriched by inventions we might never have known about without the determination of the products' inventors. [2]In 1939, for example, a professor built the first computer using "base 2," a series that was easy for a machine to identify. [3]He tried to sell his idea to IBM, but was turned down. [4]It took seven years before his idea was accepted and the first general-purpose computer was introduced. [5]Today, all computers use the system he devised. [6]Another example is the copy machine patented in 1939. [7]Its inventor tried to sell his idea to twenty different companies. [8]Because no one was interested then, the first commercial copy machine was not introduced until 1959. [9]Through the persistence of inventors such as these, our lives have been greatly improved.

Topic sentence(s): _1, 9_

➤ Review Test 4

Here is a chance to apply your understanding of topic sentences to a full-length reading. The following selection looks at a custom once followed by many families: sitting down to dinner together. The author discusses the benefits of this custom and how to find time for it. After reading the selection, answer the questions that follow on the central point and main ideas. There are also questions on vocabulary in context and supporting details.

Words to Watch

Following are some words in the reading that do not have strong context support. Each word is followed by the number of the paragraph in which it appears and its meaning there. These words are indicated in the selection by a small circle (°).

dissected (2): cut apart
grisly (2): horrible
embraced (3): adopted
exorbitant (3): extreme

peers (6): people of equal standing, as in age
demise (7): death
confronted (7): faced
struck (13): made by stamping or punching a material
rapport (13): a relationship of mutual understanding
sit-coms (13): situation comedies
bonding (14): forming a close relationship

DINNER WAS RESERVED FOR THE FAMILY

Maggie Isaacs

1   I don't know about your house, but in my home when I was a kid we all met around the dinner table once a day. Usually we didn't catch more than a glance of each other in the morning. Breakfast was a quickie: a nod, a cup of coffee, and everybody's gone. Most of us weren't home for lunch. But it was understood that at night we ate dinner together and shared our day.

2   I can still remember—and it's more than thirty years ago— explaining at the dinner table how we dissected° a frog in our high school biology class that day and, as I embellished the grisly° details for effect, secretly enjoying the look of horror on my mother's face.

3   When I had my own family, we embraced° the same custom—we ate dinner together. Sure, we sometimes had the television news on, but we talked about what was happening in the world that day. The point is, we talked. About the country, the neighborhood, the school. About our friends, teachers, the exorbitant° price of everything, the need for a new couch, the condition of the car.

4   It was here that the kids first learned about the immediate world that they were growing up in and the good and bad people in it. And they found out that you could disagree about substantial issues, like politics and religion.

5   I heard my husband ask our children at the dinner table the same question my father, years ago, had asked us: "What did you learn in school today?" And we discovered early on that we'd better have an answer to that question—as did our kids much later.

6   It now seems the family dinner hour, at least as I once knew it, is a thing of the past. And I see the results everywhere. As a college teacher, I am constantly amazed at how difficult our young adults find it to talk to anyone but their peers°. With some, every sentence contains the phrase that makes me cringe: *like, you know* . . . No, in fact, I don't know.

The demise° of the family dinner hour has made the job of watching out for our children and spotting problems sooner than later more difficult. When we are confronted° with a teenager who uses drugs or alcohol, a high school student with poor study habits, or a youthful pregnancy, we ask ourselves, why didn't we see this coming, and we run for the experts. 7

It's admirable that our politicians are promising to do more about cracking down on drugs, improving education, and upgrading child care facilities. But we can't just turn our children over to others the way we turn a car over to a mechanic—a little adjustment here, a fine-tuning there. The middle-of-the-night stark truth is that we parents are responsible for our own children. It's time to look at ourselves to prevent the problems. Teachers, counselors, psychologists can be, at best, only our helpers. 8

No one denies that sitting down together every evening is harder today because of the two-income family. When we're dead tired, how much easier to let the kids sit alone with a tray in front of the television. But it was never simple. My dad worked two jobs and somehow we managed to wait dinner for him. 9

My husband started his workday at 5 p.m. during the years he was an editor of a newspaper. Those days we had our dinner shortly after 4 p.m. Not terribly convenient, to be sure; it meant snacks for the children before bed. At various times in my life I have served family dinner anywhere from 4 in the afternoon to 9 in the evening. 10

Spending "quality time" with the children, the "in" phrase today, is not something that should be left to weekends. When we look at and talk to our children across the table and they look at and talk to us night after night after night, we find out all sorts of things. 11

My parents got an idea of whom we were spending our time with, what we were doing, and how we looked. Was someone's color bad? Was someone else's appetite off? Was another youngster constantly sniffling? Had still another's personality changed; was he or she depressed? 12

Teenagers are a complicated lot, and any parent who sees a child through those years deserves a specially struck° medal. But even with the nuisance of rearranging our schedules in order to be there at dinner-time and the knowledge that we're not likely to be a hundred percent successful in building rapport°, it's more rewarding finding out about our own family than living with all the make-believe people in the TV sit-coms°. 13

We hear much about the bonding° that takes place between a mother and newborn baby. I suggest there's another bonding that takes place at the family dinner table every night. 14

Reading Comprehension Questions

Vocabulary in Context

1. The word *embellished* in "I . . . remember . . . explaining . . . how we dissected a frog . . . and, as I embellished the grisly details . . . enjoying the look of horror on my mother's face" (paragraph 2) means
   a. ignored.
   b. exaggerated.
   c. forgot.
   d. destroyed.

2. The word *substantial* in "they found out that you could disagree about substantial issues, like politics and religion" (paragraph 4) means
   a. unknown.
   b. minor.
   c. important.
   d. creative.

3. The word *upgrading* in "our politicians are promising to do more about cracking down on drugs, improving education, and upgrading child care facilities" (paragraph 8) means
   a. improving.
   b. photographing.
   c. moving.
   d. closing.

Central Point

4. Which of the following is the topic of the entire selection?
   a. Families eating dinner together
   b. Changes in society
   c. Family customs
   d. The two-income family

5. Which sentence best expresses the central point of the entire selection?
   a. When the author was young, her family ate dinner together at night.
   b. Changes in society are challenging our families.
   c. There are numerous two-income families today.
   d. To help prevent problems with children, families should eat dinner together.

Main Ideas

6. The main idea of paragraph 1 is expressed in its
   a. first sentence.
   b. second sentence.
   c. next-to-last sentence.
   d. first sentence and last sentence.

7. The main idea of paragraph 3 is expressed in its
   (a.) first sentence.
   b. second sentence.
   c. next-to-last sentence.
   d. first sentence and last sentence.

8. A main idea may cover two or more paragraphs. Which sentence best expresses the main idea of paragraphs 9 and 10?
   a. The author's husband worked nights.
   b. Children should have a snack before bedtime.
   (c.) It's possible to share dinner even in inconvenient situations.
   d. Parents must take responsibility for neighborhood children.

Supporting Details

9. According to the author, a family dinner hour allows kids to
   (a.) learn more about the world in which they are growing up.
   b. ask for help with their homework.
   c. eat a well-balanced and nourishing meal.
   d. all of the above.

10. The author feels that parents should use the family dinner hour
    a. to discuss nutrition.
    (b.) to spot problems before they become too large to handle.
    c. to watch TV together.
    d. as an excuse to leave work early.

Mapping Activity

This selection is about a problem and a suggested solution. The main points are below. Write them in the diagram where they belong.

- Parents should re-establish the family dinner hour.
- Our children need watching over.

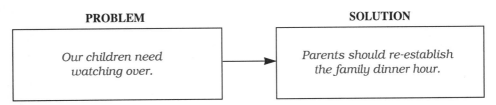

PROBLEM	SOLUTION
Our children need watching over.	*Parents should re-establish the family dinner hour.*

Discussion Questions

1. Isaacs focuses on dinner as a way for families to spend time together. What other ways are there for families to get together regularly?

2. If children aren't talking to their parents about their daily activities and problems, to whom *are* they talking? With what results? Should it matter if children don't talk about their lives to their parents?

Writing Activities

1. Write a paragraph beginning with this topic sentence: "Children benefit when parents spend time with them every day." Go on to explain and illustrate the benefits you think are most important.

2. Draw a line down the center of a notebook page. At the top of one side write, "Family Activities I Enjoyed Most." At the top of the other side write, "Family Activities I Enjoyed Least." Under the first heading, list at least two or three of your favorite family activities as a child. Under the second heading, list some of your least favorite family activities at the time. Then write a paper with this central point: "As a child, I had several favorite and least favorite family activities."

Check Your Performance			LOCATIONS OF MAIN IDEAS
Activity	*Number Right*	*Points*	*Total*
Review Test 1 (5 items)	_____	x 4 =	_____
Review Test 2 (5 items)	_____	x 4 =	_____
Review Test 3 (5 items)	_____	x 4 =	_____
Review Test 4 (10 items)	_____	x 3 =	_____
Mapping Activity (2 items)	_____	x 5 =	_____
		TOTAL SCORE =	_____%

Enter your total score onto the Reading Performance Chart: Review Tests on the inside back cover.

10

Transitions

Read the following sentences:

> I love drinking coffee. It keeps me awake at night.

The author's point in these two sentences is unclear. Does the writer love drinking coffee *because* it keeps him awake at night? Or does he like drinking coffee *even though* it keeps him awake at night? To make the author's point clear, a transition is needed. **Transitions** are words and phrases (like *because* and *even though*) that show the connections, or relationships, between ideas. They guide readers in the same way that signposts inform travelers. Here are the same two ideas, with a suitable transition added:

> I love drinking coffee *even though* it keeps me awake at night.

Now the author's point is clear. He likes drinking coffee in spite of its keeping him awake at night. Like a sign, the transition has pointed out the direction of the author's thoughts.

FIVE COMMON TYPES OF TRANSITIONS

There are five major types of transitions:

1 Words that show addition
2 Words that show time
3 Words that show comparison and/or contrast
4 Words that show illustration
5 Words that show cause and effect

Each of these transitions will be explained on the pages that follow.

1   WORDS THAT SHOW ADDITION

Put a check beside the item that is more clear:

_____   The sound on our TV set is is full of static. The picture keeps jumping out of focus.

_____   The sound on our TV set is full of static. Also, the picture keeps jumping out of focus.

The first item makes us wonder if the picture's jumping has something to do with the sound being full of static. The word *also* in the second item makes the relationship between the sentences clear. The author is discussing two separate problems with the TV set. One problem is that the sound is full of static. An *additional* problem is that the picture keeps jumping out of focus. *Also* and words like it are known as addition words.

   Addition words show you that the author is continuing in the same train of thought. They introduce ideas that *add to* what has already been mentioned. Here are some common addition words:

Addition Words

first	third	next	finally
first of all	also	in addition	last
one	another	additionally	last of all
second	moreover	furthermore	

Examples

The following examples contain addition words. Notice how these words introduce ideas that *add to* what has already been said.

   A lively workout at the end of a long day relaxes me. *Furthermore*, it makes my problems seem smaller.

   Hippos give birth underwater. They *also* nurse their young there.

   I hate my job because of the long hours. *Moreover*, my boss is often rude to me.

➤ *Practice 1*

Write a suitable addition transition from the above box in each of the following blank spaces. Try to use a variety of transitions.

   1. LaVonda's car badly needs a tuneup. _____*Furthermore*_____, the muffler needs to be replaced.

   2. _____*In addition*_____ to spoiling our softball game, the rainstorm flooded our basement.

3. Cigarettes stain your teeth, burn holes in your clothes, and give you bad breath. _____*Moreover*_____, they can kill you.

4. The human body has six pounds of skin. _____*Also*_____, it contains sixty thousand miles of blood vessels.

5. One of my hobbies is eating. _____*Another*_____ is napping.

2   WORDS THAT SHOW TIME

Put a check beside the item that is more clear:

_____ Mitch went for the job interview. He got a haircut and shaved off his mustache.

_____ Before Mitch went for the job interview, he got a haircut and shaved off his mustache.

The first item isn't clear about when Mitch got a haircut and shaved off his mustache—before or after the interview. The word *before* in the second item makes the order of the two events clear. Mitch got a shave and haircut *before* he went for the job interview. *Before* and words like it are time words.

Time words help us to understand the order in which events occur. They tell us *when* something happened in relation to something else. Here are some common time words:

Time Words

first	during	often	then
second	in the past	following	since
after	before	later	while
next	earlier	afterward	as
always	when	now	meanwhile

Examples

The following examples contain time words. Notice how these words show us *when* something takes place.

I carefully inserted a disk into the computer. *Next*, I turned on the power switch.

As I listened, Sally's story became more and more believable. *After* she finished, I was sure she had told the truth.

Following the accident, Rob was questioned by the police but was not given a ticket.

➤ *Practice 2*

Write a suitable time transition from the box on the previous page in each of the following blank spaces. Try to use a variety of transitions.

1. First paint the walls, and _____ *then* _____ install the carpeting.

2. _____ *After* _____ the death of its beloved president, the whole country mourned.

3. A change in routine _____ *often* _____ upsets my grandfather.

4. _____ *While* _____ A.J. pumped the gas, Mario checked the oil, and Richard put air in the tires.

5. Phil was furious when the TV broke _____ *during* _____ the final game of the World Series.

3   WORDS THAT SHOW COMPARISON AND/OR CONTRAST

Put a check beside the item that is more clear:

_____ For many people, the first day on a new job is a scary experience. Similarly, the first class in college can be a frightening event.

_____ For many people, the first day on a new job is a scary experience. The first class in college can be a frightening event.

In the first item, the word *similarly* makes the relationship between the sentences clear. Just as the first day on a new job can be frightening, so can being in a college class for the first time. *Similarly* and words like it or known as comparison words.

Comparison words signal that the author is pointing out a similarity between two subjects. The words tell us that the second subject is *like* the first one in some way. Here are some common comparison words:

Comparison Words

like	equal	likewise	alike
similarly	equally	in the same way	comparable
similar	identical	just as	the same as

Now again, put a check beside the item that is more clear:

_____ The dog next door is lovable. She barks a lot at night.

_____ Although the dog next door is lovable, she barks a lot at night.

The first sentence suggests that one of the lovable things about the dog is her barking. The transition *although* in the second sentence shows that the dog is lovable despite her barking. *Although* and words like it are known as contrast words.

Contrast words show that two things *differ* in one or more ways. Here are some common contrast words:

Contrast Words

in contrast	on the other hand	despite	instead
differ	however	nevertheless	unlike
even though	although	yet	but

Examples

The first two sentences below contain comparison words. Notice how these words show that things are *alike* in some way. The last two sentences contain contrast words. Notice how these words signal that one thing is *different from* another thing.

Four-year-old Kevin watched his older brother Tommy swing the bat and then tried to do it *in the same way.*

I can't stand the sound of brakes screeching. *Equally* annoying is hearing chalk squeaking on a blackboard.

The test results I got in my science lab experiment were *unlike* those reached by everyone else in the class.

Mike was angry when he didn't get a raise. His wife, *however,* took the news calmly.

➤ Practice 3

Write a suitable comparison or contrast transition from the above boxes in each of the following blank spaces. Try to use a variety of transitions.

1. I was surprised when I tried a frozen banana—it tastes just _____*like*_____ banana ice cream.

2. _____*Even though*_____ the penguin can't fly, it can swim faster than any fish.

3. Skeet is the kind of cat who waits patiently to be fed. _____*In contrast*_____, Tabby follows us around the house meowing when he's hungry.

4. _____*Despite*_____ the long winters in Minnesota, many love living there.

5. The two necklaces looked almost _____*identical*_____, yet one was worth thousands of dollars and the other cost $8.95.

4 WORDS THAT INTRODUCE EXAMPLES

Put a check beside the item that is easier to read and understand.

_____ There is too much stress in my life. For instance, I am working overtime three days a week.

_____ There is too much stress in my life. I am working overtime three days a week.

The second item makes us think that the only cause for stress is too much overtime work. The words *for instance* in the first item make it clear that the overtime work is only one of the causes of stress. *For instance* and words and phrases like it are known as example words.

Example words tell us that one or more examples will be used to illustrate a point. Here are some common example words:

Example Words

for example	to illustrate	once
for instance	such as	including

Examples

The following sentences contain example words. Notice how these words signal that one or more *examples*, or *illustrations*, are coming.

Nine states got their names from rivers that flow through them. *For example*, Minnesota is named after the Minnesota River.

Some Canadians, *including* Michael J. Fox and Peter Jennings, moved to the United States to seek their fame and fortune.

When Cesar and Mary bought an old farmhouse, they ran into many problems, *such as* rotted plumbing and a leaking roof.

➤ *Practice 4*

Write a suitable example transition from the above box in each of the following blank spaces. Try to use a variety of transitions.

1. The sun is Earth's main energy source. _____*To illustrate*_____, the sun causes seasons to change and winds to blow.

2. Some doctors feel laughing helps people who are ill. _____*For example*_____, one doctor reported that patients who joined a weekly "humor group" had less pain.

3. Nita's parents speak Spanish at times they don't want the children to understand them, _____*such as*_____ when they plan a birthday surprise.

4. This soup has some unusual vegetables, _____*including*_____ burdock and sea kale.

5. Abraham Lincoln was famous for his honesty. _____*Once*_____, when he worked at a store, he once walked several miles to return a nickel to a customer.

5 WORDS THAT SHOW CAUSE AND EFFECT

Put a check beside the item that is more clear:

_____ The baby refused to eat her breakfast. I was in a bad mood all morning.

_____ The baby refused to eat her breakfast. As a result, I was in a bad mood all morning.

In the first item, we are not sure of the relationship between the two sentences. Were there two problems: the baby's refusing to eat and the bad mood? The words *as a result* show that the bad mood was *caused* by the baby refusing to eat. *As a result* and words and phrases like it are known as cause and effect words.

Cause and effect words show that the author is discussing the *reason or reasons* something happened or the *results* of something. They signal that one event *caused* another to happen. Here are some common cause and effect words:

Cause and Effect Words

because	as a result	reason	thus
cause	result in	consequences	on account of
lead to	so	consequently	therefore
result	effect	since	due to

Examples

The following examples contain cause and effect words. Notice how these words introduce a *reason* for something or the *results* of something.

I sleep for an hour before going to night class *because* I'm very tired after work.

Since we seldom use our air conditioner, our electric bill is never too high.

Americans have become more and more interested in exercise. *As a result,* home exercise machines have become big business.

ten steps to college reading

➤ *Practice 5*

Write a suitable cause and effect transition from the box on the previous page in each of the following blank spaces. Try to use a variety of transitions.

1. Drinking enormous amounts of carrot juice can _____*cause*_____ one's skin to turn orange.

2. The teams were not finished with the game, but it had to be called _____*on account of*_____ darkness.

3. The lifeguard thought he spotted a shark. _____*Therefore*_____, the beach was closed for the day.

4. People in the Antarctic no longer wear fur _____*because*_____ quilted, layered clothing is warmer.

5. My husband likes the house to look neat. _____*Thus*_____, when things pile up on his dresser, he scrapes them all into the top drawer.

TRANSITIONS AND PATTERNS OF ORGANIZATION

You have already seen how transitions show the relationships between ideas in sentences. Similarly, entire paragraphs can be organized according to one kind of relationship. This arrangement is called the paragraph's **pattern of organization**. Each of the following five patterns of organization uses one type of transition:

1 List of items
2 Time order
3 Comparison and/or contrast
4 Definition and example
5 Cause and effect

Following are explanations of the above patterns and the type of transition each uses.

1   List of Items

A **list of items** refers to a simple series of details—such as reasons, examples, or facts—that support a point. The items are listed in any order the author feels is important. Lists of items often uses *addition* transitions, such as *first, also, another*, and *finally*. (For a longer list of addition transitions, see page 196.)

Here is an example of a paragraph organized as a list of items. The addition transitions are shown in **boldface** type.

Most people think of pizza as junk food, but pizza contains many healthful ingredients. **First of all**, the crust is rich in B vitamins, which keep the nervous system humming smoothly. **In addition**, the tomato sauce is an excellent source of vitamin A, which is essential for good vision, among other things. And **finally**, the mozzarella cheese contains protein and calcium, each of which supports good health in many ways, including keeping bones strong.

➤ Practice 6

The following paragraph is organized as a list of items. Complete the paragraph by filling in each blank with a suitable addition transition from the box. Use each transition once.

second	next	also	first

A videotape called "How to Have a Moneymaking Garage Sale" lists these tips for success. _____*First*_____, check with your insurance company to be sure that you are covered for unforeseen events such as accidents. _____*Second*_____, price your articles reasonably. Clothes should sell for about 10 percent of their original value, and appliances for 20 percent. _____*Next*_____, never publish a phone number in your advertisements. This is a good security measure and will prevent nuisance calls. _____*Also*_____, set out the items you are selling so they can all be easily seen. Customers won't buy what they cannot see.

2 Time Order

The **time order** pattern of organization presents events in the order in which they happened. The two most common kinds of time order involve 1) a series of events or stages and 2) a series of steps (directions). The time order pattern uses *time* transitions, such as *then, next*, and *after*. (For a longer list of time transitions, see page 197.)

Here is an example of a paragraph organized according to the time order pattern. The time transitions are shown in **boldface** type.

Do you have a noticeable stain or burn in your carpeting? It's easy to correct the problem. **First**, use a sharp utility knife to cut out the damaged area (but not the padding underneath). **Then** cut a patch the same size and shape from a leftover piece of carpet or a spot of carpeting that's not noticeable, such as under a radiator. **Next**, cut a piece of burlap the same size as the patch. Place the burlap where you cut out the damaged piece of carpet. **Finally**, glue the carpet patch to the burlap.

➤ *Practice 7*

The following paragraph is organized in a time order. Complete the paragraph by filling in each blank with a suitable time transition from the box. Use each transition once.

then	before	after	later

A Los Angeles lawyer named Steve is happy about the one time he didn't go to court. On a cross-country flight, the movie came on. He reached into his carry-on bag and pulled out a set of headphones. _____*Before*_____ he could put them on, a flight attendant hurried over and said that he could not use them—he had to "rent" the airline's headphones. The lawyer insisted this was not fair, and he watched the movie with his own headphones. _____*After*_____ the plane landed, airport police arrested him and charged him with "theft of the movie's soundtrack." The lawyer was detained briefly and _____*then*_____ released. The case was _____*later*_____ turned over to the local district attorney, who decided not to prosecute.

3   Comparison and/or Contrast

The **comparison and/or contrast** pattern shows how two things are similar to each other, how they differ from each other, or both. This pattern uses *comparison* transitions—such as *like, similar to*, and *just as*—and/or *contrast* words—such as *unlike, however, in contrast*. (For longer lists of comparison and contrast transitions, see pages 198 and 199.)

Here is an example of a paragraph organized according to the comparison and/or contrast pattern. The comparison transitions are shown in **boldface** type.

According to the record books, men and women can be **equally** bad drivers. On the female side is the Arkansas woman who needed 104 attempts before passing her driver's test. A **similar** driver is the Texas man who received ten tickets, drove on the wrong side of the road four times, and was involved in four hit-and-run accidents. He accomplished all this in just one year.

➤ *Practice 8*

The following paragraph both compares and contrasts. Complete the paragraph by filling in each blank with a suitable comparison or contrast transition from the box. Use each transition once.

differ	similar	however	alike

Stepfamilies and "natural" families are both alike and different in interesting ways. Both types of families have _____*similar*_____ everyday values. And both tend to have backgrounds that are _____*alike*_____ as well. _____*However*_____, the stepfamily includes more people than the natural family—ex-spouses and ex-in-laws. In addition, the conflicts each type of family faces _____*differ*_____. For example, stepchildren are likely to have bitter, angry feelings toward their stepparents. Children don't have those same feelings about their natural parents.

4   Definition and Example

In the **definition and example** pattern of organization, a textbook author introduces and defines a new term. Then he or she gives one or more examples to make sure the definition is clear. The definitions are generally introduced with *example* transitions, such as *for instance* and *to illustrate*. (For a longer list of example transitions, see page 200.)

Here is an example of a paragraph organized according to the definition and example pattern. The term being defined is shown in *italics*. The example transitions are shown in **boldface** type.

Regeneration is the ability which some animals, **such as** fish and insects, have to renew lost body parts. **For instance**, an octopus can regrow lost tentacles. And a spider can regrow lost legs. This ability can come in very handy when a limb is lost in an accident or in a fight.

➤ *Practice 9*

The following paragraph is organized in the definition and example pattern. First, underline the term being defined. Then complete the paragraph by filling in each blank with a suitable example transition from the box. Use each transition once.

including	such as	for instance

A phobia is an irrational and extreme fear of some object or situation. *For instance*, when people are so afraid of heights that they cannot cross a bridge without trembling, they are said to have a phobia. There are many other common phobias, *including* fears of snakes, water, and enclosed places. While these fears are rather common, some are more rare, *such as* the fear of hair and the fear of peanut butter sticking to the roof of one's mouth.

5 Cause and Effect

The **cause and effect** pattern involves questions such as "Why did this event happen?" or "What would be the result of doing this?" In other words, it deals with the causes and/or the effects of an event. This pattern uses *cause and effect* transitions, such as *because, as a result,* and *since.* (For a longer list of cause and effect transitions, see page 201.)

Here is an example of a paragraph organized according to the cause and effect pattern. The cause and effect transitions are shown in **boldface** type.

Go ahead and laugh—it's good for you. Laughing relaxes the facial muscles, **causing** you to look and feel less tense. It also increases the oxygen in the brain, **resulting in** a light-headed sense of well-being. In addition, laughing is a proven stress-reducer; **thus** it decreases your chances of getting stress-related illnesses.

➤ *Practice 10*

The following paragraph is organized in the cause and effect pattern. Complete the paragraph by filling in each blank with a suitable cause and effect transition from the box. Use each transition once.

consequences	so	effects	result in

Do you often raid the refrigerator at midnight? Research has shown that nighttime eating has _____*consequences*_____ most people would prefer to avoid. According to one researcher, "Eating at night . . . burns fewer calories than eating a snack in the morning." Burning fewer calories, in turn, will _____*result in*_____ putting on more weight. On any one evening, this process may put very little weight on a person. Over time, however, the _____*effects*_____ may be significant. _____*So*_____ if you often feel like munching at night, try having something light, such as an apple or a cup of herbal tea.

➤ Practice 11

Identify the pattern used in each item below. Write the letter of one of the following patterns of organization in the space provided. Each pattern is used twice.

a List of items
b Time order
c Comparison and/or contrast
d Definition and example
e Cause and effect

_____*e*_____ 1. Because he wanted to prove that he was an exceptional athlete, Deion Sanders decided to play both professional baseball and professional football.

_____*d*_____ 2. In geography, a panhandle is a strip of territory extending like the handle of a pan. The Oklahoma panhandle, for example, is a narrow part of the state that projects westward over Texas.

_____*b*_____ 3. Famous lawman Wyatt Earp was born in Monmouth, Illinois, in 1848. In 1881, he was involved in the controversial gunfight at the OK Corral. Earp died in 1929 in Los Angeles, California.

_____*c*_____ 4. Walking and gardening have similar benefits for me. Both give me exercise and let me enjoy the outdoors.

_____*a*_____ 5. Blanchard's Furniture Store is having a super sale on sofas, dining room sets, and bedroom furnishings. Coffee tables are also on sale.

_____*d*_____ 6. A stereotype is an overly generalized image of members of a group. One common stereotype, for instance, is the image of all professors as being absentminded.

_c_ 7. Glossy and flat paints have different virtues. A glossy paint is easier to keep clean than a flat paint, but a flat paint covers flaws in the wall better than a glossy one does.

_b_ 8. Toby decided he needed a day off. He stayed in bed until noon, watched game shows on TV all afternoon, then called out for a pizza for dinner. Afterward, he read until it was time for bed.

_a_ 9. Mark's family believes in volunteering. His mother delivers food to shut-ins, and his father works with the Boy Scouts. In addition, his older sister plays the piano at nursing homes.

_e_ 10. A professor of hearing sciences at Ohio University has discovered that the reason for some people's speech problems is that they lack feeling in their tongues. Thus they have trouble placing their tongues in the correct position for certain sounds.

➤ Review Test 1

To review what you've learned in this chapter, answer each of the following questions. Circle the letter of the answer you think is correct, or fill in the blank.

1. Transitions are words or phrases that signal
   a. main ideas.
   b. relationships between ideas.
   c. the importance of ideas.

2. _F_ TRUE OR FALSE? An example transition shows that two things differ.

3. _T_ TRUE OR FALSE? A cause and effect transition signals the reason that something happened or the result of something.

4. The transitions *likewise* and *similarly* are _____comparison_____ words.

5. The transitions *another* and *furthermore* are _____addition_____ words.

➤ *Review Test 2*

Complete each sentence with the appropriate transition word or phrase shown in the margin. Then circle the kind of transition you have used.

1. a. An active volcano offers some amazing sights, _____*including*_____ red-hot fountains that may burst 150 feet into the air.

   b. The transition shows:
   (illustration)   comparison   contrast

   likewise
   even though
   including

2. a. _____*Although*_____ Tom is a so-so-student himself, he pushes his little brother to study hard.

   b. The transition shows:
   time   (contrast)   cause and effect

   Although
   Often
   Since

3. a. First it started to rain. _____*Then*_____ the weather reporter said showers were likely.

   b. The transition shows:
   (time)   contrast   illustration

   However
   For instance
   Then

4. a. _____*Because*_____ Marta liked the instructor, she decided to take her for another course.

   b. The transition shows:
   comparison   time   (cause and effect)

   For example
   Because
   Just as

5. a. To avoid drunk drivers, I stay home on New Year's Eve. I _____*also*_____ stay off the road late at night.

   b. The transition shows:
   (addition)   time   contrast

   however
   also
   in contrast

6. a. Bad habits _____*such as*_____ nail biting and overeating often begin in childhood.

   b. The transition shows:
   time   contrast   (illustration)

   in contrast
   such as
   before

7. a. I hung up the phone, and _____ *then* _____ I
      began to cry.

   therefore
   then
   instead

   b. The transition shows:

      (time)   contrast   cause and effect

8. a. The wife of the inventor of the telephone couldn't use
      her husband's invention _____ *because* _____ she
      was deaf.

   and
   because
   yet

   b. The transition shows:
      addition   contrast   (cause and effect)

9. a. Stainless steel never rusts or cracks. _____ *Moreover* _____,
      it can take great changes in temperature.

   Moreover
   After
   However

   b. The transition shows:

      (addition)   time   illustration

10. a. The sailboat sped through the water _____ *like* _____
       a hot knife cutting through warm butter.

    despite
    like
    because

    b. The transition shows:
       contrast   cause and effect   (comparison)

➤ *Review Test 3*

A. Fill in each blank with the appropriate transition in the box. Use each transition once.

so	moreover	even though
such as	before	

1. My ten-year-old car needs transmission work. _____ *Moreover* _____, it could use a whole new set of tires.

2. Cheryl hasn't received a raise _____ *even though* _____ she has worked at the company now for three years.

3. The first telephone booths were mistaken for other things, _____ *such as* _____ elevators.

4. _____*Before*_____ Ella leaves her apartment, she makes sure the answering machine is turned on.

5. No one did well on the test. _____*So*_____ the teacher decided to spend more class time on the material.

B. The paragraph below includes a mixture of relationships. Fill in each blank with the appropriate transition in the box. Use each transition once.

however	leads to	like
second	therefore	

      Many women have the goal of a "perfect" body. Fitness centers know this fact. (6)_____*Therefore*_____, they run ads that feature tall, shapely models who suggest this message: "Join our center, and you'll look (7)_____*like*_____ me." Such a message is disturbing for two reasons. First, it sets up a goal that few women can reach. And (8)_____*second*_____, the main point of fitness centers should be health, not looks. It is true that physical fitness (9)_____*leads to*_____ improved looks. (10)_____*However*_____, the ads should show fit women with many types of shapes. Then more women will come to like their own body type.

➤ Review Test 4

Here is a chance to apply your understanding of transitions to a full-length reading. In this selection, the author tells about a young man who had to overcome more and work harder than most people to reach his goals. Tri Lee's story shows just how long a journey we can make if we are determined enough.

      Following the reading are questions on transitions. There are also other reading comprehension questions to help you continue to reinforce the skills taught in previous chapters.

Words to Watch

Following are some words in the reading that do not have strong context support. Each word is followed by the number of the paragraph in which it appears and its meaning there. These words are indicated in the story by a small circle (°).

    valedictorian (12): student with the highest grades in a class who gives a graduation speech *paranoid* (22): overly suspicious

immersed (23): deeply involved

protagonist (26): the main character of a story

antagonist (26): opponent

irony (26): the contrast between what is said and what is meant

persevered (27): kept on trying

diverse (28): varied

THE VOYAGE OF TRI LEE

John Kellmayer

Tri Lee came a long way in six years.   1

In 1983, at the age of twelve, Tri Lee boarded a small fishing boat,   2
about ninety feet long. There were eighty-four other Vietnamese refugees
on the boat when it departed from Cantho, Vietnam, at 4 a.m. The sea
was rough and choppy, and waves splashed over the side of the boat. The
fishing boat towed another, much smaller boat. No one was in the second
boat, only some clothes and supplies. The night was bitingly cold, and
the moon was hidden by thick clouds. The fishing boat's destination was
international waters, off the coast of Malaysia. Communist patrol boats
fired at the fishing boat as it pulled out of the harbor.

More frightened than ever, Tri watched with sad brown eyes as   3
the coast of his homeland, Vietnam, slowly disappeared from sight.

Tri, separated from his parents, was accompanied by two male   4
cousins, seventeen and eighteen years old. He had no money and few
belongings. Neither he nor his cousins spoke English. The other people
on the boat were strangers to him.

It took four days before the two boats reached their destination.   5
The eighty-five refugees then were forced to enter the smaller boat,
about forty feet long. The boat people had paid the owners of the larger
fishing boat to transport them to international waters. Once there, they
were on their own.

The eighty-five refugees crowded in the small boat faced a   6
perilous situation. Their supply of food and drinking water was limited.
There was a good chance they might never see land again.

After a few days at sea, however, they spotted a British oil rig. At   7
first, the British refused to pick up the Vietnamese. The British were
headed toward another destination and didn't want to be bothered with
the refugees. Instead, they offered only supplies and directions to

Malaysia. Then, after wishing the refugees good luck, the British got under way.

A desperate young Vietnamese woman picked up an axe and smashed a hole in the fishing boat, which immediately began to fill with water. 8

The fishing boat was rapidly sinking. Tri said a silent prayer and prepared himself for the worst. Faced with witnessing eighty-five humans drown, the English sailors then relented. The oil rig turned around, and the Vietnamese refugees were picked up. 9

Tri climbed aboard the oil rig. Standing on its deck, he looked back to watch the fishing boat disappear under water. 10

He would never look back again. 11

Six years later, Tri Lee stood on a much different platform and looked out onto a much different scene. He had been named co-valedictorian° of the senior class of a high school in a New Jersey suburb. Tri told his classmates, their parents, families, and friends about his experiences in Vietnam. He spoke about freedom, opportunities, goals, believing in yourself, and the value of hard work. 12

"I'm just a person with average ability who works as hard as I can," said Tri with a noticeable accent. "I'm not a hero by any stretch of the imagination. I'm just determined to take advantage of the opportunities that are there for me. Anybody can accomplish what I did. They just have to want it badly enough." 13

The rest of Tri Lee's story shows just how motivated he was. 14

After being rescued by the British oil rig, Tri was sent to a United Nations refugee camp on a small island called Bindong, in Malaysia. There were twenty thousand other Vietnamese refugees in the camp. Tri was separated from his cousins, who were sent to a U.N. camp in the Philippines. 15

Tri lived in the Bindong camp for four months. He describes life there as "horrible" and recalls unsanitary conditions, unappetizing foods, and sleeping on the wooden floor of a crowded hut. And there was so much conflict and fighting among the refugees that armed guards had to patrol the camp twenty-four hours a day. 16

Tri spent most of his time at Bindong studying English and trying to convince the authorities that he should be allowed to enter America. Many refugees had been turned down, but Tri had three factors in his favor. First, two older sisters had followed the same route out of Vietnam a year earlier. They, too, had passed through the camp at Bindong and had been allowed to immigrate to America. Second, Tri, 17 who studied most of the day and much of the night, had quickly learned some English. He impressed the authorities with his intelligence and motivation. Third, Tri's age was an advantage. United States immigration officials realized that it would be much easier for a twelve-year-old than for a middle-aged person to make a new start in America.

Eventually, Tri's request to enter America was granted. However, 18 he was first sent to another refugee camp in the Philippines for a few months. There he was reunited with his two cousins. He was then put on flights from Malaysia to Hong Kong, San Francisco, and Philadelphia.

The Catholic Church arranged for Tri to be placed with a foster 19 family in Voorhees, New Jersey. His two sisters were already living there with another family and attending Eastern Regional High School. Tri enrolled at the Voorhees Middle School.

Although Tri had excelled in English at the refugee camps, 20 attempting to speak and understand English well enough to fit in with American teenagers proved very difficult. As a result of his language difficulties and the problems of adjusting to a much different culture, Tri withdrew and kept to himself. In the beginning, he had few friends. He was homesick and lonely and wondered if his parents, who were still in Vietnam, were alive.

"It was a rough time for me," Tri recalls. "Back in the refugee 21 camps, we were taught sentence structure, grammar, punctuation, and formal conversational English. Everything changed, though, when I arrived in America. When people spoke fast, I had problems understanding what they were saying. Also, I couldn't begin to understand slang or street English. And American teenagers use a lot of slang and street English," he says with a smile. "In addition, I missed my home and my parents an awful lot, especially in the beginning. Still, as rough a time as I went through, it couldn't compare to what I had gone through in Vietnam, on the boat, and in the refugee camps.

"Anyhow, when I didn't understand, I thought people were 22 talking about me, maybe saying bad things about me. I thought they didn't like me, or they didn't think I belonged in their country. I suppose I got a little paranoid° for a while."

Tri was placed in a class for non-English-speaking students. He 23 received intensive instruction in reading, writing, and speaking English. Determined to overcome the language barrier, Tri excelled in his lessons and studied constantly at home. Also, he became a voracious reader. "I would read anything I could get my hands on," explains Tri. "I particularly liked reading the classics. Even today, I still prefer to read serious literature. Two of my favorite books are *All Quiet on the Western Front* and *Lord of the Flies*. I remember I read a lot of books about sports, hunting and fishing, and airplanes, too. In addition, my foster parents spoke only English. In order to survive in America, I had to learn English. I was totally immersed° in the language. In fact, if I had to give one bit of advice to non-English-speaking students, it's get rid of your native language dictionaries as soon as you can. Don't let them become too much of a crutch for you."

Once Tri felt more comfortable with informal English, he became   24
more trusting and started to make friends. Also, athletics helped Tri gain acceptance among his American classmates. An outstanding runner, Tri joined the track and cross-country teams.

When Tri entered Eastern Regional High School, his special   25
English classes were discontinued, and he was placed in the college preparatory curriculum. Tri will always remember the day during his freshman year when he realized he was finally completely comfortable with English. "I listen to the radio a lot. The way I look at it, the more English I hear, the better. In addition, I like rock music. I enjoy groups such as Van Halen and U2. Anyhow, one morning when I was in the ninth grade, I was listening to the radio and it dawned on me that I had stopped translating everything from Vietnamese into English. I had actually started *thinking in English!*"

When Tri entered his sophomore year at Eastern Regional, he   26
signed up for all honors classes. He remembers his first homework assignment in honors English II. "We had to read five short stories and identify the protagonist°, the antagonist°, the conflict, and the irony° in each story. The assignment was due the following morning. I kept going over and over those stories, afraid that I didn't know what I was doing and that I was making a lot of stupid mistakes. I put at least six hours into that assignment. I had other homework that night, too. Needless to say, I didn't get a whole lot of sleep that night."

But Tri persevered°. He continued to sign up for the most difficult   27
honors courses. And in order to devote himself exclusively to his studies, he quit the track and football teams. His course schedule was the most rigorous that the school could offer. In his senior year, Tri's schedule included honors English and French, Advanced Physics, Advanced Placement Calculus, and Pascal (a computer language course).

And Tri was no longer withdrawn. He became so popular with his   28
classmates that he was elected Student Council treasurer in his junior and senior years. He had a diverse° group of friends in high school and became a close observer of Western culture.

He noticed three significant differences between American and 29
Asian students. First, Tri was surprised at the way American young
people speak to their elders. He recalls being startled at how some of
his classmates would talk about, and sometimes to, their parents or
teachers. Also, he wasn't used to the ease with which Americans
express their feelings. Class discussions in which classmates shared
personal feelings were a completely new experience for him.
According to Tri, Vietnamese children are taught to keep their feelings
to themselves. Finally, Tri believes that American high school students
don't place the same value on education as do Asian students.

"American teenagers have so much given to them—new cars, 30
nice clothes, a comfortable place to live—that some of them get
spoiled. They take too many things for granted. My parents constantly
stressed how important school was to my sisters and me. They told me
that education is the most important thing in the world. In addition, my
background as a Vietnamese boat person makes me appreciate the
opportunities I have in America. I don't mean to criticize American
young people; they just don't know what it's like to live in a country
that was torn apart by war. They don't know what it's like to be a
refugee, to have to leave your homeland, to have your father arrested
by the Communists. They don't know how good they have it here."

Tri admits that math and science come easily to him, but he still 31
has to struggle sometimes with English. Consequently, he continues to
work hard to improve his language skills. "I make sure I read the
newspaper every day. And I'm always reading a book or magazine. The
best English teachers I've ever had have been my friends. They'll go
out of their way to help me improve my English. All along, even back
when I was struggling in junior high school, I had friends who would
tutor me and give me extra help with assignments.

"There were times I probably aggravated my friends, always 32
asking them what something meant. But they never got tired of my
questions. They never got impatient with me. As a result, I gained more
confidence. I think the confidence I acquired with my use of English
carried over to all the other areas of my life."

What was the end result of Tri's devotion to his studies? Over 33
four years at Eastern Regional High, Tri received straight A's in all
subjects. He was named to the National Honor Society during his junior
and senior years. And, of course, he was then chosen co-valedictorian
of his class.

Eventually, Tri's family was reunited in America. The 34
Communists had arrested Tri's father, an army surgeon, and placed him
in a "reeducation camp" for two years. When Tri's father was released,

he and his wife joined the growing numbers of Vietnamese boat people and followed their children to America.

Tri feels he's been changed by his experiences in America. Like 35 many American teenagers, he prefers to wear T-shirts, jeans, and sneakers. Also, he enjoys many of the same activities his American friends do. For instance, Tri goes to a lot of movies. He particularly likes the James Bond films. He attends rock concerts and major league baseball games. Tri likes to shop at the malls and enjoys talking to friends on the phone.

Tri's Americanization, however, has occasionally created conflict 36 with his parents. "My parents were close to fifty years old when they immigrated to America. When I left Viet Nam, I was a little boy. When our family was reunited in America, I had become a teenager—an American teenager. Sometimes I'll say or do something that I know makes my parents wonder about me. Still, they understand that I've been exposed to a much different culture and that some of my ideas have changed a lot. We still have a real good relationship, though. They've always been very supporting of me. And one thing that hasn't changed is that my parents constantly stress the importance of education."

Today, Tri attends Princeton University, where he is majoring in 37 mechanical engineering. His journey from a small fishing boat adrift in international waters to the Princeton campus shows the value of a firm will and hard work.

Tri shares his story on these pages in hopes that others, 38 immigrants or native-born Americans, may be uplifted and encouraged when they face hardship.

It's his way of saying thanks to America. 39

Vocabulary Questions

A. Use context clues to help you decide on the best definition for each italicized word. Then circle the letter of each choice.

1. The word *perilous* in "The eighty-five refugees crowded in the small boat faced a perilous situation. Their supply of food and drinking water was limited" (paragraph 6) means
   a. weather.
   b. dangerous.
   c. calm.
   d. guilty.

2. The word *relented* in "Faced with witnessing eighty-five humans drown, the English sailors then relented. The oil rig turned around, and the Vietnamese refugees were picked up" (paragraph 9) means
   a. cheered.
   b. turned away.
   c. hardened in attitude.
   d. gave in.

3. The word *voracious* in "he became a voracious reader. 'I would read anything I could get my hands on,' explains Tri" (paragraph 23) means
   a. science.
   b. careless.
   c. confused.
   d. very eager.

4. The word *rigorous* in "His course schedule was the most rigorous that the school could offer. In his senior year, Tri's schedule included honors English and French, Advanced Physics, Advanced Placement Calculus, and Pascal (a computer language course)" (paragraph 27) means
   a. difficult.
   b. necessary.
   c. expensive.
   d. clear.

5. The word *acquired* in "the confidence I acquired with my use of English carried over to all the other areas of my life" (paragraph 32) means
   a. avoided.
   b. gained.
   c. designed.
   d. remembered.

B. Below are words or forms of words from "Words to Watch." Write in the one that best completes each sentence.

diverse	immersed	paranoid
persevere	valedictorian	

6. Hawaii boasts of its _____*diverse*_____ ethnic groups living together in harmony.

7. Julie's long hours of study have made her the top student in the class so far. She is therefore a candidate for class _____*valedictorian*_____.

8. Peter doesn't seem to trust anyone anymore—he's become completely _____*paranoid*_____.

9. Tanya was so _____*immersed*_____ in playing the piano that she forgot to eat lunch.

10. To reach a worthwhile goal, one must _____*persevere*_____, for there may be many obstacles and setbacks.

Reading Comprehension Questions

Central Point and Main Ideas

1. Which sentence best expresses the central point of the selection?
   a. Tri Lee still has to struggle with his English at times.
   b. In just six years, Tri Lee went from a non-English-speaking refugee to the top of his high school class.
   c. Tri Lee is studying mechanical engineering at Princeton University.
   d. Many immigrants become successful Americans.

2. The main idea of paragraph 29 is expressed in its
   a. first sentence.
   b. second sentence.
   c. next-to-last sentence.
   d. last sentence.

3. Which sentence best expresses the main idea of paragraph 35?
   a. Tri has become a typical American teenager in many ways.
   b. Tri is always busy.
   c. Tri has American friends.
   d. Tri likes James Bond movies and ballgames.

4. Which sentence best expresses the main idea of paragraph 36?
   a. Tri's parents were almost fifty years old when they came to live in America.
   b. Tri was a little boy when he and his parents were separated.
   c. Tri's relationship with his parents remains good, but they are uncomfortable with some of his American ways.
   d. As always, Tri's parents remain very supportive of him and stress the importance of education.

Supporting Details

5. Tri Lee came to the United States
   a. after a few days at sea in a small boat.
   b. soon after being rescued by a British oil rig.
   c. with his entire family.
   d. after escaping from Vietnam and spending months in refugee camps.

6. According to Tri Lee, in comparison with Asian students, American students
   a. take less for granted.
   b. place greater value on their education.
   c.) have an easier time expressing their feelings.
   d. speak more respectfully to and about their elders.

Transitions

7. Each of the three differences between American and Asian students explained in paragraph 29 is introduced with an addition transition. Write those transitions below.

   _____ *First* _____   _____ *Also* _____   _____ *Finally* _____

8. The relationship of the two sentences below is one of
   a. addition.
   b. time.
   c. illustration.
   d.) cause and effect.

   . . . he still has to struggle sometimes with English. Consequently, he continues to work hard to improve his language skills. (Paragraph 31)

9. The transition that begins the sentence below signals
   a. an addition.
   b. an example.
   c.) a comparison.
   d. a contrast.

   Like many American teenagers, he prefers to wear T-shirts, jeans, and sneakers. (Paragraph 35)

10. The transition starting the second sentence below signals
    a. an addition.
    b.) an example.
    c. a comparison.
    d. a contrast.

    . . . he enjoys many of the same activities his American friends do. For instance, Tri goes to a lot of movies. (Paragraph 35)

Mapping Activity

Just as a paragraph can be mainly organized according to one pattern, so can longer selections. The main pattern of organization of this selection is time order: first one thing happened, then another, then another, and so on. We can divide those events into three main parts. Two parts are summarized in the diagram below. In the empty box, write a summary of the missing part of Tri Lee's story.

Central point: With hard work and dedication, Tri Lee overcame hardships to change himself from a refugee who knew no English to a star American student.

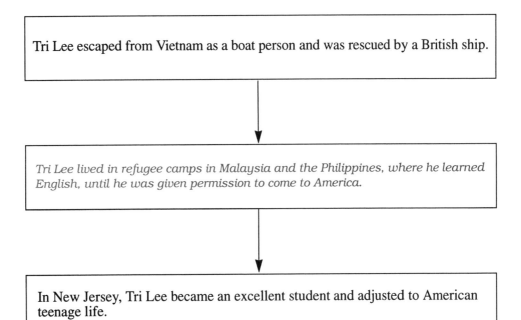

Tri Lee escaped from Vietnam as a boat person and was rescued by a British ship.

Tri Lee lived in refugee camps in Malaysia and the Philippines, where he learned English, until he was given permission to come to America.

In New Jersey, Tri Lee became an excellent student and adjusted to American teenage life.

Discussion Questions

1. Tri Lee did whatever he had to—study for hours, get little sleep, quit sports—to get good grades. What goal are you determined to reach? How do you intend to reach it?

2. Many people have come to America to escape frightening conditions in their native countries. For some like Tri Lee, the journey was difficult, even dangerous. How and when did your family (or your ancestors) come to America? What hardships, if any, did they face?

Writing Activities

1. What special goal are you determined to reach? Write a paper explaining that goal and how you intend to reach it. List the steps you plan to take and what difficulties you are prepared to face in order to make your plan a success.

2. Tri Lee faced great dangers and discomforts during his journey to America. Have you ever been in a dangerous situation? A very uncomfortable one? Write a narrative (a description of a series of events) of a time when you were in an unusual situation of danger and/or discomfort. Before starting your narrative, reread paragraphs 1–11. Note how the author uses specific details to recreate the events in Tri Lee's dramatic escape from Vietnam. Then try to include the same type of specific details in your narrative.

Check Your Performance   TRANSITIONS

Activity	Number Right	Points	Total
Review Test 1 (5 items)	_____	x 2 =	_____
Review Test 2 (10 items)	_____	x 2 =	_____
Review Test 3 (10 items)	_____	x 2 =	_____
Review Test 4 (20 items)	_____	x 2 =	_____
Mapping Activity (1 item)	_____	x 10 =	_____
	TOTAL SCORE	=	_____ %

Enter your total score onto the Reading Performance Chart: Review Tests on the inside back cover.

Part II

MASTERY TESTS

CONSONANTS: Test 1

A. Show with a check whether the boldfaced letter in each word has the soft or hard sound of **c** or **g**.

	Soft sound (as in *city* or *gem*)	Hard sound (as in *can* or *game*)
1. **c**oat		✓
2. re**c**ent	✓	
3. i**g**nite		✓
4. pa**g**e	✓	
5. fi**g**ure		✓

B. (6–10.) Fill in each blank space with the word that contains a consonant blend.

Some very *(unusual, strange)* _____*strange*_____ messages have been *(found, seen)* _____*found*_____ on gravestones. For example, the gravestone of one *(educator, professor)* _____*professor*_____ reads, "School is out. Teacher has gone home." Written on another *(grave, tomb)* _____*grave*_____ is this message: "I told you I was sick!" And here's one that is even *(odder, briefer)* _____*briefer*_____: "That is all."

C. (11–20.) Circle each word that contains a consonant digraph (a pair of consonants with only one sound). There are ten such words.

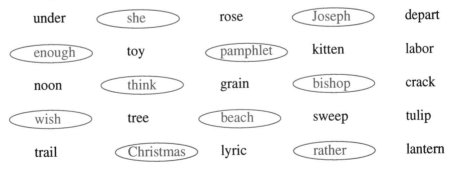

under   (she)   rose   (Joseph)   depart

(enough)   toy   (pamphlet)   kitten   labor

noon   (think)   grain   (bishop)   crack

(wish)   tree   (beach)   sweep   tulip

trail   (Christmas)   lyric   (rather)   lantern

(Continues on next page)

D. Complete each sentence with the word that contains a silent consonant.

21. To relax, my sister sometimes likes to *(paint, knit)* _____*knit*_____.

22. The chief of a Midwestern Native American tribe was buried *(sitting, lying)* _____*sitting*_____ on his favorite horse.

23. Leaving my homework where the dog could get at it was a *(stupid, dumb)* _____*dumb*_____ mistake.

24. By the time we finished playing tennis, I was soaked with sweat. Even my *(wristband, headband)* _____*wristband*_____ was all wet.

25. Dr. Frank N. Stein was late for the brain transplant because he was *(lost, stuck)* _____*stuck*_____ in traffic.

CONSONANTS: Test 2

A. Complete each sentence with the word which has the hard sound of **c** (as in *can*) or **g** (as in *game*).

1. My grandmother always added *(celery, cabbage)* _____*cabbage*_____ to her bean soup.

2. Zena's hair stuck straight up, and the ends were tinted *(gold, orange)* _____*gold*_____.

3. The *(castle, palace)* _____*castle*_____ had a secret room, where the prince kept his diary.

4. *(Corinne, Alice)* _____*Corinne*_____ felt out of place at her father's high school reunion.

5. Many *(geniuses, greats)* _____*greats*_____ did poorly in school, including Thomas Edison and Albert Einstein.

B. (6–10.) Circle each word that contains one or more consonant blends. There are five such words.

comet   (glad)   (grin)   parade   pathway

(prank)   redwood   silly   (skill)   (slim)

C. Find each word that contains a consonant digraph (a pair of consonants with only one sound), and write it in the appropriate blank space.

> Phil had planned for this day for two years. He had worked evenings and summers, saving all he could. Finally, he had enough money to buy a car he had dreamed of. He walked into a local showroom, pointed to a red Corvette, and wrote a check for a down payment.

11. _____*Phil*_____   14. _____*showroom*_____

12. _____*this*_____   15. _____*check*_____

13. _____*enough*_____

(Continues on next page)

D. (16–25.) Circle each word in the box that contains a silent consonant. All of the words are either straight across or straight down. Here are the words to look for:

comb	duck	knock	knot	numb
sign	tack	wrap	wreck	write

w	r	a	p		s	i	g	n
z	f	w	f	l	g	o	f	h
c	h	r	t	a	c	k	p	z
o	u	i	m	s	t	p	q	f
m	c	t	s	w	r	e	c	k
b	n	e	h	o	t	z	o	n
q	u	e	d	u	c	k	o	o
z	m	t	h	e	i	u	m	c
o	b	k	k	n	o	t	t	k

CONSONANTS: Test 3

A. Show with a check whether the boldfaced letter in each word has the soft or hard sound of **c** or **g**.

	Soft sound (as in *city* or *gem*)	Hard sound (as in *can* or *game*)
1. sa**g**a		✓
2. **c**eiling	✓	
3. **g**inger	✓	
4. lettu**c**e	✓	
5. re**c**ord		✓

B. (6–10.) Fill in each blank space with the word that contains a consonant blend.

Have you been to the zoo lately? If your answer is no, you are in for a *(surprise, shock)* _____surprise_____ on your next visit. Zoos are changing. They were first *(created, used)* _____created_____ to show off rare animals, which were housed in *(tiny, small)* _____small_____ cages. Now, zoos *(raise, breed)* _____breed_____ animals in danger of disappearing. Also, the animals are now housed in spaces that are larger and more like the *(environments, areas)* _____environments_____ they are used to in their homelands.

(Continues on next page)

C. (11–20.) Circle each word in the box that contains a consonant digraph (a pair of consonants with only one sound). All of the words are either straight across or straight down. Here are the words to look for:

ashore	bath	chip	death	dish
gopher	photo	show	them	tough

a	b	a	t	h	q	u	u	w
c	r	x	h	n	u	s	d	t
h	f	d	e	a	t	h	c	o
i	p	u	m	g	r	o	f	u
p	h	n	f	o	b	w	r	g
g	o	p	h	e	r	z	y	h
l	t	m	g	p	c	w	z	m
g	o	t	a	s	h	o	r	e
d	i	s	h	u	i	n	g	b

D. (21–25.) Circle each word that contains a silent consonant. There are five such words.

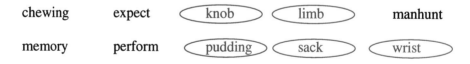

chewing	expect	knob	limb	manhunt
memory	perform	pudding	sack	wrist

CONSONANTS: Test 4

A. Find each word that contains a hard **c** (as in *can*) or **g** (as in *game*), and write it in the appropriate blank space.

> The concert to benefit earthquake victims was worth the price we paid. The music was great. I just wish that George and I had been able to sit nearer to the stage. We were so far away we were barely able to see the groups that played.

1. _____*concert*_____   4. _____*great*_____

2. _____*victims*_____   5. _____*groups*_____

3. _____*music*_____

B. (6–15.) Circle each word in the box that contains a consonant blend. All of the words are either straight across or straight down. Here are the words to look for:

blush	brief	faint	hunt	round
skate	sneeze	special	stamp	trip

h	o	h	o	s	t	a	m	p
u	f	t	x	n	w	h	y	s
n	b	r	i	e	f	n	k	f
t	h	i	s	e	v	n	t	a
i	o	p	b	z	x	s	l	i
s	k	a	t	e	f	r	q	n
k	a	t	r	o	u	n	d	t
b	l	u	s	h	i	h	e	r
r	u	s	p	e	c	i	a	l

(Continues on next page)

C. (16–20.) Circle each word that contains a consonant digraph (a pair of consonants that have only one sound). There are five such words.

(blush)   bullfrog   cartoon   (cheap)   desk

eagle   (phase)   (rough)   (thousand)   violet

D. (21–25.) Fill in each blank with the answer that contains at least one silent consonant.

Have you ever tried to *(compose, write)* _____*write*_____ an

essay only to stare at a blank sheet of paper because no ideas come to your

mind? This happens to everyone, even *(well-known, famous)*

_____*well-known*_____ authors. Some say it is helpful to get away from the

project for a while and do something *(entirely, wholly)*

_____*wholly*_____ different. Others say that is a *(wrong, poor)*

_____*wrong*_____ approach. They prefer to jot down anything on

the paper. They feel that *(with luck, in time)* _____*with luck*_____ ,

jotting will help them to gather their thoughts and get on with the writing.

CONSONANTS: Test 5

A. Complete each sentence with the word that has a soft **c** (as in *city*) or **g** (as in *gem*).

1. A common *(practice, custom)* _____*practice*_____ in many households is to give thanks for food before a meal.

2. I like Al's Supermarket because the salesclerks there are very *(courteous, civil)* _____*civil*_____.

3. Martina was proud when she was named the outstanding *(educator, principal)* _____*principal*_____ of her district.

4. The *(vegetation, garden)* _____*vegetation*_____ in back has been ignored too long and is now wild and overgrown.

5. In ancient *(England, Egypt)* _____*Egypt*_____, a person who killed a cat could be punished by death.

B. Complete each sentence with the word that has at least one consonant blend.

6. President Teddy Roosevelt once said, "Speak *(softly, low)* _____*softly*_____ and carry a big stick."

7. When I need to relax, I sit down and play my *(harp, guitar)* _____*harp*_____.

8. If you *(run, bump)* _____*bump*_____ into another car, it is a good idea to check for damage.

9. Nora was in a rush, so she ordered only coffee and a *(bran, cherry)* _____*bran*_____ muffin.

10. Whenever my father said, "This will hurt me more than you," I knew he was about to *(punish, spank)* _____*spank*_____ me.

(Continues on next page)

C. Complete each sentence with the word that has a consonant digraph.

11. Some *(fish, birds)* _____*fish*_____ can be frozen alive and then brought back to life by being defrosted.

12. Maleek decided to include a *(diagram, graph)* _____*graph*_____ in his research paper.

13. If you are not satisfied with your meal in a restaurant, send it back to the *(chef, cook)* _____*chef*_____.

14. Boris *(believed, thought)* _____*thought*_____ he looked tough when his beard had three days' growth.

15. When her class *(giggled, laughed)* _____*laughed*_____, Professor McNee realized that she was lecturing on the wrong subject.

D. Complete each sentence with the word that has at least one silent consonant.

16. Even experienced skaters sometimes *(fall, trip)* _____*fall*_____.

17. I liked Tom Hanks's latest movie, but my sister thought it was *(dumb, stupid)* _____*dumb*_____.

18. In Africa, there is a large bearded antelope called a *(gnu, wildebeast)* _____*gnu*_____.

19. When my boss starts *(coughing, wheezing)* _____*wheezing*_____, she knows she's catching a cold.

20. We could tell it was Harold at the door because of his unusual way of *(knocking, pounding)* _____*knocking*_____.

CONSONANTS: Test 6

A. (1–5.) Fill in each blank with the word that has at least one hard **c** or **g** sound.

A number of professional sports are competing for the attention of the American *(audience, public)* _____*public*_____ . Baseball and football used to be the most popular sports. However, labor problems have resulted in fewer fans. This change has opened the door for other sports. Basketball has begun to win over *(increasing, large)* _____*increasing*_____ numbers of fans. Hockey, the national sport of *(Iceland, Canada)* _____*Canada*_____ , has seen its popularity *(advance, grow)* _____*grow*_____ , as well. And on the horizon is the world's most popular sport, (auto races, soccer) _____*soccer*_____ .

B. (6–10.) Fill in each blank with the word that contains at least one consonant blend.

Because he had to stay late at the *(bank, office)* _____*bank*_____ where he worked, Antonio would be late for his date with *(Cary, Brenda)* _____*Brenda*_____ . He decided it would be *(best, wise)* _____*best*_____ to call her and *(explain, reveal)* _____*explain*_____ his problem. He told her to go on to the movie without him. He would meet her at the *(front, side)* _____*front*_____ door of the theater as soon as he could.

C. (11–15.) Fill in each blank with the word that contains at least one consonant digraph.

Even though Mavis and Travis were twins, they had different goals. Both wanted to help people, but not in the same way. Mavis wanted to become a *(professor, teacher)* _____*teacher*_____ . She felt that teaching would enable her to help people to gain *(enough, sufficient)* _____*enough*_____ knowledge to reach their own goals. However, Travis had a different *(view, philosophy)* _____*philosophy*_____ . He *(wanted, wished)* _____*wished*_____ to become *(prosperous, wealthy)* _____*wealthy*_____ and use part of his fortune to help people to start their own businesses.

(Continues on next page)

D. (16–20.) Fill in each blank with the word that contains a silent consonant.

      Parker Ranch is on the island of Hawaii. It is the *(biggest, largest)* _____*biggest*_____ privately owned cattle ranch in the United States. The ranch was once open space used mostly by Hawaiian *(ducks, geese)* _____*ducks*_____. It became a ranch over a hundred years ago *(after, when)* _____*when*_____ the king of Hawaii was given a gift of five cows and a bull. The animals multiplied, and the king needed help in *(controlling, managing)* _____*controlling*_____ them. He asked a friend, Mr. Parker, to oversee the animals. Parker did so, and the king *(signed over, granted)* _____*signed over*_____ to him two acres of land for his own ranch. The ranch continued to grow and is now over 330 square miles.

VOWELS: Test 1

A. For each item below, write a word from the box with the vowel sound listed. When you are finished, you will have used all the words in the box.

cute	grant	not	rope	skip
slide	stage	stun	tent	three

1. Short **a** sound: _____grant_____

2. Long **a** sound: _____stage_____

3. Short **e** sound: _____tent_____

4. Long **e** sound: _____three_____

5. Short **i** sound: _____skip_____

6. Long **i** sound: _____slide_____

7. Short **o** sound: _____not_____

8. Long **o** sound: _____rope_____

9. Short **u** sound: _____stun_____

10. Long **u** sound: _____cute_____

B. Here are the rules for long vowel sounds:

a	When a word ends in a vowel-consonant-**e**, the vowel before the consonant is long and the final **e** is silent.
b	When two of certain vowels are together in a word, the first one is long and the second is silent.
c	A single vowel at the end of a word (other than a silent **e**) usually has a long sound.

Beside each word, write the letter of the rule that applies. Write a short explanation as well. Note the example.

Example

boat	_b_	*The "o" is long and the "a" is silent.*
11. hope	_a_	*The "o" is long and the "e" is silent.*
12. she	_c_	*The "e" is long.*
13. neat	_b_	*The "e" is long and the "a" is silent.*
14. cane	_a_	*The "a" is long and the "e" is silent.*
15. goal	_b_	*The "o" is long and the "a" is silent.*

(Continues on next page)

C. Here are the rules for **y** as a vowel:

> **a** In the middle of a word, **y** usually sounds like short **i**.
> **b** At the end of a one-syllable word, **y** sounds like long **i**.
> **c** At the end of a word with more than one syllable, **y** sounds like long **e**.

Beside each word, identify the **y** sound by writing in one of the following:

ĭ (short **i**)   ī (long **i**)   ē (long **e**)

Write a short explanation as well. Note the example.

Example

empty   ē   *At end of word with more than one syllable*

16. ply   ī   *At end of one-syllable word*

17. happy   ē   *At end of word with more than one syllable*

18. syrup   ĭ   *In middle of word*

19. worry   ē   *At end of word with more than one syllable*

20. try   ī   *At end of one-syllable word*

VOWELS: Test 2

A. Beside each word, write its vowel sound.

If the vowel is short, write **ă, ĕ, ĭ, ŏ,** or **ŭ**.

If the vowel is long, write **ā, ē, ī, ō,** or **ū**.

If the vowel is followed by **r**, write **r**.

1. bleed	ē		6. pot	ŏ
2. trick	ĭ		7. stay	ā
3. park	r		8. write	ī
4. check	ĕ		9. cute	ū
5. stump	ŭ		10. fork	r

B. Complete each sentence with the word with a *short* vowel. (Remember that vowels followed by an **r** are neither long nor short.)

11. When the dog relaxes, her ears *(drape, drop, droop)* _____ drop _____.

12. The term paper took *(four, five, ten)* _____ ten _____ hours longer than Adriana expected.

13. The fifty-year-old tree in back is full of *(sap, leaves, life)* _____ sap _____.

14. On weekends, Francisco often unwinds by taking a long *(drive, run, hike)* _____ run _____ in the country.

15. A glass window pane and a(n) *(oak, steel, brick)* _____ brick _____ wall are made with the same main ingredient: sand.

(Continues on next page)

C. Here are the rules for long vowel sounds:

> **a** When a word ends in a vowel-consonant-**e**, the vowel before the consonant is long and the final **e** is silent.
>
> **b** When two of certain vowels are together in a word, the first one is long and the second is silent.
>
> **c** A single vowel at the end of a word (other than a silent **e**) usually has a long sound.

Use the rules to help you place the following words in the right spaces.

hi	treat	snake	wrote	soap

*Silent-**e** Rule*	*Two-Vowels-Together Rule*	*Final Vowel Rule*
16. _snake_	18. _treat_	20. _hi_
17. _wrote_	19. _soap_	

D. Show with a check whether the **oo** in each word is long or short.

	Long oo	*Short oo*
21. room	✓	
22. crook		✓
23. noon	✓	
24. stood		✓
25. proof	✓	

VOWELS: Test 3

A. Circle each word in the box that contains a short vowel sound. All of the words appear either straight across or straight down. Then write each word under the correct heading below.

Here are the words to look for:

add	bench	chin	flat	nun
plod	quilt	romp	smell	stuff

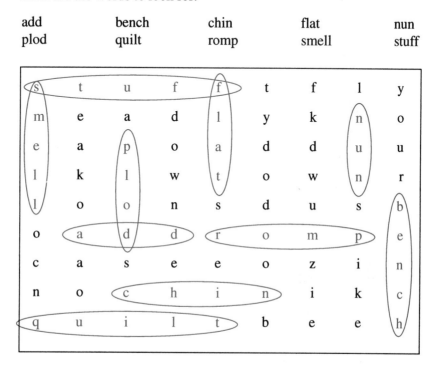

	Short a		*Short e*		*Short i*		*Short o*		*Short u*
1.	add	3.	bench	5.	chin	7.	plod	9.	nun
2.	flat	4.	smell	6.	quilt	8.	romp	10.	stuff

B. Complete each sentence with the word that has a *long* vowel sound. (Remember that vowels followed by an **r** are neither long nor short.)

11. The tune-up on my car at Harry's Rapid Service Shop was (*fast, quick, speedy*) _____ speedy _____ but poorly done.

12. I asked the waitress to give the check to (*him, her, you*) _____ you _____.

(Continues on next page)

13. After a rain, the children like to *(push, float, sink)* _____*float*_____ paper boats in the sidewalk puddles.

14. Eager to make hot cocoa, we hurried in from the *(bite, chill, numbing)* _____*bite*_____ of the winter wind.

15. If you *(put, install, place)* _____*place*_____ a special radio signal in your car, the police can trace the car if it's stolen.

C. Show with a check whether the **y** in each word sounds like ĭ, ī, or ē.

	Short i	*Long i*	*Long e*
16. holy			✓
17. spy		✓	
18. symbol	✓		
19. funny			✓
20. cry		✓	

D. Find the five words that contain **oo** in the paragraph below. Write the words in the blank spaces and use a check to show whether each **oo** has a long or short sound.

Laura's new apartment had drawbacks. Her bed just barely fit in the bedroom, and the bath area was so small that she had trouble finding space for toothpaste and shampoo. Also, a look around revealed how much of the place was in need of repair. She needed to get out her tools.

	Long oo	*Short oo*
21. _____*bedroom*_____	✓	
22. _____*toothpaste*_____	✓	
23. _____*shampoo*_____	✓	
24. _____*look*_____		✓
25. _____*tools*_____	✓	

VOWELS: Test 4

A. Circle each word in the box that contains a *long* vowel sound. All of the words appear either straight across or straight down. Then write each word under the correct heading below.

Here are the words to look for:

boat	cheese	claim	cute	few
glide	stain	sweet	toast	wise

s	s	w	e	e	t	g	w	c
s	f	e	w	k	o	l	i	h
t	o	n	v	y	w	i	s	e
a	p	t	c	a	n	d	k	e
i	b	p	l	q	n	e	v	s
n	o	n	a	n	u	n	e	e
q	a	c	i	l	i	t	x	n
r	t	o	m	o	c	u	t	e
y	d	t	o	a	s	t	o	n

Long *a*		Long *e*		Long *i*		Long *o*		Long *u*	
1. claim	3.	cheese	5.	glide	7.	boat	9.	cute
2. stain	4.	sweet	6.	wise	8.	toast	10.	few

B. Complete each sentence by writing in the word with a *short* vowel. (Remember that vowels followed by **r** are neither long nor short.)

11. My plants all *(die, wilt, droop)* _____wilt_____ from being watered either too much or too little.

12. Enrique was not looking forward to spending two weeks with his aunt in *(New York, Montana, Ohio)* _____Montana_____.

(Continues on next page)

13. Heart disease accounts for one *(half, third, fourth)* _____*half*_____ of all American deaths each year.

14. I turned to tell my *(wife, date, sister)* _____*sister*_____ that I thought the play was boring, but she was asleep.

15. Even though I was lost, I knew that if I kept driving *(north, west, east)* _____*west*_____, I would reach the ocean.

C. Here are the rules for long vowel sounds:

a	When a word ends in a vowel-consonant-e, the vowel before the consonant is long and the final **e** is silent.
b	When two of certain vowels are together in a word, the first one is long and the second is silent.
c	A single vowel at the end of a word (other than a silent **e**) usually has a long sound.

Beside each word, write the letter of the rule that applies.

16. beef __*b*__   21. grime __*a*__

17. shape __*a*__   22. we __*c*__

18. no __*c*__   23. slope __*a*__

19. bail __*b*__   24. train __*b*__

20. cream __*b*__   25. loaf __*b*__

VOWELS: Test 5

A. Complete each sentence with a word that has a *short* vowel sound. (Remember that vowels followed by an **r** are neither long nor short.)

1. Sharri's *(apple, peach, date)* _____apple_____ tree bore so much fruit that she gave much of it away.

2. Now a democracy, Australia was once ruled by a *(king, queen, czar)* _____king_____.

3. Amad keeps a spare key *(over, near, under)* _____under_____ a big rock by his back door.

4. A triathlon consists of three *(parts, events, sports)* _____events_____: a swim, a bike ride, and a run.

5. It takes four hours to hard-boil a(n) *(crane, ostrich, lark)* _____ostrich_____ egg.

B. Complete each sentence with the word that has a *long* vowel sound. (Remember that vowels followed by an **r** are neither long nor short.) Then, using the rules for long vowel sounds below, write the letter of the rule the word follows.

Here are the rules for long vowel sounds:

a	When a word ends in a vowel-consonant-**e**, the vowel before the consonant is long and the final **e** is silent.
b	When two of certain vowels are together in a word, the first one is long and the second is silent.
c	A single vowel at the end of a word (other than a silent **e**) usually has a long sound.

6. Although gorillas can *(maim, kill, crush)* _____maim_____ just about anything, they are very gentle creatures.

7. The word you chose follows this rule: ___b___

8. The way Mimi remembers a phone number is to repeat it *(six, seven, nine)* _____nine_____ times.

9. The word you chose follows this rule: ___a___

(Continues on next page)

245

10. My daughter's favorite TV (*character, actor, hero*) _____hero_____ is Mr. Rogers.

11. The word you chose follows this rule: __c__

12. When it started raining hard, Chim was forced to (*race, dash, run*) _____race_____ across the parking lot to his car.

13. The word you chose follows this rule: __a__

14. Scientists continue to (*goad, prod, urge*) _____goad_____ us to eat breakfast, as it is the most important meal of the day.

15. The word you chose follows this rule: __b__

C. Complete the sentence with the word that has a **y** that sounds like a short **i**.

16. Many scientists believe that tales of the hairy humanlike creature called Bigfoot are just (*myth, fantasy, yarns*) _____myth_____.

D. Complete each sentence with the word that has a **y** that sounds like a long **i**.

17. Wily's (*crafty, sly, sneaky*) _____sly_____ ways got him in trouble with his family and friends.

18. The weather report called for continued (*cloudy, dry, foggy*) _____dry_____ conditions.

E. Complete each sentence with the word that has a **y** that sounds like a long **e**.

19. When the fire started, there was no time to (*delay, dally, stay*) _____dally_____ — everyone had to leave fast.

20. Ever since she got a toy piano, my little sister wants to (*carry, play, try*) _____carry_____ it morning, noon, and night.

VOWELS: Test 6

A. (1–5.) Fill in each blank with the word that has a *short* vowel sound.

Most owls nest in trees and come out at night to *(eat, fly, hunt)* _____*hunt*_____. An exception is the burrowing owl. This *(little, tiny, wee)* _____*little*_____ owl is only about *(six, eight, nine)* _____*six*_____ inches high. As its name suggests, it digs its nests underground. This owl hunts during the day and can be seen sitting on fenceposts near its *(home, mate, nest)* _____*nest*_____. Once common throughout the Southwest, the burrowing owl is in danger of extinction due mostly to *(huge, large, vast)* _____*vast*_____ development projects.

B. (6–15.) In the following paragraph, ten words are boldfaced. Each word is pronounced according to one of the rules or sounds listed below. Write the words in the appropriate spaces.

Where would **we** be without the **fish** in the sea? Half of the world's population depends on fish for its **main** source of food. **Yet** there are danger signs that the oceans are being overfished. Four of the richest fishing areas of the **world** include the **west** coast of Australia, the west **coast** of South America, the Mediterranean Sea, and the **east** coast of Asia. In the past **five** years, the fish catch in each of **these** areas has declined significantly.

Silent-e Rule	*Two-Vowels-Together Rule*	*Final Single Vowel Rule*
6. *five*	8. *main*	11. *we*
7. *these*	9. *coast*	
	10. *east*	

Short Vowel Sounds	*Sounds of Vowels Followed by r*
12. *fish*	15. *world*
13. *Yet*	
14. *west*	

(Continues on next page)

C. Find the five words that contain **oo** in the paragraph below. Write the words in the blank spaces and use a check to show whether each **oo** has a long or short sound.

> The hot summer day was too much for Salvatore. Rather than stay around the house and watch TV all day, he thought it might be nice to take the family on a picnic. "We'll pick up some food on the way and relax by a babbling brook." Salvatore's wife, Diana, loved the idea. The last thing she wanted to do was cook in a hot kitchen. And the kids liked the idea, as well. Sal Jr. figured it was a great opportunity to play touch football. And Dee Dee saw herself sitting beneath a large oak tree, reading a romance novel.

		Long oo	Short oo
16.	too	✓	
17.	food	✓	
18.	brook		✓
19.	cook		✓
20.	football		✓

SYLLABLES: Test 1

A. Using the rules shown in the box, divide the following words into syllables. For each word, also write the number of the rule that applies. Note the example.

---

1. Divide between two consonants.

2. Divide before a single consonant.

	Syllable Division	Rule Number
Example: climate	cli-mate	2
1. forward	for-ward	1
2. occur	oc-cur	1
3. complex	com-plex	1
4. welcome	wel-come	1
5. unite	u-nite	2
6. angel	an-gel	2

B. Using the rules shown in the box, divide the following words into syllables. For each word, also write the number of the rule that applies. Note the example.

---

3. Divide before a consonant followed by *le*.

4. Divide after prefixes and before suffixes.

5. Divide between the words in a compound word.

	Syllable Division	Rule Number
Example: moonlight	moon-light	5
7. cripple	crip-ple	3
8. gladly	glad-ly	4
9. hallway	hall-way	5
10. distrust	dis-trust	4
11. puzzle	puz-zle	3
12. cloudburst	cloud-burst	5
13. goodness	good-ness	4

(Continues on next page)

C. Complete each sentence by underlining the compound word. Then, in the space provided, break the compound word into syllables.

14. Kenny's first stop in registering for classes was the school (<u>fieldhouse</u>, *auditorium, gymnasium*).

   field-house

15. Studies show that single men are more likely than husbands to have an emotional (*disorder,* <u>breakdown</u>, *collapse*).

   break-down

16. The mugger ran off with Brenda's purse, removed the wallet, and then tossed the purse onto the (*avenue, pavement,* <u>sidewalk</u>).

   side-walk

17. A tidal wave begins with a(n) (<u>landslide</u>, *movement, shaking*) on the ocean floor.

   land-slide

D. Underline the three words below that have a prefix or suffix. Then, in the spaces provided, write those words, dividing them into syllables.

<u>movement</u>   kneepad   <u>depart</u>
statue   <u>badly</u>   pilot

18. ____*move-ment*____   19. ____*de-part*____   20. ____*bad-ly*____

SYLLABLES: Test 2

A. Using the rules shown in the box, divide the following words into syllables. For each division, also write the number of the rule that applies. Note the example.

> 1. **Divide between two consonants.**
> 2. **Divide before a single consonant.**

	Syllable Division	*Rule Numbers*	
Example: abandon	*a-ban-don*	*2*	*1*
1. entertain	*en-ter-tain*	*1*	*1*
2. diplomat	*dip-lo-mat*	*1*	*2*
3. absolute	*ab-so-lute*	*1*	*2*
4. hibernate	*hi-ber-nate*	*2*	*1*
5. alcohol	*al-co-hol*	*1*	*2*
6. terminal	*ter-mi-nal*	*1*	*2*

B. Using the rules shown in the box, divide the following words into syllables. For each division, also write the number of the rule that applies. Note the example.

> 3. **Divide before a consonant followed by *le*.**
> 4. **Divide after prefixes and before suffixes.**
> 5. **Divide between the words in a compound word.**

	Syllable Division	*Rule Numbers*	
Example: subtitle	*sub-ti-tle*	*4*	*3*
7. unfriendly	*un-friend-ly*	*4*	*4*
8. outfielder	*out-field-er*	*5*	*4*
9. previewing	*pre-view-ing*	*4*	*4*
10. rattlesnake	*rat-tle-snake*	*3*	*5*
11. newlywed	*new-ly-wed*	*4*	*5*
12. grandmother	*grand-moth-er*	*5*	*4*
13. puzzlement	*puz-zle-ment*	*3*	*4*

(Continues on next page)

C. Complete each sentence by underlining the word with a prefix or suffix. Then, in the space provided, break the underlined word into syllables.

14. I saw enough of the (<u>preview</u>, ad, plotline) to know that I didn't want to see the movie.

    pre-view

15. Dr. Nomo is known as a (splendid, <u>skillful</u>, superb) surgeon.

    skill-ful

16. The (<u>report</u>, article, newscast) said that the steam pipe explosion was heard more than a mile away.

    re-port

17. Only when we pay for college (credit, <u>instruction</u>, coursework) do we appreciate high-school's cost-free education.

    in-struc-tion

D. Underline the three compound words below. Then break those words into syllables in the spaces provided.

pasture   <u>daybreak</u>   hundred
<u>schoolroom</u>   magnet   <u>pathway</u>

18.   *day-break*   19.   *school-room*   20.   *path-way*

SYLLABLES: Test 3

A. Using the rules shown in the box, divide the following words into syllables. Then write the numbers of the two rules that apply. For each word, first use any of rules 3–5 that apply before using rule 1 or 2.

> 1. **Divide between two consonants.**
> 2. **Divide before a single consonant.**
> 3. **Divide before a consonant followed by *le*.**
> 4. **Divide after prefixes and before suffixes.**
> 5. **Divide between the words in a compound word.**

		Syllable Division	*Rule Numbers*	
1.	tomato	to-ma-to	2	2
2.	algebra	al-ge-bra	1	2
3.	disconnect	dis-con-nect	4	1
4.	sincerely	sin-cere-ly	1	4
5.	incubate	in-cu-bate	4	2
6.	housekeeping	house-keep-ing	5	4
7.	solution	so-lu-tion	2	4
8.	belonging	be-long-ing	2	4
9.	anklebone	an-kle-bone	3	5
10.	photograph	pho-to-graph	2	5

B. Complete each of the words below with one of the following **-le** combinations. Use each **-le** combination once.

-ble	**-dle**	**-gle**	**-ple**	**-tle**

11. nee _____nee-dle_____   14. tur _____tur-tle_____

12. dim _____dim-ple_____   15. jug _____jug-gle_____

13. fum _____fum-ble_____

(Continues on next page)

C. Circle the ten compound words in the puzzle. All of the words run either straight across or straight down. Then write each word in the space provided, breaking it into syllables. Here are the words you are looking for:

airport	blueprint	doorstop	downtown	necktie
postcard	restroom	snowball	suitcase	wishbone

n	o	s	u	i	t	c	a	s	e
e	b	l	s	o	o	u	i	o	r
c	l	u	e	w	h	y	r	h	o
k	u	e	w	h	e	n	p	t	o
t	e	w	i	s	h	b	o	n	e
i	p	o	s	t	c	a	r	d	v
e	r	d	o	o	r	s	t	o	p
d	i	r	e	s	t	r	o	o	m
s	n	o	w	b	a	l	l	l	a
s	t	d	o	w	n	t	o	w	n

16.	air-port	21.	post-card
17.	blue-print	22.	rest-room
18.	door-stop	23.	snow-ball
19.	down-town	24.	suit-case
20.	neck-tie	25.	wish-bone

SYLLABLES: Test 4

A. Using the rules shown in the box, divide the following words into syllables. Then write the numbers of the two rules that apply. For each word, first use any of rules 3–5 that apply before using rule 1 or 2.

> 1. **Divide between two consonants.**
> 2. **Divide before a single consonant.**
> 3. **Divide before a consonant followed by *le*.**
> 4. **Divide after prefixes and before suffixes.**
> 5. **Divide between the words in a compound word.**

	Syllable Division	*Rule Numbers*	
1. outstanding	out-stand-ing	5	4
2. rearrange	re-ar-range	4	1
3. settlement	set-tle-ment	3	4
4. incorrect	in-cor-rect	4	1
5. following	fol-low-ing	1	4
6. unholy	un-ho-ly	4	4
7. electron	e-lec-tron	2	1
8. expensive	ex-pen-sive	4	1
9. vanilla	va-nil-la	2	1
10. pillowcase	pil-low-case	1	5

B. Underline the five words that end in a consonant followed by **-le**. Then break up the words into syllables in the blank spaces below.

>   See if you can solve this <u>riddle</u>. In a <u>terrible</u> car accident, a father is killed and his young son seriously hurt. The boy is rushed to the hospital, where the surgeon on duty takes one look at the <u>horrible</u> sight and says, "I'm <u>unable</u> to operate on this boy. He's my son." How is this <u>possible</u>? The answer, of course, is this: The surgeon is the boy's mother.

11. _____rid-dle_____   14. _____un-a-ble_____

12. _____ter-ri-ble_____   15. _____pos-si-ble_____

13. _____hor-ri-ble_____

(Continues on next page)

C. Circle the ten words with prefixes and suffixes in the puzzle. All of the words run either straight across or straight down. Then write each word in the space provided, breaking it into syllables. Here are the words you are looking for:

awful	decode	expose	pavement	prepay
return	sadly	suction	unwed	waiting

s	a	d	l	y	n	e	w	c	o
u	u	p	u	n	w	e	d	s	l
c	n	p	a	v	e	m	e	n	t
t	t	r	e	l	x	w	c	o	w
i	u	e	u	e	p	o	o	w	a
o	n	p	n	a	o	r	d	b	i
n	c	a	o	r	s	k	e	a	t
p	l	y	h	n	e	q	u	l	i
r	e	a	d	r	e	t	u	r	n
e	a	w	f	u	l	w	h	o	g

16. _____aw-ful_____   21. _____re-turn_____

17. _____de-code_____   22. _____sad-ly_____

18. _____ex-pose_____   23. _____suc-tion_____

19. _____pave-ment_____   24. _____un-wed_____

20. _____pre-pay_____   25. _____wait-ing_____

Name _____

Section _____ Date_____

SCORE: (Number correct) _____ x 5 = _____%

SYLLABLES: Test 5

A. Using the rules shown in the box, divide the following words into syllables. Then write the numbers of the two rules that apply. For each word, first use any of rules 3–5 that apply before using rule 1 or 2.

> 1. **Divide between two consonants.**
> 2. **Divide before a single consonant.**
> 3. **Divide before a consonant followed by *le*.**
> 4. **Divide after prefixes and before suffixes.**
> 5. **Divide between the words in a compound word.**

		Syllable Division	*Rule Numbers*	
1.	meaningless	*mean-ing-less*	4	4
2.	incomplete	*in-com-plete*	4	1
3.	unlawful	*un-law-ful*	4	4
4.	sunbonnet	*sun-bon-net*	5	1
5.	refinement	*re-fine-ment*	4	4
6.	equipment	*e-quip-ment*	2	4
7.	newsweekly	*news-week-ly*	5	4
8.	belittle	*be-lit-tle*	2	3
9.	opening	*o-pen-ing*	2	4
10.	submarine	*sub-ma-rine*	4	2

(Continues on next page)

B. Complete each sentence by underlining the compound word. Then, in the space provided, divide the word into syllables.

11. When I'm hungry, I know I can find a snack in the *(cupboard, refrigerator)*.
    _____cup-board_____

12. Ellis decided to be an active *(father, househusband)* and care for his infant for a year. _____house-hus-band_____

13. It was a difficult ascent, but the climbers finally made it to the *(summit, mountaintop)*. _____moun-tain-top_____

14. Though she was an excellent athlete, Darlene was a(n) *(commonplace, ordinary)* student. _____com-mon-place_____

15. Please explain your *(reasoning, viewpoint)* to me. _____view-point_____

C. Complete each sentence by underlining the word that has both a prefix and a suffix. Then, in the space provided, divide the word into syllables.

16. On the curb was a baby wrapped in a *(coverlet, pillowcase, comforter)*.
    _____com-fort-er_____

17. In his jeans and red T-shirt, Umberto was a(n) *(casual, unlikely, friendly)*-looking insurance salesperson. _____un-like-ly_____

18. Raoul is a *(mechanic, designer, principal)*. _____de-sign-er_____

19. *(Dislodging, Loosening, Moving)* the fallen tree from the roadway took three full hours. _____dis-lodg-ing_____

20. Most car accidents are *(harmless, deadly, preventable)*. _____pre-vent-a-ble_____

SYLLABLES: Test 6

A. Using the rules shown in the box, divide the following words into syllables. Then write the numbers of the two rules that apply. For each word, first use any of rules 3–5 that apply before using rule 1 or 2.

---

1. **Divide between two consonants.**
2. **Divide before a single consonant.**
3. **Divide before a consonant followed by *le*.**
4. **Divide after prefixes and before suffixes.**
5. **Divide between the words in a compound word.**

	Syllable Division	*Rule Numbers*	
1. rebuttal	re-but-tal	2	1
2. cardholder	card-hold-er	5	4
3. Eskimo	Es-ki-mo	1	2
4. outpouring	out-pour-ing	5	4
5. leisurely	lei-sure-ly	2	4
6. marketplace	mar-ket-place	1	5
7. cannibal	can-ni-bal	1	2
8. jamboree	jam-bo-ree	1	2
9. vacancy	va-can-cy	2	1
10. rollaway	roll-a-way	5	2

(Continues on next page)

B. Complete the passage by underlining each word in parentheses that has both a prefix and a suffix. Then, in the space provided, break each of these words into syllables.

> When people vacation, one of the most popular destinations is the island chain of Hawaii. But did you ever wonder what vacation spots the residents of Hawaii find *(relaxing, attractive)*? One of their favored destinations is Las Vegas, Nevada, with its shows full of *(excitement, activity)* and its *(agreeable, delightful)* weather. Another is Seattle, Washington, where the cold, damp, rainy climate is *(totally, completely)* different from the subtropics of Hawaii. However, the vacation spot Hawaiians consider most *(worthwhile, desirable)* is the favorite of many Americans: Disneyland.

11. _____*re-lax-ing*_____   14. _____*com-plete-ly*_____

12. _____*ex-cite-ment*_____   15. _____*de-sir-a-ble*_____

13. _____*de-light-ful*_____

C. Underline the five words below that have three syllables. Then, in the space provided, divide each word into syllables.

> A revealing public survey on doctors was recently released. Only 42% of patients thought that their doctor explained things well. Also, 63% felt that physicians make too much money. Only 31% felt that doctors spend sufficient time with patients. And 69% said they were starting to lose confidence in doctors.

16. _____*re-veal-ing*_____   19. _____*suf-fi-cient*_____

17. _____*re-cent-ly*_____   20. _____*con-fi-dence*_____

18. _____*phy-si-cians*_____

WORD PARTS: Test 1

Use the word parts in the box to complete the words in the sentences below. Use each word part only once.

auto — self	**ped** — foot
bene — good, well	**re** — again, back
er — a person who does something	**ion** — act of
ex — out, from	**un** — not
mono — one	**ven** — come

1. The *(research . . .)* _____*researcher*_____ found that students tend to learn better when lectures contain some humor.

2. Some lakes and rivers have become so *(. . . clean)* _____*unclean*_____ that they have actually caught fire.

3. My new *(. . . matic)* _____*automatic*_____ camera advances the film by itself each time I take a picture.

4. A skirt with an elastic waistband can *(. . . pand)* _____*expand*_____ to fit women of many sizes.

5. Before starting my car in cold weather, I need to pump the gas *(. . . al)* _____*pedal*_____ a few times.

6. Jay Leno performs alone at the beginning of the *Tonight Show*, when he gives his *(. . . logue)* _____*monologue*_____.

7. Whenever my mother tells me that the *(. . . fits)* _____*benefits*_____ will outweigh the drawbacks, I know she's about to ask me to do something unpleasant.

8. Sometimes course *(registrat . . .)* _____*registration*_____ seems to last longer than the courses themselves.

(Continues on next page)

9. To (*. . . fresh*) _____*refresh*_____ themselves, some Japanese workers take yawn breaks: They all raise their arms and yawn at the same time—for thirty seconds.

10. Many people attended the spy *(con . . . tion)* _____*convention*_____; however, no one was willing to wear a name-tag.

WORD PARTS: Test 2

Use the word parts in the box to complete the words in the following passage. Read the passage through one time before trying to complete the words. Use each word part once.

er — a person who does something	**ist** — a person skilled at something
ex — out, from	**ly** — in a certain manner
ful — full of	**re** — again
in — within	**spect** — look
ion — state of being	**tele** — far, over a distance

When a murder takes place, how do the police get information about the killer? First, they *(in . . .)* _____ *inspect* _____ the scene of the crime. Maybe the murderer left fingerprints on a *(. . . phone)* _____ *telephone* _____, an ashtray, or a glass. Other clues that point to specific individuals *(. . . clude)* _____ *include* _____ footprints (perhaps showing the pattern of wear in a shoe), hairs, and traces of blood. A close examination of the victim's body can also be very *(use . . .)* _____ *useful* _____. A stab wound may be matched to the blade of a particular knife. *(Similar . . .)* _____ *Similarly* _____, *(special . . . s)* _____ *specialists* _____ can determine from a bullet wound the kind of gun that was used and the distance from which the bullet was fired. And once the bullet is *(. . . tracted)* _____ *extracted* _____ from the body, it too will show marks that link it to only one gun. Increasingly, the methods for tracking down *(kill . . . s)* _____ *killers* _____ offer more than clues; they offer sure

(Continues on next page)

(identificat . . .) _____identification_____. It is hoped such exact police methods will persuade many would-be criminals to *(. . . consider)* _____reconsider_____ their plans.

WORD PARTS: Test 3

Use the word parts in the box to complete the words in the sentences below. Use each word part only once.

able — able to be	**mono** — one
audi — hear	**pre** — before
ish — similar to	**sub** — below, under
ly — in a certain manner	**super** — over, above, beyond
mis — badly, wrong	**tele** — far, over a distance

1. The *(. . . ence)* _____*audience*_____ starting clapping as soon as they heard the famous actress begin to speak.

2. When the bus turned on its side, several passengers were *(serious . . .)* _____*seriously*_____ injured.

3. Looking through the powerful *(. . . scope)* _____*telescope*_____, we could see Saturn's rings.

4. According to a survey, the average person spends about a year of his or her life searching for *(. . . placed)* _____*misplaced*_____ objects.

5. Because she was *(. . . occupied)* _____*preoccupied*_____ with an earlier assignment, Laurel didn't hear the teacher ask her a question.

6. Today, many reporters travel with a small *(port . . .)* _____*portable*_____ computer.

7. The lecturer spoke in such a *(. . . tone)* _____*monotone*_____ that he almost put the students to sleep.

8. The scholarship is awarded on the basis of both financial need and *(. . . ior)* _____*superior*_____ grades.

(Continues on next page)

9. The car was so (. . . *standard*) _____*substandard*_____ that within months the fuel pump needed replacing and the bumper fell off.

10. Whenever I catch my (*devil* . . .) _____*devilish*_____ son snatching a piece of candy, he says, "I was taking it for you, Mommy."

WORD PARTS: Test 4

Use the word parts in the box to complete the words in the following passage. Read the passage through one time before trying to complete the words. Use each word part once.

aud — hear	**man** — hand
ex — out, from	**ment** — state of being
ful — full of	**pre** — before
in — within	**re** — again, back
ly — in a certain manner	**spect** — look

Last night in a dream, an angel came to me and asked, "Would you like to see hell?" After *(. . . paring)* _____*preparing*_____ myself to see a terrible *(. . . acle)* _____*spectacle*_____, I went with the angel. Suddenly we stood *(. . . side)* _____*inside*_____ a large room draped with blue velvet. In the middle of this *(beauti . . .)* _____*beautiful*_____ room was a huge golden pot filled with sweet-smelling food. Many people sat around the pot. Each held a spoon of silver. The spoons' handles were so long that the people could reach the pot and scoop out food. They couldn't, however, *(. . . age)* _____*manage*_____ to bring the food to their mouths. The only *(. . . ible)* _____*audible*_____ sounds were moans of pain. I realized that everyone was starving.

"Now would you like to see heaven?" asked the angel. I *(eager. . .)* _____*eagerly*_____ agreed. To my *(amaze . . .)* _____*amazement*_____, the next room I saw looked just like the first—with the same golden pot and the same silver spoons. However, here everyone appeared to be *(. . . tremely)* _____*extremely*_____ happy. The people were talking and laughing and looked well-fed.

(Continues on next page)

Puzzled, I said, "In the other room there was only misery. Here there is only joy. How can this be?" With a wise smile, the angel *(. . . plied)* _____replied_____, "Here they feed each other."

WORD PARTS: Test 5

A. Use the word parts in the box to complete the words in the sentences below. Use each word part only once.

bio — life	**less** — without
ism — a belief or practice	**port** — carry
ist — a person skilled at something	

1. The stock-market crash of 1929 left many people *(penni . . .)* _____*penniless*_____—they had no money at all.

2. Actor and *(humor . . .)* _____*humorist*_____ Robin Williams is known for his zany sense of humor.

3. One type of *(vegetarian . . .)* _____*vegetarianism*_____ excludes all dairy products and eggs.

4. To know about chemical reactions in the body, doctors must study *(. . . chemistry)* _____*biochemistry*_____.

5. When the elevator broke down, the *(. . . er)* _____*porter*_____ had to walk up four flights of stairs to get our luggage to us.

(Continues on next page)

B. (6–10.) Use the word parts in the box to complete the words in the following passage. Read the passage through one time before trying to complete the words. Use each word part once.

er — a person who does something	**sub** — below, under
ful — full of	**un** — not
spect — look	

The Labrador retriever has been named by the American Kennel Club as the nation's most popular breed. What does this mean if you want a Lab puppy? Be very *(care...)* _____*careful*_____ before you buy. When a breed is named number one, a flood of people look for puppies. *(...fortunately)* _____*Unfortunately*_____, this usually attracts the dishonest type of *(breed...)* _____*breeder*_____ who raises *(...standard)* _____*substandard*_____ puppies just for the profit. These dogs have few of the qualities that made the breed popular. The best advice is to buy a puppy from a reputable source, and always *(in...)* _____*inspect*_____ the puppy first.

WORD PARTS: Test 6

A. Use the word parts in the box to complete the words in the sentences below. Use each word part only once.

un — not	**pre** — before
ible — able to be	**tele** — far, over a distance
pod — foot	

1. The kitten at the animal shelter looked so *(. . . loved)* _____*unloved*_____ that I just had to adopt her.

2. The woman's feet hurt, so she went to the *(. . . iatrist)* _____*podiatrist*_____ to have her corns removed.

3. The judge warned the jury not to *(. . . judge)* _____*prejudge*_____ the defendant, but to wait for all the facts before judging.

4. The acrobat is so *(flex . . .)* _____*flexible*_____ that he can wrap his legs around his head.

5. The Learning Center contains a *(. . . conference)* _____*teleconference*_____ room where staff members can talk on a special TV to people on other campuses.

(Continues on next page)

B. (6–10.) Use the word parts in the box to complete the words in the following passage. Read the passage through one time before trying to complete the words. Use each word part once.

ful — full of	**post** — after
less — without	**re** — again, back
ly — in a certain manner	

High school reunions provide an opportunity to *(. . . acquaint)* _____*reacquaint*_____ yourself with former classmates. However, some people are a little nervous when attending them. So here are some tips for a *(success . . .)* _____*successful*_____ reunion. First, pamper yourself; make yourself look your best. Second, wear something that makes a statement. Buy a stunning *(strap . . .)* _____*strapless*_____ dress or a sharp silk suit. Next, try to be outgoing. Keep in mind that you are a worthwhile person and speak to others *(confident . . .)* _____*confidently*_____. But even if you have had a fantastic life, don't act superior. Take the time to find out what your classmates have done in their *(. . .-high school)* _____*post-high school*_____ years. Finally, go with the attitude that you are going to have a good time. That is the main reason for attending reunions.

DICTIONARY USE: Test 1

A. Below are three pairs of dictionary guidewords. Each pair is followed by a series of other words. Circle the two words in each series which would be found on the page with the guidewords.

1–2. **coverage / crab**

~~cow~~   cornice   cool-headed   crack   ~~cozy~~

3–4. **festive / fiberboard**

~~feud~~   fight   fiend   fiberglass   ~~few~~

5–6. **japan / Jefferson**

~~jasmine~~   ~~jeer~~   jelly   janitor   jive

B. Answer the questions below about the following dictionary entry for *cite*.

cite (sīt) *v.* **cit•ed, cit•ing. 1.** To quote as an authority or example. **2.** To mention as support, illustration, or proof. **3.** To commend officially for meritorious action, esp. in military service. **4.** To summon before a court of law.

7. The part of speech of *cite* is
   (a.) verb.
   b. noun.
   c. adjective.

8. The past tense of *cite* has
   a. one syllable.
   (b.) two syllables.
   c. three syllables.

9. The definition of *cite* that fits the sentence below is
   a. definition 1.   c. definition 3.
   b. definition 2.   (d.) definition 4.

   The judge himself is on trial; he was cited for taking bribes from local union officials.

10. The definition of *cite* that fits the sentence below is
   a. definition 1.   c. definition 3.
   (b.) definition 2.   d. definition 4.

   To back up my point that homemakers work hard, I cited a study which shows that most spend over fifty hours a week on household chores.

(Continues on next page)

C. Use your dictionary and the spelling hints on page 92 to find the correct spelling of the following words.

11. hury   *hurry*   14. eazy   *easy*

12. sertain   *certain*   15. bote   *boat*

13. procead   *proceed*   16. beleive   *believe*

D. Use the following pronunciation key to answer the questions below.

Pronunciation Key

ă pat	ā pay	â care	ä father	ĕ pet	ē bee	ĭ pit
ī pie, by	î pier	ŏ pot	ō toe	ô paw, for		oi noise
ŏŏ took	ōō boot	ou out	th thin	*th* this		ŭ cut
û urge	yōō abuse	zh vision	ə about, item, edible, gallop, circus			

17. In *elbow* (ĕl′bō′), the **e** is pronounced like the **e** in what common word?

         pet

18. In *elbow* (ĕl′bō′), the **o** is pronounced like the **o** in what common word?

         toe

19. In *bloodstream* (blŭd′strēm′), the **oo** is pronounced like the **u** in what common word?

         cut

20. In *bloodstream* (blŭd′strēm′), the **ea** is pronounced like the **ee** in what common word?

         bee

DICTIONARY USE: Test 2

Use your dictionary as needed to answer the questions below.

A. Put dots between the syllables in each word. Then write out the word with the correct pronunciation symbols, including accent marks.

1. c r e d i t   *cred•it*   krĕd′ĭt   4. n e e d l e   *nee•dle*   nēd′l

2. l e g a l   *le•gal*   lē′gəl   5. t w i l i g h t   *twi•light*   twī′līt′

3. p l e a s a n t   *pleas•ant*   plĕz′ənt

B. List the parts of speech for the following words.

6. bend   _____ *verb, noun* _____

7. plain   _____ *adjective, noun, adverb* _____

8. minor   _____ *adjective, noun, verb* _____

C. Write the irregular plural forms for the following words.

9. tooth   _____ *teeth* _____

10. life   _____ *lives* _____

11. party   _____ *parties* _____

D. Write in the dictionary definitions of *crook* that fit the following sentences:

12. A well-known television preacher turned out to be a crook.

_____ *A thief; swindler* _____

13. Holding the umbrella by the crook of its handle, Hector swung it back and forth as he walked down the street, paying no attention to the rain.

_____ *A curve or bend* _____

E. Use your dictionary to answer the following questions.

14. A *coyote* is
   (a.) a small wolf-like predator.
   b. a large dog-like predator.
   c. native to South America.
   d. a member of the cat family.

(Continues on next page)

15. *Mecca* is a city in
    a. Germany.
    b. East Africa.
    c. West Saudi Arabia.
    d. New South Wales, Australia.

F. Use the following pronunciation key to answer questions about the four words below.

Pronunciation Key

ă pat	ā pay	â care	ä father	ě pet	ē bee	ǐ pit
ī pie, by	î pier	ǒ pot	ō toe	ô paw, for		oi noise
ǒǒ took	ōō boot	ou **out**	th **thin**	*th* **this**		ŭ cut
û **urge**	yōō abuse	zh vision	ə about, item, edible, gallop, circus			

a•brupt (ə-brŭpt′)   **gen•der** (jěn′dər)
an•ec•dote (ăn′ĭk-dōt′)   **ep•i•dem•ic** (ěp′ĭ-děm′ĭk)

16. Which two words have the sound of **ě**, as in *pet*?
    _____*gender, epidemic*_____

17. Which two words have the sound of **ǐ**, as in *pit*?
    _____*anecdote, epidemic*_____

18. Which two words have a schwa sound?
    _____*abrupt, gender*_____

19. Which two words have both a stronger and a weaker accent?
    _____*anecdote, epidemic*_____

20. Which word has four syllables?
    _____*epidemic*_____

Name _____

Section _____ Date_____

SCORE: (Number correct) _____ x 5 = _____%

DICTIONARY USE: Test 3

A. Below are three pairs of dictionary guidewords. Each pair is followed by a series of other words. Circle the two words in each series which would be found on the page with the guidewords.

1–2. **divinity / docile**

distance   (doable)   divine   (dizzy)   dock

3–4. **gate / gear**

garter   (gather)   (gave)   gearshift   general

5–6. **treatise / trestle**

treacherous   treason   (trench)   together   (trespass)

Answer the questions below about the following dictionary entry for *baby*.

ba•by (bā′bē) *n., pl.* **-bies. 1.a.** A very young child; infant. **b.** The youngest member of a family or group. **c.** A very young animal. **2.** One who behaves in an infantile way. **3.** *Slang.* A girl or young woman. **4.** *Slang.* An object of personal concern: *The project is your baby.* — *v.* **-bied, -by•ing**. To treat overindulgently; pamper.

7. *Baby* is accented on
   (a.) its first syllable.
   b. its second syllable.
   c. both syllables.

8. *Fill in the blank:* The plural of *baby* is _____ *babies* _____.

9. The definition of *baby* that applies to the sentence below is
   a. definition 1c.   c. definition 3.
   (b.) definition 2.   d. definition 4.

   "You're such a baby," screamed Rhonda. "You always want your own way."

10. The definition of *baby* that fits the sentence below is
    (a.) definition 1b.   c. definition 3.
    b. definition 2.   d. definition 4.

    It's hard to believe that Elena, the baby in our family, just became a teenager.

(Continues on next page)

C. Use your dictionary and the spelling hints on page 92 to find the correct spelling of the following words.

11. reciept _____*receipt*_____ 14. klean _____*clean*_____

12. writting _____*writing*_____ 15. wispor _____*whisper*_____

13. dicide _____*decide*_____ 16. actshun _____*action*_____

D. Use the following pronunciation key to answer the questions below.

Pronunciation Key

ă pat	ā pay	â care	ä father	ĕ pet	ē bee	ĭ pit
ī pie, by	î pier	ŏ pot	ō toe	ô paw, for		oi noise
ŏŏ took	ōō boot	ou out	th thin	*th* this		ŭ cut
û urge	yōō abuse	zh vision	ə about, item, edible, gallop, circus			

17. In *dignity* (dĭg′nĭ-tē), the **y** is pronounced like the **ee** in what common word?

_____*bee*_____

18. In *dignity* (dĭg′nĭ-tē), the **i**'s are pronounced like the **i** in what common word?

_____*pit*_____

19. In *firetrap* (fīr′trăp′), the **i** is pronounced like the **i** in what common word?

_____*pie*_____

20. In *firetrap* (fīr′trăp′), the **a** is pronounced like the **a** in what common word?

_____*pat*_____

DICTIONARY USE: Test 4

Use your dictionary as needed to answer the questions below.

A. Put dots between the syllables in each word. Then write out the word with the correct pronunciation symbols, including accent marks.

1. e x e r c i s e *ex•er•cise* ĕk'sər-sīz' 4. s u s p e n s e *sus•pense* sə-spĕns'

2. i n q u i r e *in•quire* ĭn-kwīr' 5. w e l c o m e *wel•come* wĕl'kəm

3. m o d i f y *mod•i•fy* mŏd'ə-fī'

B. List the parts of speech for the following words.

6. loose _____*adjective, adverb, verb*_____

7. glow _____*verb, noun*_____

8. total _____*noun, adjective, verb*_____

C. Write the irregular plural forms for the following words.

9. knife _____*knives*_____

10. hero _____*heroes*_____

11. city _____*cities*_____

D. Write in the dictionary definitions of *quick* that fit the following sentences:

12. You are not going to learn a new language quickly.

_____*Occurring or achieved in a brief period of time*_____

13. My boss has a quick temper.

_____*Hasty or sharp in reacting*_____

E. Use your dictionary to answer the following questions.

14. A *Pullman* would be most likely to be found on
   a. a desk.
   b. a bicycle.
   c. a train.
   d. a racetrack.

(Continues on next page)

15. The *leeward* side of an island is
    a. facing the wind.
    (b.) away from the wind.
    c. the highest part of the island.
    d. the lowest part of the island.

F. Use the following pronunciation key to answer questions about the four words below.

Pronunciation Key

ă pat	ā pay	â care	ä father	ĕ pet	ē bee	ĭ pit
ī pie, by	î pier	ŏ pot	ō toe	ô paw, for		oi noise
ŏŏ took	ōō boot	ou out	th thin	*th* this		ŭ cut
û urge	yōō abuse	zh vision	ə about, item, edible, gallop, circus			

fab•ric (făb′rĭc)   **strat•e•gy** (străt′ə-jē)
pon•der (pŏn′dər)   **nec•es•sar y** (nĕs′ĭ-sĕr′ē)

16. Which two words have the sound of ĭ, as in *pit*?
                         fabric, necessary

17. Which two words have the sound of ă, as in *pat*?
                         fabric, strategy

18. Which two words have a schwa sound?
                         ponder, strategy

19. Which word has three syllables?
                         strategy

20. Which word has both a stronger and a weaker accent?
                         necessary

DICTIONARY USE: Test 5

A. Below are three pairs of dictionary guidewords. Each pair is followed by a series of other words. Circle the two words in each series which would be found on the page with the guidewords.

1–2. **devil / diabolical**

determine   ⬭devise⬭   ⬭dextrose⬭   diaper   digital

3–4. **index / indispensable**

⬭indignation⬭   indorse   ⬭indicate⬭   indeed   in-depth

5–6. **quitclaim / Rabat**

raccoon   quince   ⬭quiver⬭   ⬭quote⬭   Rabbi

B. Answer the questions below about the following dictionary entry for *instant*.

in•stant (ĭn′stənt) *n.* **1.** A very brief space of time; moment. **2.** A particular point in time. — *adj.* **1.** Immediate. **2.** Imperative; urgent: *an instant need.* **3.** Designed or processed for quick preparation: *instant coffee.*

7. The **i** in *instant* is pronounced as a
   a. long **i**.
   (b.) short **i**.
   c. schwa.

8. *Instant* is accented on
   (a.) its first syllable.
   b. its second syllable.
   c. both syllables.

9. The definition of *instant* that applies to the sentence below is
   (a.) noun definition 1.   c. adjective definition 1.
   b. noun definition 2.   d. adjective definition 2.

   For just an instant, Alphonse thought he would be bumped from his flight.

10. The definition of *instant* that fits the sentence below is
    (a.) noun definition 2.   c. adjective definition 2.
    b. adjective definition 1.   d. adjective definition 3.

    Just at the instant we were sitting down for dinner, both the telephone and the doorbell rang.

(Continues on next page)

C. Use your dictionary and the spelling hints on page 92 to find the correct spelling of the following words.

11. fullfil   _____*fulfill*_____   14. froun   _____*frown*_____

12. freind   _____*friend*_____   15. capible   _____*capable*_____

13. ordurly   _____*orderly*_____   16. lable   _____*label*_____

D. Use the following pronunciation key to answer the questions below.

Pronunciation Key

ă pat	ā pay	â care	ä father	ĕ pet	ē bee	ĭ pit
ī pie, by	î pier	ŏ pot	ō toe	ô paw, for		oi noise
ŏŏ took	ōō boot	ou out	th thin	*th* this		ŭ cut
û urge	yōō abuse	zh vision	ə about, item, edible, gallop, circus			

17. In *haggard* (hăg′ərd), the first **a** is pronounced like the **a** in what common word?

_____*pat*_____

18. In *koala* (kō-ä′lə), the first **a** is pronounced like the **a** in what common word?

_____*father*_____

19. In *mechanics* (mǐ-kăn′ǐks), the **e** is pronounced like the **i** in what common word?

_____*pit*_____

20. In *onyx* (ŏn′ǐks), the **y** is pronounced like the **i** in what common word?

_____*pit*_____

DICTIONARY USE: Test 6

A. Put dots between the syllables in each word. Then write out the word with the correct pronunciation symbols, including accent marks.

1. d e b a u c h   *de•bauch*   dĭ-bôch′

2. h o r t i c u l t u r e   *hor•ti•cul•ture*   hôr′tĭ-kŭl′chər

3. o p p o s i t e   *op•po•site*   ŏp′ə-zĭt

4. r e s o l u t i o n   *res•o•lu•tion*   rĕz′ə-lōō′shən

5. s t r a i g h t a w a y   *straight•a•way*   strāt′ə-wā′

B. List the parts of speech for the following words.

6. game   *noun, verb, adjective*

7. neck   *noun, verb*

8. prime   *adjective, noun, verb*

C. Write the irregular forms of the following words.

9. chewy   *chewier, chewiest*

10. crisis   *crises*

11. hit   *hit, hitting*

D. Write the dictionary definitions of *hitch* that fit the following sentences:

12. When my car broke down on the freeway, I had to hitch a ride.

To obtain (a free ride)

13. Stefan spent four years in the Army, but decided not to sign up for another hitch.

A term of military service

E. Use your dictionary to answer the following questions.

14. Which of the following illustrates the word *homonym*?
a. *Light / dark*
b. *Bear / bare*
c. *Bar / bark*
d. *Night / evening*

(Continues on next page)

283

15. Which of the following is most *mobile*?
    a. A building
    b. A car manufacturing plant
    c. An apple tree
    (d.) A wheelchair

F. Answer the questions about the four words below.

foot•ball (fŏŏt′bôl′)   **of•fi•cial** (ə-fĭsh′əl)
hyp•no•tize (hĭp′nə-tīz′)   **vi•ta•min** (vī′tə-mĭn)

16. Which word has the short sound of **oo**, as in *took*?

   _____ *football* _____

17. Which two words have long vowel sounds?

   _____ *hypnotize, vitamin* _____

18. Which word has two schwa sounds?

   _____ *official* _____

19. Which word has the fewest syllables?

   _____ *football* _____

20. Which two words have both a stronger and a weaker accent?

   _____ *football, hypnotize* _____

VOCABULARY IN CONTEXT: Test 1

A. Using context clues for help, circle the letter of the meaning of each word in italics.

1. Cleo is a *chronic* complainer. She even complains if I say she complains too much.

   Chronic means

   a. rare.   b. constant.   c. messy.

2. In a hospital emergency room, it is common to see such *gruesome* sights as burned skin and bleeding wounds.

   Gruesome means

   a. shocking.   b. common.   c. false.

3. "Your paper should be more *coherent*," my English teacher wrote. "In places, it is poorly organized and lacking in logic."

   Coherent means

   a. disorganized.   b. detailed.   c. organized and logical.

4. Would weeds make a good *supplement* to your diet? Yes, a daily addition of certain weeds would give you all you need of vitamins A and C.

   Supplement means

   a. substitute.   b. addition.   c. flavoring.

5. Sometimes people with *contrary* qualities are attracted to each other. For example, quiet Imelda goes steady with Ferdinand, who is loud.

   Contrary means

   a. similar.   b. unusual.   c. opposite.

(Continues on next page)

B. Using context clues for help, write the definition of each word in italics. Choose from the definitions in the box below. Each will be used once.

pieces of business	make longer	start
brief and clear	difficult experience	

6. To *prolong* your life, get married. Married people tend to live longer than singles.

   Prolong means to _____ *make longer* _____

7. Everyday *transactions* include buying food and clothing and signing papers to rent an apartment.

   Transactions are _____ *pieces of business* _____

8. Our mayor has decided to *initiate* a recycling program. Soon our newspapers, bottles, and cans will be re-used instead of dumped.

   Initiate means to _____ *start* _____

9. There is a special chair that eases the *ordeal* of giving birth. Most women who use the chair say they feel less pain and give birth more quickly than when lying down.

   An *ordeal* is a _____ *difficult experience* _____

10. My wordy cousin said, "It is my opinion that the level of heat has gone beyond what I am able to consider comfortable." Why can't he just be more *concise* and say, "I'm hot"?

    Concise means _____ *brief and clear* _____

VOCABULARY IN CONTEXT: Test 2

Figure out the meanings of the following five words by studying them in context.
Then complete the matching and fill-in test that follows.

1 **apathy**
(ăp′-ə-thē)

When the topic of taxes came up, Carmen's *apathy* about elections changed to sharp interest.

The students showed all the signs of *apathy*, including doodling and writing notes to one another.

2 **appropriate**
(ə-prō′prē-ĭt)

Today it is thought *appropriate* for a woman to ask a man on a date, yet most women don't do it.

It is not *appropriate* to wear cut-off jeans to most job interviews.

3 **illusion**
(ĭ-lōō′zhən)

Soap opera is a made-for-TV *illusion.* Yet many fans of one show were so convinced of its reality that they sent gifts when a character got married.

My aunt has no wish to create the *illusion* of never-ending youth. Why should she hide her silver hair or the smile wrinkles around her eyes?

4 **phobia**
(fō′bē-ə)

Rosario has a *phobia* about heights. She can't look down from the top of a tall building without feeling terror.

Perhaps no *phobia* is stranger than the fear of having peanut butter stick to the roof of your mouth.

5 **vigorous**
(vĭg′ər-əs)

Healthy elderly people can enjoy *vigorous* activities, such as jogging and biking.

I felt so lazy today that the most *vigorous* thing I did all day was brush my teeth.

Note: A key to pronunciation is on page 94.

A. Match each word with its definition.

1. apathy   __2__ proper
2. appropriate   __5__ lively; energetic
3. illusion   __4__ a continuing abnormal fear
4. phobia   __1__ lack of interest
5. vigorous   __3__ appearance of reality; a false impression

(Continues on next page)

B. Fill in each blank with one of the words from the box. Use each word once.

apathy	appropriate	illusion
phobia	vigorous	

6. I can't understand why it's not considered ___*appropriate*___ to put one's elbows on the dinner table.

7. To get your heart beating, a slow stroll won't do; your walk must be ___*vigorous*___.

8. I thought I saw my mother walk past my apartment window, but it was just an ___*illusion*___ caused by moving shadows and my own imagination.

9. The ___*apathy*___ of parents is often one reason behind juvenile crime. Parents should pay more attention to their children's activities.

10. There are many odd ___*phobia*___s. One cabdriver, for example, had to change his job because of a deep fear of red lights.

Name _____

Section _____ Date_____

SCORE: (Number correct) _____ x 10 = _____%

VOCABULARY IN CONTEXT: Test 3

A. Using context clues for help, circle the letter of the meaning of each word in italics.

1. Sports seem to be as *vital* to my husband as are food and air.

   Vital means

   a. difficult.　　　(b.) necessary.　　　c. unimportant.

2. When an Asian volcano burst in 1883, the sound was *audible* 3,000 miles away.

   Audible means

   a. able to be seen.　　(b.) able to be heard.　　c. able to be felt.

3. Ms. Landis is a very easy teacher. Her idea of being *severe* is refusing to accept a paper that is more than a month late.

   Severe means

   (a.) strict.　　　b. in charge.　　　c. gentle.

4. One usually *rational* football fan became so crazy when his team lost the Super Bowl that he shot the TV.

   Rational means

   a. insane.　　　b. very popular.　　　(c.) reasonable.

5. It was said that no *obstacle*—whether extreme heat, snow, or rocky land—could keep the Pony Express from delivering the mail on time. When Indians killed one rider, the horse went on to deliver the mail alone.

   Obstacle means

   (a.) something that gets in the way.　　b. temperature.　　c. animal.

(Continues on next page)

B. Using context clues for help, write the definition of each word in italics. Choose from the definitions in the box below. Each will be used once.

unskilled	short story	similar
fate	lack of basic needs and comforts	

6. Ice is harder than most people think; its hardness is *comparable* to that of concrete.

   Comparable means _____ similar _____

7. My sister is such an *inept* cook that she never needs to call the family to supper. We just come to the table when the smoke alarm goes off.

   Inept means _____ unskilled _____

8. As a boy, my grandfather suffered great *deprivation*. For example, his shoes always had holes in them, and meat was a rare treat.

   Deprivation means a _____ lack of basic needs and comforts _____

9. Whenever something bad happens to Gabriela, she says it's the fault of *destiny*. But I prefer to take charge of my own life rather than blame fate.

   Destiny means _____ fate _____

10. My father died when I was a baby, but Mom told me so many stories about him that I feel I knew him. For example, one *anecdote* was about how he cried with joy when I was born.

    Anecdote means a _____ short story _____

VOCABULARY IN CONTEXT: Test 4

Figure out the meanings of the following five words by studying them in context.
Then complete the matching and fill-in test that follows.

1 **accelerate**
(ăk-sĕl′ə-rāt′)

Tidal waves sometimes *accelerate* until reaching a speed of 450 miles an hour.

I thought I put my foot on the brake, but the car *accelerated* instead of stopping.

2 **controversy**
(kŏn′trə-vûr′sē)

Whether smoking should be illegal in all public places is a matter of *controversy*. Two people were arguing about it on TV just the other day.

There aren't many topics of greater *controversy* in our country than abortion.

3 **data**
(dāt′ə)

Data about the moon's surface includes information gained from photos and soil samples.

According to scientific *data*, laughing is good for us. For example, evidence shows that laughing exercises the heart.

4 **immunity**
(ĭ-myo͞o′nĭ-tē)

Certain foreign officials in this country have *immunity* to our laws; they can't even be arrested for murder.

It's not fair that supervisors have *immunity* from the rule against smoking in the restrooms.

5 **versatile**
(vûr′sə-təl)

A *versatile* food processor does everything but cook—it slices, chops, shreds, and blends.

Ivan is a wonderful piano player. But Joel is more *versatile*; he sings, acts, and plays the piano.

Note: A key to pronunciation is on page 94.

A. Match each word with its definition.

1. accelerate   _3_ information

2. controversy   _5_ able to do many things well

3. data   _1_ speed up

4. immunity   _2_ argument

5. versatile   _4_ freedom from something required of others

(Continues on next page)

B. Fill in each blank with one of the words from the box. Use each word once.

accelerate	controversy	data
immunity	versatile	

6. According to one researcher's _____*data*_____, all pregnant woman tend to dream about the same things.

7. As the roller coaster headed downward and began to _____*accelerate*_____, the entire carload of passengers screamed at once.

8. The kids wanted to stay outside even though it was raining. But after the first flash of lightning, there was no _____*controversy*_____. They all agreed we should move the picnic indoors.

9. With just a few pieces of clothing, Ling has put together a _____*versatile*_____ wardrobe. By matching just the right pieces and jewelry, she has casual, work, and dressy outfits.

10. After I failed the driving test, I asked for _____*immunity*_____ from the required ten-day wait before taking it again. My license was about to run out, so I needed a new one quickly.

VOCABULARY IN CONTEXT: Test 5

Using context clues for help, circle the letter of the meaning of each word in italics.

1. Senator Duenas claims to be an *advocate* of a clean environment, but she has yet to vote for any bills to clean up polluted waterways in her state.

    An *advocate* is a person who

    a. gets elected.   (b.) supports something.   c. cleans things up.

2. Because certain plants are poisonous to animals, pet owners should keep *antidotes* handy to prevent their pets from suffering and perhaps dying.

    An *antidote* is a

    (a.) medicine.   b. weapon.   c. poison.

3. When asked about possible scandals, most politicians are less than *candid*. They will say anything to convince voters that their behavior has not been improper.

    Candid means

    a. pleasing.   b. happy.   (c.) honest.

4. Anyone who *encounters* a wild animal in the woods should stay calm and leave as quickly as possible.

    To *encounter* means to

    a. admire.   (b.) meet.   c. get away from.

5. A complicated lecture can be *illuminated* with logical examples and clear-cut explanations.

    Illuminated means

    (a.) made clear.   b. practiced.   c. confused.

6. It is hard to be *impartial* when you listen to two people arguing. Usually you want to take one person's side.

    Impartial means

    a. interested.   b. friendly.   (c.) not favoring one side over another.

(Continues on next page)

7. Reiko figured she had only two *options*: either stay in college or work for minimum wages the rest of her life.

   Options means

   (a.) choices.   b. wishes.   c. habits.

8. Veronica's decision to study instead of going out for pizza with her friends was *prudent*. She got an A on the exam, while her friends all got D's.

   Prudent means

   a. generous.   (b.) wise.   c. unfortunate.

9. I *procrastinated* so long in getting a babysitter for New Year's Eve that all of our sitters were busy for that night by the time I called.

   Procrastinated means

   a. worked.   b. changed.   (c.) delayed.

10. Because the prisoner showed no *remorse* for his crime, the judge sentenced him to the longest possible prison term.

    Remorse means

    (a.) regret.   b. pleasure.   c. purpose.

VOCABULARY IN CONTEXT: Test 6

Figure out the meanings of the following five words by studying them in context. Then complete the matching and fill-in test that follows.

1 **ambivalent**
(ăm-bĭv′ə-lənt)

Heidi was *ambivalent* about her career choice. She wasn't sure if she should study to be a nurse or an accountant.

Darren is not usually *ambivalent*, but this evening he can't make up his mind about what he wants for dinner.

2 **apprehensive**
(ăp′rĭ-hĕn′sĭv)

People are often *apprehensive* about new situations. Their fear lessens as they become more familiar with the situation.

Ernesto was *apprehensive* about the upcoming final exam. Unless he did well, he would be disqualified from playing football.

3 **elated**
(ĭ-lā′tĭd)

My sister was *elated* when she heard she was finally pregnant.

Ramon was *elated* when he was offered a promotion and a big raise.

4 **nostalgia**
(nŏ-stăl′jə)

Music from the 1960s fills my parents with *nostalgia* because it reminds them of when they first met.

Willis has feelings of *nostalgia* when he thinks about the happy days of his childhood, before his father died.

5 **vivid**
(vĭv′ĭd)

It is common to have *vivid* memories of a special event. You can almost see yourself reliving the occasion.

Shanna's recollection of the car crash was all too *vivid*. She could recall all the terrible details of the impact and the resulting injuries.

Note: A key to pronunciation is on page 94.

A. Match each word with its definition.

1. ambivalent   __4__ a desire for something in the past

2. apprehensive   __3__ delighted; overjoyed

3. elated   __1__ uncertain

4. nostalgia   __2__ afraid; anxious

5. vivid   __5__ full of lifelike images

(Continues on next page)

B. Fill in each blank with one of the words from the box. Use each word once. Read through the passage at least once before starting to fill in the blanks.

ambivalent	apprehensive	elated
nostalgia	vivid	

Marta was (6)_____*ambivalent*_____ about her upcoming trip. On the one hand, she was (7)_____*apprehensive*_____ because she had never been on an airplane before. She would be flying all the way from Los Angeles to Miami. On the other hand, she was (8)_____*elated*_____ at the thought of seeing Uncle Christos again. Marta had not seen her uncle for ten years, but her memories of times with this special man were as (9)_____*vivid*_____ as if they had happened last week. She could still see Christos gathering her brothers and sisters and entertaining them with stories about life in the old country. Such memories usually filled Marta with great (10)_____*nostalgia*_____, but now they only made her more excited about her visit to Miami.

MAIN IDEAS: Test 1

A. Each group of words below consists of one general idea and four specific ideas. The general idea includes all the specific ideas. Underline the general idea in each group.

1. jazz	blues	rap	<u>music</u>	rock
2. <u>science</u>	biology	physics	chemistry	zoology
3. fry	boil	<u>cook</u>	bake	steam
4. chapter	contents	<u>book</u>	index	page
5. murder	<u>crime</u>	stealing	speeding	kidnapping
6. bonnet	turban	<u>hat</u>	baseball cap	helmet
7. granola	oatmeal	raisin bran	<u>cereal</u>	bran flakes
8. <u>pants</u>	cuffs	pockets	buttons	zipper
9. mortgage	VISA bill	<u>debt</u>	child support	car loan

B. In each pair below, one idea is general and the other is specific. The general idea includes the specific one. Do two things:

1) Underline the idea in each pair that you think is more general.
2) Then write in one more specific idea that is covered by the general idea.

10. <u>Mexican food</u>	taco	*burrito*
11. comics section	<u>newspaper</u>	*sports section*
12. Miami	<u>city</u>	*Dallas*
13. <u>weapon</u>	knife	*gun*
14. iron	<u>metal</u>	*copper*
15. <u>monster</u>	Dracula	*Wolfman*
16. high chair	<u>children's furniture</u>	*stroller*
17. poker	<u>card game</u>	*gin rummy*
18. <u>good-luck charm</u>	four-leaf clover	*horseshoe*

(Other answers are possible.)

(Continues on next page)

297

C. Each group of three items below contains three levels of ideas. Write a *1* by the most general idea in each group, a *2* by the less general idea, and a *3* by the most specific idea.

19. __3__ Gloria Estefan   __1__ singer   __2__ pop singer

20. __1__ color   __3__ red   __2__ bright color

21. __3__ lawn mower   __2__ garden tool   __1__ tool

22. __3__ *The Tonight Show* __1__ TV program   __2__ talk show

23. __3__ oak floor   __1__ flooring   __2__ wood floor

24. __1__ store   __2__ department store __3__ Wal-Mart

25. __2__ telephone call   __3__ long-distance call __1__ communication

MAIN IDEAS: Test 2

A. Each group of words below consists of one general idea and four specific ideas. The general idea includes all the specific ideas. Underline the general idea in each group.

1. envelope	can	box	<u>container</u>	bottle
2. banana	ice cream	syrup	cherries	<u>banana split</u>
3. <u>high-risk job</u>	astronaut	firefighter	policeman	miner
4. insurance	dead bolt	guard dog	<u>protection</u>	suntan lotion
5. microwaves	take-out food	high-speed trains	<u>time savers</u>	express mail
6. burnt toast	<u>minor problems</u>	boring date	flat tire	a cold

B. After each paragraph are three subjects. Label each subject with one of the following:

> *T*—for the topic of the paragraph
> *B*—for the subject that is too broad
> *N*—for the subject that is too narrow

7–9. The United States accepts close to two million legal immigrants each year. California is the top destination. It accepts almost 40 percent. Texas is next, accepting 12 percent. These two states are followed by New York, Florida, and Illinois as favorite destinations.

   B   Immigration

   N   Legal immigrants in California

   T   Legal immigrants to the United States

(Continues on next page)

10–12. People who favor laws against handguns have several reasons. They argue, for example, that handguns make it easier to kill people. Other weapons, such as knives, may cause less damage. Also, people who own guns could leave a loaded handgun within reach of a small child. Children do not know the difference between a toy gun and the real thing. Finally, half of all the guns used in crimes have been stolen. This means that criminals get many of their weapons from people who bought guns to protect themselves.

   <u> B </u> Weapons

   <u> T </u> Handgun laws

   <u> N </u> One way criminals get handguns

C. (13–20.) Each group of items below includes one topic, one main idea (topic sentence), and two supporting details. Label each item with one of the following:

      T —for the topic
      MI—for the main idea
      SD—for the supporting details

Group 1

   <u> SD </u> Eating buttercups or irises can give someone extreme indigestion.

   <u> MI </u> If eaten, certain common garden plants can make people very ill.

   <u> SD </u> If eaten, lilies of the valley cause an irregular heartbeat.

   <u> T </u> Certain common garden plants.

Group 2

   <u> SD </u> Imagine your former sweetheart wearing a diaper or covered with smelly garbage.

   <u> T </u> Recovering from a broken romance.

   <u> MI </u> Certain methods can help you recover from a broken romance.

   <u> SD </u> Each time you find yourself thinking of the other person, stop yourself by banging a fist on the table.

MAIN IDEAS: Test 3

A. In each pair below, one idea is general and the other is specific. The general idea includes the specific one. Do two things:

   1) Underline the idea in each pair that you think is more general.
   2) Then write in one more specific idea that is covered by the general idea.

1. <u>hot beverage</u>　　tea　　　　　　　　　*coffee*

2. senator　　<u>elected official</u>　　　　　*mayor*

3. <u>reading material</u>　　news magazine　　*book*

4. sweat pants　　<u>exercise clothing</u>　　*T-shirt*

5. <u>baseball player</u>　　catcher　　　　　*pitcher*

6. <u>achievement</u>　　grade of A in a course　*winning a spelling contest*

   (Other answers are possible.)

B. After each paragraph are three subjects. Label each subject with one of the following:

   T—for the topic of the paragraph
   B—for the subject that is too broad
   N—for the subject that is too narrow

7–9. Many employees steal small items from their workplaces. The most common stolen goods are office supplies. People who would never steal a pen from a supermarket shelf think nothing of taking one home from work. Also, many office workers consider personal use of the office copying machine a benefit of the job. And then there are specialists. One famous story concerns an appliance plant worker. He regularly helped himself to parts from the assembly line. Eventually, he had enough to build his own refrigerator.

   _*B*_ Crime

   _*T*_ Employee theft

   _*N*_ Employee theft of office supplies

(Continues on next page)

10–12. Although people dream of being celebrities, the disadvantages of fame are great. First, the famous must look perfect all the time. There's always someone ready to photograph a celebrity looking dumpy in old clothes. The famous also give up their privacy. Their divorces and other problems end up on the evening news and in headlines. Even worse, famous people are often in danger. They get threatening letters and are sometimes attacked.

    __N__   The dangers of fame

    __T__   The disadvantages of fame

    __B__   The advantages and disadvantages of fame

C. (13–20.) Each group of items below includes one topic, one main idea (topic sentence), and two supporting details. Label each item with one of the following:

         T —for the topic
         MI—for the main idea
         SD—for the supporting details

Group 1

    __T__   Occupations and walking.

    __SD__   Nurses walk the most, over five miles a day.

    __MI__   One study found occupations influence how much people walk.

    __SD__   Dentists walk the least, under a mile each day.

Group 2

    __SD__   Staying in the sun too long can cause sunstroke.

    __SD__   People develop skin cancer after years of working on their suntans.

    __T__   Being in the sun.

    __MI__   Spending time in the sun can be dangerous.

MAIN IDEAS: Test 4

A. Each group of three items contains three levels of ideas. Write a *1* by the most general idea in each group, a *2* by the less general idea, and a *3* by the most specific idea.

1. _3_ Ireland   _1_ country   _2_ European country

2. _2_ sentence   _1_ paragraph   _3_ word

3. _1_ organizations   _3_ Four-H Clubs   _2_ youth organizations

4. _1_ buildings   _3_ church   _2_ houses of worship

5. _3_ *Gone with the Wind* _1_ entertainment   _2_ movie

6. _1_ household chores   _3_ washing floors   _2_ cleaning

B. After each paragraph are three subjects. Label each subject with one of the following:

> *T*—for the topic of the paragraph
> *B*—for the subject that is too broad
> *N*—for the subject that is too narrow

7–9. Flea markets and garage sales appeal to people for a couple of reasons. First, of course, a used item costs less than a new one. Many people on a budget have wonderful wardrobes they have assembled with good used clothing. Second, many who shop at flea markets and garage sales are collectors. There are people who collect old hats, 1950s toasters, toaster covers, salt and pepper shakers, comic books, and just about anything else you can think of.

   _N_ Collecting items sold at flea markets and garage sales

   _T_ Flea markets and garage sales

   _B_ Places to shop

(Continues on next page)

10–12. Some people think an only child is lucky because of the material goods and attention he or she receives. But only children have their problems too. For one thing, they have no privacy. Parents always feel entitled to know everything that's going on in an only child's life. Also, only children miss the companionship of brothers and sisters. They can be lonely, and they may have trouble making friends later in life because they never learned to get along with a brother or sister.

    _T_   Only children

    _B_   Children

    _N_   The loneliness of only children

C. (13–20.) Each group of items below includes one topic, one main idea (topic sentence), and two supporting details. Label each item with one of the following:

        T —for the topic
        MI—for the main idea
        SD—for the supporting details

Group 1

    _SD_   Fresh vegetables in season cost less than canned or frozen vegetables.

    _T_   Fresh, frozen, and canned vegetables.

    _SD_   Canning and freezing vegetables robs them of important vitamins and minerals.

    _MI_   Fresh vegetables have advantages over frozen and canned vegetables.

Group 2

    _SD_   The word *trombone* comes from the French word for *pull* and *push*.

    _MI_   The names of many musical instruments come from the way they are played.

    _T_   The names of musical instruments.

    _SD_   *Violin* is Latin for "to skip like a calf."

MAIN IDEAS: Test 5

A. After each paragraph are three subjects. Label each with one of the following:

> *T*—for the topic of the paragraph
> *B*—for the subject that is too broad
> *N*—for the subject that is too narrow

1–3. Losers in presidential elections often fade away after one attempt at the White House. But some unsuccessful presidential nominees try more than once. Richard Nixon was defeated by John F. Kennedy in 1961, yet was successful six years later. Adlai Stevenson lost to Dwight Eisenhower in 1954 and then tried again in 1958. He was unsuccessful again. But Henry Clay and William Jennings Bryan can top that. Each was nominated three times and lost each time.

    T   Some unsuccessful presidential nominees

    N   Richard Nixon and John F. Kennedy

    B   Nominees for the presidency

4–6. Herding dogs share certain characteristics that make them excellent watchdogs. They are large dogs. Among the purebreds classified as herding dogs by the American Kennel Club are collies, sheepdogs, and German shepherds. Also, herding dogs are bred to work closely with humans. They are fast learners, eager to please, and like to dominate situations.

    T   Herding dogs

    B   Dogs

    N   Collies, sheepdogs, and German shepherds

(Continues on next page)

B. Circle the letter of the correct topic of each of the following paragraphs. Then find the sentence in which the author states the main idea about that topic, and circle the letter of that topic sentence.

> ¹Businesses leaving the United States do so for various reasons. ²Lower cost for plants and labor is a major reason. ³Being purchased by a foreign company is another reason for a business to leave the U.S. ⁴Other reasons are high taxes in the U.S. and special incentives offered by a host country.

7. The topic is
   a. businesses that are leaving the United States.
   b. American businesses.
   c. businesses that leave the U.S. because they are purchased by a foreign company.

8. The main idea is stated in sentence
   a. 1.
   b. 2.
   c. 4.

> ¹The average monthly earnings of people who don't complete high school are less than $500. ²A high school graduate averages slightly more than $1,000 per month. ³A college graduate averages over $2,000 per month. ⁴A person with a master's degree makes even more. ⁵These statistics from the U.S. Census Bureau show that the more education you get, the more you are likely to earn.

9. The topic is
   a. education and earning power.
   b. our system of education.
   c. the earning power of a master's degree.

10. The main idea is stated in sentence
    a. 1.
    b. 2.
    c. 5.

MAIN IDEAS: Test 6

A. After each paragraph are three subjects. Label each with one of the following:

> *T*—for the topic of the paragraph
> *B*—for the subject that is too broad
> *N*—for the subject that is too narrow

1–3. The television audience during prime time is divided up unevenly among all the available channels. During those hours, most people watch the national networks. Over 70 percent of sets are tuned to ABC, CBS, NBC, or Fox. Cable stations account for 20 percent of viewers. Pay TV takes up another 5 percent. Public TV is viewed by only 3 percent of the public during prime time.

   _B_   The television audience

   _T_   The television audience during prime time

   _N_   The prime time audience for cable stations

4–6. Secondhand smoke—smoke from someone else's cigar or cigarette—can cause breathing illnesses and even lung cancer. According to the government, there are several ways to avoid the dangers of secondhand smoke. First, don't allow smoking at all in your home. Second, do not permit people to smoke outdoors in areas where nonsmokers pass by. Third, in restaurants that allow smoking, ask to be seated as far away from the smoking area as possible.

   _B_   Smoking

   _N_   Sitting far from the smoking area in restaurants

   _T_   The dangers of secondhand smoke

(Continues on next page)

B. Circle the letter of the correct topic of each of the following paragraphs. Then find the sentence in which the author states the main idea about that topic, and circle the letter of that topic sentence.

> [1]Gasoline is the most common product made from petroleum. [2]However, about three thousand products other than gasoline are also made from petroleum. [3]Some of the others are bubble gum, crayons, floor polish, house paint, and eyeglasses. [4]Ping-pong paddles and loudspeakers also contain petroleum.

7. The topic is
   a. gasoline as a product of petroleum.
   b. products.
   c. products made from petroleum.

8. The main idea is stated in sentence
   a. 1.
   b. 2.
   c. 4.

> [1]Children who don't read during summer vacation will lose six months of their reading level by September. [2]There are several things parents can do to help children maintain their reading levels during summer vacation. [3]First, turn the TV off when it is not being watched. [4]Second, set up a daily reading time for children. [5]Third, be a role model by reading novels, magazines, or newspapers. [6]Leave them around the house so that children will see reading materials around. [7]Fourth, show an interest in what your child is reading by asking questions or by taking turns reading out loud. [8]Also remember that writing and reading go together. [9]Leave notes for your child that require a written response. [10]Buy notebooks in which children can keep a journal of their activities and thoughts.

9. The topic is
   a. reading.
   b. maintaining children's reading levels during summer vacation.
   c. being a good role model for reading during summer vacation.

10. The main idea is stated in sentence
    a. 1.
    b. 2.
    c. 3.

SUPPORTING DETAILS: Test 1

A. (1–5.) Major and minor supporting details are mixed together in the list below. The details of this list support the main idea shown. Separate the major, more general details from the minor ones by filling in the outline. One detail has been filled in for you.

- Have the names and dates of your educational background in mind or on paper.
- Come prepared to fill in certain commonly requested information.
- Make sure the application is easy to read.
- Print or write clearly.
- Be prepared to provide names and dates of your previous jobs.
- Use a pen.

Main idea: There are a number of things to remember when filling out a job application.

Major detail: 1. *Make sure the application is easy to read.*

Minor details: a. *Print or write clearly.*

b. *Use a pen.*

Major detail: 2. *Come prepared to fill in certain commonly requested information.*

Minor details: a. *Have the names and dates of your educational background in mind or on paper.*

b. *Be prepared to provide names and dates of your previous jobs.*

(Continues on next page)

B. (6–10.) In the spaces provided, complete the notes on each paragraph: For the first paragraph, complete the heading, including the word that ends in *s*. Then fill in the two missing major details. For the second paragraph, fill in the two missing major details. In each paragraph, the topic sentence is boldfaced.

1. A respectful parent guides and instructs more than he or she punishes. **To be a respectful parent, there are several don'ts you should remember.** First, don't yell a lot at children. Yelling will tell a child that the parent is out of control. Or it will result in a shouting match that loses respect. Second, don't lay down too many rules. Growing up is not a boot camp. Too many rules will prevent children from understanding what is really important. Third, don't show disrespect to a child. This will create resentment. Fourth, don't order children around. They will not learn responsibility if they feel they have to do what you want at the instant you command it. Finally, don't neglect to acknowledge good behavior. Praise and hugs work wonders in promoting responsibility and respect.

    Heading: _____ *Several Don't* _____ s for Parents to Remember

    List of major details:

    1. Don't yell a lot at children.

    2. Don't lay down too many rules.

    3. *Don't show disrespect to a child.*

    4. Don't order children around.

    5. *Don't neglect to acknowledge good behavior.*

2. **For various reasons, veterinarians are implanting computer microchips under the skin of pets.** First, the chips can be used to recognize an animal that has been lost or stolen. Second, they can be used to identify purebred animals that have come from breeders. Breeders who guarantee that an animal is free from defects can identify the animal later in life. And third, the animal's history can be kept on the chip. This means that if a pet changes vets, the new doctor can see what treatments the animal has undergone.

    Heading: Various Reasons Vets Are Implanting Computer Microchips Under the Skin of Pets

    List of major details:

    1. *The chips can be used to recognize a lost or stolen animal.*

    2. Implanted microchips can identify animals for breeders.

    3. *The animal's history can be kept on the chip.*

SUPPORTING DETAILS: Test 2

A. (1–4.) In the spaces provided, complete the notes on each paragraph: For the first paragraph, complete the heading, including the word that ends in *s*. Then fill in the missing major detail. For the second paragraph, fill in the two missing major details. In each paragraph, the topic sentence is boldfaced.

1. **There are a couple of important steps to take when choosing a puppy.** One is to check out a pup's physical condition carefully. Being cute isn't enough. The animal's eyes should be clear and bright, and its gums should be pink and firm. Also, get an idea of the puppy's personality. Watch it play with other pups. If it's very timid or aggressive, it might not make a good pet.

   Heading: _____*Important Step*_____s to Take When Choosing a Puppy

   List of major details:

   1. Check out a pup's physical condition carefully.

   2. *Get an idea of the pup's personality.* _____

2. Many people continue to work after "retiring." **There are two main reasons many senior citizens continue to work after "retiring."** First, of course, some work mainly for the money. According to one survey, 32 percent of older workers fall into this category. The others, however, work mainly because they like to. One retired mechanic, for instance, loves his $4.75-an-hour job at a fast-food restaurant. And a teacher who had always wanted to be a doctor went into medicine after "retirement," as a nurse.

   Heading: Two Main Reasons "Retired" People Continue to Work

   List of major details:

   1. *For money* _____

   2. *Because they like to* _____

(Continues on next page)

B. Read the paragraph below and then answer the questions that follow. The topic sentence is boldfaced.

> **While we lack the instincts of animals, humans do share several powerful motives.** One is the drive to achieve. This desire is what urges us to set athletic records or to try out for the starring role in a play. Another human motive is the urge to use power. People with a strong power drive may join a campus activity in order to become its leader. The desire to associate with other people is a third powerful motive. This motive brings people to join organizations, work on committees, socialize, and marry.

5. The major details of this paragraph involve several
   a. instincts that people share.
   b. motives that people share.
   c. habits that people share.

6. The major details are indicated by the signal words
   a. *one, another,* and *third.*
   b. *first, second,* and *finally.*
   c. *achieve, power,* and *associate.*

7. The major details of this paragraph are human drives to
   a. set records, star in plays, and join organizations.
   b. achieve, use power, and associate with others.
   c. join organizations, work on committees, socialize, and marry.

8. When people join a campus activity in order to become its leader, they are motivated by the drive to
   a. achieve.
   b. use power.
   c. socialize.

9. The desire to associate with others motivates people to
   a. set athletic records.
   b. lead a campus activity.
   c. socialize and marry.

10. When people try out for a play, they are motivated by the drive to
    a. achieve.
    b. use power.
    c. socialize.

SUPPORTING DETAILS: Test 3

Answer the questions that follow each paragraph. The topic sentence of each paragraph is boldfaced.

A. ¹**Various pests destroy vegetation across the country.** ²The Mediterranean fruit fly attacks over 250 types of fruits and vegetables nationwide. ³Its cousin, the Mexican fruit fly, can cause damage to over 50 varieties of vegetation. ⁴The boll weevil, which once did enormous damage to the cotton industry in the South, is still active in some areas. ⁵It attacks cotton only. ⁶The gypsy moth strips the leaves off over 500 kinds of trees, shrubs, and garden plants. ⁷Also destructive is the Japanese beetle, which strikes over 250 kinds of trees, fruits, and vegetables.

1. __T__ TRUE OR FALSE? The Mexican fruit fly is related to the Mediterranean fruit fly.

2. __F__ TRUE OR FALSE? According to the passage, the cotton industry in the South was greatly damaged by the Mexican fruit fly.

3. The idea below is
   a. true according to the paragraph.
   b. false according to the paragraph.
   (c.) not mentioned in the paragraph.

   The Japanese beetle came from Japan.

4. *Circle the letter of the missing detail:* The _____ damages over 500 kinds of trees, shrubs, and garden plants.
   a. Mediterranean fruit fly
   b. boll weevil
   (c.) gypsy moth

5. The answer to question 4 can be found in sentence
   a. 4.
   b. 5.
   (c.) 6.
   d. 7.

(Continues on next page)

B.   ¹When winter approaches, influenza (the flu) is not far behind. ²**To protect against influenza, doctors recommend that people—especially those in high-risk groups—get vaccinated as early as possible.** ³An early shot gives the body time to develop the antibodies necessary to fight the flu. ⁴Among the groups at greater than average risk of getting the flu are senior citizens and children. ⁵People with long-term health problems are in danger, as well. ⁶Those who belong to these high-risk groups should get a flu shot every year.

6. __*T*__ TRUE OR FALSE? Children are at greater than average risk of getting influenza.

7. The answer to question 1 can be found in sentence
   (a.) 4.
   b. 5.
   c. 6.
   d. 8.

8. The idea below is
   a. true according to the paragraph.
   (b.) false according to the paragraph.
   c. not mentioned in the paragraph.

   Senior citizens do not need a flu shot every year.

9. *Circle the letter of the missing detail:* _____ will let your body develop antibodies in time to fight the flu.
   a. A yearly flu shot
   (b.) An early flu shot
   c. Several flu shots

10. *Complete the sentence:* Members of three high-risk groups who should get yearly flu shots include those with _____*long-term*_____ health problems.

SUPPORTING DETAILS: Test 4

Answer the questions that follow each paragraph. The topic sentence of each paragraph is boldfaced.

A.   [1]**In both fiction and reality, ventriloquists become quite attached to their dummies.** [2]In the 1929 movie *The Great Gabbo*, a ventriloquist goes mad and destroys his dummy. [3]He spends the rest of his life on the run, believing he is wanted for murder. [4]There are real-life stories of ventriloquists who are buried with their dummies. [5]Other accounts tell of ventriloquists who left money to their dummies in their wills. [6]One ventriloquist, Herbert Dexter, spent more time with his dummy, Charlie, than with his wife and used it to cruelly mock her. [7]In the 1930s, his wife sued him for divorce, naming Charlie as having successfully competed for her husband's affections. [8]She claimed that she had thoughts of "murdering" Charlie. [9]"I would have thrown him out of the window had I been able to unlock the coffin-like trunk in which he was kept," she testified. [10]The divorce was granted.

1. The movie *The Great Gabbo* is about a ventriloquist who
    a. is buried with his dummy.
    b. is wanted for murder.
    c. destroys his dummy.

2. __T__ TRUE OR FALSE? According to the author, some ventriloquists are buried with their dummies.

3. Some real-life ventriloquists have reportedly
    a. destroyed their dummies.
    b. committed murder.
    c. left money in their wills to their dummies.

4. The answer to question 3 can be found in sentence
    a. 4.
    b. 5.
    c. 6.
    d. 7.

5. Herbert Dexter
    a. was buried with his dummy, Charlie.
    b. sued his wife for divorce.
    c. used his dummy to make fun of his wife.

(Continues on next page)

B. ¹**Adults should help children follow a good financial plan.** ²First, children should be taught ways to earn money. ³Baby-sitting, newspaper routes, or household chores may be options. ⁴Then, children should be shown how to save money for something special. ⁵A plan can be developed that allows them to use a little of the money they earn for minor purchases, such as birthday cards and candy. ⁶The rest of the money they earn can be put in the bank. ⁷When there is enough, the child can make that special purchase. ⁸A money management plan taught early can prevent children from wasting money later in life.

6. __T__ TRUE OR FALSE? According to the author, children should be taught how to save money for a special purchase.

7. The answer to question 6 can be found in sentence
   a. 2.
   b. 3.
   c. 4.
   d. 6.

8. The idea below is
   a. true according to the paragraph.
   b. false according to the paragraph.
   c. not mentioned in the paragraph.

   Children can be permitted to use some of the money they earn for minor purchases.

9. The author considers birthday cards to be
   a. expensive.
   b. useless.
   c. minor purchases.

10. __T__ TRUE OR FALSE? The author feels early training in money management can help children handle their money well as adults.

SUPPORTING DETAILS: Test 5

Read each paragraph below and then answer the questions that follow it. The topic sentence is boldfaced.

A.   [1]**Parts of our environment affect the way we behave and feel.** [2]First, there is temperature. [3]Most people prefer temperatures in the 70s. [4]When it is hotter than the 70s, they become less active and less alert. [5]Lighting also affects us. [6]In the classroom or on the job, bright light encourages work. [7]In contrast, the low lighting of a restaurant relaxes us and encourages informal conversation. [8]Last is color. [9]For example, red is felt as exciting, blue as calming, and yellow as cheerful.

1. As the topic sentence suggests, the major details of this paragraph are
   a. various temperatures.
   b. places where we work and relax.
   (c.) parts of our environment that affect our behavior and moods.

2. Specifically, the major details of this paragraph are
   a. cool, hot, and just-right temperatures.
   b. the classroom, the job, and the restaurant.
   (c.) temperature, lighting, and color.

3. The signal words that introduce the major details are
   (a.) *first, also,* and *last.*
   b. *most, when,* and *and.*
   c. *in contrast, for example,* and *as.*

4. Most people become less alert
   a. in bright light.
   (b.) in temperatures over the 70s.
   c. in restaurants with low lighting.

5. The last sentence of the paragraph provides
   a. a major detail.
   (b.) minor details.
   c. both major and minor details.

(Continues on next page)

B. [1]**Intelligence includes several basic mental abilities.** [2]One is language skill. [3]People strong in this ability do well on reading tests and have large vocabularies. [4]Another such ability is a quick memory. [5]People talented in this skill may learn the words to a popular song after hearing it only once or twice. [6]A third basic mental skill allows us to make sense of visual information. [7]People strong in this ability can quickly see similarities and differences between designs and pictures.

6. The major details of this paragraph are
   a. types of mental abilities.
   b. types of language abilities.
   c. types of similarities and differences.

7. The signal words that introduce the major details are
   a. *several, mental,* and *abilities.*
   b. *one, another,* and *third.*
   c. *first, also,* and *another.*

8. Specifically, the major details of this paragraph are
   a. designs and pictures.
   b. language, memory, and visual abilities.
   c. reading tests, large vocabularies, and unscrambling mixed-up sentences.

9. The ability to learn quickly the words to a popular song shows a strong
   a. language ability.
   b. memorizing ability.
   c. visual ability.

10. The ability to see quickly how designs and pictures are alike shows a strong
    a. language ability.
    b. memorizing ability.
    c. visual ability.

SUPPORTING DETAILS: Test 6

Read each paragraph below and then answer the questions that follow it. The topic sentence is boldfaced.

A. **¹The National Board of Medical Examiners recently released a number of alarming facts about doctors.** ²First, the amount of time doctors spend examining patients is down dramatically from previous years. ³Twenty years ago, doctors spent eleven minutes with patients. ⁴Today they take only seven minutes. ⁵Second, it was found that a large number of patients have been switching doctors. ⁶Within the past year, for instance, 25 percent of patients reported changing doctors. ⁷The most common reason given was that patients did not feel comfortable with the doctor they left. ⁸Finally, medical students' reasons for wanting to become a doctor were unexpected. ⁹The most common reason given was to make a good living. ¹⁰Working with people ranked third.

1. The opening phrase that describes the major supporting details is
    a. "The National Board of Medical Examiners."
    (b.) "a number of alarming facts about doctors."
    c. "the amount of time doctors spend examining patients."

2. The first major supporting detail is signaled by the addition word or words
    a. *a number of.*
    b. *only.*
    (c.) *first.*

3. The second major detail is introduced in sentence
    a. 3.
    (b.) 5.
    c. 6.

4. The third major detail is introduced in sentence
    a. 7.
    (b.) 8.
    c. 9.

5. Circle the letter of the outline that best reflects the paragraph.

    A. Main idea: The National Board of Medical Examiners recently released a number of alarming facts about doctors.
       1. Twenty years ago, doctors spent eleven minutes examining patients.
       2. Today, on the average, doctors spend seven minutes examining patients.
       3. Within the past year, 25 percent of patients reported changing doctors, in most cases because of discomfort with the doctor.
       4. The reasons medical students give for wanting to become a doctor were unexpected.   *(Continues on next page)*

Ⓑ Main idea: The National Board of Medical Examiners recently released a number of alarming facts about doctors.
1. Doctors today spend less time examining patients than they did twenty years ago.
2. A large number of patients have been switching doctors.
3. Medical students rank making a good living as a more important reason to become a doctor than working with people.

B. ¹**There are different ways to handle embarrassing moments.** ²One way is to reduce the significance of the embarrassing moment. ³For instance, if you don't make a big deal about spilling your coffee, other people probably won't. ⁴Another way is to disown your behavior. ⁵After the embarrassing moment, say something like "That's not the real me, you know." ⁶And a third way to handle an embarrassing moment is to get help. ⁷For example, if you spill food at a restaurant, don't try to clean it up yourself. ⁸Have a friend or a waiter help you to clean up the mess.

6. The major supporting details for this paragraph are
   a. 1) embarrassing moments, 2) disowning yourself, and 3) spilling food at a restaurant.
   (b.) 1) reduce the significance of the event, 2) disown your behavior, and 3) get help.
   c. 1) don't make a big deal out of spilling your coffee, 2) say, "That's not the real me, you know," and 3) let somebody else clean up a spill at a restaurant.

7. The first major supporting detail is signaled by the addition word or words
   (a.) *one.*
   b. *also.*
   c. *another.*

8. The last major supporting detail is signaled by the addition word or words
   a. *another.*
   (b.) *third.*
   c. *for example.*

9. Sentence 3 provides
   a. a major detail.
   (b.) a minor detail.

10. Sentence 4 provides
    (a.) a major detail.
    b. a minor detail.

LOCATIONS OF MAIN IDEAS: Test 1

The five paragraphs that follow are on the first level of difficulty. Write the number of each topic sentence in the space provided.

1. ^{1}In many homes, the refrigerator door is the family bulletin board. ^{2}On it, people place things they don't want to lose. ^{3}These may include the phone number of the local police or of a favorite baby sitter. ^{4}Also kept there are reminders, including notes about social events. ^{5}Finally, the refrigerator is a favorite spot to display things, such as a child's art work.

    Topic sentence: _____1_____

2. ^{1}Do you want to lose weight? ^{2}Then try eating in only one place and at regular times. ^{3}This will help you cut down on snacking. ^{4}Also, eat slowly. ^{5}The trick is to get as much pleasure as possible from the smallest amount of food. ^{6}You want to give your body time to let you know when you've had enough. ^{7}Last, make exercise part of your daily schedule. ^{8}You will have more success losing weight if you follow these diet guidelines.

    Topic sentence: _____8_____

3. ^{1}Few things are more boring than standing in line. ^{2}Luckily, ways have been found to make some otherwise boring waits more bearable. ^{3}Airlines now hire people to make sure customers don't waste time in the wrong lines. ^{4}In some places, live entertainment cheers customers in long lines. ^{5}It seems that being able to look at oneself also makes waiting easier. ^{6}In large buildings, complaints about slow elevators decrease when mirrors are put up nearby.

    Topic sentence: _____2_____

4. ^{1}When their costs go up, gas stations try new ways of making a profit. ^{2}To stir up business, some have gone back to giving away free glasses with a fill-up. ^{3}Also, at some stations, customers can have their cars washed, rent a video, or leave film to be developed. ^{4}There are even stations with stores that sell many quick-stop needs, from doughnuts to dog food.

    Topic sentence: _____1_____

(Continues on next page)

5.   ¹Have you ever wondered why we are attracted to certain people as friends and lovers? ²One key is physical closeness. ³We are more likely to be interested in people we see often. ⁴What we think of as good looks are also important. ⁵We tend to like people whose looks we like. ⁶We also are drawn to people with whom we share similar backgrounds, interests, and values. ⁷Several factors, then, help explain our attractions to other people.

Topic sentence: _____7_____

LOCATIONS OF MAIN IDEAS: Test 2

The five paragraphs below are on the first and second levels of difficulty. Write the number of each topic sentence in the space provided. For the one case in which there are two topic sentences, write in both numbers.

1. ¹Do you keep your eyes open when you kiss? ²If so, you're in the minority. ³There are several explanations for the fact that most people close their eyes when kissing. ⁴One explanation is that it is simply tradition. ⁵We learned to kiss that way and continue. ⁶Another is that closing our eyes helps us focus on our sense of touch. ⁷A third explanation says that when we kiss we are so close that we could not look at each other without crossing our eyes.

   Topic sentence(s): _____3_____

2. ¹William Henry Harrison had one of the most fascinating careers of all the presidents of the United States. ²He was the only president to study medicine. ³Before getting his degree, he left school and joined the Army, where he rose to the rank of general. ⁴He was elected president at age sixty-eight. ⁵Until Ronald Reagan, this was the oldest a man had been elected president. ⁶He gave one of the longest inaugural addresses on record, close to two hours. ⁷Shortly after his speech, he caught pneumonia. ⁸Harrison died a little more than a month after taking office.

   Topic sentence(s): _____1_____

3. ¹Hot dogs are as American as any food. ²Unfortunately, they are also high in fat and salt. ³Since the country has become more health-conscious, some companies have introduced hot dogs that are more nutritious. ⁴First came chicken and turkey frankfurters, which have been on the market for some time. ⁵These are lower in fat than the traditional beef and pork hot dogs. ⁶There are now also franks that have tofu added to them to reduce fat 20 percent or more. ⁷Some companies have cut out nitrates, preservatives that have been linked to cancer. ⁸Still others have lowered the salt content of their hot dogs.

   Topic sentence(s): _____3_____

(Continues on next page)

4.   [1]The traditional American dream has included getting married, buying a home, and raising a family. [2]While marriage may still be the goal of most men, an Ohio University survey suggests that it appeals to fewer women. [3]The survey asked single men and women between the ages of eighteen and thirty-four if they ever wanted to get married. [4]Two out of three men said they wanted to get married. [5]Only 50 percent of the women surveyed indicated a desire to get married.

Topic sentence(s): _____2_____

5.   [1]It is often difficult for foreign students to adjust to life in America. [2]For one thing, they may be uncomfortable with the casual relationship that exists between American teachers and students. [3]In many countries, students treat teachers much more formally. [4]In addition, foreign students have the language problem to deal with. [5]Their English classes may not have prepared them to understand fast-paced conversation filled with slang expressions. [6]Foreign students' social lives can be difficult as well. [7]Having a background so different from that of other students can make it hard to find friends. [8]For various reasons, then, life in America can be hard on foreign students.

Topic sentence(s): _____1, 8_____

LOCATIONS OF MAIN IDEAS: Test 3

The five paragraphs below are on the second level of difficulty. Write the number of each topic sentence in the space provided. For the one case in which there are two topic sentences, write in both numbers.

1. ¹The ease in opening and closing Velcro has given it some interesting uses. ²For instance, astronauts have used it to keep objects—and themselves—from falling into space. ³They also have had small pieces of Velcro stuck inside their helmets so they could scratch an itchy nose. ⁴Today, the fabric is used to fasten the fireproof suits of race-car drivers. ⁵This allows a driver to jump out of a suit in seconds if necessary. ⁶Velcro is also used to join two parts of the artificial heart.

    Topic sentence(s): _____1_____

2. ¹Studies show that a dog or cat creates a more relaxed home environment which can help to end family arguments. ²In addition, pets often serve as an emotional outlet for older men. ³The men share thoughts and feelings with the pets that they don't share with the rest of the family. ⁴Pets also ease life's stressful times, including the death of a loved one. ⁵Furthermore, pets have been used with proven success in increasing the will to live among older people. ⁶Clearly, pets can be good for our mental health.

    Topic sentence(s): _____6_____

3. ¹If you want to improve your running ability, lifting weights will help. ²Weight training increases strength, which will help propel you forward more efficiently. ³Weights will also prepare you to run longer distances, since muscle is where fuel is stored. ⁴And, combined with stretching activities, weights will cut down on injuries. ⁵Even though you may not see many muscle-bound runners, working with weights will help you run.

    Topic sentence(s): _____1, 5_____

4. ¹Every week, guns kill several hundred Americans. ²To cut down on these deaths, some say we should stop the sale of guns, or at least of the worst kinds. ³Since so many people already own guns, others suggest we require a permit to carry a gun outside the home. ⁴Many gun owners call for yet another solution: tough penalties for those who use guns in crimes. ⁵These are just a few of the many ideas on how to reduce the dangers of guns in America.

    Topic sentence(s): _____5_____

(Continues on next page)

5. [1]The reason we shiver and get goosebumps when we are shocked has to do with our animal nature. [2]When animals see or hear something threatening, their fur stands on end. [3]This reaction makes them look larger and thus more dangerous to an enemy. [4]In addition, extra blood flows to their muscles, getting them ready for action. [5]Humans react in the same way. [6]When we sense danger, goosebumps appear where our fur would stand on end if we had any. [7]Also, the blood flow to our skin is reduced in favor of our muscles, making us feel cold. [8]Unlike other animals, we have no fur to warm us, so we shiver to get warm.

    Topic sentence(s): _____*1*_____

LOCATIONS OF MAIN IDEAS: Test 4

The five paragraphs below are on the third level of difficulty. Write the number of each topic sentence in the space provided. For the one case in which there are two topic sentences, write in both numbers.

1. [1]Can watching television influence how we think? [2]Research shows that people who watch a lot of TV are influenced by its unrealistic representation of sex roles. [3]For example, male characters outnumber females by three to one in prime-time TV. [4]Also, men play a far greater variety of roles than women. [5]And fewer than 20 percent of married mothers on television work outside the home; in real life, over 50 percent do. [6]No wonder so many heavy TV viewers agree that "women should take care of running their homes and leave running the country to men."

    Topic sentence(s): _____2_____

2. [1]The question of who holds the power in a marriage is more complex than it used to be. [2]Husbands once had more power in marriages. [3]They earned more, were better educated, and had jobs with more prestige. [4]But as women get better jobs and earn more, they gain power at home. [5]Another factor in the balance of power is whether or not both partners care the same about the marriage. [6]If the husband, for example, cares more about staying married than the wife does, the wife will have more power. [7]That is because the husband will do more to please her. [8]Thus the power structure of marriage has become more complicated in recent years.

    Topic sentence(s): _____1, 8_____

3. [1]What steps can you take if you turn an ankle or strain a muscle? [2]Many sports physicians recommend the "RICE" formula for sprains and strains: Rest, Ice, Compression, and Elevation. [3]First, rest the joint or muscle that hurts. [4]Secondly, apply ice to the injured area. [5]Ice may be used at regular times for two days. [6]A compression bandage, such as an Ace bandage, will also ease the pain. [7]Finally, elevating an injured ankle or knee will keep pressure off it and prevent further damage. [8]Of course, if the pain stays or if the injury swells, you should see a doctor at once.

    Topic sentence(s): _____2_____

(Continues on next page)

4.   ¹Until recently, the mountain town of Katy, West Virginia, was too far away to pick up television signals. ²But then cable TV was installed. ³Now all but three of the 170 houses in Katy have television. ⁴The introduction of TV to Katy has influenced local students in both helpful and harmful ways. ⁵On the plus side, students now express themselves better. ⁶They also understand others and world events better. ⁷But on the minus side, students' attention span has shortened. ⁸And they are now so used to a TV being on that they have trouble working in quiet classrooms.

Topic sentence(s): _____4_____

5.   ¹The distance we like to keep between ourselves and others depends on the other people, according to one researcher. ²The space within about one foot from us is "intimate" space. ³We share it willingly only with loved ones. ⁴If forced to share it with strangers (in a crowded elevator, for instance), we feel uncomfortable. ⁵Between one and four feet away is our "personal" space, which we share with friends. ⁶This is about how far apart we sit at a restaurant, for example. ⁷Between about four and ten feet away is "social" space. ⁸This is the distance we keep from strangers at parties and other gatherings. ⁹Finally, over ten feet away is "public" space, a distance at which we can pretty much ignore others.

Topic sentence(s): _____1_____

LOCATIONS OF MAIN IDEAS: Test 5

The five paragraphs below are on the third and fourth levels of difficulty. Write the number of each topic sentence in the space provided. For the one case in which there are two topic sentences, write in both numbers.

1. ¹People wonder why home burglar alarms often go off even when no trespassers are entering the houses. ²False alarms in home security systems occur for a variety of reasons. ³Police in Texas report that cockroaches sometimes get into systems and trigger the alarm. ⁴A firm in Arkansas learned that a system that kept going off was home to a spider. ⁵Whenever the spider moved by a sensing device, the alarm went off. ⁶A company in Dallas discovered that a system was continually being set off by a banner set up to motivate salespeople. ⁷Whenever the air conditioning came on, the banner blew back and forth, setting off a motion detector. ⁸Almost all companies report that the most common cause is human error. ⁹Two out of three false alarms occur when people forget their code or open doors and windows without turning off the system.

    Topic sentence(s): _____2_____

2. ¹Our life stages may be set by biology, but how we view those stages is shaped by society. ²During the Middle Ages, for example, children dressed—and were expected to act—like little adults. ³Adolescence became a separate stage of life only fairly recently, when a teenage subculture appeared. ⁴Before that, young people were "children" until about age sixteen. ⁵Then they went to work, married, and had their own children. ⁶Today, young adulthood has become a new stage of life, covering about ages twenty to thirty. ⁷And now that people live longer and spend years in active retirement, older adulthood has also become a distinct life stage.

    Topic sentence(s): _____1_____

3. ¹In California, a "Victim's Bill of Rights" was passed recently. ²This law broadened the type of evidence that could be used in court. ³The idea was to keep criminals from going free due to legal loopholes. ⁴But defense lawyers soon learned that they, too, could use this law. ⁵In rape trials especially, the new law could be used to move part of the blame onto the victim. ⁶This was done by presenting evidence, not permitted before, that the victim was careless or sexually "loose." ⁷A law intended to protect crime victims thus turned out to have just the opposite effect.

    Topic sentence(s): _____7_____

(Continues on next page)

4.   [1]Zoos used to be places where unhappy-looking animals paced back and forth in small cages. [2]But today, many zoos have large "natural" areas in which animals can live as if they were in the wild. [3]In some zoos, for example, chimpanzees and gorillas live in large areas that look like rain forests. [4]Huge animals such as elephants wander freely on "African plains" in the heart of New York City and San Diego. [5]Zookeepers sometimes use such environments to allow animals to work for their food, as in the wild. [6]In one zoo, for instance, honey is hidden in a fake anthill. [7]Chimpanzees scoop the honey out with a stiff piece of hay, a process similar to how they "fish" for insects in Africa.

Topic sentence(s): _____2_____

5.   [1]While parents of different countries use different languages, parental speech patterns appear to be much the same throughout the world. [2]A Stanford University study found that when mothers want to warn their babies, they use short, sharp words such as *no* in English and *nyet* in Russian. [3]When parents want to praise their babies, the message first rises in pitch and then falls. [4]American mothers, for instance, stretch the word *good* into *"Goo-ood!"* [5]When the baby needs comforting, a long, soothing sound such as *shhh* is used. [6]And to call attention to something, parents begin with a low tone and end on a high note, as in "Look at THIS!" [7]When it comes to communicating with children, there is apparently a universal language.

Topic sentence(s): _____1, 7_____

LOCATIONS OF MAIN IDEAS: Test 6

The five paragraphs below are on the fourth level of difficulty. Write the number of each topic sentence in the space provided. For the one case in which there are two topic sentences, write in both numbers.

1. [1]Photo radar is increasing the efficiency of ticket giving. [2]With photo radar, a beam is directed at oncoming traffic. [3]When a speeder is detected, a picture of the front of the vehicle is taken. [4]The license number is matched with the car's owner, and a ticket is sent. [5]The arresting officer does not have to take time explaining the situation to one motorist while others speed by. [6]Also, the load on traffic courts is lessened since people are sent a copy of the picture that was taken. [7]Photo radar has shown itself to be a practical and effective means of enforcing speed limits.

   Topic sentence(s): _____1, 7_____

2. [1]It is not uncommon for depression to set in after a divorce. [2]A recent study shows that a condition called "move down" contributes to post-divorce depression. [3]"Move down" refers to the economizing that is done by the person moving out of the residence. [4]The person who moves out has a tendency to move into a house or apartment that is of lower quality. [5]The study compared divorced people who moved down with those who maintained a home of the same quality. [6]Those who did not move down were less stressed and had less chance of depression setting in.

   Topic sentence(s): _____2_____

3. [1]A bullfighter usually kneels in front of the bull before a fight begins. [2]Audience members are amazed at his courage. [3]However, the truth is that by kneeling, the bullfighter tricks the bull into being gentle. [4]Among animals, when two males fight, one can signal he gives up by taking a yielding position. [5]The animal drops to the ground and raises his backside. [6]This position tells the other male that he has won and thus reduces his instinct to fight. [7]For this reason, the bull thinks the kneeling bullfighter is giving up. [8]Therefore the bull does not attack.

   Topic sentence(s): _____3_____

(Continues on next page)

4. ¹The Great Flood of 1993 caused extreme destruction in states along the Mississippi River. ²There is strong evidence that humans were a major contributor to the destruction during the Great Flood. ³The longest river in the U.S., the Mississippi begins in Minnesota and empties into the Gulf of Mexico in Louisiana. ⁴Before Europeans settled along its banks, the river responded to floods by widening. ⁵Workers changed that by building levees to protect the towns along the river's banks. ⁶Engineers straightened the river. ⁷Both changes made the river move faster. ⁸When floods come, the water has no place to go and presses against the levees. ⁹When the pressure becomes too great, the levees break, flooding towns. ¹⁰If the levees hold, there is a danger that the water will become higher than the levees, and this results in floods as well.

    Topic sentence(s): _____2_____

5. ¹There are 170 million acres of federally owned land used by ranchers to graze cattle and sheep. ²The government recognizes that two-thirds of that land is overgrazed. ³A new technique called "holistic resource management" may put an end to overgrazing and return lands to their original state. ⁴The technique, called HRM for short, is modeled on a pattern that existed before cattle herds trampled the prairies. ⁵Buffalo used to move into an area, consume grasses and plant life, fertilize the area, then move on to new areas. ⁶Followers of HRM try to imitate this pattern by moving herds along at a set speed and time.

    Topic sentence(s): _____3_____

TRANSITIONS: Test 1

Complete each sentence with the appropriate transition word or phrase. Then circle the kind of transition you have used.

1. a. _____*While*_____ digging in his garden, Lonnie discovered an old tin box full of coins.

   b. The transition signals

   ⟨time.⟩   contrast.   addition.

   To illustrate
   Although
   While

2. a. Both Presidents Lincoln and Kennedy were killed on a Friday. _____*Furthermore*_____, each was in a large crowd and with his wife when killed.

   b. The relationship of the second sentence to the first is one of

   cause and effect.   illustration.   ⟨addition.⟩

   Furthermore
   In contrast
   As a result

3. a. _____*Just as*_____ human infants suck their thumbs, baby elephants suck their trunks.

   b. The relationship between the two parts of the sentence is one of

   cause and effect.   time.   ⟨comparison.⟩

   Although
   Just as
   Because

4. a. The chef stuffed steel wool into the cracks of the restaurant _____*so*_____ mice could no longer get into the kitchen.

   b. The transition shows

   comparison.   ⟨cause and effect.⟩   time.

   so
   similarly
   in contrast

5. a. Nita planned to become a stewardess _____*until*_____ she discovered she got airsick.

   b. The transition shows

   cause and effect.   ⟨time.⟩   contrast.

   because
   in the same way
   until

(Continues on next page)

6. a. Arnie's recent camping trip was a disaster. _____For example_____, one morning he scared a skunk and sat in poison ivy.

   As a result
   For example
   In addition

   b. The transition signals a relationship of
   addition.   cause and effect.   (illustration.)

7. a. Roberto was so hungry that he ordered two Whoppers. _____Also_____, he asked for a large chocolate shake.

   In contrast
   For example
   Also

   b. The transition shows
   contrast.   illustration.   (addition.)

8. a. Movie audiences usually dislike film monsters. _____However_____, filmgoers pitied King Kong and even shed tears at his death.

   In addition
   However
   Likewise

   b. The relationship of the two sentences is one of
   (contrast.)   comparison.   addition.

9. a. You can be insured against just about anything. _____For instance_____, comedians Abbott and Costello once insured themselves against any member of their audience dying of laughter.

   In addition
   On the other hand
   For instance

   b. The relationship of the second sentence to the first sentence is one of
   addition.   contrast.   (illustration.)

10. a. The zookeeper put a large mirror in the peacock's cage. _____As a result_____, the bird spread its tail and showed off for the "other" peacock.

    As a result
    Furthermore
    In the same way

    b. The transition signals a relationship of
    addition.   comparison.   (cause and effect.)

TRANSITIONS: Test 2

A. Fill in each blank with the appropriate transition in the box. Use each transition once.

Note: You may find it helpful to check (✓) each transition after you insert it into a sentence.

also	during	for instance
because	similar	

1. At 21, Claudia saw a photo of her mother at the same age. She was amazed to see how _____*similar*_____ they looked.

2. I'm not going to invite Brad and Gerry to the same party _____*because*_____ they are not on speaking terms.

3. Thousands of years ago, the Earth was very different. _____*For instance*_____, much of Europe was once covered with ice.

4. In his forties, Chun had more trouble than ever losing weight. _____*Also*_____, his hairline started to move back.

5. _____*During*_____ an interview, former President Jimmy Carter was asked how he would feel if his daughter had a love affair. He answered, "Shocked. She's only seven."

(Continues on next page)

B. Fill in each blank with the appropriate transition in the box. Use each transition once.

Note: You may find it helpful to check (✓) each transition after you insert it into a sentence.

because	but	such as
first	when	

There are some interesting facts about the peanut butter in your pantry. (6)_____*First*_____, about 63 percent of all the peanuts grown are made into peanut butter. Second, over 500 million pounds of peanut butter are made in the United States alone. That would make 7 billion peanut-butter-and-jelly sandwiches! It's true we use some peanut butter for other things, (7)_____*such as*_____ cookies, candies, and eating right out of the jar when nobody is looking. (8)_____*But*_____ there's still enough left for a lot of sandwiches. Those sandwiches are good for you (9)_____*because*_____ peanut butter is full of protein. Most people, however, don't even think about this nutritional benefit. They just know that (10)_____*when*_____ they spread peanut butter on bread, their tastebuds are about to be happy.

TRANSITIONS: Test 3

Complete each sentence with the appropriate transition word or phrase. Then circle the kind of transition you have used.

1. a. The first apartment that we looked at was dirty, _____*but*_____ the second one had been recently painted.

   furthermore
   but
   so

   b. The transition shows
   addition.   cause and effect.   (contrast.)

2. a. Wind whipped the ocean around, ____*resulting in*____ huge, rough waves.

   resulting in
   despite
   instead of

   b. The transition signals a relationship of
   contrast.   time.   (cause and effect.)

3. a. My rabbit, Jack, has definite food preferences. ____*For example*____, he'll ignore an apple if there are peanuts in his dish.

   Similarly
   For example
   However

   b. The relationship of the second sentence to the first is one of
   (illustration.)   contrast.   comparison.

4. a. ____*During*____ the 1960s, American college students protested against the Vietnam War.

   Like
   Instead of
   During

   b. The transition shows
   comparison.   (time.)   contrast.

5. a. Jan was happy with the clock radio he won in the contest ____*even though*____ he would rather have won the portable TV.

   even though
   because
   additionally

   b. The transition signals a(n)
   comparison.   (contrast.)   addition.

(Continues on next page)

6. a. The river had overflowed onto the road I take to
   school. _____As a result_____, I had to drive out of my
   way to get to my class.

   In addition
   As a result
   Similarly

   b. The relationship between the two sentences is one of
   addition.   (cause and effect.)   comparison.

7. a. The great magician Houdini claimed to be extremely
   strong. _____To illustrate_____, he would invite
   members of the audience to hit him in the stomach
   with all their strength.

   Furthermore
   On the other hand
   To illustrate

   b. The relationship of the second sentence to the first is
   one of
   (illustration.)   contrast.   addition.

8. a. Oil spills in rivers and lakes cause great problems for
   wildlife. _____Moreover_____, the oil is a threat to
   our own water supply.

   Moreover
   Instead
   To illustrate

   b. The relationship of the second sentence to the first is
   one of
   (addition.)   illustration.   contrast.

9. a. A newborn tiger and a newborn domestic cat are
   _____similar_____ in some ways. Both are born
   with their eyes closed, and both are dependent upon
   their mother for a long time.

   in contrast
   similar
   next

   b. The transition signals
   contrast.   time.   (comparison.)

10. a. Computers can determine how poisonous something is
    by examining its makeup. _____Furthermore_____,
    computers can predict which part of the body a poison
    will affect.

    Furthermore
    However
    For example

    b. The relationship of the second sentence to the first is
    one of
    contrast.   illustration.   (addition.)

TRANSITIONS: Test 4

A. Complete each sentence with the appropriate transition from the box. Use each transition once.

Note: You may find it helpful to check (✓) each transition after you insert it into a sentence.

even though	for example	now
because	moreover	

1. In rodeos, a horse jumps and bucks _____*because*_____ it is in pain from the sharp spurs on the cowboy's boots and the strap pulled tight around its groin.

2. Colleges have started to serve the needs of handicapped students. _____*For example*_____, some schools provide tutors and notetakers for the handicapped.

3. _____*Even though*_____ many diseases are closely tied to eating habits, the average U.S. doctor receives less than three hours of training in nutrition.

4. In the past, fingerprints were needed to positively identify a criminal. _____*Now*_____, the genetic code of a single cell is enough to do the same.

5. Widespread drug use by athletes has led to calls for random testing. _____*Moreover*_____, some authorities are proposing much stiffer penalties for athletes who abuse drugs.

(Continues on next page)

B. Fill in each blank with the appropriate transition from the box. Use each transition once.

Note: You may find it helpful to check (✓) each transition as you insert it into a sentence.

although	also	such as
therefore	however	

Mark Twain, creator of colorful characters (6)_____*such as*_____ Tom Sawyer, loved to tell stories. He (7)_____*also*_____ loved an audience. But did you know he spent hours telling tales to someone who never heard a single word he said? He probably never had a better audience than his special young friend, Helen Keller. Helen was both blind and deaf. (8)_____*However*_____, she could feel the shapes and movements of his lips and (9)_____*therefore*_____ could make out the words. Her enjoyment of his tales was clear. "She interrupted all along and in the right places, with chuckles and bursts of laughter," Twain recalled. He admired Helen's patience and skill in learning to read, write, and speak. (10)_____*Although*_____ Twain was forty-five years older than Helen, they became good friends.

TRANSITIONS: Test 5

A. This part of the test will check your ability to recognize the relationships (signaled by transitions) within and between sentences. Read each passage and answer the questions that follow.

Passage 1

¹Travel by airplane is safer than travel by car. ²Yet I am still nervous whenever I fly. ³When I get on a plane, I make sure I know where all the safety features are on the plane. ⁴I look for my life raft and the fire extinguishers. ⁵I also look around to spot all of the emergency exits.

1. The relationship of sentence 2 to sentence 1 is one of
   a. illustration.
   b. time.
   c. addition.
   d. contrast.

2. The relationship of sentence 5 to sentence 4 is one of
   a. cause and effect.
   b. addition.
   c. illustration.
   d. comparison.

Passage 2

¹McDonald's is the largest fast-food chain in the United States. ²McDonald's can also be found in Mexico, throughout Europe, and even in Russia. ³In fact, the busiest McDonald's in the world is in Moscow. ⁴To illustrate how busy this restaurant is, it serves more than 40,000 customers a day. ⁵In three weeks, this restaurant sells more food than the average McDonald's does in a year.

3. The relationship of sentence 2 to sentence 1 is one of
   a. addition.
   b. contrast.
   c. illustration.
   d. cause and effect.

4. The relationship expressed by sentence 4 is one of
   a. addition.
   b. time.
   c. illustration.
   d. contrast.

(Continues on next page)

Passage 3

[1]The world's population grows by 250,000 each day. [2]Most births occur in the poorest parts of the world. [3]For instance, almost 140,000 people are born each day in Asia. [4]An additional 75,000 are born daily in Africa. [5]However, on any one day in North America, Europe and Australia, only 13,000 will be born.

5. The relationship of sentence 3 to sentence 2 is one of
   a. illustration.
   b. contrast.
   c. cause and effect.
   d. time.

6. The relationship of sentence 5 to sentence 4 is one of
   a. addition.
   b. comparison.
   c. illustration.
   d. contrast.

B. Fill in each blank with the appropriate transition from the box. Use each transition once.

Note: You may find it helpful to check (✓) each transition as you insert it into a sentence.

as a result for example	another	although

(7)_____*Although*_____ environmental news is not usually very good, there are some success stories worth noting. (8)_____*For example*_____, many companies in Tokyo, Japan, are allowing workers to use computers to work from home. (9)_____*As a result*_____, there is less pollution from automobiles. Similar success stories are being reported in the U.S. The air quality in Los Angeles has improved greatly in the past twenty years. (10)_____*Another*_____ example is a river in Cleveland that was once so polluted that it routinely caught fire. It has been cleaned up and is no longer a fire hazard.

TRANSITIONS: Test 6

A. This part of the test will check your ability to recognize the relationships (signaled by transitions) within and between sentences. Read each passage and answer the questions that follow.

Passage 1

¹We may curse honeybees while we are having a picnic, but we should be thankful for them as we eat. ²Honeybees are responsible for pollinating 60 percent of the fruit and vegetables we eat. ³For instance, honeybees routinely pollinate apple and orange trees, tomatoes, and carrots. ⁴Without them, lettuce might sell for five dollars a head, and fruit would be an occasional luxury.

1. The relationship of the last part of sentence 1 to the first part is one of
   a. time.
   b. cause and effect.
   c. addition.
   d. contrast.

2. The relationship of sentence 3 to sentence 2 is one of
   a. addition.
   b. illustration.
   c. cause and effect.
   d. time.

Passage 2

¹Bicycle riding can be a good way to get exercise. ²It can also be a pleasant way to see the countryside. ³Not so pleasant is getting a flat tire miles from home. ⁴A new product may change that. ⁵An airless tire is now available for biking enthusiasts. ⁶Made of polyurethane, it is lightweight and durable. ⁷Moreover, it comes with a lifetime guarantee that the tire will never go flat.

3. The relationship of sentence 2 to sentence 1 is one of
   a. addition.
   b. illustration.
   c. cause and effect.
   d. comparison.

4. The relationship of sentence 7 to sentence 6 is one of
   a. time.
   b. cause and effect.
   c. addition.
   d. contrast.

(Continues on next page)

Passage 3

¹Some officials in California recently released water from a dam down a river. ²They wanted to improve the environment for wildlife. ³Instead of helping wildlife, however, they harmed it. ⁴Over five thousand fish were killed, including salmon, trout and catfish. ⁵A study revealed that the water which was released carried more sediment and waste than officials had realized.

5. The relationship of sentence 3 to sentence 2 is one of
   a. time.   (c.) contrast.
   b. addition.   d. comparison.

6. The relationship of the last half of sentence 4 to the first part is one of
   a. addition.   (c.) illustration.
   b. contrast.   d. time.

B. Fill in each blank with the appropriate transition from the box. Use each transition once.

Note: You may find it helpful to check (✓) each transition as you insert it into a sentence.

in addition	another	however
often		

The Philippine Islands have some of the richest coral reefs in the world. (7)_____*However*_____, scientists are concerned that fishermen are destroying the reefs. One common practice used to catch a large number of fish is to throw explosives into the water. This kills schools of fish and destroys the reef where they live. (8)_____*Another*_____ practice is used to catch certain fish for use in aquariums overseas. Fishermen throw poison into the water around the reef. The poison stuns the fish, which float to the surface and are easily netted. The poison destroys the reef. (9)_____*In addition*_____, it is fatal to the fish, which are poisoned slowly. It (10)_____*often*_____ takes as long as three months for the fish to die. By that time, the fish are in aquariums of unsuspecting fish collectors who wonder what they did wrong.

COMBINED SKILLS: Test 1

A. [1]In 1991, a total eclipse of the sun occurred over Mexico, providing scientists with a rare opportunity. [2]The duration of the event was over six minutes. [3]Birds stopped singing. [4]Bees stopped flying. [5]Furthermore, flowers began to close their petals. [6]Grazing animals began to head home. [7]Scientists were able to gather data that they will be studying for years. [8]The next total eclipse in North America will not occur until 2017.

1. Which word or words have a hard **c** sound?
   a. *Eclipse*
   b. *Mexico*
   c. *Occur*
   (d.) All of the above

2. In sentence 2, the word *duration* means
   a. fear.
   b. location.
   c. memory.
   (d.) length of time.

3. The main idea of this paragraph is expressed in sentence
   (a.) 1.
   b. 2.
   c. 6.
   d. 8.

4. The statement below is
   a. true, according to the paragraph.
   (b.) false, according to the paragraph.
   c. not mentioned in the paragraph.

   Birds sang louder than usual during the eclipse.

5. The relationship of sentence 5 to sentence 4 is one of
   a. time order.
   (b.) addition.
   c. illustration.
   d. contrast.

(Continues on next page)

B.   ¹Fire-walking involves taking five steps over hot coals. ²The traditional belief is that in order to walk over the hot coals, you must condition your mind. ³The theory is that with proper mental fitness, the pain will not be felt. ⁴Yet science has come up with another explanation. ⁵The coals that are used are made of wood. ⁶Though they look hot, they do not conduct heat well. ⁷Thus taking five short steps over the coals is not enough time to get burned toes or blisters on the bottom of the feet.

6. Which syllable rule applies to the words *over*, *belief*, and *enough*?
   a. When two consonants come between two vowels, divide between the consonants.
   (b.) When a single consonant comes between two vowel sounds, divide before the consonant.
   c. Compound words are always divided between the words they contain.

7. In sentence 2, the word *condition* means
   a. close.
   b. search.
   (c.) prepare.
   d. notice.

8. Which of the following statements best expresses the main idea of the paragraph?
   a. Fire-walking is dangerous.
   (b.) Tradition and science have differing explanations for fire-walking.
   c. Difficult activities can be accomplished with proper mental fitness.
   d. Traditional beliefs are usually contradicted by science.

9. According to tradition, the act of fire-walking is
   a. unhealthy.
   b. lengthy.
   c. a religious experience.
   (d.) a mental challenge.

10. The relationship of sentence 4 to sentence 3 is one of
   a. time.
   b. addition.
   c. comparison.
   (d.) contrast.

COMBINED SKILLS: Test 2

Read each passage below and then answer the questions that follow.

A.   ¹The Worm Concern is an unusual recycling business that is benefiting the environment in various ways. ²The business takes in waste such as lawn clippings, tree trimmings, table scraps, and manure. ³All of this is then fed to six acres of common earthworms. ⁴The worms convert the garbage into an inexpensive rich fertilizer. ⁵This organic recycling has cut down on the amount of trash dumped into landfills. ⁶Also, it has provided a first-class soil for lawns and gardens.

1. Which group is made up of words with a long vowel sound?
   a. *An, that, clippings*
   b. *Ways, tree, also*
   c. *Earthworms, landfills, first-class*
   d. *Convert, rich, cut*

2. In sentence 4, the word *convert* means
   a. change.
   b. put.
   c. carry.
   d. permit.

3. The main idea of this paragraph is best expressed in sentence
   a. 1.
   b. 2.
   c. 5.
   d. 6.

4. According to the paragraph, organic recycling
   a. is expensive.
   b. results in more room in landfills.
   c. requires chemicals.
   d. is a nonprofit activity.

5. The relationship between sentences 2 and 3 is one of
   a. time.
   b. addition.
   c. comparison.
   d. contrast.

(Continues on next page)

B. ¹The odor of food draws bears. ²As a result, bears are often found around campsites. ³Fish and Game officials have suggestions on what to do and not to do if you see a bear. ⁴First of all, they suggest that if the bear has not sensed your presence, back away downwind. ⁵Do not run, as the bear is likely to give chase. ⁶If the bear sees you, stand up and raise your arms, so that you look as large as you can. ⁷Don't crouch down thinking the bear will avoid you if you appear small. ⁸If the bear charges, try yelling forcefully and throwing rocks at the bear. ⁹Don't run away even then—the bear is faster than you. ¹⁰If the animal attacks you, cover your head and neck and bring your legs up into your chest. ¹¹Don't lie flat on the ground looking as if you are dead. ¹²The bear is not likely to fall for this.

6. Which group is made up of words that contain a digraph?
   a. *Suggest, large, charges*
   b. *Fish, chase, throwing*
   c. *Food, do, you*
   d. *Campsites, downwind*

7. The word *throwing* would be found on a dictionary page with which guide-words?
   a. throaty / thunderclap
   b. thine / thorax
   c. thundercloud / tidewater

8. The main idea of this paragraph is expressed in sentence
   a. 1.
   b. 2.
   c. 3.
   d. 10.

9. According to the paragraph, if a bear sees you, you should
   a. run as fast as you can.
   b. make yourself look as large as possible.
   c. play dead.
   d. try to get downwind of the animal.

10. The relationship between sentences 1 and 2 is one of
    a. time.
    b. comparison.
    c. illustration.
    d. cause and effect.

COMBINED SKILLS: Test 3

Read each passage below and then answer the questions that follow.

A. ¹A drought can be disastrous to farmers. ²Crops that don't get enough water fail to grow properly, leading to little or no income for the farmers. ³Some farmers have found crops that are drought-resistant. ⁴One is canola, a plant whose oil is being touted as a healthy cooking oil. ⁵Another plant requiring much less water than most plants is buffalo gourd. ⁶It needs to be planted only once and continues to produce plants yearly. ⁷Lubricating oil and fuel can be made from buffalo gourd. ⁸Kenaf, another hearty grower, can be used in the production of newspapers. ⁹It prevents newsprint from coming off on readers' hands. ¹⁰Several drought-resistant plants, then, hold special promise for farmers.

1. Which word has a digraph that sounds like **f**?
   a. *if*
   b. *enough*
   c. *healthy*
   d. *kenaf*

2. In sentence 4, the word *touted* means
   a. promoted.
   b. replaced.
   c. avoided.
   d. rejected.

3. The main idea of this paragraph is expressed in sentence
   a. 1.
   b. 2.
   c. 7.
   d. 10.

4. Buffalo gourd is a source of
   a. a healthy cooking oil.
   b. lubricating oil.
   c. a special kind of newsprint.
   d. wateı.

5. Sentence 2 expresses a relationship of
   a. time.
   b. comparison and/or contrast.
   c. illustration.
   d. cause and effect.

(Continues on next page)

349

B. [1]In ice hockey, skaters using special sticks try to knock a hard rubber disk called a "puck" into a net that is guarded by a player called a goalie. [2]Goalies wear helmets and masks to protect them from being hurt if they are hit by a puck. [3]They began to wear such protective gear after Bobby Hull started playing in the National Hockey League. [4]Hull had a shot that put fear into goalies. [5]It was clocked at a hundred miles per hour. [6]While the shot terrorized everyone around Hull, he said that once he made a shot that scared even him. [7]That time, Hull wound up and slapped the puck, which took off toward the goalie and then rose. [8]The goalie tried to get out of the way, but could not. [9]As he tried to move, the puck hit him on the side of the face and then ripped into his ear. [10]The ear was severed and so had to be sewn back on. [11]From then on, that goalie began wearing a facemask whenever his team played against Hull. [12]Other goalies followed, and eventually all goalies were wearing helmets and masks.

6. Which syllable rule applies to the word *helmet*?
   a. When two consonants come between two vowels, divide between the consonants.
   b. When a single consonant comes between two vowel sounds, divide before the consonant.
   c. Compound words are always divided between the words they contain.

7. Which definition of *shot* applies in sentence 6?
   a. The firing or discharge of a weapon
   b. A throw, hit, or drive in a sporting event
   c. A photograph
   d. A drink of liquor

8. Which statement best expresses the main idea of this paragraph?
   a. A National Hockey League goalie once had his ear cut off by a puck.
   b. Unusual events often change the way a game is played.
   c. One of Bobby Hull's shots led to goalies wearing helmets and masks.
   d. Bobby Hull's shots put terror into the hearts of National Hockey League goalies.

9. According to the paragraph, goalies did not wear helmets and masks
   a. until after Bobby Hull came into the league.
   b. until the league required it.
   c. unless Bobby Hull was playing.
   d. because they were not allowed to.

10. The relationship of sentence 11 to sentence 10 is one of
    a. time.
    b. contrast.
    c. comparison.
    d. illustration.

COMBINED SKILLS: Test 4

A.   ¹A Bowling Green University poll surveyed young men and women to find out what they considered romantic. ²The survey, which listed the top ten activities for men and women, found some similarities and some differences. ³Kissing, cuddling, hugging, and taking walks were favored by both men and women. ⁴Both also chose sending or receiving flowers, candle-lit dinners, and sending or receiving cards or love letters. ⁵Saying "I love you," getting surprise gifts, and slow dancing rounded out the women's list, but were not on the men's list. ⁶On the other hand, sitting by the fireplace, holding hands, and making love were found on the men's list but not on the women's.

1. In which word does **y** sound like long **i**?
   a. *Young*
   b. *They*
   c. *Saying*
   d. *By*

2. In sentence 5, the words *rounded out* mean
   a. were omitted from.
   b. ruined.
   c. completed.
   d. fully described.

3. Which statement best expresses the main idea of this paragraph?
   a. A survey found that there are more similarities than differences in what men and women find romantic.
   b. One survey shows how differently men and women think about romance.
   c. Young men and women agree and disagree about a variety of things, including romance.
   d. Women have a better understanding of what is romantic than men.

4. According to the paragraph,
   a. hugging was on the women's list, but not the men's.
   b. making love was on both lists.
   c. slow dancing was on the women's list, but not the men's.
   d. taking walks was on the women's list, but not the men's.

5. The relationship between sentences 5 and 6 is one of
   a. time.
   b. comparison.
   c. cause and effect.
   d. contrast.

(Continues on next page)

B.   ¹How can you tell if someone is lying? ²The polygraph test is designed to be a simple way to prove if someone is lying or telling the truth. ³The test involves a machine that is hooked up to a person by wires and straps. ⁴Questions are asked, and bodily responses are recorded. ⁵Usually, no more than ten questions are asked. ⁶Two or three of the questions are pointed, as in "Did you steal the picture?" ⁷The remaining questions may not seem important, but they help the questioner to determine the truthfulness of the subject. ⁸Supporters of polygraph tests claim that they have a 95 percent accuracy rating. ⁹However, opponents of polygraph tests dispute this view. ¹⁰They say that a good liar and anyone accustomed to taking the test can beat one, thus making the tests useless.

6. Which word from the paragraph has a word part meaning "without"?
   a. *Responses*
   b. *Questions*
   c. *Supporters*
   d. *Useless*

7. In sentence 9, the word *dispute* means
   a. agree with.
   b. notice.
   c. deny.
   d. use.

8. Which sentence best expresses the main idea of this paragraph?
   a. The polygraph is a machine used as a lie detector.
   b. People who operate polygraph tests must be very skilled in the operation of the machine and in asking questions.
   c. An important part of a polygraph test is a series of questions intended to help the questioner discover dishonesty.
   d. There is disagreement over the accuracy of the polygraph test, which is designed to sense when people are lying.

9. According to the paragraph, during a polygraph test
   a. no more than ten questions are ever asked.
   b. the subject's legs are hooked up to the polygraph machine.
   c. a person used to taking polygraph tests will finish more quickly than someone unaccustomed to the tests.
   d. some physical responses of the person taking the test are recorded.

10. The relationship between sentences 8 and 9 is one of
    a. time.
    b. contrast.
    c. comparison.
    d. illustration.

COMBINED SKILLS: Test 5

Read each passage below and then answer the questions that follow.

A. ¹The Food and Drug Administration recently opened a new division called the Office of Criminal Investigations. ²The office was set up to discover consumer cheating. ³The first task for the office was to check claims by people who said they found syringes in cans of Pepsi-Cola. ⁴One hundred investigators tried to verify the truth about hundreds of reports nationwide. ⁵The examiners used techniques that would get fast results. ⁶In most cases, people admitted within two days that their claims were untrue. ⁷Not one of the claims about cans of Pepsi has been proven true. ⁸Moreover, over forty of those who made claims have been arrested for trying to cheat the company.

1. The Two-Vowels-Together Rule applies to which word?
    a. *Opened*
    b. *Division*
    c. *Claims*
    d. *Moreover*

2. In sentence 4, the word *verify* means
    a. hide.
    b. prove.
    c. delay.
    d. read about.

3. Which statement best expresses the main idea of this paragraph?
    a. A new federal division demonstrated great skill in its very first case.
    b. There are many divisions within the Food and Drug Administration.
    c. In the Pepsi-Cola investigation, no consumers told the truth.
    d. It took the most experienced investigators in the government to solve a difficult case.

4. The Office of Criminal Investigations
    a. found that few claims in the Pepsi-Cola fraud case were true.
    b. has been paid for by the Pepsi-Cola company.
    c. had as its first case a Pepsi-Cola investigation.
    d. was recently transferred to the Food and Drug Administration.

5. The relationship of sentence 8 to the two sentences before it is one of
    a. time.
    b. addition.
    c. contrast.
    d. illustration.

(Continues on next page)

353

B.   ¹Two of America's most beloved presidents were assassinated—Abraham Lincoln and John F. Kennedy. ²There are a number of striking coincidences in President Lincoln's and President Kennedy's lives. ³Lincoln was elected president in 1860, one hundred years before Kennedy was elected president. ⁴Both had vice presidents named Johnson. ⁵Andrew Johnson was Lincoln's vice president. ⁶Lyndon Johnson was Kennedy's. ⁷Both Johnsons were Southern Democrats who had served in the U.S. Senate. ⁸Andrew Johnson was born in 1808, and Lyndon Johnson was born in 1908. ⁹Furthermore, both Lincoln and Kennedy supported civil rights and racial equality. ¹⁰Both were shot in the head, both on a Friday and in the presence of their wives. ¹¹John Wilkes Booth, Lincoln's killer, was born in 1839, a hundred years before Kennedy's killer, Lee Harvey Oswald, was born. ¹²Both assassins were themselves killed before they could be brought to justice.

6. Which syllable rule applies to the words *hundred* and *assassins*?
    a. When two consonants come between two vowels, divide between the consonants.
    b. When a single consonant comes between two vowel sounds, divide before the consonant.
    c. Divide after prefixes and before suffixes.

7. In sentence 2, the word *striking* means
    a. hitting.
    b. dull.
    c. common.
    d. remarkable.

8. The main idea of this paragraph is expressed in sentence
    a. 1.
    b. 2.
    c. 3.
    d. 10.

9. According to the paragraph, Lincoln and Kennedy
    a. were both born in Illinois.
    b. had the same birthday.
    c. had vice presidents who had served in the Senate.
    d. were both Southerners.

10. The relationship of sentence 9 to several of the sentences before it is one of
    a. time.
    b. contrast.
    c. illustration.
    d. addition.

COMBINED SKILLS: Test 6

Read each passage below and then answer the questions that follow.

A. ¹San Francisco Bay isn't what it used to be. ²Sailing ships from around the world have brought with them diverse sea animals. ³These different organisms have changed the population of the bay. ⁴For instance, New Zealand slugs with no natural enemies have eliminated the oysters once plentiful in the bay. ⁵Russian jellyfish are eating microscopic organisms that native fish eat. ⁶Green crabs from the Atlantic Ocean were brought in by a company that had packaged lobsters in seaweed. ⁷The crabs hid in the seaweed and began multiplying when the seaweed was thrown into the bay. ⁸Scientists report that very few original inhabitants remain in the bay.

1. The Rule for a Final Single Vowel applies to which group of words?
   a. *Francisco, by, very*
   b. *Bay, these, the*
   c. *Sea, have, are*
   d. *Sailing, oysters, seaweed*

2. In sentence 2, the word *diverse* means
   a. varied.
   b. local.
   c. single.
   d. dead.

3. Which of the following best expresses the main idea of this paragraph?
   a. San Francisco Bay has an unusual mixture of sea animals.
   b. Sea animals from around the world have changed the population of San Francisco Bay.
   c. The original inhabitants of San Francisco Bay have chosen to leave it.
   d. Creatures with no natural enemies have taken over San Francisco Bay and will soon spread to other locations.

4. The New Zealand slugs
   a. are eaten by fish.
   b. hide in seaweed.
   c. have no natural enemies.
   d. are original inhabitants of the bay.

5. The relationship of sentence 4 to sentence 3 is one of
   a. addition.
   b. time.
   c. contrast.
   d. illustration.

(Continues on next page)

B. [1]Air travel today is made possible by a powerful and efficient engine developed over fifty years ago. [2]In 1939, the jet engine was developed at the same time by two inventors who had never met or spoken to each other. [3]Hans von Ohain was a German inventor. [4]His counterpart was a British citizen named Frank Whittle. [5]Though each had thought up the same invention, the lives of these men took different routes. [6]In Germany, Hans von Ohain was able to continue his work with government support. [7]He convinced Adolf Hitler that World War II would be won if he could perfect a quiet turbine engine that would make planes fly faster. [8]Von Ohain's progress was slowed as Germany began to lose the war, and Germany never used the jet engine. [9]In contrast, Frank Whittle's government responded less positively. [10]Whittle was unable to convince the British government that the jet engine he developed would revolutionize flying. [11]Nevertheless, he continued to work on the engine throughout the war. [12]Once the war ended, Whittle found buyers for his invention.

6. Which word has a word part that means "a person who does something"?
   a. *Possible*
   b. *Powerful*
   c. *Inventor*
   d. *Support*

7. In sentence 4, the words *his counterpart* mean
   a. someone with a role similar to his.
   b. a friend he once had.
   c. a coworker.
   d. a person that he knew well.

8. Which statement best expresses the main idea of this paragraph?
   a. Due to its inability to develop a jet engine, Germany lost World War II.
   b. The two inventors of the jet engine had different career paths.
   c. The jet engine is an invention that has changed the world.
   d. It usually takes many years for inventions to become accepted by the world.

9. According to the paragraph, Frank Whittle
   a. knew of the work being done by Hans von Ohain.
   b. was not liked by the British government.
   c. kept working on the jet engine throughout World War II.
   d. was tempted to move from Britain to Germany.

10. The relationship of sentence 11 to sentence 10 is one of
    a. addition.
    b. example.
    c. contrast.
    d. comparison.

Part III

TEN READING SELECTIONS

1

Life Over Death
Bill Broderick

Preview

When the author saw a cat lying in the middle of the road, he stopped his car. All he expected to do was to move a dead animal off the road. When he found that the cat was still alive, his day became a complicated one. But the trouble he went through was worth it. The chance to save a life doesn't come along every day.

Words to Watch

grimaced (2): made a twisted face
immobile (2): not moving
ligament (5): a band of tissue which connects bones or supports organs
tendon (5): a tissue which connects muscles to bones and other parts of the body
good Samaritan (6): someone who helps others unselfishly
resignation (9): acceptance without resistance
dejected (11): depressed
pathetic (11): pitiful

My reaction was as it always is when I see an animal lying in the   1
roadway. My heart sank. And a lump formed in my throat at the
thought of a life unfulfilled. I then resolved to move him off the road,
to ensure that one of God's creations does not become a permanent part
of the pavement. Some might ask what difference it makes. If it's
already dead, why not just leave it there? My answer is that I believe in
death with dignity, for people and for animals alike.

So I pulled my car over to the side of the road and walked back to 2
where the cat lay motionless. Two cars passed over him, managing to
avoid running him over. With no other cars in sight, I made my way to
the lifeless form just as a jogger went by. The jogger grimaced° at the
sight of the immobile° cat, blood dripping from his mouth. "How'd it
happen?" he asked. I replied that I didn't know; he probably got hit by
some careless driver. I just wanted to get him off the road. I reached
down for the cat and got the surprise of my life. The little creature
lifted his head ever so slightly and uttered a pitiful, unforgettable little
"meow." He was still alive.

What was I going to do now? I was already late for work. All I 3
had intended to do was move the cat off the road. I didn't need this. But
I knew I had no choice. I sighed deeply, then reached down and
carefully cradled the cat in my hands. I asked the jogger to open my car
trunk and remove the things from a small box. Then I gently placed the
cat in the box. He was in shock, so he probably could not feel the pain
from his obvious injuries. "Kinda funny lookin', isn't he?" asked the
jogger. I was annoyed by his question, but I had to admit that he was
right. This cat looked peculiar. Not ugly, mind you. But he seemed to
have a comical look on his face, even at such a dreadful time.

"What are you gonna do with him?" the jogger asked. I told him I 4
would take the cat to the local vet and let him decide what to do.

The vet was only five minutes away. My wife and I had been 5
bringing our animals to him for several years, and I knew I could rely
on him to do what was best for the cat. I brought the cat into the
reception room and placed it on the counter. As this was an emergency,
the vet was summoned right away. He examined the cat thoroughly,
listing the injuries for his assistant to write down. "Broken jaw, that'll
have to be set. Two teeth broken. A couple more loose. Possible
internal injuries, but they don't look too bad. Uh-oh. This doesn't look
good. He doesn't appear to have any movement in his right front leg.
Possible break, definite ligament° and tendon° damage."

The vet completed his examination, then looked at me and asked 6
what I wanted to do. I knew what he meant. Did I want to have the cat
"put to sleep"? I became uneasy. I clumsily explained that I was hoping
to get advice from him on what to do. Fair enough. The jaw would have
to be wired shut for six weeks, and the cat would have to wear a cast on
its leg for three months. There was no way of knowing if the damage to
the leg was permanent. He could have the cast removed and still not be
able to use the leg. The cost of all the surgery would be high, but I would
get a 50 percent "good Samaritan°" discount if I went ahead with it.

Now I was really at a loss. If I went ahead with the surgery, I'd be 7
paying for a cat which wasn't mine, whose owner I'd probably never

find, and who might end up with the use of only three legs. And on top of it, this was one of the funniest-looking cats ever born. Black and white, spotted where it shouldn't be, kinked tail, and a silly half-smile on its face. I chuckled at that and the entire situation.

"What do you want to do, Bill?" asked the vet.   8

I shrugged my shoulders in resignation°. "Dan, I'll choose life   9
over death every time. Let's give it our best shot."

I called back later in the day and learned that the surgery had been   10
successful. "You can pick up your cat tomorrow morning," I was told.
My cat. I started to say that he was not my cat, but I knew otherwise.

The next morning, my wife and I drove to the vet and picked up   11
the cat. He looked ghastly. His jaw was now bandaged, and a cast
covered one leg entirely and wrapped around his midsection. We were
dejected°. But, as we drove him home, we began thinking that perhaps
this cat was not as pathetic° as he looked. As frightened as he must have
been, as much pain as he must have felt, he sat calmly in my wife's lap.
He purred and stared out the window with his curious half-smile.

When we got home, we introduced him to our two Siamese cats,   12
who stared in disbelief at this strange creature. They sensed it might be
a cat, but they had never seen one like this. It took him very little time
to get used to his new surroundings. It took him longer to get used to
the cast, which made even walking a chore. Surely he must have been
embarrassed. After all, an animal normally able to glide around quietly
should not make a resounding thump every time he moves.

In due time, the cast came off. To our relief, Pokey, as we now   13
called him, had about 90 percent mobility in the leg. He got around okay,
but he limped whenever he tried to move any faster than a slow walk.

All this occurred four years ago. Pokey is still with us today. In   14
fact, he has become our most beloved cat. Because of his injury, he is
strictly an indoor cat. This does not seem to bother him at all. It is hard
to believe that any cat has ever enjoyed himself more. Maybe it's
because he had been slowed after being hit by a car, or perhaps he just
has a special individuality. He is never bored. At times he will race
around the house like he is leading the Indy 500. Or he'll leap into the
air at an imaginary foe. Or he'll purr loudly at the foot of our bed,
staring into space with that silly grin on his face. And he couldn't care
less that he still looks funny.

It would have been easy to let Pokey lie in the middle of the road.   15
And it would have been just as simple to have the vet put him to sleep.
But when I think of all the pleasure this cat has given us, and of how
much fun he has living with us, I know the right decision was made.
And I'd do it again in a second. I'll take life over death every time.

WORD SKILLS QUESTIONS

A. Use your knowledge of phonics, word skills, and the dictionary to answer the questions below.

Consonants

1. In *grimaced* in "The jogger grimaced at the sight of the immobile cat" (paragraph 2), the letter **c**
   a. has the hard sound of **c** as in *can*.
   b. has the soft sound of **c** as in *city*.

Vowels

2. In *reached* in "I reached down for the cat . . ." (paragraph 2), the letter **a**
   a. has the sound of short **a**.
   b. has the sound of long **a**.
   c. is silent.

Syllables

3. The word in the sentence below which follows the syllable rule to "divide before a single consonant" is
   a. *because*.
   b. *strictly*.
   c. *indoor*.

   "Because of his injury, he is strictly an indoor cat. This does not seem to bother him at all." (Paragraph 14)

Word Parts

4. *Motionless* in "I . . . walked back to where the cat lay motionless" (paragraph 2) means
   a. without movement.
   b. full of movement.
   c. able to be moved.

Dictionary Use

5. *Pathetic* in "perhaps this cat was not as pathetic as he looked" (paragraph 11) is accented on the
   a. first syllable.
   b. second syllable.
   c. third syllable.

   pa·thet·ic (pə-thĕt′ĭk)

B. Use context clues to help you decide on the best definition for each italicized word. Then circle the letter of each choice.

6. The word *resolved* in "I then resolved to move him off the road, to ensure that one of God's creations does not become a permanent part of the pavement" (paragraph 1) means
   a. forgot.
   b. hid.
   c. decided.
   d. drove.

7. The word *summoned* in "As this was an emergency, the vet was summoned right away. He examined the cat thoroughly" (paragraph 5) means
   a. informed.
   b. called for.
   c. telephoned.
   d. thought of.

8. The word *ghastly* in "He looked ghastly. His jaw was now bandaged, and a cast covered one leg entirely" (paragraph 11) means
   a. clever.
   b. appealing.
   c. terrible.
   d. marvelous.

9. The word *disbelief* in "our two Siamese cats . . . stared in disbelief at this strange creature. They sensed it might be a cat, but they had never seen one like this" (paragraph 12) means
   a. uncertainty.
   b. time.
   c. pleasure.
   d. hatred.

10. The word *resounding* in "After all, an animal normally able to glide around quietly should not make a resounding thump every time he moves" (paragraph 12) means
   a. soft.
   b. brave.
   c. relaxed.
   d. loud.

READING COMPREHENSION QUESTIONS

Central Point and Main Ideas

1. Which sentence best expresses the central point of the selection?
   a. Drivers should be on the alert for animals on the road.
   b. Every life is valuable.
   c. Cats make great pets.
   d. Pokey is strictly an indoor cat because of his injury.

2. Which sentence best expresses the main idea of paragraphs 3 and 4?
   a. The author didn't know what to do.
   b. The author was willing to take responsibility for the cat.
   c. The author was annoyed at the jogger's questions.
   d. The cat was funny looking.

3. Which sentence best expresses the main idea of paragraph 14?
   a. Pokey enjoys life a great deal now.
   b. Pokey sometimes leaps into the air at imaginary enemies.
   c. Pokey must spend the rest of his life indoors.
   d. Pokey was injured four years ago.

Supporting Details

4. The author
   a. saw a car hit the cat.
   b. was very surprised that the cat was still alive.
   c. was surprised that the jogger came by.
   d. thought that the cat was ugly.

5. The author
   a. had heard about the vet.
   b looked for the nearest vet.
   c. knew and trusted the vet.
   d. drove for hours till he found a vet.

6. For Pokey's surgery, the vet charged the author
   a. nothing.
   b. little.
   c. half the usual cost.
   d. his usual charge.

7. The author is
   a. never going to stop for a hurt animal again.
   b. glad that he saved the cat.
   c. worried that Pokey will always have a limp.
   d. sure that Pokey wants to go outside.

Transitions

8. The transition word *then* in the sentence below signals
   a. an example.
   (b.) time.
   c. comparison.
   d. contrast.

   > I sighed deeply, then reached down and carefully cradled the cat in my hands. (Paragraph 3)

9. The second sentence below begins with a transition that shows
   a. addition.
   (b.) contrast.
   c. an example.
   d. cause and effect.

   > He looked ghastly. . . . But, as we drove him home, we began thinking that perhaps this cat was not as pathetic as he looked. (Paragraph 11)

10. The sentence below begins with a transition that signals
    a. time.
    b. contrast.
    c. comparison.
    (d.) cause and effect.

    > Because of his injury, he is strictly an indoor cat. (Paragraph 14)

MAPPING ACTIVITY

This selection is organized by time: first one thing happened; then another; after that, another; and so on. The major events are scrambled in the list below. Write the letters of the events in their correct order in the diagram below.

    A. The author chooses surgery for the cat.
    B. The cat is taken to the author's home to recover.
    C. The cat is taken to the vet, who offers the choice of putting the animal to sleep or doing expensive surgery.
    D. The cat recovers and stays on as a happy and welcome household pet.
    E. A very badly injured cat is found.

Central point: A decision in favor of life is always best, as Pokey's recovery and rich life make clear.

E → C → A → B → D

DISCUSSION QUESTIONS

1. In the first paragraph, the author uses the expression "death with dignity." What does he mean?

2. Can and should something be done to make the world a better place for hurt and homeless creatures like Pokey? Explain your answer.

WRITING ACTIVITIES

1. Write a paragraph about an animal that has played a role in your life. First introduce the animal, and then explain what it was like or what it meant to you. Include examples to make clear any qualities you mention. For instance, if you write that the animal was clever, describe one or two events which are good examples of that cleverness.

2. The author felt he had to help the injured cat because he "had no choice." Write a letter to Broderick describing a time you also did something because you felt it was the only right thing to do. Describe the situation and explain your decision. Here is an example of a topic sentence for this assignment: "When my sister lost her job, I had no choice—I had to invite her and her children to live with me for a while."

Check Your Performance			**LIFE OVER DEATH**
Skill	*Number Right*	*Points*	*Total*
WORD SKILLS QUESTIONS			
Phonics, Word Parts, Dictionary (5 items)	_____	x 10 =	_____
Vocabulary in Context (5 items)	_____	x 10 =	_____
		SCORE =	_____ %
COMPREHENSION QUESTIONS			
Central Point and Main Ideas (3 items)	_____	x 7 =	_____
Supporting Details (4 items)	_____	x 7 =	_____
Transitions (3 items)	_____	x 7 =	_____
Mapping (5 items)	_____	x 6 =	_____
		SCORE =	_____ %

FINAL SCORES: Word Skills _____ %   Comprehension _____ %

Enter your final scores onto the reading performance chart on the inside back cover.

2

Cipher in the Snow
Jean Mizer Todhunter

Preview

In every school, there are some students whom nobody really knows. We may be aware of their names but little else about them. No one seems to really care about who they are. This selection looks at one such student, who led a short, unhappy life. The question raised is whether the people around him could have made his life a better one.

Words to Watch

cipher (title): a person or thing of no importance
lurched (1): staggered
blurted out (11): said suddenly
bleakly (14): gloomily
peaked (17): thin and tired
veiled (17): hidden
resolve (20): determination

> On most snowy mornings on my way to the high school where I   1
> teach, I drive behind the school bus. I was trailing the bus on one biting
> cold February morning when it veered and stopped short at the town
> hotel. It had no business doing this, and I was annoyed as I had to bring
> my car to an unexpected stop. A boy lurched° out of the bus, reeled,
> stumbled, and collapsed on the snowbank at the curb. The bus driver
> and I reached him at the same moment. His thin, hollow face was white
> even against the snow.
>
> "He's dead," the driver whispered.   2

It didn't register for a minute. I glanced quickly at the scared 3
young faces staring down at us from the school bus. "A doctor! Quick!
I'll phone from the hotel . . ."

"No use. I tell you he's dead." The driver looked down at the 4
boy's still form. "He never even said he felt bad," he muttered, "just
tapped me on the shoulder and said, real quiet, 'I'm sorry. I have to get
off at the hotel.' That's all. Polite and apologizing like."

At school the giggling, shuffling morning noise quieted as the 5
news went down the halls. I passed a huddle of girls. "Who was it? Who
dropped dead on the way to school?" I heard one of them half whisper.

"Don't know his name; some kid from Milford Corners," was the 6
reply.

It was like that in the faculty room and the principal's office. "I'd 7
appreciate your going out to tell the parents," the principal told me.
"They haven't a phone, and anyway, somebody from school should go
there in person. I'll cover your classes."

"Why me?" I asked. "Wouldn't it be better if you did it?" 8

"I didn't know the boy," the principal admitted levelly. "And in 9
last year's sophomore personalities column I noted that you were listed
as his favorite teacher."

I drove through the snow and cold down the bad canyon road to 10
the Evans place and thought about the boy, Cliff Evans. His favorite
teacher! Why, he hasn't spoken two words to me in two years! I could
see him in my mind's eye all right, sitting back there in the last seat in
my afternoon literature class. He came in the room by himself and left
by himself. "Cliff Evans," I muttered to myself, "a boy who never
talked." I thought a minute. "A boy who never smiled. I never saw him
smile once."

The big ranch kitchen was clean and warm. I blurted out° my 11
news somehow. Mrs. Evans reached blindly for a chair. "He never
said anything about bein' ailing."

His stepfather snorted. "He ain't said nothin' about anything 12
since I moved in here."

Mrs. Evans got up, pushed a pan to the back of the stove, and 13
began to untie her apron. "Now hold on," her husband snapped. "I got
to have breakfast before I go to town. Nothin' we can do now anyway.
If Cliff hadn't been so dumb, he'd have told us he didn't feel good."

After school I sat in the office and stared bleakly° at the records 14
spread out before me. I was to close the boy's file and write his
obituary for the school paper. The almost bare sheets mocked the effort.
"Cliff Evans, white, never legally adopted by stepfather, five half
brothers and sisters." These meager strands of information and the list
of D grades were about all the records had to offer.

Cliff Evans had silently come in the school door in the mornings 15
and gone out of the school door in the evenings, and that was all. He
had never belonged to a club. He had never played on a team. He had
never held an office. As far as I could tell, he had never done one
happy, noisy kid thing. He had never been anybody at all.

How do you go about making a boy into a zero? The grade school 16
records showed me much of the answer. The first and second grade
teachers' annotations read "sweet, shy child"; "timid but eager." Then
the third grade note had opened the attack. Some teacher had written in
a good, firm hand, "Cliff won't talk. Uncooperative. Slow learner." The
other academic sheet had followed with "dull"; "slow-witted"; "low
IQ." They became correct. The boy's IQ score in the ninth grade was
listed at 83. But his IQ in the third grade had been 106. The score
didn't go under 100 until the seventh grade. Even timid, sweet children
have resilience. It takes time to break them.

I stomped to the typewriter and wrote a savage report pointing out 17
what education had done to Cliff Evans. I slapped a copy on the
principal's desk and another in the sad, dog-eared file; slammed the
file; and crashed the office door shut as I left for home. But I didn't feel
much better. A little boy kept walking after me, a boy with a peaked°
face, a skinny body in faded jeans, and big eyes that had searched for a
long time and then had become veiled°.

I could guess how many times he'd been chosen last to be on a 18
team, how many whispered child conversations had excluded him. I
could see the faces and hear the voices that said over and over, "You're
dumb. You're dumb. You're just a nothing, Cliff Evans."

A child is a believing creature. Cliff undoubtedly believed them. 19
Suddenly it seemed clear to me: When finally there was nothing left at
all for Cliff Evans, he collapsed on a snowbank and went away. The
doctor might list "heart failure" as the cause of death, but that wouldn't
change my mind.

We couldn't find ten students in the school who had known Cliff 20
well enough to attend the funeral as his friends. So the student body
officers and a committee from the junior class went as a group to the
church, looking politely sad. I attended the service with them and sat
through it with a lump of cold lead in my chest and a big resolve°
growing in me.

I've never forgotten Cliff Evans or that resolve. He has been my 21
challenge year after year, class after class. Each September, I look up
and down the rows carefully at the unfamiliar faces. I look for veiled
eyes or bodies scrunched into a seat in an alien world. "Look, kids," I
say silently, "I may not do anything else for you this year, but not one
of you is going out of here a nobody. I'll work or fight to the bitter end

doing battle with society and the school board, but I won't have one of you leaving here thinking yourself into a zero."

Most of the time—not always, but most of the time—I've 22 succeeded.

WORD SKILLS QUESTIONS

A. Use your knowledge of phonics and dictionary study to answer the questions below. The questions are based on the following passage from the selection.

[Cliff] has been my challenge year after year, class after class. Each September, I look up and down the rows carefully at the unfamiliar faces. I look for veiled eyes or bodies scrunched into a seat in an alien world. "Look, kids," I say silently, "I may not do anything else for you this year, but not one of you is going out of here a nobody. I'll work or fight to the bitter end doing battle with society and the school board, but I won't have one of you leaving here thinking yourself into a zero." (Paragraph 21)

Consonants

1. In the word *challenge*, **g** has
   a. the hard sound of **g** as in *game*.
   b. the soft sound of **g** as in *gem*.
   c. a silent sound.

Vowels

2. The words *each, seat, year,* and *leaving* all contain examples of which rule for long vowel sounds?
   a. When a word ends in a vowel-consonant-**e**, the first vowel is long and the **e** is silent.
   b. When two of certain vowels are together in a word, the first one is long and the second is silent.
   c. A single vowel at the end of a word usually has a long sound.

Syllables

3. The word *September* is divided into syllables
   a. between double consonants.
   b. before single consonants.
   c. as a compound word.

Word Parts

4. *Unfamiliar* means
    a. before becoming familiar.
    b. familiar again.
    (c.) not familiar.

Dictionary Use

5. The definition that fits *alien* in the passage on the previous page is
    a. definition 1.
    (b.) definition 2.

    > a•li•en (ā′lē-ən) *adj.* **1.** Owing allegiance to another country or government. **2.** Not one's own; unfamiliar: an *alien* culture.

B. Use context clues to help you decide on the best definition for each italicized word. Then circle the letter of each choice.

6. The word *veered* in "the bus . . . veered and stopped short at the town hotel" (paragraph 1) means
    a. went in reverse.
    (b.) turned suddenly.
    c. sped up.
    d. closed its doors.

7. The word *reeled* in "a boy lurched out of the bus, reeled, stumbled, and collapsed on the snowbank at the curb" (paragraph 1) means
    a. jumped.
    b. laughed.
    (c.) moved unsteadily.
    d. pushed.

8. The word *meager* in "these meager strands of information and the list of D grades were about all the records had to offer" (paragraph 14) means
    a. impressive.
    b. injured.
    (c.) few.
    d. proud.

9. The word *annotations* in "the . . . teachers' annotations read 'sweet, shy child'; 'timid but eager' " (paragraph 16) means
    (a.) written comments.
    b. lies.
    c. excuses.
    d. criticisms.

10. The word *resilience* in "even timid, sweet children have resilience. It takes time to break them" (paragraph 16) means
    a. pleasant voices.
    b. illnesses.
    (c.) ability to recover.
    d. secrets.

READING COMPREHENSION QUESTIONS

Central Point and Main Ideas

1. Which sentence best expresses the central point of the selection?
    a. A boy nobody knew died on the way to school.
    (b.) As Cliff's story shows, children need to feel valued.
    c. Stepparents must value their stepchildren.
    d. The doctor felt Cliff died of heart failure.

2. Which sentence best expresses the main idea of paragraph 16?
    a. Cliff's first grade teacher thought Cliff was a "sweet, shy child."
    b. Cliff was later described as a "slow learner" and as having a "low IQ."
    c. Cliff's IQ did not go below 100 until the seventh grade.
    (d.) Cliff became a "zero" because his teachers must have treated him as one.

3. Which sentence best expresses the main idea of paragraph 17?
    (a.) The author was angered and upset by what the school had done to Cliff.
    b. The author didn't feel well.
    c. The school never helped Cliff.
    d. The author disliked doing paperwork.

4. Which sentence best expresses the main idea of paragraph 19?
    a. Cliff died of heart failure.
    b. Children are innocent.
    (c.) Cliff's heart failed because others convinced him he was nothing.
    d. The doctor listed Cliff's cause of death as "heart failure."

Supporting Details

5. ___F___ TRUE OR FALSE? Cliff was labeled as a slow learner at the end of his first year in school.

6. Cliff had
    (a.) never been adopted by his stepfather.
    b. been one of the author's favorite students.
    c. a small group of close friends.
    d. been very sick for a long time.

7. At the funeral,
    a. everyone was sad and cried.
    b. the author saw many of Cliff's teachers.
    c. the author became determined to help other students like Cliff.
    d. ten of Cliff's friends showed up.

Transitions

8. The sentence below begins with a transition that shows
    a. time.
    b. comparison.
    c. contrast.
    d. cause and effect.

    Then the third grade note had opened the attack. (Paragraph 16)

9. The transitional word *but* in the sentence below signals
    a. addition.
    b. comparison.
    c. contrast.
    d. cause and effect.

    The doctor might list "heart failure" as the cause of death, but that wouldn't change my mind. (Paragraph 19)

10. The second sentence below begins with a transition that shows
    a. addition.
    b. time.
    c. cause and effect.
    d. illustration.

    We couldn't find ten students in the school who had known Cliff well enough to attend the funeral as his friends. So the student body officers and a committee from the junior class went as a group to the church, looking politely sad. (Paragraph 20)

MAPPING ACTIVITY

This selection is organized by time: first one thing happened, then another, then another, and so on. Major events of the selection are scrambled in the list below. Write them in their correct order in the diagram based on the reading.

- Visit to Cliff's home
- What the records revealed
- Teacher's decision (to keep other students from becoming like Cliff)
- Funeral
- Unexpected bus stop
- Search in school records

Central point: People had so convinced Cliff that he was a zero that he gave up and died.

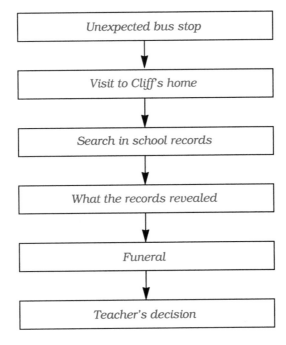

DISCUSSION QUESTIONS

1. From the article, what information do you learn and infer about Cliff's home life? How do you think he was treated by his mother? His stepfather?

2. Todhunter states that Cliff "had never been anybody at all." What does she mean? What is needed for a person to be "somebody"— either in school or out of school?

WRITING ACTIVITIES

1. The author asks, "How do you go about making a boy into a zero?" How did Cliff become a zero? Write a paragraph explaining why he thought so little of himself. You might begin with this topic sentence: "The attitudes and behavior of people around Cliff Evans convinced him that he was a zero." Then you could go on to explain briefly how teachers, students, and family influenced Cliff's poor self-image.

2. What would you say to Cliff's mother or stepfather if you had the chance? Write a letter to either, or both, explaining how you think each might have influenced Cliff. Use whatever tone you wish—angry, sad, questioning, or sympathetic.

Check Your Performance   CIPHER IN THE SNOW

Skill	Number Right	Points	Total
WORD SKILLS QUESTIONS			
Phonics, Word Parts, Dictionary (5 items)	_____	x 10 =	_____
Vocabulary in Context (5 items)	_____	x 10 =	_____
		SCORE =	_____%
COMPREHENSION QUESTIONS			
Central Point and Main Ideas (4 items)	_____	x 7 =	_____
Supporting Details (3 items)	_____	x 7 =	_____
Transitions (3 items)	_____	x 7 =	_____
Mapping (6 items)	_____	x 5 =	_____
		SCORE =	_____%

FINAL SCORES: **Word Skills** _____%   **Comprehension** _____%

Enter your final scores onto the reading performance chart on the inside back cover.

3

Friendship and Living Longer
Vicky Chan

Preview

Maybe the old saying should be changed from "An apple a day . . ." to "Friendship each day keeps the doctor away." As this selection explains, strong social ties appear to be good preventive medicine. How do we know that family and friends keep us healthier? And why would a strong social life make for a strong body? Vicky Chan offers some interesting evidence.

Words to Watch

subjects (2): people being studied in an experiment
confirms (4): supports
tend (5): are likely
responsive (5): reacting easily
abrupt (9): sudden
literally (11): actually

> Do you want to be healthier and live longer? Spend time with your friends. That is the prescription given by several medical studies. These surveys show that people with strong social ties—to friends, family and loved ones, even pets—live longer and enjoy better health than lonely people.   1

One study in California, for example, followed 7,000 people over a period of nine years. The subjects° were asked to describe their social ties. Some said that they were isolated from others. These subjects had death rates two or three times higher than people with families and friends. 2

The stronger the social ties to others, the study found, the lower the death rate. This pattern held true for men and women, young and old, rich and poor. The race of the subject did not change the result. It also applied to people with different lifestyles. Cigarette smokers who had friends lived longer than friendless smokers. Joggers involved with other people lived longer than joggers who lived isolated lives. 3

Another study confirms° this result. The University of Michigan looked at 2,754 adults in Tecumseh, Michigan. The researchers carefully measured their subjects' health at the beginning of the study. The lonely, isolated people started out as healthy as the others. But over ten years, they were two to four times as likely to die. 4

Other findings also show the health value of personal ties. Married men and women tend° to live longer than single, divorced, or widowed people of the same age. In nursing homes, patients became more aware and responsive° when they played with cats and dogs. Pet owners are more likely to survive heart attacks than people without pets. 5

Another kind of proof that social ties support good health comes from Japan. Most Japanese people live hectic lives in cities as crowded, noisy, and polluted as ours. Such a way of life seems unhealthy. Yet the Japanese are among the healthiest and longest-lived people in the world. One reason may be their diet. Another reason, though, is their way of life. Japanese have strong ties to family and coworkers. These ties are rarely broken. For example, companies tend to move coworkers as a group, rather than one at a time. Thus the work groups remain the same. 6

Studies of Japanese-Americans support the importance of the role of Japanese social life in preserving their health. Japanese-Americans who live in strongly Japanese neighborhoods and have mainly Japanese friends tend to live longer than those who do not. Both groups eat mostly American-style food, and many in both groups smoke and drink. Thus it appears to be the strong social ties of Japanese communities that keep their members healthy. 7

Why is it more healthy to have friends and loved ones? We don't know, exactly. But it is probably a combination of several explanations. In part, people with strong social ties may simply have more to live for. They have loved ones or family who share their lives. They have friends who call them and ask them how they're doing. They have get-togethers to look forward to. 8

Social contacts also provide us with a buffer against the shocks of 9
life. At some point, each of us moves, changes a job, or loses a loved
one. Such abrupt° changes tend to cause increases in the rates of many
diseases. These include heart disease, cancer, strokes, and mental
illnesses. Accidents are also more likely to happen to people whose
lives have suddenly changed. Friends, loved ones, even a loyal dog can
help us to get through the otherwise very rough changes that we must
deal with in life.

Finally, friends and loved ones can affect our health in still 10
another way. If we are smokers, they may help us to quit. If we overeat,
they may urge us to cut back. They can remind us to go for medical
checkups. And if we have fears or sadnesses bottled up inside us,
friends can help us face and overcome them. By caring for us, in other
words, friends and family help us to care for ourselves.

Close human ties make life not only fuller, but also longer. Caring 11
for others, and being cared for by them, is literally° a more healthy way
to live.

WORD SKILLS QUESTIONS

A. Use your knowledge of phonics, word parts, and the dictionary to answer the
questions below.

Consonants

1. Words from paragraph 9 with consonant blends include
   a. *social, loved,* and *illnesses.*
   b. *provide, against,* and *include.*
   c. *shocks, likely,* and *otherwise.*

Vowels

2. Words from paragraph 6 that contain a long **e** sound include
   a. *noisy, Japanese,* and *reason.*
   b. *yet, ties,* and *same.*
   c. *another, life,* and *time.*

Syllables

3. *Tecumseh* in paragraph 4 is divided into syllables
   a. between two consonants.
   b. before a single consonant.
   c. using both of the above rules.

Word Parts

4. *Friendless* in "Cigarette smokers who had friends lived longer than friendless smokers" (paragraph 3) means
   a. able to be a friend.
   b. one who makes friends.
   c. without friends.

Dictionary Use

5. The definition of *tie* that applies in "The subjects were asked to describe their social ties" (paragraph 2) is
   a. definition 1.
   b. definition 2.
   c. definition 3.
   d. definition 4.

   tie (tī) *n.* **1.** A means by which something is tied, as a cord or string. **2.** Something that unites; bond: *marital ties.* **3.** A necktie. **4.** A beam or rod that joins parts and gives support.

B. Use context clues to help you decide on the best definition for each italicized word. Then circle the letter of each choice.

6. The word *surveys* in "Spend time with your friends. That is the prescription given by several medical studies. These surveys show that people with strong social ties . . . live longer" (paragraph 1) means
   a. prescriptions.
   b. friends.
   c. studies.
   d. ties.

7. The word *isolated* in "Some said that they were isolated from others. These subjects had death rates two or three times higher than people with families and friends" (paragraph 2) means
   a. joined.
   b. coming.
   c. separated.
   d. taking.

8. The word *hectic* in "Most Japanese people live hectic lives in cities as crowded, noisy, and polluted as ours" (paragraph 6) means
   a. boring and empty.
   b. busy and rushed.
   c. brief and happy.
   d. long and peaceful.

9. The word *buffer* in "Social contacts also provide us with a buffer against the shocks of life" (paragraph 9) means
   a. protection.
   b. bad attitude.
   c. honesty.
   d. problem.

10. The words *bottled up* in "if we have fears or sadnesses bottled up inside us, friends can help us face and overcome them" (paragraph 10) mean
    a. fully repaired.
    b. balanced.
    c. welcomed.
    d. held in.

READING COMPREHENSION QUESTIONS

Central Point and Main Ideas

1. Which sentence best expresses the central point of the selection?
   a. Everyone wants to be healthy and live a long life.
   b. People are healthier and live longer when they have strong social relationships.
   c. The Japanese are among the healthiest people in the world.
   d. Friends and loved ones help get us through hard times.

2. Which is the topic sentence of paragraph 5?
   a. The first sentence
   b. The second sentence
   c. The third sentence
   d. The fourth sentence

3. Which sentence best expresses the main idea of paragraph 10?
   a. The second sentence
   b. The third sentence
   c. The next-to-the-last sentence
   d. The last sentence

Supporting Details

4. According to the reading, a married man is more likely to live longer than a
   a. married woman.
   b. smoker.
   c. divorced man.
   d. friend.

5. _T_ TRUE OR FALSE? Japanese-Americans who live in Japanese communities and have mainly Japanese friends are likely to live longer than Japanese-Americans who do not.

6. People with strong social ties
   a. may have more to live for.
   b. never experience sudden changes.
   c. need fewer medical checkups.
   d. all of the above.

7. According to Chan, people whose lives suddenly change are more likely than others to
   a. have friends.
   b. have accidents.
   c. quit smoking.
   d. smoke.

Transitions

8. The transitions which introduce paragraphs 4, 5, and 6 signal
   a. addition.
   b. time.
   c. cause and effect.
   d. illustration.

9. The relationship of the second sentence below to the first is one of
   a. addition.
   b. comparison.
   c. contrast.
   d. cause and effect.

   Such a way of life seems unhealthy. Yet the Japanese are among the healthiest and longest-lived people in the world. (Paragraph 6)

10. The relationship of the two sentences below is one of
   a. time.
   b. comparison.
   c. contrast.
   d. cause and effect.

   . . . the Japanese are among the healthiest and longest-lived people in the world. One reason may be their diet. (Paragraph 6)

MAPPING ACTIVITY

This selection is made up of a central point along with evidence and possible explanations for that point. Complete the diagram below by filling in the scrambled items that follow.

- According to a University of Michigan study, lonely people tend to die sooner.
- Friendship leads to better health and longer lives.
- Strong ties may give people more to live for.
- Social contacts buffer us against life's shocks.

Central point: _Friendship leads to better health and longer lives._

_____

Evidence for the Point

1. According to a California study, the stronger the social ties, the lower the death rate.

2. _According to a University of Michigan study, lonely people tend to die sooner._

3. Studies show that married people tend to live longer and that relationships with pets make people stronger.

4. Studies show that Japanese-Americans with strong social ties are healthier than other Americans.

Possible Explanations for the Point

1. _Strong ties may give people more to live for._

_____

2. _Social contacts buffer us against life's shocks._

_____

3. By caring for us, friends often help us care for ourselves.

DISCUSSION QUESTIONS

1. Do you agree that "social contacts . . . provide us with a buffer against the shocks of life"? What are some of the ways that these contacts keep us from feeling pain? Give an example.

2. How can people who have trouble making friends cope with crisis? In what ways could they form more social ties?

WRITING ACTIVITIES

1. "Friendship and Living Longer" states that we need friends and relatives when we face major changes in our lives. Think back to when you lost a loved one, moved to a new town, began a new job, changed schools, started college, or experienced any other difficult change. Whom did you rely on to soften the shock? Write about what happened and how this person helped you adjust. Following is one example of a topic sentence for this paper: "Without the help of my best friend, Andy, I would never have been able to deal with the death of my father."

2. While we need friends and family, we also require privacy at times. How do you find privacy? Walk around a park alone? Meditate in your bedroom? Write a paper in which you list and explain ways you find privacy. Or instead list and explain the benefits that private time gives you.

Check Your Performance   FRIENDSHIP AND LIVING LONGER

Skill	*Number Right*	*Points*	*Total*
WORD SKILLS QUESTIONS			
Phonics, Word Parts, Dictionary (5 items)	_____	x 10 =	_____
Vocabulary in Context (5 items)	_____	x 10 =	_____
		SCORE =	_____%
COMPREHENSION QUESTIONS			
Central Point and Main Ideas (3 items)	_____	x 7 =	_____
Supporting Details (4 items)	_____	x 7 =	_____
Transitions (3 items)	_____	x 7 =	_____
Mapping (4 items)	_____	x 7.5 =	_____
		SCORE =	_____%

FINAL SCORES: **Word Skills** _____%   **Comprehension** _____%

Enter your final scores onto the reading performance chart on the inside back cover.

4

The Lost Teens
Richard McCaffery Robinson

Preview

It is often hard to understand some teenagers' self-destructive behavior, such as getting pregnant and drug and alcohol abuse. Why in the world do young people harm their lives so carelessly? The answer, says Richard McCaffery Robinson, lies in their vision of their future.

Words to Watch

disaster (2): terrible event
armored (3): protected
wedlock (7): marriage
day-in, day-out (8): constant
flashy (8): fancy
foothills (9): low hills at the foot of a mountain
role models (11): people whom others want to be like
achieved (11): reached

A sixteen-year-old girl waits, awkward and anxious, in a   1
pregnancy clinic. The receptionist calls her name and ushers her into a
private room. "Don't worry," says the clinic worker with a smile. "Your
test came back negative. You're not pregnant."

But instead of being relieved, the girl is disappointed. For many   2
other girls her age, becoming a teenaged single mother would be a
disaster°. It would disrupt their lives and limit their future
opportunities. For this girl, though—and for thousands like her across
America—becoming pregnant seems exciting. To have her own baby to

hold and take care of would be an adventure. She would really be someone, for the first time in her life.

In another part of town, a fifteen-year-old boy stands holding a   3
paper bag. He looks anxiously over his shoulder, then ducks into a house. Inside the house is a steel-armored° door. He presses a buzzer, and a small, barred window opens in the door. The boy hands the paper bag through. A moment later a different bag is handed back to him. Inside this bag is a roll of green bills—five hundred dollars in twenties. The boy grins and runs out of the house. He has just made his first cocaine delivery.

He doesn't know what he's getting himself into—not really. He   4
knows that he might end up dead. In his neighborhood, kids end up dead all the time. But he also imagines that he might end up with a BMW, with expensive clothes, with a beautiful woman on his arm.

What do the disappointed girl at the pregnancy clinic and the   5
excited boy at the crack house have in common? They are both caught up in one of America's greatest social problems. They are both victims of the lack of opportunity, hope, and goals faced by a growing number of young Americans. Teenage pregnancy and teenage drug abuse occur, most often, because the young people involved feel they have nothing to lose.

Some teenagers stay away from sex and drugs because of   6
religious or moral beliefs. Many others are careful because they have goals for their lives. They may want to go to college, or become musicians, or play pro basketball. If they have a baby (or their girlfriends do), or they get mixed up with drugs, they know that their plans will go out the window. They'll be "stuck."

But all too many teenagers feel that they are already stuck. Today,   7
one out of three American children grows up in poverty. As teenagers, these children are three times more likely than other teens to have a child out of wedlock°. They are also the young people most at risk from drugs.

A girl may imagine the joys of having a baby of her own to hold   8
and love. But she may not think about the hard parts. How will she feed and clothe a child? How will she take care of a child who is sick? She is not really aware of the day-in, day-out° demands of parenthood. For a teenaged boy, drug dealing may be the only route he thinks will take him to the "good life" he sees on TV. After all, flashy° clothes, fast cars, big houses, Caribbean vacations cost a lot of money. He doesn't think of years in prison, or of being gunned down on a street corner.

Not only the poorest American teenagers feel hopeless and   9
aimless, however. Sometimes the richest young Americans feel the

same way. Pacific Palisades is an expensive Los Angeles neighborhood in the foothills° above the Pacific Ocean. Teenagers at Palisades High School don't have to dream about big houses and BMWs. They live in big houses and drive BMWs to school. But often their lives seem empty. They see little of their parents, who are too busy making money so they can afford the "good life." They have nothing interesting and useful to do. So they escape into sex, drugs, and alcohol. Recently, four Palisades High students were killed when their speeding car went off the road and crashed. Three, including the driver, had been drinking. Another girl left a party drunk. She was found shot to death the next morning.

These children of wealth "had everything," people said. But in 10 one respect, they are just like the poorest kids. The teenagers of Pacific Palisades often feel they have nothing to look forward to. They have everything but goals, everything but hope.

How can we deal with the problems of sex, pregnancy, and drug 11 abuse among the young? Parents and politicians sometimes offer an easy answer: they tell them to "just say no." This may be good advice, but it is not enough. Teenagers also need to have something that they can say "yes" to. In poor neighborhoods, young people have to be offered more opportunities for wholesome recreation and work. Also, rich and poor teens alike need role models°—other young people who have achieved° success as well as inspiring, caring adults. And teenagers have to be shown that there is more to the truly good life than the things money can buy. They need school and community programs that can help them learn the values of developing one's talents, of building rich personal relationships, and of planning for a hopeful future.

WORD SKILLS QUESTIONS

A. Use your knowledge of phonics, word parts, and the dictionary to answer the questions below.

Consonants

1. The word with a soft sound of **g** (as in *gem*) in the sentence below is
   a. *getting.*
   b. *imagines.*
   c. *might.*

   "He doesn't know what he's getting himself into . . . . In his neighborhood, kids end up dead all the time. But he also imagines that he might end up with a BMW." (Paragraph 4)

Vowels

2. The word *goals* in "Many others are careful because they have goals for their lives" (paragraph 6) is an example of which rule for long vowel sounds?
   a. When a word ends in a vowel-consonant-*e*, the first vowel is long and the **e** is silent.
   b. When two of certain vowels are together in a word, the first one is long and the second is silent.
   c. A single vowel at the end of a word usually has a long sound.

Syllables

3. The word *opportunities* in "young people have to be offered more opportunities" (paragraph 11) is divided into syllables
   a. between double consonants.
   b. before single consonants.
   c. both of the above.

Word Parts

4. *Aimless* in "Not only the poorest American teenagers feel . . . aimless" (paragraph 9) means
   a. without purpose.
   b. similar to a purpose.
   c. able to have a purpose.

Dictionary Use

5. The definition that fits *empty* in "They live in big houses and drive BMWs to school. But often their lives seem empty" (paragraph 9) is
   a. definition 1.
   b. definition 2.
   c. definition 3.

   > **emp·ty** (ĕmp′-tē) *adj.* **-ti·er, ti·est. 1.** Containing nothing. **2.** Having no occupants or inhabitants; unoccupied. **3.** Lacking purpose, substance, value, or effect.

B. Use context clues to help you decide on the best definition for each italicized word. Then circle the letter of each choice.

   6. The word *ushers* in "The receptionist calls her name and ushers her into a private room" (paragraph 1) means
      a. worries.
      b. guides.
      c. completes.
      d. loses.

7. The word *relieved* in ". . . instead of being relieved, the girl is disappointed" (paragraph 2) means
    a. sorry.
    b. comforted.
    c. praised.
    d. dependable.

8. The word *disrupt* in ". . . becoming . . . teenaged single mother[s] . . . would disrupt their lives and limit their future opportunities" (paragraph 2) means
    a. make more interesting.
    b. put an end to.
    c. improve.
    d. disturb.

9. The word *demands* in "How will she feed and clothe a child? How will she take care of a child who is sick? She is not really aware of the day-in, day-out demands of parenthood" (paragraph 8) means
    a. cries.
    b. pleasures.
    c. questions.
    d. requirements.

10. The word *respect* in "But in one respect, they are just like the poorest kids. The teenagers of Pacific Palisades often feel they have nothing to look forward to" (paragraph 10) means
    a. state.
    b. detail.
    c. advantage.
    d. household.

READING COMPREHENSION QUESTIONS

Central Point and Main Ideas

1. Which sentence best expresses the central point of the selection?
    a. Teenagers have more problems today than ever before.
    b. For all of today's teens, life seems hopeless.
    c. Many teenaged girls want to have babies.
    d. To keep teens out of trouble, we must help them find goals and hopes.

2. Which sentence best expresses the main idea of paragraph 7?
    a. One of every three American children grows up poor.
    b. Poor teenagers are more likely to have babies.
    c. Many poor teenagers already feel they are stuck without a future and behave accordingly.
    d. Poor teenagers are more at risk from drugs than other teenagers.

3. Which sentence best expresses the main idea of paragraph 10?
   a. People think that wealthy kids have everything.
   b. Wealthy teenagers have nothing in common with poor teenagers.
   (c.) Many wealthy kids lack goals and hope, just as poor kids do.
   d. All wealthy teenagers are lacking goals.

Supporting Details

4. The author tells us that the fifteen-year-old boy who has just delivered the cocaine
   (a.) has never delivered drugs before.
   b. is afraid he will be arrested.
   c. will go on to become a major drug dealer.
   d. will be dead before he reaches his sixteenth birthday.

5. Some teenagers stay away from sex and drugs because they
   a. are rich.
   b. are poor.
   (c.) have goals.
   d. have friends.

6. ___*F*___ TRUE OR FALSE? Teenagers from wealthy homes always get to spend a lot of time with their parents.

7. The author feels that teenagers need to know all of the following except:
   a. Sex, drugs, and alcohol don't make problems go away.
   (b.) The good life requires lots of money.
   c. Raising a baby isn't easy.
   d. Dealing drugs is dangerous.

Transitions

8. Paragraph 2 begins with a transition that shows
   a. addition.
   (b.) contrast.
   c. an example.
   d. cause and effect.

9. The relationship of the second sentence below to the first sentence is one of
   a. time.
   b. contrast.
   c. an example.
   (d.) cause and effect.

   They have nothing interesting and useful to do. So they escape into sex, drugs and alcohol. (Paragraph 9)

10. The transition *like* in the sentence below signals
    a. addition.
    b. time.
    c. contrast.
    (d.) comparison.

> But in one respect, [these children of wealth] are just like the poorest kids. (Paragraph 10)

MAPPING ACTIVITY

This selection describes a problem and suggests a solution. Complete the diagram of the problems and the suggested solution by filling in the missing points, which are scrambled below.

- American teenagers who feel hopeless and aimless have babies and get involved with drugs.
- Many of these teenagers, whose parents are too busy making money, have nothing useful to do.
- Many feel they have nothing to gain by staying away from pregnancy and drugs.
- To fight the problems of pregnancy and drug abuse among the young, we must give teenagers something to say "yes" to.

GENERAL PROBLEM:

American teenagers who feel hopeless and aimless have babies and get involved with drugs.

Problem of Poor Teenagers

Many feel they have nothing to gain by staying away from pregnancy and drugs.

Problem of Rich Teenagers

Many of these teenagers, whose parents are too busy making money, have nothing useful to do.

SUGGESTED SOLUTION:

To fight the problems of pregnancy and drug abuse among the young, we must give teenagers something to say "yes" to.

DISCUSSION QUESTIONS

1. According to the article, all teens need role models. Who were (or are) your role models? What about them did (or do) you admire?

2. The author states in paragraph 11 that telling teenagers to "just say no" to drugs and casual sex is not enough. Why not? Instead of telling teens to "just say no," what sort of campaign might work?

WRITING ACTIVITIES

1. In "The Lost Teens," the author writes of a sixteen-year-old girl who is disappointed at not being pregnant. Write a letter to the girl explaining why she should not be disappointed. Here are some issues you may wish to discuss in your letter: a) time needed for child care; b) younger versus older parents; c) financial responsibilities of parenthood.

2. Write about one person who has been a role model for you. Begin with a topic sentence such as "My mother has been a special role model for me for many years." Your supporting details should explain what you've admired about your role model and how he or she influenced your character and goals. Use specific examples.

Check Your Performance   THE LOST TEENS

Skill	*Number Right*	*Points*	*Total*
WORD SKILLS QUESTIONS			
Phonics, Word Parts, Dictionary (5 items)	_____	x 10 =	_____
Vocabulary in Context (5 items)	_____	x 10 =	_____
		SCORE =	_____ %
COMPREHENSION QUESTIONS			
Central Point and Main Ideas (3 items)	_____	x 7 =	_____
Supporting Details (4 items)	_____	x 7 =	_____
Transitions (3 items)	_____	x 7 =	_____
Mapping (4 items)	_____	x 7.5 =	_____
		SCORE =	_____ %

FINAL SCORES: Word Skills _____ %   **Comprehension** _____ %

Enter your final scores onto the reading performance chart on the inside back cover.

5

Room with a New View
Steve Lopez

Preview

Nameless, almost faceless, homeless people camp on the streets of every American city. Here's the story of one such man who came to have a name and a face for the people who saw him daily on one Philadelphia street. By responding to him as a real person, the people on his street changed his life and their own.

Words to Watch

inspiration (6): encouragement
oblivious to (6): unaware of
distribution (10): supply
barrier (11): something that separates
apparently (14): seeming to be
alcove (15): small space off to the side
maintaining (16): keeping in good condition
fragments (21): pieces
displaced (24): away from home

Three years ago, architect Peter Fox is fresh out of college and catches a bus for his first day on the job. The bus pulls up to 20th and Chestnut, the door opens, and there's some guy camped out on the sidewalk like he owns the property.   1

Next day, same thing. And the next day, and the next.   2

"I had to step over him every morning," Fox says.   3

Fox would continue on to work, where he sat against a window 4 one flight above 20th Street. Sometimes he'd design a new swimming pool for someone who was unhappy with their old swimming pool. And when his work didn't seem to reflect reality, there was always the window.

Three years later, the man is still out there. Peter Fox is still 5 looking.

They don't know each other. But Fox has found comfort and 6 inspiration° in just looking. And the man—oblivious to° his starring role in the drama Fox sees through his window—is comfortable with his own invisibility.

The man outside says he is John Madison, Vietnam veteran. 7

"Shortly after I started," Fox wrote in a letter, "a Korean fruit stand 8 opened. At first the street guy would bum them for food and money."

It looked like only a matter of time before one of them drove out 9 the other. But that didn't happen.

"Pretty soon they had him helping unload their truck in the 10 morning when it arrived from the food distribution° center."

This despite a language barrier°. On some level, maybe because 11 both Madison and the Koreans were on the edge of things, they made a connection.

"Next, he was sweeping the sidewalk, then driving the truck for 12 them, all the time his appearance improving."

Partly because he was getting paid by the Korean fruit vendors. A 13 couple bucks here, a couple bucks there. What was emerging, gradually, was the new John Madison.

"Better clothes, haircut, apparently° now off the street. And the 14 wild look disappearing from his eyes."

What Fox didn't know—nobody knew—was that Madison had 15 taken to camping in a quiet alcove° near the Boy Scouts of America office several blocks away. Though it was still the street, to him it was a fancier address, fit for a man of his upward mobility.

"As the fortunes of the vendors improved, they, along with their 16 relatives, bought several shops on the block, and the street guy became responsible for maintaining° all the shops, as well as the street and sidewalk along the entire block."

Fox watched as the John Madison Corporation conquered new 17 territory. With a household broom, he had staked out the west side of 20th Street from Market to Chestnut. He had the sidewalk so clean you had to look twice to figure out what was wrong with the picture. He even dug cigarette butts out of cracks.

And he was diversifying. 18

"He is now holding down two jobs—collecting trash for a private 19
hauler in the early morning and then arriving (usually hanging off the
side of the trash truck) to work for the Koreans and other merchants."

Madison's abilities did not escape the notice of the management 20
of Nuts to You, one of the few remaining non-Korean businesses on the
block. Manny Radbill, the owner, occasionally had Madison clean his
van. One time Madison found money in it and immediately gave it to
Radbill. Debbie Alexander, Radbill's manager, remembers the time she
handed Madison a Christmas bonus. He refused.

To John Madison, words and possessions are confusing 21
fragments° of a complicated world. His luxury is to need so little.

His only vice, Radbill says, is a beer or two on a warm afternoon, 22
a habit the Koreans do not seem to appreciate. Most of them, however,
see in Madison a little bit of themselves. He works hard, says Hyun Jin.
What else is there?

There is Peter Fox, watching the whole thing out the window. 23
And there's Madison, the man he used to step over.

"It has been very inspiring to watch all of this happen. It's a great 24
reflection of the Korean merchants, refugees themselves, who in
establishing themselves and their families in this country have found
room in their plan to reach down to someone more displaced° than
themselves and pull him up with them."

Madison says he's off the streets now and rents space in a North 25
Philadelphia house for $3 a night. He liked hearing that people have
seen the change in him and appreciate what he's done for the block.

As Madison smiled at the thought, broom in hand, Peter Fox 26
watched through the window.

WORD SKILLS QUESTIONS

A. Use your knowledge of phonics, word parts, and the dictionary to answer the
questions below. The questions are based on the following passage from the
selection.

> Madison's abilities did not escape the notice of the management of
> Nuts to You, one of the few remaining non-Korean businesses on the block.
> Manny Radbill, the owner, occasionally had Madison clean his van. One
> time Madison found money in it and immediately gave it to Radbill. Debbie
> Alexander, Radbill's manager, remembers the time she handed Madison a
> Christmas bonus. He refused. (Paragraph 20)

Consonants

1. The word containing both a consonant blend and a silent **c** is
   a. *escape.*
   b. *block.*
   c. *clean.*

Vowels

2. The words *escape, time,* and *gave* all are examples of which rule for long vowel sounds?
   a. When a word ends in a vowel-consonant-**e**, the first vowel is long and the **e** is silent.
   b. When two of certain vowels are together in a word, the first one is long and the second is silent.
   c. A single vowel at the end of a word usually has a long sound.

Syllables

3. *Remembers* is divided into syllables
   a. between two consonants.
   b. before a single consonant.
   c. using both of the above rules.

Word Parts

4. *Bonus* contains a word part that means
   a. in a certain manner.
   b. again.
   c. good.

Dictionary Use

5. The word *van* can be found on a dictionary page with the guidewords
   a. vacuous / value.
   b. valve / vaporous.
   c. versus / veto.

B. Use context clues to help you decide on the best definition for each italicized word. Then circle the letter of each choice.

6. The word *vendors* in "a Korean fruit stand opened. . . . Pretty soon they had him helping unload their truck. . . . he was getting paid by the Korean fruit vendors" (paragraphs 8–13) means
   a. pickers.
   b. sellers.
   c. machines.
   d. tasters.

7. The word *emerging* in "all the time his appearance improving. . . . What was emerging, gradually, was the new John Madison" (paragraphs 12–13) means
   a. appearing.
   b. hurting.
   c. ending.
   d. playing.

8. The phrase *upward mobility* in "it was a fancier address, fit for a man of his upward mobility" (paragraph 15) means
   a. expensive tastes.
   b. great needs.
   c. improving position.
   d. extreme poverty.

9. The word *diversifying* in "And he was diversifying. 'He is now holding down two jobs . . .'" (paragraphs 18–19) means
   a. doing more.
   b. earning less.
   c. becoming harder to manage.
   d. collecting trash.

10. The word *vice* in "His only vice . . . is a beer or two on a warm afternoon, a habit the Koreans do not seem to appreciate" (paragraph 22) means
    a. fear.
    b. change.
    c. fault.
    d. strength.

READING COMPREHENSION QUESTIONS

Central Point and Main Ideas

1. Which sentence best expresses the central point of the selection?
   a. Peter Fox enjoys looking out his window at John Madison and others.
   b. Homeless men should be put to work.
   c. Some Korean merchants helped John Madison begin a new life.
   d. Everyone needs to earn a living.

2. Which sentence best expresses the main idea of paragraphs 8–10?
   a. Some Koreans opened a fruit stand.
   b. Madison asked the Koreans for money and food.
   c. Fox expected trouble between Madison and the Koreans.
   d. New Korean businessmen got Madison to work for them.

3. Which sentence best expresses the main idea of paragraphs 12–17?
   a. At first, Madison helped the Korean businessmen unload their truck.
   b. Madison was getting paid by the Korean fruit vendors.
   (c.) Madison worked more and more for the Koreans, and his personal life improved.
   d. Madison cleaned the sidewalks so well that they looked strange.

Supporting Details

4. According to the author, the Koreans
   a. were afraid of Madison.
   b. kept asking Madison to move.
   c. taught Madison to drive a truck.
   (d.) did well in their businesses.

5. As life improved for the Koreans,
   a. they no longer had to work so hard.
   (b.) life also improved for Madison.
   c. Peter Fox became successful, as well.
   d. the other store owners became jealous of them.

6. ___F___ TRUE OR FALSE? Madison was glad to have the Christmas bonus from Nuts to You.

7. As a result of his efforts, Madison
   a. has convinced Peter Fox to give money to the homeless.
   b. now works for the Boy Scouts of America.
   (c.) is now living in a house in North Philadelphia.
   d. is finding jobs for other homeless men.

Transitions

8. The transition *after* in the sentence below signals
   (a.) addition.
   b. contrast.
   c. time.
   d. cause and effect.

   "Shortly after I started," Fox wrote in a letter, "a Korean fruit stand opened." (Paragraph 8)

9. In the sentences below, the transition *because* introduces one of the ____causes____ (causes or *effects?*) of Madison's improving appearance.

   "Next, he was sweeping the sidewalk, then driving the truck for them, all the time his appearance improving." Partly because he was getting paid by the Korean fruit vendors. (Paragraphs 12–13)

10. The transition *however* in the sentence below signals
    a. time.
    b.) contrast.
    c. an example.
    d. cause and effect.

> His only vice . . . is a beer or two on a warm afternoon, a habit the Koreans do not seem to appreciate. Most of them, however, see in Madison a little bit of themselves. (Paragraph 22)

MAPPING ACTIVITY

This selection is organized by time: first one thing happened; then another; after that, another; and so on. Four major events are scrambled in the list below. Write them in the diagram in their correct order.

- Madison then takes on more jobs and improves his appearance.
- Madison camps on the street.
- Madison moves off the street.
- Korean businessmen pay him for odd jobs.

Central point: By offering work to John Madison, a homeless man, Korean businessmen start a new life for him.

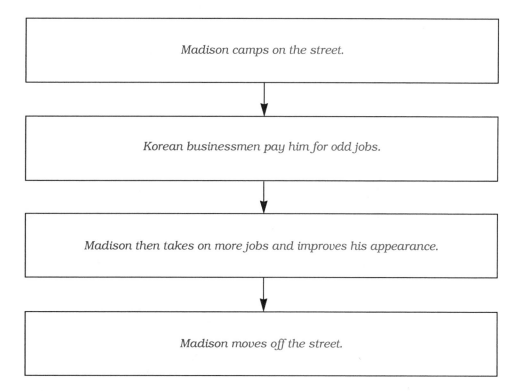

Madison camps on the street.

↓

Korean businessmen pay him for odd jobs.

↓

Madison then takes on more jobs and improves his appearance.

↓

Madison moves off the street.

DISCUSSION QUESTIONS

1. John Madison found money in a van and returned it. He also refused to accept a Christmas bonus. What do these facts tell us about him? Would you have done the same? Why or why not?

2. The author states that John Madison's "luxury is to need so little." What does this mean? How much—or how little—do you need to make you happy?

WRITING ACTIVITIES

1. Write a paragraph in which you list and explain the reasons why you think that many are homeless. Begin the paragraph with your topic sentence.

2. Write about someone who, like the Korean businessmen, went to some trouble to help someone else overcome a problem. Like Lopez, first describe the problem, and then go on to explain how the situation got better.

Check Your Performance   ROOM WITH A NEW VIEW

Skill	Number Right	Points	Total
WORD SKILLS QUESTIONS			
Phonics, Word Parts, Dictionary (5 items)	_____	x 10 =	_____
Vocabulary in Context (5 items)	_____	x 10 =	_____
		SCORE =	_____ %
COMPREHENSION QUESTIONS			
Central Point and Main Ideas (3 items)	_____	x 7 =	_____
Supporting Details (4 items)	_____	x 7 =	_____
Transitions (3 items)	_____	x 7 =	_____
Mapping (4 items)	_____	x 7.5 =	_____
		SCORE =	_____ %

FINAL SCORES: **Word Skills** _____ %   **Comprehension** _____ %

Enter your final scores onto the reading performance chart on the inside back cover.

6

Classroom Notetaking
Clarissa White

Preview

What do you do during a classroom lecture? Do you sit and stare at the instructor, wondering if he or she will ever stop? Do you look at the person next to you, trying to figure out what he could possibly be writing when you haven't heard anything interesting? Do you try to write down everything that is said, but can't keep up? Knowing what to do and how to do it during a lecture is a skill. Mastering this skill will make you a better student. Keep that in mind as you read the next selection, which gives you tips on how to make the best use of class time.

Words to Watch

deaden (3): dull
glazed (3): glassy
launching pad (7): starting point
groping (8): reaching
cement (14): fix firmly

How would you feel if you were forced to spend 1800 hours—the 1 equivalent of 75 days in a row—sitting in a hard-backed chair, eyes wide open, listening to the sound of someone else's voice? You wouldn't be allowed to sleep, eat, or smoke. You couldn't leave the room. To make matters worse, you'd be expected to remember every important point the speaker made, and you'd be punished for forgetting. And, to top it off, you'd have to pay thousands of dollars for the experience.

Sound like the torture scene from the latest spy thriller? Actually, 2
it's nothing of the kind. It's what all college students do who take a full
load of five courses for four years. Those 1800 hours are the time
they'll spend in the lecture room.

Unfortunately, many students do regard these hours as torture, and 3
they do all sorts of things to deaden° the pain. Some of them sit through
class with glazed° eyes, minds wandering to the athletic field or the
movie theater. Others hide in the back of the room, sneaking glances at
the newspaper or the book they're being tested on in their next class.
Still others reduce the pain to zero: they simply don't come to class.
These students do not realize that if they don't listen in class—and take
notes—they're missing out on one of the most important aspects of
their education.

WHY TAKE LECTURE NOTES?

One reason you should take lecture notes is that lectures add to 4
what you read in textbooks. Lecturers combine the material and
approaches of many texts, saving you the trouble of researching an entire
field. They keep up to date with their subjects and can include the latest
studies or discoveries in their presentations; they needn't wait for the next
edition of the book to come out. They can provide additional examples or
simplify difficult concepts, making it easier for you to master tricky
material. And the best lecturers combine knowledge with expert
showmanship. Both informative and entertaining speakers, they can make
any subject, from ancient civilizations to computers, leap vividly to life.

True, you say, but isn't it good enough just to listen to these 5
wonderful people without writing down what they say? Actually, it
isn't, which leads us to another reason for taking lecture notes. Studies
have shown that after two weeks, you'll forget 80 percent of it. And
you didn't come to the lecture room just to be entertained. You came to
learn. The only way to keep the material in your head is to get it down
in permanent form—in the form of lecture notes.

HOW TO TAKE LECTURE NOTES

There are three steps to mastering the art of taking good lecture 6
notes: the preparation, the notetaking process itself, and the post-lecture
review.

Preparation

First, mentally prepare yourself to take good notes. Examine your 7
attitude. Remember, you're not going to the lecture room to be bored,

tortured, or entertained; you're going there to learn. Also, examine the material the lecture will cover. Read the textbook chapter in advance. If your instructor's lecture usually follows the organization of the textbook, you'll be familiar with the material and won't have to spend half the lecture wondering what it's about or how to spell a key term. If, however, your instructor merely uses the textbook as a launching pad° and devotes most of the lecture to supplementary material, at least you'll have the background to follow what is being said.

Second, prepare yourself physically. Get a good night's sleep, and 8
get to class—on time. Even better, get to class early, so you can get a good seat near the front of the room. You'll hear better there and be less tempted to let your mind wander. You'll also have time to open your notebook to a new page, find your pen, and write the date, course, and topic of the lecture at the top. This way, you won't still be groping° under your chair or flipping through pages when the instructor begins to speak.

Process

When you take class notes, always use 8½" x 11" paper, preferably 9
in a looseleaf notebook so you can insert handouts. Write on only one side of the paper. Later, you might want to spread all your notes out in front of you. Have a pen to write with rather than a pencil, which moves more slowly across a page and is not as legible.

Be prepared to do a good deal of writing in class. A good rule of 10
thumb for taking notes is "When in doubt, write it down." After class, you will have time to go over your notes and make decisions about what is important enough to study and what is not. But in the midst of a lecture, you don't always have time to decide what is really important and what is quite secondary. You don't want to miss getting down a valuable idea that the instructor does not repeat later.

Be sure to always write down what the instructor puts on the 11
board. If he or she takes the time to write something on the board, it is generally safe to assume that such material is important. And don't fall into the trap that some students fall into. They write down what is on the board but nothing more. They just sit and listen while the instructor explains all the connections between those words that have been chalked on the board. Everything may be perfectly clear to a student then, but several days later, chances are that all the connecting material will be forgotten. If you write down the explanations in class, it will be much easier for you to make sense of the material and to study it later.

As much as possible, organize your notes by starting main points 12
at the margin. Indent secondary points under the main points and indent

examples even further. Skip lines between main sections. Wherever possible, number the points. If the instructor explains three reasons for poverty, or four results of the greenhouse effect, make sure you number each of those reasons or results. The numbers help organize the material and make it easier for you to study and remember it.

Here are some other hints for taking good classroom notes: 13

- If you miss something, don't panic. Leave space for it in your notes and keep going. Later, get the missing information from a classmate or your textbook.

- Be alert for signals that something is an important point ("A major cause of anxiety is . . ."), a new topic ("Another problem of urban living is . . ."), the beginning of an enumeration ("There are seven warning signals . . ."), or a summary ("In conclusion . . ."). These signals will help you organize your note-taking. If your instructor says, "The point I am trying to make is . . . ," be sure you *get the point*—in your notes.

- Use abbreviations in order to save time. Put a key for abbreviated words in the top margin of your notes. For instance, in a business class, *com* could stand for *communication; info* for *information.* In a psychology class, *beh* could stand for *behavior; mot* for *motivation.* You can also abbreviate certain common words, using a "+" for *and,* a "*w/*" for *with,* and an "*ex*" for *example.*

- Finally, don't ignore the very beginning and end of class. Often, instructors devote the first five minutes of their lectures to a review of material already covered or a preview of the next day's lecture. The last five minutes of a lecture can contain a clear summary of the class—or ten more major points the instructor simply *has* to make before the bell rings. Don't spend the first five minutes of class getting your materials out and the last five minutes putting them away. If you do, you'll probably miss something important.

Post-Lecture Review

Taking good notes lets you bring the lecture home with you. The   14 real learning takes place after class. As soon as you have time, sit down and reread your notes. Fill in anything unclear or missing while it's still fresh in your mind. Then, in the left-hand column of each page, write a few key words and phrases that summarize the points of the lecture. Cover your notes, and, using only these key words, try to reconstruct as much of the lecture as you can. This review will cement° the major points in your memory—and will save significant time when you study for the exam.

To sum all this up, be prepared to go into class and be not just an active listener but an active notetaker as well. Being in class and taking good notes while you are there are the most valuable steps you can take to succeed in college. 15

WORD SKILLS QUESTIONS

A. Use your knowledge of phonics, word parts, and the dictionary to answer the following questions.

Consonants

1. A word from paragraph 14 in which **c** has a soft sound (as in *city*) is
   a. *column.*
   b. *reconstruct.*
   c. *cement.*

Vowels

2. The **o** in *devote* in "Often, instructors devote the first five minutes of their lectures to a review . . . or a preview" (paragraph 13)
   a. has a long sound.
   b. has a short sound.
   c. is silent.

Syllables

3. The correct syllable division of *reconstruct* in "Cover your notes, and . . . try to reconstruct as much of the lecture as you can" (paragraph 14) is
   a. rec-ons-truct.
   b. re-constr-uct.
   c. re-con-struct.

Word Parts

4. A *post-lecture review* in "There are three steps to mastering the art of taking good lecture notes: the preparation, the notetaking process itself, and the post-lecture review" (paragraph 6) is a review that takes place
   a. before the lecture.
   b. during the lecture.
   c. after the lecture.

Dictionary Use

5. The accented syllable in *equivalent* is
   a. the first syllable.
   b. the second syllable.
   c. the third syllable.
   d. the fourth syllable.

e·quiv·a·lent (ē-kwĭv'ə-lənt)

B. Use context clues to help you decide on the best definition for each italicized word. Then circle the letter of your choice.

6. The word *equivalent* in "1800 hours—the equivalent of 75 days in a row" (paragraph 1) means
   a. rest.
   b. equal.
   c. difference.
   d. first.

7. The word *showmanship* in "And the best lecturers combine knowledge with expert showmanship. . . . they can make any subject, from ancient civilizations to computers, leap vividly to life" (paragraph 4) means
   a. dramatic skill.
   b. handwriting.
   c. research ability.
   d. popularity.

8. The word *vividly* in "entertaining speakers, they can make any subject, from ancient civilizations to computers, leap vividly to life" (paragraph 4) means
   a. in a quiet way.
   b. in a lively way.
   c. in a civilized way.
   d. in a confusing way.

9. The word *supplementary* in "If, however, your instructor merely uses the textbook as a launching pad and devotes most of the lecture to supplementary material, at least you'll have the background to follow what is being said" (paragraph 7) means
   a. textbook.
   b. unimportant.
   c. additional.
   d. boring.

10. The word *enumeration* in "Be alert for signals that something is . . . the beginning of an enumeration ('There are seven warning signals . . . ')" (paragraph 13) means
    a. a new topic.
    b. a signal.
    c. a list.
    d. a beginning.

READING COMPREHENSION QUESTIONS

Central Point and Main Ideas

1. Which sentence best expresses the central point of the selection?
   a. Students can learn more from lectures than from reading textbooks.
   b. Taking lecture notes is an important skill involving three main steps.
   c. College lectures are more than just entertainment.
   d. Use lecture notes to learn after class.

2. The main idea of paragraph 4 can be found in its
   a. first sentence.
   b. second sentence.
   c. third sentence.
   d. last sentence.

3. Which sentence best expresses the main idea of paragraph 14?
   a. Notetaking allows you to bring a copy of the lecture home with you.
   b. Always fill in the blanks in your notes as soon as class ends.
   c. Completing and reviewing lecture notes soon after class will help you remember the material.
   d. Reread your notes soon after class, filling in any missing information and making unclear information clear.

Supporting Details

4. According to the essay, lecturers
   a. bring together information from many different sources.
   b. include new as well as old material in their lectures.
   c. keep students entertained as well as informed.
   d. all of the above.

5. _T_ TRUE OR FALSE? Students need to prepare for class both physically and mentally.

6. When taking classroom notes, students should always
   a. write on both sides of the notebook page.
   (b.) write in ink.
   c. write on index cards.
   d. write words out fully.

7. Numbering lecture points
   a. helps organize material.
   b. makes it easier for you to study the material.
   c. makes it easier for you to remember the points.
   (d.) all of the above.

Transitions

8. Paragraphs 7 and 8 both begin with transitions that show
   (a.) addition.
   b. contrast.
   c. illustration.
   d. cause and effect.

9. The transition beginning the second sentence below signals
   a. an addition.
   b. a comparison.
   (c.) an example.
   d. a cause and effect.

   Put a key for abbreviated words in the top margin of your notes. For instance, in a business class, *com* could stand for *communication.* . . . (Paragraph 13)

10. The first word of the last item marked by a bullet (•) in paragraph 13 signals
    (a.) addition.
    b. contrast.
    c. comparison.
    d. an example.

MAPPING ACTIVITY

This selection is organized into lists—a list of reasons for taking lecture notes and a list of steps for lecture notetaking. Complete the diagram on the next page by filling in the five missing points.

Central point: Students should take lecture notes, a skill that involves three main steps.

Note: Wording of missing points will vary.

A. Reasons for Taking Classroom Notes

1. Lectures add to what you read in textbooks.
2. *Without notes, you'll forget most of the lecture.*

B. *How to Take Lecture Notes*

1. Prepare yourself mentally and physically.
2. Follow a careful notetaking process.
   a. Write in ink on one side of looseleaf notebook paper.
   b. When in doubt, write it down in your notes.
   c. Always write what the instructor puts on the board and the explanations of that material.
   d. *Organize your notes through margins and numbering.*
   e. If you miss something, just leave space for it.
   f. *Be alert for signals.*
   g. Use abbreviations.
   h. *Don't ignore the beginning and end of class.*
3. Complete and review notes after class.

DISCUSSION QUESTIONS

1. Of all the advice in this article, what three points will be the most helpful for you to remember and practice?

2. Besides knowing how to take lecture notes, what other study skills do you think are important for students to know and practice? For example, what skills are useful when reading, studying material, or taking a test?

WRITING ACTIVITIES

1. Draw a line down the middle of a notebook page. On the top left hand side, write the words "Things I do." On the top right hand side, write the words "Things I don't do." In the "Things I do" column, list tips the author gives which you already do while taking notes. In the "Things I don't do" column, list those things you don't do now but, according to the article, might help you take better notes. Then write a paragraph on the tips you know help you take notes and those you haven't tried yet but hope will help you take better notes.

2. White says that the best lecturers "combine knowledge with expert showmanship" and are "informative and entertaining speakers" who "can make any subject . . . leap vividly to life." If you're lucky, you've known at least one teacher who is both well-informed and entertaining. Write about this teacher, listing and illustrating two or three of his or her ways of keeping students interested. As an alternative, describe a teacher you've known who was not effective.

Check Your Performance   **CLASSROOM NOTETAKING**

Skill	*Number Right*	*Points*	*Total*
WORD SKILLS QUESTIONS			
Phonics, Word Parts, Dictionary (5 items)	_____	x 10 =	_____
Vocabulary in Context (5 items)	_____	x 10 =	_____
		SCORE =	_____%
COMPREHENSION QUESTIONS			
Central Point and Main Ideas (3 items)	_____	x 7 =	_____
Supporting Details (4 items)	_____	x 7 =	_____
Transitions (3 items)	_____	x 7 =	_____
Mapping (5 items)	_____	x 6 =	_____
		SCORE =	_____%

FINAL SCORES: Word Skills _____%   **Comprehension** _____%

Enter your final scores onto the reading performance chart on the inside back cover.

7

Knowledge Is Power
Anna-Maria Petricic

Preview

When Anna-Maria Petricic read the words "Knowledge is real power" as a student in Croatia, she was intrigued by the phrase. She wasn't sure of its meaning, but she knew that its message was an important one. This is the story of the author's struggle to unlock the secret of that phrase.

Words to Watch

proclaimed (1): announced
essence (1): central point
dismayed (4): discouraged
objective (5): unaffected by personal feelings
certified (8): guaranteed as authentic
terse (9): short and direct
pretentious (10): flashy and egotistical; inclined to show off
imprinted (10): fixed
formidable (13): difficult
shrouded (16): covered
resolved (16): firmly decided
earnestly (17): seriously
steadfast (17): firm; unbending
quest (21): pursuit
ascended (22): climbed

> "Knowledge is real power," proclaimed° the bold letters on a   1
> bookmark showing Superman soaring upward from between two
> blocks of books. As I read this, a wave of energy swept over me. I

studied the bookmark, trying to comprehend its exact meaning. It seemed like the essence° of life was revealed on that small piece of red and blue paper. But, as a teenager in high school, I had no idea what it meant. I only knew that this great excitement I was experiencing had something to do with knowledge. I wanted the power that knowledge brought. For that to happen, I knew I had to attend college. I also knew that this would not be easy.

As a high school student in Sisak, a town near Zagreb, Croatia, all   2
I heard were horror stories about college. "First you sweat preparing for the entrance exams. If you survive that and are lucky enough to be accepted into college, you must deal with your teachers. They will be your enemies for the next four years. The first lesson they teach is that they will do everything they can to crush your confidence, to break your spirit, to make you quit." Such tales were commonly whispered in the high school hallways by students aspiring to go to college.

I was shocked. Surely these stories could not be true. College was   3
supposed to build my confidence in the process of attaining knowledge. Teachers were supposed to encourage me with their wisdom and compassion. They should prepare me for all challenges, not turn me against learning. The more I heard the whispers, the more convinced I became that I must not attend college in my homeland. If I wanted knowledge, I must attend a university in America.

I read all I could about colleges in the U.S. I was dismayed°. The   4
costs were staggering. Then I read about a small, private university in Iowa that was offering work-study scholarships for international students. The school would cover tuition, room, and board in exchange for a twenty-hour-per-week work commitment. In return, students had to show the university that they had sufficient funds in the bank for health insurance and personal expenses. Including airfare from Croatia to America, I calculated that I would need $2,000 per year.

I could hardly contain myself. I dashed into the kitchen that cold   5
winter evening to proudly announce the news to my mother. "I am going to school in America!" My mother looked up at me while still working in the foamy sink full of dirty dishes. "Yes? And who is going to pay for that?" My mother's voice was heavy yet coolly objective°. In my excitement, I overlooked the fact that my mother hardly made enough money to provide for our immediate needs. I brushed that thought aside, not willing to let it spoil my enthusiasm. I wanted my mother's support. Everything else would work out somehow.

I eagerly wrote a letter of inquiry to the American university.   6
Within a couple of weeks, I received a thick envelope. My mother stood beside me while I ripped it open and spread the contents on the table. I picked up the letter on top. It was from the dean of the College

of Arts and Sciences. I was blinded with tears as I read the words of encouragement and warm invitation to attend the college. I felt that at this school, my desire for education would be sacredly cherished and respected. My educational heaven was waiting in America. To get there, I knew that I had to be prepared to wage a long, hard battle. And I had to start now.

7   When she saw how understanding the university was, my mother took a strong stand of support. She vowed to do all she could to help make my dream become reality. She pointed to a row of dictionaries on the bookshelf. I reached for the Croatian-English dictionary and began the first of many long, difficult, and sometimes discouraging steps.

8   Although my English was quite good, the application forms sent by the college included many words I didn't understand. After a few hours of trying to interpret meanings and of translating, my head was spinning. I needed to take the Test of English as a Foreign Language (TOEFL) and the Scholastic Aptitude Test (SAT). I also needed to send a certified° translation of my high school transcripts. The application deadline was in April. I was not even going to get my high school diploma until June. Suddenly, everything was moving so fast. I couldn't keep up. "Maybe I should postpone this until next year," I thought. We had little money, and I wasn't even sure I could get accepted. I could attend the University of Zagreb for a year, and then transfer the units. My mother suggested that I send a letter to the admissions officer explaining the situation.

9   After sending the letter, I went to a branch of the University of Zagreb to get information about the entrance exams. I waited for an hour in a small, crowded room thick with cigarette smoke. Two ladies behind the admissions desk provided meager answers to students' questions. The women were apparently upset that all these students were wasting their precious gossip time. Their sharp, terse° responses offered no help. Instead, they managed to make the students feel guilty for even asking. I gave up in my attempt to find out about the entrance exams.

10   As I walked toward the exit, I stopped to observe the college students who were in the hallway. They wore torn jeans, and they spoke in pretentious° sentences. Their eyes were dull and they had lifeless smiles imprinted° on pale faces. Burning cigarette butts between their fingers were their only well-defined feature. I did not know whether to feel pity for them or for myself. As I left the building, I was both disappointed and humiliated. I had only been there for an hour, and I wondered how I would feel after four years of classes here. My dream had spoiled me. I wanted the luxury of being treated like a human being, and I knew just the place where that would happen.

Shortly, I received a new letter from my admissions officer in   11
Iowa that provided encouragement. He asked me to continue my
application process and said that I should not worry about my high
school transcripts. They could be mailed as soon as I graduated. What
was needed at this time were my test results.

A month later, I took the TOEFL and SAT at the American school   12
in Zagreb. I had studied hard and was satisfied with my performance.
The results of both tests were sent directly to the university in America.
When the admissions officer received them, he called me to offer
congratulations. I had done well. My application was almost complete.
Besides my transcripts, which I knew would not be a problem, I needed
only one more thing: the money.

My mother joined forces with me in this last, but most   13
formidable°, obstacle. She borrowed money from a friend and deposited
it in my account so that I could obtain the bank's confirmation that I had
the funds required by the university. However, at the last minute, my
mother's friend decided that he needed his money back. I was forced to
withdraw the money.

When I returned home from the bank, I found my mother   14
unwrapping our old paintings, works of art by Vladimir Kirin, a famous
Croatian artist who was now deceased. Mother had collected his work
for as long as I can remember and had planned to open an art gallery in
the artist's memory. As I walked across the room, my mother's words
stopped me in my tracks. "You have to write an ad for the weekend
paper," she said. These paintings meant more than anything to my
mother. Yet she was prepared to sell them so that I could live my
dream.

The ad was placed. All we had to do was wait for the phone calls.   15
But none came. After two weeks, we ran the ad again, but nothing
happened.

I suddenly felt afraid. Even though I could see myself walking   16
around the campus of my new college, even though I could visualize
my new classrooms and teachers, it was all still just a dream. I felt like
I was looking at slowly dissolving fog. The dream world was fading
away, leaving the old, gray reality. I was trapped in truth that I could
not accept. I became paralyzed as I imagined myself slowly sinking
into ignorance and despair. I would become one of those lifeless, gray
faces that walked daily to the bus station through the smog-shrouded°
streets. I would work with people who can only afford to think about
survival, people who see no values beyond the crispness of bills in their
wallets. The ignorant world threatened to swallow me. Though scared

to death, I resolved° not to yield. I was not just fighting for money; I was fighting for principle. I would not live a life of deliberate humiliation. I refused to expect from life only as much as others thought I should expect. I alone was responsible to make the best of my life. I had to continue my fight.

17 For the first time in my life, I earnestly° prayed for myself. I went to church in the early afternoon when I knew nobody would be there. My wooden-soled shoes echoed on the cold floor that led to the main altar. I knelt down and prayed. I prayed for *money*. That humiliated me because I have always thought it was selfish to pray for myself. My prayers had always been devoted to my friends, family, and to those who suffered. I never prayed for anything for myself because I believed that if God took care of the world, I would be taken care of. Now, I prayed for the most selfish thing of all, and I hated myself for it. Full of shame, I prayed, my eyes steadfast° on the ground. Finally, I gained enough strength to look up at the crucifix. I surrendered completely. I forgot all of my thoughts, and my mind began to flow toward some new space. The pressure dissolved. I felt as if I'd been let out of prison. I was free. My guilt and shame were gone, and my heart was beating with a new force. Everything was going to be fine.

18 In the meantime, my mother continued to search for funds. She called an old friend who owned a jewelry store. He had known me since I was a little girl and bragged that he would do anything for me. He fell silent when he heard my mother's request. He was sorry, but he had just invested all of his money in a new project. He tried to comfort my mother. "I would teach her myself if she were my daughter," he boasted. "School in America. Who does she think she is? She doesn't need college. A woman shouldn't be too smart. She can marry either of my two sons. I promise she will have the freedom to go to church whenever she wants. What more could she need?" Struggling to remain civil, my mother thanked him sarcastically and walked away.

19 Time was slipping by. I had already obtained a U.S. visa, and I had made my air reservation. The travel agent found a cheap student rate. Despite strict regulations, she was willing to sell me a one-way ticket. My hopes were raised, but even the low-cost ticket had to be paid for. And there was precious little time.

20 That evening, my mother, brother, grandmother, and I gathered in the living room of our small apartment. I stared at the wall. My brother leaned against the doorway cursing fate. My grandmother tightly held her prayer book, her lips moving slowly. Gloomy silence threatened to break down the walls. Then, as if by magic, words I did not think about came from my lips. "Mother, what about a credit card?" Unlike

America, it was not easy to obtain a credit card in Croatia. Yet my mother knew an influential officer of a local bank. Could he help us? My mother sighed and acknowledged that it was worth a try. Once again my hopes were raised.

21 I returned home from school the next day to find a sense of calm that our household had not known for weeks. Before I had a chance to ask, my mother smiled and nodded her head. My prayers had been answered. My quest° for knowledge was to become a reality.

22 Later that summer, I was on a flight to America. As the plane ascended° into the clouds, my thoughts turned from the quickly disappearing city I was leaving to the destination I knew so little about. I suddenly realized that I was all alone. I was on my own. Everything that happened from that moment on would be the result of my own actions. I was not afraid. My dream had come true, and I was about to begin living a different reality.

23 That reality turned out to be all that I wanted: loving teachers, a real chance to pursue knowledge, and wonderful friends from all over the world. My life as a college student is better than I ever dreamed. It has not been easy. In my job with the University Food Service, I have had to work very hard. I have also had to deal with some irresponsible and disinterested students who refuse to carry out their assignments or pretend they don't understand simple instructions. I must remind myself that this is the only way to keep my scholarship. But my work has many rewards. I have become assistant director of Food Services. I have also received the first Outstanding Student-Employee Award presented by the university, and my work has been recognized by the Board of Trustees.

24 And I have begun the study of literature. This has opened up a new world for me. Every reading assignment, each class discussion has deepened my understanding of life. I am getting to know myself. I can feel the power growing inside me as I complete each assignment. I am beginning to live the magic of knowledge. In everything I learn, I find the same lesson: I can never know everything, but with what I know, I can accomplish anything. The old Superman bookmark is pasted on my door: "Knowledge is real power." Now I know what it means.

WORD SKILLS QUESTIONS

A. Use your knowledge of phonics, word parts, and the dictionary to answer the questions below. The questions are based on the following passage from the selection.

> Shortly, I received a new letter from my admissions officer in Iowa that provided encouragement. He asked me to continue my application process and said that I should not worry about my high school transcripts. They could be mailed as soon as I graduated. What was needed at this time were my test results. (Paragraph 11)

Consonants

1. A word that contains a consonant digraph is
   a. *letter.*
   b. *process.*
   c. *should.*
   d. *what.*

Vowels

2. A word that follows the silent-e rule is
   a. *new.*
   b. *letter.*
   c. *he.*
   d. *time.*

Syllables

3. The words *received*, *about*, and *results* are divided into syllables according to which rule?
   a. When two consonants come between two vowels, divide between the consonants.
   b. When a single consonant comes between two vowel sounds, divide before the consonant.
   c. Compound words are divided between the words they contain.

Word Parts

4. The word *application* means
   a. act of applying.
   b. after applying.
   c. similar to applying.

Dictionary Use

5. The word *continue* would appear on a page with which two guidewords?
   a. consist / constitutional
   b. constitutive / contaminate
   c. contd. / continuum
   d. contort / control

B. Use context clues to help you decide on the best definition for each italicized word. Then circle the letter of your choice.

6. The word *comprehend* in "I studied the bookmark, trying to comprehend its exact meaning" (paragraph 1) means
   a. forget.
   b. write down.
   c. understand.
   d. pass by.

7. The word *aspiring* in "Such tales were commonly whispered in the high school hallways by students aspiring to go to college" (paragraph 2) means
   a. paying.
   b. hoping.
   c. remembering.
   d. forgetting.

8. The word *attaining* in "College was supposed to build my confidence in the process of attaining knowledge" (paragraph 3) means
   a. recognizing.
   b. creating.
   c. pleasing.
   d. gaining.

9. The word *meager* in "Two ladies behind the admissions desk provided meager answers to students' questions. The women were apparently upset that all these students were wasting their precious gossip time" (paragraph 9) means
   a. complicated and difficult.
   b. complete.
   c. careful.
   d. brief and inadequate.

10. The word *civil* in "Struggling to remain civil, my mother thanked him sarcastically and walked away" (paragraph 18) means
    a. outraged.
    b. feminine.
    c. polite.
    d. superior.

READING COMPREHENSION QUESTIONS

Central Point and Main Ideas

1. Which sentence best expresses the central point of the selection?
   a. There are big differences between Croatia and America.
   b. Education is better in the United States than in Croatia.
   c. By not giving up, the author has achieved the college experience she dreamed of.
   d. Colleges and universities should provide more low-cost opportunities for foreign students.

2. Which sentence best expresses the main idea of paragraph 2?
   a. Petricic spent her high school years in Croatia.
   b. As a high school student, Petricic heard horror stories about college.
   c. Petricic was told that college entrance exams were very difficult.
   d. Petricic was warned that college teachers would be her enemies.

3. Which sentence best expresses the main idea of paragraph 23?
   a. Even though she has become a successful college student, Petricic is disappointed with life in America.
   b. Despite difficulties, Petricic is happy with how things have turned out in America.
   c. Petricic's hard work in Food Services has paid off with an award and official recognition.
   d. Petricic must work hard to keep her scholarship.

Supporting Details

4. _F_ TRUE OR FALSE? According to the author, in order to be accepted to the university, all she needed to show was that she had enough money.

5. According to the author,
   a. one of her mother's friends was able to help her go to college in the United States.
   b. selling precious paintings helped her raise the money she needed.
   c. the University of Zagreb was willing to offer her a scholarship.
   d. she was able to raise the money to begin college in the United States through a credit card.

6. When Petricic's mother called an old friend who owned a jewelry store,
   a. he promised to help.
   b. he said he had just invested his money in another project.
   c. he said he would have helped if Anna-Maria were a boy instead of a girl.
   d. he promised to give Anna-Maria jewelry if she married one of his sons.

7. _T_ TRUE OR FALSE? Petricic has to keep her job with the University Food Service in order to keep her scholarship.

Transitions

8. The relationship between the second part of the sentence below and the first part is one of
   a. cause and effect.
   b. comparison.
   c. contrast.
   (d.) time.

   > After sending the letter, I went to a branch of the University of Zagreb to get information about the entrance exams. (Paragraph 9)

9. The sentence below expresses a relationship of
   a. time.
   b. comparison.
   c. contrast.
   (d.) cause and effect.

   > I never prayed for anything for myself because I believed that if God took care of the world, I would be taken care of. (Paragraph 17)

10. The transition in the second sentence below signals
   (a.) an addition.
   b. a comparison.
   c. an example.
   d. a cause and effect.

   > In my job with the University Food Service, I have had to work very hard. I have also had to deal with some irresponsible and disinterested students who refuse to carry out their assignments or pretend they don't understand simple instructions. (Paragraph 23)

MAPPING ACTIVITY

This selection was written according to a time order. Complete the map on the next page by filling in the following statements that divide the reading into a few parts.

- Petricic decides to go to college.
- She decides that going to a special college in the U.S. would be better than attending the University of Zagreb.
- Finally in the U.S., Petricic has found her new life to be all that she had hoped for.
- As a high school student, Petricic is inspired by the words "Knowledge is real power."
- After much struggle, Petricic and her family find the money needed to get to the U.S.

Central point: With persistence and support, Petricic has achieved the education she wished for.

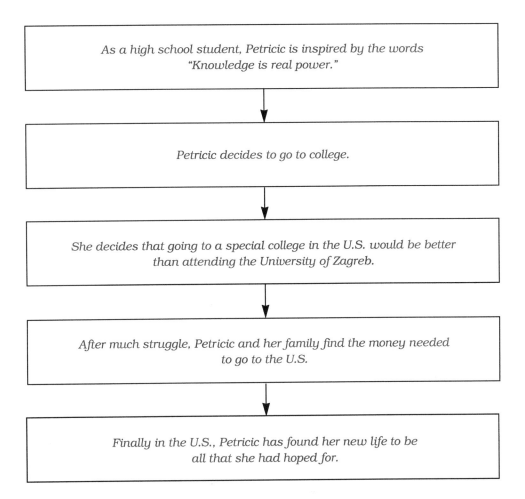

As a high school student, Petricic is inspired by the words "Knowledge is real power."

Petricic decides to go to college.

She decides that going to a special college in the U.S. would be better than attending the University of Zagreb.

After much struggle, Petricic and her family find the money needed to go to the U.S.

Finally in the U.S., Petricic has found her new life to be all that she had hoped for.

DISCUSSION QUESTIONS

1. The author writes that when she went to high school, students told horror stories about college. When you were in high school, what was your perception of college? Now that you are in college, has your perception changed? If so, in what ways?

2. At the conclusion of the selection, Petricic writes that she now knows the meaning of the words "Knowledge is real power." What do these words mean to you?

WRITING ACTIVITIES

1. The author knew that coming to America would not be easy. There were times when she was afraid her dream would not be realized. Write a paragraph telling of something you wanted very badly, but were afraid you would not be able to attain. Tell of the struggles you had to overcome to get to your goal. How did you finally reach it?

2. Petricic would not have been able to come to America without the support of her mother. Who has helped you the most in your quest for education? Write a paper explaining who this person is and how he or she has helped you. Use the kind of specific detail Petricic has used in her essay to dramatize your story for your readers.

Check Your Performance   **KNOWLEDGE IS POWER**

Skill	Number Right	Points	Total
WORD SKILLS QUESTIONS			
Phonics, Word Parts, Dictionary (5 items)	_____	x 10 =	_____
Vocabulary in Context (5 items)	_____	x 10 =	_____
		SCORE =	_____ %
COMPREHENSION QUESTIONS			
Central Point and Main Ideas (3 items)	_____	x 7 =	_____
Supporting Details (4 items)	_____	x 7 =	_____
Transitions (3 items)	_____	x 7 =	_____
Mapping (5 items)	_____	x 6 =	_____
		SCORE =	_____ %

FINAL SCORES: **Word Skills** _____ %   **Comprehension** _____ %

Enter your final scores onto the reading performance chart on the inside back cover.

8

A Brother's Lesson
Christopher de Vinck

Preview

We can learn from the most unexpected sources. This story tells what one man learned from his brother, who was blind and could not speak. What could you possibly learn from such a helpless human being? Quite a lot, as you will discover from this reading.

Words to Watch

mute (1): not able to speak
stammered (3): spoke with pauses or repetitions without meaning to
confirmed (10): admitted (someone) to full membership in the church
insight (11): understanding
hyperactive (12): overly active
sheepishly (14): in an embarrassed way

I grew up in the house where my brother was on his back in his 1
bed for almost 33 years, in the same corner of his room, under the same
window, beside the same yellow walls. Oliver was blind, mute°. His
legs were twisted. He didn't have the strength to lift his head or the
intelligence to learn anything.

Today I am an English teacher, and each time I introduce my class 2
to the play about Helen Keller, *The Miracle Worker*, I tell my students

about Oliver. One day, during my first year teaching, a boy in the last row raised his hand and said, "Oh, Mr. de Vinck. You mean he was a vegetable."

I stammered° for a few seconds. My family and I fed Oliver. We   3
changed his diapers, hung his clothes and bed linen on the basement line in winter, and spread them out white and clean on the lawn in the summer. I always liked to watch the grasshoppers jump on the pillowcases.

We bathed Oliver. Tickled his chest to make him laugh.   4
Sometimes we left the radio on in his room. We pulled the shade down over his bed in the morning to keep the sun from burning his tender skin. We listened to him laugh as we watched television downstairs. We listened to him rock his arms up and down to make the bed squeak. We listened to him cough in the middle of the night.

"Well, I guess you could call him a vegetable. I called him Oliver,   5
my brother. You would have liked him."

One October day in 1946, when my mother was pregnant with   6
Oliver, her second son, she was overcome by fumes from a leaking coal-burning stove. My oldest brother was sleeping in his crib, which was quite high off the ground so the gas didn't affect him. My father pulled them outside, where my mother revived quickly.

On April 20, 1947, Oliver was born. A healthy looking, plump,   7
beautiful boy.

One afternoon, a few months later, my mother brought Oliver to a   8
window. She held him there in the sun, the bright good sun, and there Oliver looked and looked directly into the sunlight, which was the first moment my mother realized that Oliver was blind. My parents, the true heroes of this story, learned, with the passing months, that blindness was only part of the problem. So they brought Oliver to Mt. Sinai Hospital in New York for tests to determine the extent of his condition.

The doctor said that he wanted to make it very clear to both my   9
mother and father that there was absolutely nothing that could be done for Oliver. He didn't want my parents to grasp at false hope. "You could place him in an institution," he said. "But," my parents replied, "he is our son. We will take Oliver home of course." The good doctor answered, "Then take him home and love him."

Oliver grew to the size of a 10-year-old. He had a big chest, a   10
large head. His hands and feet were those of a five-year-old, small and soft. We'd wrap a box of baby cereal for him at Christmas and place it under the tree; pat his head with a damp cloth in the middle of a July heat wave. His baptismal certificate hung on the wall above his head. A bishop came to the house and confirmed° him.

Even now, five years after his death from pneumonia on March 11
12, 1980, Oliver still remains the weakest, most helpless human being I
ever met, and yet he was one of the most powerful human beings I ever
met. He could do absolutely nothing except breathe, sleep, eat and yet
he was responsible for action, love, courage, insight°. When I was
small my mother would say, "Isn't it wonderful that you can see?" And
once she said, "When you go to heaven, Oliver will run to you,
embrace you, and the first thing he will say is 'Thank You.'" I
remember, too, my mother explaining to me that we were blessed with
Oliver in ways that were not clear to her at first.

So often parents are faced with a child who is severely retarded, 12
but who is also hyperactive°, demanding or wild, who needs constant
care. So many people have little choice but to place their child in an
institution. We were fortunate that Oliver didn't need us to be in his
room all day. He never knew what his condition was. We were blessed
with his presence, a true presence of peace.

When I was in my early 20s I met a girl and fell in love. After a 13
few months I brought her home to meet my family. When my mother
went to the kitchen to prepare dinner, I asked the girl, "Would you like
to see Oliver?" for I had told her about my brother. "No," she
answered.

Soon after, I met Roe, a lovely girl. She asked me the names of 14
my brothers and sisters. She loved children. I thought she was
wonderful. I brought her home after a few months to meet my family.
Soon it was time for me to feed Oliver. I remember sheepishly° asking
Roe if she'd like to see him. "Sure," she said.

I sat at Oliver's bedside as Roe watched over my shoulder. I gave 15
him his first spoonful, his second. "Can I do that?" Roe asked with
ease, with freedom, with compassion, so I gave her the bowl and she
fed Oliver one spoonful at a time.

The power of the powerless. Which girl would you marry? Today 16
Roe and I have three children.

WORD SKILLS QUESTIONS

A. Use your knowledge of phonics, words parts, and the dictionary to answer the questions below. The questions are based on the following passage from the selection.

> One October day in 1946, when my mother was pregnant with Oliver, her second son, she was overcome by fumes from a leaking coal-burning stove. My oldest brother was sleeping in his crib, which was quite high off the ground so the gas didn't affect him. My father pulled them outside, where my mother revived quickly. (Paragraph 6)

Consonants

1. Which of the following words from the paragraph have consonant digraphs?
   a. *pregnant, from, stove*
   b. *mother, she, which*
   c. *oldest, quite, didn't*

Vowels

2. The word *stove* is an example of which rule for long vowel sounds?
   a. When a word ends in a vowel-consonant-**e**, the vowel before the consonant is long and the final **e** is silent.
   b. When two of certain vowels are together in a word, the first one is long and the second is silent.
   c. A single vowel at the end of a word (other than a silent **e**) usually has a long sound.

Syllables

3. The word *pregnant* is divided into syllables
   a. between two consonants.
   b. before single consonants.
   c. as a compound word.

Word Parts

4. Which of the following has a word part meaning "again or back"?
   a. *overcome*
   b. *affect*
   c. *revived*

Dictionary Use

5. The word *crib* can be found on a dictionary page with the guidewords
   a. cup / current.
   b. contort / control.
   c. Crete / Croatia.

B. Use context clues to help you decide on the best definition for each italicized word. Then circle the letter of each choice.

6. The word *tender* in "We pulled the shade down over his bed in the morning to keep the sun from burning his tender skin" (paragraph 4) means
    a. strong.
    b. easily hurt.
    c. rough.
    d. very clear.

7. The word *overcome* in ". . . she was overcome by fumes from a leaking coal-burning stove" (paragraph 6) means
    a. warmed.
    b. protected.
    c. impressed.
    d. overpowered.

8. The word *revived* in "she was overcome by fumes. . . . My father pulled them outside, where my mother revived quickly" (paragraph 6) means
    a. died.
    b. laughed loudly.
    c. fell asleep.
    d. returned to consciousness.

9. The words *grasp at* in "He didn't want my parents to grasp at false hope" (paragraph 9) mean
    a. reach for.
    b. fear.
    c. turn away from.
    d. be responsible for.

10. The word *severely* in "So often parents are faced with a child who is severely retarded, but who is also hyperactive, demanding or wild, who needs constant care" (paragraph 12) means
    a. quietly.
    b. seriously.
    c. not at all.
    d. religiously.

READING COMPREHENSION QUESTIONS

Central Point and Main Ideas

1. Which sentence best expresses the central point of the selection?
    a. Parents are often forced to place very hyperactive and retarded children in institutions.
    b. Oliver's condition was caused by his mother's exposure to fumes from a coal stove.
    c. The author married Roe because she was nice to Oliver.
    (d.) Despite Oliver's total helplessness, de Vinck and his family benefited greatly from Oliver's presence.

2. Which sentence best expresses the main idea of paragraph 4?
    a. Despite his condition, Oliver liked to watch television.
    b. Oliver's skin was sensitive to sunlight.
    (c.) Oliver received lots of attention from his family.
    d. Oliver's family worried whenever he coughed.

3. Sometimes a main idea covers several paragraphs. Which sentence best expresses the main idea of paragraphs 13–16?
    a. The first girlfriend the author brought home did not want to see Oliver.
    b. The second girlfriend the author brought home did want to see Oliver and then asked to feed him.
    (c.) His girlfriends' reactions to Oliver helped de Vinck decide to marry his second girlfriend.
    d. The author fell in love with two girls when he was in his early 20s.

Supporting Details

4. Oliver's parents
    a. considered putting Oliver in an institution.
    b. wanted to put Oliver in an institution, but could not afford it.
    (c.) preferred to care for Oliver themselves at home.
    d. were ordered by a doctor not to care for Oliver at home.

5. Oliver
    a. enjoyed watching television.
    b. never laughed.
    c. was hyperactive, wild and demanding.
    (d.) did not require full-time care.

6. When Roe first came to visit Oliver's house, she
    a. refused to see Oliver.
    b. started feeding Oliver immediately.
    (c.) asked the author if she could feed Oliver.
    d. acted embarrassed and uncomfortable.

7. _F_ TRUE OR FALSE? Oliver died when he was ten years old.

Transitions

8. The relationship of the first sentence below to the ones that follow it is one of
   a. addition.
   b. comparison.
   (c.) contrast.
   d. cause and effect.

   > "You could place him in an institution," he said. "But," my parents replied, "he is our son. We will take Oliver home of course." (Paragraph 9)

9. The transitions at the beginning of the sentences below signal
   (a.) time.
   b. comparison.
   c. examples.
   d. cause and effect.

   > When I was in my early 20s I met a girl and fell in love. After a few months I brought her home to meet my family. (Paragraph 13)

10. The transition *so* in the sentence below signals a relationship of
    a. time.
    b. comparison.
    c. contrast.
    (d.) cause and effect.

    > Roe asked with ease, with freedom, with compassion, so I gave her the bowl and she fed Oliver one spoonful at a time. (Paragraph 15)

MAPPING ACTIVITY

Major events of the selection are scrambled in the list below. Write them in the diagram in the order in which they happened.

- Oliver's mother finds out that Oliver is blind.
- Roe feeds Oliver, and de Vinck eventually marries her.
- Oliver dies.
- The author's mother is overcome by fumes.
- Oliver is born.

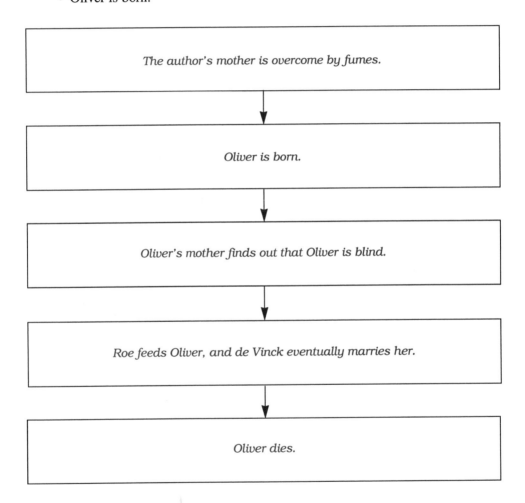

The author's mother is overcome by fumes.

↓

Oliver is born.

↓

Oliver's mother finds out that Oliver is blind.

↓

Roe feeds Oliver, and de Vinck eventually marries her.

↓

Oliver dies.

DISCUSSION QUESTIONS

1. The author states that Oliver was "the weakest, most helpless human being I ever met, and yet he was one of the most powerful human beings I ever met." What do you think he means by this statement?

2. What was de Vinck's girlfriend trying to avoid by not seeing Oliver? What did it show about her as a person? How was her response different from Roe's?

WRITING ACTIVITIES

1. Oliver had a powerful influence on de Vinck's views of "action, love, courage, insight." Who has had a great influence on your views of life? Describe this person, and explain how he or she has affected your values and/or goals. Include at least one example of how you have been influenced by this person—just as de Vinck shows how Oliver influenced his choice of a wife.

2. The author feels his parents were "true heroes." Do you know someone who, in a difficult situation, has acted "heroically"? Write a paper about this person. Explain both the difficult situation and the person's behavior. You can write about a short-term situation—a car accident, being fired, and so on. Or you can write about a long-term problem, such as the one deVinck's parents faced. In either case, include enough detail to show the difficulty of the problem and the character of the person you're writing about.

Check Your Performance		A BROTHER'S LESSON	
Skill	*Number Right*	*Points*	*Total*
WORD SKILLS QUESTIONS			
Phonics, Word Parts, Dictionary (5 items)	_____	x 10 =	_____
Vocabulary in Context (5 items)	_____	x 10 =	_____
		SCORE =	_____ %
COMPREHENSION QUESTIONS			
Central Point and Main Ideas (3 items)	_____	x 7 =	_____
Supporting Details (4 items)	_____	x 7 =	_____
Transitions (3 items)	_____	x 7 =	_____
Mapping (5 items)	_____	x 6 =	_____
		SCORE =	_____ %

FINAL SCORES: Word Skills _____ %   Comprehension _____ %

Enter your final scores onto the reading performance chart on the inside back cover.

9

Looking Back on Our Youth
Darrell Sifford

Preview

A common complaint of the not-so-young is "I wish I'd known years ago the things I know today." Life would be so much easier if we all didn't have to make the same mistakes to gain the wisdom of experience. In this selection, columnist Darrell Sifford tries to save young readers from some of these mistakes. He passes along some of what he's learned through the years.

Words to Watch

midlife (1): middle age
prosper (6): succeed
adversity (6): misfortune
reciprocating (7): paying back
mentors (8): guides
nurture (10): nourish
adequate (11): enough
moderation (11): avoidance of extremes
modify (11): change
excessive (12): too much
blue funk (14): bad mood
solely (15): only

Well, here you are—in midlife° or wherever—and, as you look 1
back, do you realize how little you knew in the bloom of youth, even
though you thought you knew it all?
Do you ever wish that you could go back to those early years and 2

do it all over again—knowing what you now know?

That's not possible, of course. But what may be possible—and what I had the opportunity to do not long ago—is to appear before an audience of high school juniors and seniors and talk to them about "what I wish somebody had told me when I was 17 or 18." 3

What would you say to students? In forty-five minutes, what would you single out as the most important things for them to take away from the meeting? 4

Let me share with you some of what I talked about: 5

The world is not always fair. As adults, some of us know this, but, as adolescents, most of us didn't. We had the sense that good input always resulted in good outcome, that if we did our part, the result would be in line with what we expected. It would be nice if things worked this way, but they don't. The world can be—and often is—a friendly place in which we can prosper°, but, at times, it can be hostile and unfair. People who expect this and who aren't disabled when adversity° strikes them for no reason are way ahead of everybody else. Bad things do happen to good people, and, occasionally, nothing makes sense. 6

Parenting is a tough job—maybe the toughest—and it's helpful to realize sooner than later that parents, for all their flaws, probably are doing the best they can. Try to share with your parents, even if they don't share back with you. *Tell* them you love them and *show* them you love them, even if they aren't comfortable reciprocating°. Question your parents. When it's appropriate, challenge them. But don't grind them down. Don't polish their guilt. Most parents, I'm convinced, feel guilty to some extent about not doing more or doing better for their children. 7

It's important to find mentors° at various stages throughout life. Latch onto somebody who is older and wiser, and let that person guide you around the potholes. What's in it for the mentor? A feeling of satisfaction in helping somebody. Remember that the mentor gets something out of it, too—so don't be afraid of trying to recruit a mentor. 8

We need goals throughout life and plans for pursuing our goals. Goals never stop changing, if we're lucky. We accomplish one goal, and then we move on to the next. Don't ever be without goals, short-range and long-range. They are the fuel that keeps us going. 9

We need relationships. Barbra Streisand says it all in the song: "People who need people are the luckiest people in the world." In the final analysis, the relationships that we nurture° with the few core people in our lives are the most precious things we have. Don't ever get too busy to take time to care for and feed relationships with people who matter. 10

434 TEN READING SELECTIONS

Our bodies are marvelous works of nature, but it's our 11
responsibility to care for them. It's important to get adequate° rest, to
eat reasonably, to act in moderation°. The patterns we set in childhood
often are the patterns we carry into adulthood, so take a look at what
you're doing now—and modify° it if that's called for.

It's a serious world much of the time, but don't be afraid to have 12
fun—and don't ever feel guilty about having fun. The psychologist
Arnold Lazarus, on hearing of the death of a friend, always says the
same thing: "I hope he had enough fun." He doesn't say that he hopes
the person had enough money, a big-enough title, an office with enough
windows. But enough *fun*. How much is enough? Only you can decide
how much is enough for you. Fun doesn't come at the expense of
reasonable responsibility. It comes at the expense of excessive°
seriousness.

What you think about yourself is far more important than what 13
others think about you. If you remember this, you'll never feel the need
to live your life in ways that you *think* will win approval from others.
You can live your life in a way that makes sense to you, that meets your
needs and goals. It's said that life is not for amateurs, and I believe that.
Amateurs are those of us who let others tell us how to run our lives.

People will disappoint you at times and fall short of your 14
expectations. If you always expect perfection or even reasonable
behavior, you're going to find yourself in a blue funk° much of the
time. But if you accept that others, just like you, sometimes shoot
themselves in the foot, you'll consume less Maalox and sleep more
soundly.

You can't control anybody else, but you can control how you react 15
to other people. It's a waste of time and energy to try to change another
person. Use that same time and energy to work on yourself—and you'll
find that life is a lot sweeter for everybody. This is true now and
forevermore. You alone can define what success means to you. Don't
let anybody else try to define success for you. This was what John
Ehrlichman told me was the most important thing he learned from his
Watergate experience. His sin, he said, was letting others sell him their
value systems. How do I now define success? The achievement of a life
that contains a balance of love, work and play. That's a far different
definition than I might have offered twenty years ago, when the focus
solely° was on work.

There's no need to be in any hurry to get married. It's wise to get 16
your life somewhat in place before you complicate it by incorporating
with another person. Marriages that come later seem to prosper more
than marriages that come sooner.

People are more alike than they are different. You're probably 17
more typical than you think you are—so when you feel like an outsider
who is staring in through the window, remember that a lot of other
people feel that way, too. You're probably not odd or weird, just
typical.

If you need help, don't be afraid to ask for it. It's a tremendous 18
burden to go through life with the feeling that you have to do it all by
yourself. There's some virtue, as Frank Sinatra sings, in doing it your
way, but doing it your way doesn't mean that you can't find a firm
shoulder to lean on at times. The strongest people, in my opinion, are
those who know when to ask for help.

Well, that's what I said to the students. How about you? 19

WORD SKILLS QUESTIONS

A. Use your knowledge of phonics, word parts, and the dictionary to answer the
questions below. The questions are based on words taken from the selection.

Consonants

1. A word containing a digraph (a pair of consonants with only one sound) with
   the sound of **f** is
   a. *friend.*
   b. *enough.*
   c. *seriousness.*

Vowels

2. Words pronounced with a short **u** are
   a. *much, fun, enough,* and *money.*
   b. *serious, guilty,* and *you.*
   c. *hearing, only,* and *expense.*

Syllables

3. Words in which prefixes and suffixes are separate syllables include
   a. *expense, reasonable,* and *excessive.*
   b. *always, enough,* and *office.*
   c. *money, windows,* and *doesn't.*

Word Parts

4. The word with a word part that means "a person skilled at something" is
   (a.) *psychologist.*
   b. *person.*
   c. *friend.*

Dictionary Use

5. *Excessive* is accented on the
   a. first syllable.
   (b.) second syllable.
   c. third syllable.

   > **ex·ces·sive** (ĭk-sĕs′ĭv) *adj.* Exceeding [that is, going beyond] what is normal, proper, or reasonable.

B. Use context clues to help you decide on the best definition for each italicized word. Then circle the letter of each choice.

6. The word *hostile* in "The world can be . . . a friendly place . . . , but, at times, it can be hostile and unfair" (paragraph 6) means
   a. generous.
   b. holy.
   c. active.
   (d.) unfriendly.

7. The word *flaws* in "Parenting is a tough job . . . and it's helpful to realize . . . that parents, for all their flaws, probably are doing the best they can" (paragraph 7) means
   a. friends.
   b. talents.
   c. controls.
   (d.) faults.

8. The word *recruit* in "Latch onto somebody who is older and wiser. . . . don't be afraid of trying to recruit a mentor" (paragraph 8) means
   (a.) get.
   b. fire.
   c. teach.
   d. bribe.

9. The word *core* in "the relationships that we nurture with the few core people in our lives are the most precious things we have" (paragraph 10) means
   a. hard-working.
   b. educated.
   (c.) central.
   d. young.

10. The word *incorporating* in "There's no need to be in any hurry to get married. It's wise to get your life somewhat in place before you complicate it by incorporating with another person" (paragraph 16) means
    a. buying.
    b. joining.
    c. meeting.
    d. arguing.

READING COMPREHENSION QUESTIONS

Central Point and Main Ideas

1. Which sentence best expresses the central point of the selection?
   a. The author's experience has taught him what advice to give the young.
   b. Young people need to be told what to do.
   c. Young people think they know everything.
   d. Most people would like a second chance in life.

2. Which sentence best expresses the main idea of paragraph 6?
   a. Young people expect life to be fair.
   b. It would be nice if life were fair.
   c. It's best to realize life is not always fair.
   d. The real world is sometimes a friendly place.

3. The main idea of paragraph 12 can be found in its
   a. first sentence.
   b. second sentence.
   c. next-to-the-last sentence.
   d. last sentence.

Supporting Details

4. _F_ TRUE OR FALSE? According to Sifford, mentors are the most precious things we have.

5. The author tells us that all people have
   a. the same definition of success.
   b. the same goals throughout life.
   c. very little control over the way other people behave.
   d. very little control over the way they react to others.

6. It's a poor idea to
   a. find mentors.
   b. nurture important relationships.
   c. expect perfection in others.
   d. ask for help when you need it.

7. _T_ TRUE OR FALSE? Sifford feels that it is possible to be too serious.

Transitions

8. The transition *even though* in the sentence below signals
   a. addition.
   b. contrast.
   c. an example.
   d. cause and effect.

   > Well, here you are . . . and, as you look back, do you realize how little you knew in the bloom of youth, even though you thought you knew it all? (Paragraph 1)

9. The sentence below contains
   a. a time signal.
   b. a contrast signal.
   c. an example signal.
   d. a cause-and-effect signal.

   > We had the sense . . . that if we did our part, the result would be in line with what we expected. (Paragraph 6)

10. The transition in the middle of the sentence below signals
    a. addition.
    b. time.
    c. contrast.
    d. an example.

    > How do I now define success? (Paragraph 15)

MAPPING ACTIVITY

The ideas in this selection are organized mainly in a list. Five points in that list are missing in the diagram on the next page. Complete the diagram by writing in a brief summary of the missing points.

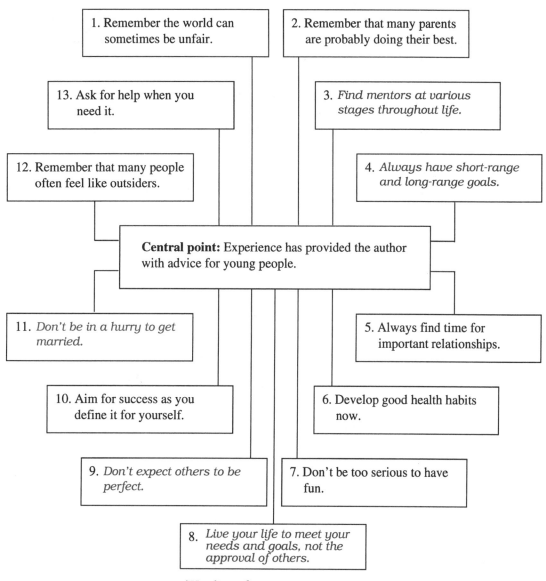

1. Remember the world can sometimes be unfair.

2. Remember that many parents are probably doing their best.

13. Ask for help when you need it.

3. *Find mentors at various stages throughout life.*

12. Remember that many people often feel like outsiders.

4. *Always have short-range and long-range goals.*

Central point: Experience has provided the author with advice for young people.

11. *Don't be in a hurry to get married.*

5. Always find time for important relationships.

10. Aim for success as you define it for yourself.

6. Develop good health habits now.

9. *Don't expect others to be perfect.*

7. Don't be too serious to have fun.

8. *Live your life to meet your needs and goals, not the approval of others.*

(Wording of answers may vary.)

DISCUSSION QUESTIONS

1. Sifford says that "the world is not always fair" and that "bad things do happen to good people." Do you agree? When, in your experience, has the world seemed unfair to you?

2. Of all the things Sifford says, which piece of advice do you think would be hardest for a high school audience to accept? Why did you make the choice you did?

WRITING ACTIVITIES

1. As the author says, it is not possible to go back in life and change things. But what if we could? Write about one thing you have done which you would change if you could. Possible topics include deciding to marry (or not to marry) a certain person at a certain age, deciding to stay at home or to leave home and move into your own place, taking (or not taking) a particular job when it was offered to you, and deciding on a particular career direction.

2. Choose one of Sifford's points and write about an experience that proved its truth to you. For example, you could tell about a time in your life that showed that the world can be unfair, that it's difficult to be a parent, or that people need important relationships. Your topic sentence will be the point you choose from the reading. Your support will be a narrative of the experience that proves the point.

Check Your Performance   LOOKING BACK ON OUR YOUTH

Skill	*Number Right*	*Points*	*Total*
WORD SKILLS QUESTIONS			
Phonics, Word Parts, Dictionary (5 items)	_____	x 10 =	_____
Vocabulary in Context (5 items)	_____	x 10 =	_____
		SCORE =	_____ %
COMPREHENSION QUESTIONS			
Central Point and Main Ideas (3 items)	_____	x 7 =	_____
Supporting Details (4 items)	_____	x 7 =	_____
Transitions (3 items)	_____	x 7 =	_____
Mapping (5 items)	_____	x 6 =	_____
		SCORE =	_____ %

FINAL SCORES: Word Skills _____ %   Comprehension _____ %

Enter your final scores onto the reading performance chart on the inside back cover.

10

How to Write Clearly
Edward T. Thompson

Preview

Do you like to write? Or is writing, in your opinion, pure torture? If you answered "torture," cheer up: you're about to receive some valuable help. Certain tricks of the trade can make writing easier and more effective for everyone. In this selection, the editor-in-chief of *Reader's Digest* shares with you his ideas on how to write what you mean—clearly and briefly.

Words to Watch

clarity (9): clearness
objective (10): unbiased
detract (10): take away from
ironically (14): contrary to what is expected
delete (17): remove
mentality (19): mind
biota (21): living things
mortality (21): death
endeavoring (22): trying
artistry (28): the work of an artist
excess (28): extra
anecdotes (28): brief stories
belabor (28): to explain in too much detail
invariably (28): always

If you are afraid to write, don't be.   1

If you think you've got to string together big fancy words and   2
high-flying phrases, forget it.

To write well, unless you aspire to be a professional poet or 3
novelist, you only need to get your ideas across simply and clearly.

It's not easy. But it is easier than you might imagine. 4

There are only three basic requirements: 5

First, you must *want* to write clearly. And I believe you really do, 6
if you've stayed this far with me.

Second, you must be willing to *work hard*. Thinking means 7
work—and that's what it takes to do anything well.

Third, you must know and follow some *basic guidelines.* 8

If, while you're writing for clarity°, some lovely, dramatic or 9
inspired phrases or sentences come to you, fine. Put them in.

But then with cold, objective° eyes and mind ask yourself: "Do 10
they detract° from clarity?" If they do, grit your teeth and cut the frills.

FOLLOW SOME BASIC GUIDELINES

I can't give you a complete list of "do's and don'ts" for every 11
writing problem you'll ever face.

But I can give you some fundamental guidelines that cover the 12
most common problems.

1. Outline what you want to say.

I know that sounds grade-schoolish. But you can't write clearly 13
until, *before you start*, you know where you will stop.

Ironically°, that's even a problem in writing an outline (i.e., 14
knowing the ending before you begin).

So try this method: 15

- On 3″ x 5″ cards, write—one point to a card—all the points you
  need to make.

- Divide the cards into piles—one pile for each group of points
  closely related to each other. (If you were describing an
  automobile, you'd put all the points about mileage in one pile,
  all the points about safety in another, and so on.)

- Arrange your piles of points in a sequence. Which are most
  important and should be given first or saved for last? Which
  must you present before others in order to make the others
  understandable?

- Now, *within* each pile, do the same thing—arrange the *points* in
  logical, understandable order.

There you have your outline, needing only an introduction and 16
conclusion.

This is a practical way to outline. It's also flexible. You can add, 17
delete° or change the location of points easily.

2. Start where your readers are.

How much do they know about the subject? Don't write to a level 18
higher than your readers' knowledge of it.

CAUTION: Forget that old—and wrong—advice about writing to 19
a twelve-year-old mentality°. That's insulting. But do remember that
your prime purpose is to *explain* something, not prove that you're
smarter than your readers.

3. Avoid jargon.

Don't use words, expressions, phrases known only to people with 20
specific knowledge or interests.

Example: A scientist, using scientific jargon, wrote, "The biota° 21
exhibited a one hundred percent mortality° response." He could have
written: "All the fish died."

4. Use familiar combinations of words.

A speech writer for President Franklin D. Roosevelt wrote, "We 22
are endeavoring° to construct a more inclusive society." F.D.R. changed
it to, "We're going to make a country in which no one is left out."

CAUTION: By familiar combinations of words, I do *not* mean 23
incorrect grammar. *That* can be unclear. Example: John's father says he
can't go out Friday. (Who can't go out? John or his father?)

5. Use "first-degree" words.

These words immediately bring an image to your mind. Other 24
words must be "translated" through the first-degree word before you
see the image. Those are second/third-degree words.

First-degree words	Second/third-degree words
face	visage, countenance
stay	abide, remain, residue
book	volume, tome, publication

First-degree words are usually the most precise words, too. 25

6. Stick to the point.

Your outline—which was more work in the beginning—now   26
saves you work. Because now you can ask about any sentence you
write: "Does it relate to a point in the outline? If it doesn't, should I add
it to the outline? If not, I'm getting off the track." Then, full steam
ahead—on the main line.

7. Be as brief as possible.

Whatever you write, shortening—*condensing*—almost always   27
makes it tighter, straighter, easier to read and understand.

Condensing, as *Reader's Digest* does it, is in large part artistry°.   28
But it involves techniques that anyone can learn and use.

- *Present your points in logical ABC order:* Here again, your
  outline should save you work because, if you did it right, your
  points already stand in logical ABC order—A makes B understandable, B makes C understandable and so on. To write in a
  straight line is to say something clearly in the fewest possible
  words.

- *Don't waste words telling people what they already know:*
  Notice how we edited this: "Have you ever wondered how
  banks rate you as a credit risk? ~~You know, of course, that it's
  some combination of facts about your income, your job, and so
  on. But actually,~~ Many banks have a scoring system. . . ."

- *Cut out excess° evidence and unnecessary anecdotes°:* Usually,
  one fact or example (at most, two) will support a point. More
  just belabor° it. And while writing about something may remind
  you of a good story, ask yourself: "Does it really help to tell the
  story, or does it slow me down?"

  (Many people think *Reader's Digest* articles are filled with
  anecdotes. Actually, we use them sparingly and usually for one
  or two reasons: either the subject is so dry it needs some
  "humanity" to give it life; or the subject is so hard to grasp, it
  needs anecdotes to help readers understand. If the subject is
  both lively and easy to grasp, we move right along.)

- *Look for the most common word wasters:* windy phrases.

Windy phrases	Cut to . . .
at the present time	now
in the event of	if
in the majority of instances	usually

- *Look for passive verbs you can make active:* Invariably°, this produces a shorter sentence. "The cherry tree was chopped down by George Washington." (Passive verb and nine words.) "George Washington chopped down the cherry tree." (Active verb and seven words.)

- *Look for positive/negative sections from which you can cut the negative:* See how we did it here: "The answer ~~does not rest with carelessness or incompetence. It lies largely in~~ is having enough people to do the job."

- Finally, to write more clearly by saying it in fewer words: *when you've finished, stop.*

WORD SKILLS QUESTIONS

A. Use your knowledge of phonics, word parts, and the dictionary to answer the following questions.

Consonants

1. Words with digraphs (two consonants with only one sound) in paragraph 28 are
   a. *people, hard,* and *grasp.*
   b. *think, phrases, shorter,* and *enough.*
   c. *actually, write, words,* and *stop.*

Vowels

2. The words *actually, sparingly, usually*, and *humanity* in paragraph 28 are examples of which pattern for **y** as a vowel?
   a. In the middle of a word, **y** usually sounds like short **i**.
   b. At the end of a one-syllable word, **y** sounds like long **i**.
   c. At the end of a word with more than one syllable, **y** sounds like long **e**.

Syllables

3. *Practical* in "This is a practical way to outline" (paragraph 17) is divided into syllables
   a. between double consonants.
   b. before a single consonant.
   c. using both of the above rules.

Word Parts

4. The word in "The biota exhibited a one hundred percent mortality response" (paragraph 21) that contains a word part meaning "life" is
   a. *biota.*
   b. *exhibited.*
   c. *response.*

Dictionary Use

5. The definition of *jargon* that applies in paragraphs 20 and 21 is
   a. definition 1.
   b. definition 2.

> **jar·gon** (jär′-gən) *n.* **1.** Nonsensical or incoherent talk. **2.** The specialized or technical language of a profession or group.

B. Use context clues to help you decide on the best definition for each italicized word. Then circle the letter of each choice.

6. The word *aspire* in "To write well, unless you aspire to be a professional poet or novelist, you only need to get your ideas across simply and clearly" (paragraph 3) means
   a. pretend.
   b. wish.
   c. neglect.
   d. sweat.

7. The word *fundamental* in "I can't give you a complete list of 'do's and don'ts'. . . . But I can give you some fundamental guidelines that cover the most common problems" (paragraphs 11–12) means
   a. unusual.
   b. extra.
   c. boring.
   d. basic.

8. The word *sequence* in "Arrange your piles of points in a sequence. Which are most important and should be given first or saved for last? Which must you present before others . . . ?" (paragraph 15) means
   a. circle.
   b. time.
   (c.) order.
   d. space.

9. The word *prime* in "do remember that your prime purpose is to *explain* something, not prove that you're smarter than your readers" (paragraph 19) means
   (a.) main.
   b. old.
   c. easy.
   d. not required.

10. The word *sparingly* in "*Cut out excess evidence and unnecessary anecdotes.* . . . Many people think *Reader's Digest* articles are filled with anecdotes. Actually, we use them sparingly" (paragraph 28) means
    a. at the beginning.
    (b.) in a limited way.
    c. pleasantly.
    d. frequently.

READING COMPREHENSION QUESTIONS

Central Point and Main Ideas

1. Which sentence best expresses the central point of the selection?
   a. Many people are afraid to write.
   (b.) Clear writing has three basic requirements.
   c. Good writers know when to stop writing.
   d. Everyone wants to write clearly.

2. Which sentence best expresses the main idea of paragraph 15?
   (a.) Try an outlining method that uses 3″ x 5″ cards.
   b. Write one point to a card.
   c. Put the cards into piles, with each pile containing closely related points.
   d. Arrange the piles in an order.

3. Which sentence best expresses the main idea of paragraph 28?
   a. Present your points in a logical order.
   b. Don't tell people what they already know.
   (c.) There are a few techniques to writing briefly.
   d. Look for and eliminate common word wasters.

Supporting Details

4. The author states that writing well requires
   a. hard work.
   b. getting your ideas across simply and clearly.
   c. learning some basic guidelines for writing.
   d. all of the above.

5. Brief writing
   a. is very boring to read.
   b. is easy to read and understand.
   c. avoids using any examples or anecdotes.
   d. will usually confuse readers.

6. ___F___ TRUE OR FALSE? According to the author, an outline should not be changed after it is written.

7. A clear writer
   a. tells people what they already know.
   b. prefers passive verbs.
   c. makes every sentence relate to the point.
   d. uses big words and fancy phrases.

Transitions

8. Paragraphs 6, 7, and 8 all begin with
   a. addition signals.
   b. comparison signals.
   c. example signals.
   d. cause and effect signals.

9. The transition word that begins the second sentence below shows
   a. comparison.
   b. contrast.
   c. an example.
   d. cause and effect.

   I can't give you a complete list of "do's and don'ts" for every writing problem you'll ever face. But I can give you some fundamental guidelines that cover the most common problems. (Paragraphs 11–12)

10. The relationship of the second sentence below to the first sentence is one of
    a. addition.
    b. time.
    c. comparison.
    d. contrast.

    This is a practical way to outline. It's also flexible. (Paragraph 17)

MAPPING ACTIVITY

The suggestions in this selection are organized into lists of requirements and guidelines. Complete the diagram of the selection below by filling in the missing points—one requirement and four guidelines. *Note: Wording of answers may vary.*

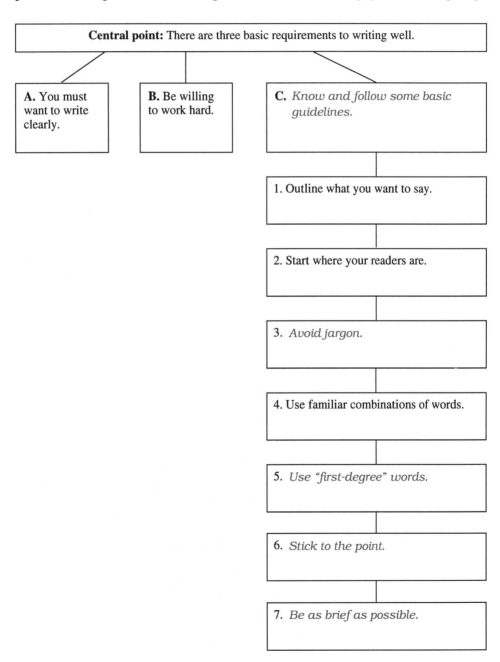

Central point: There are three basic requirements to writing well.

A. You must want to write clearly.

B. Be willing to work hard.

C. *Know and follow some basic guidelines.*

1. Outline what you want to say.

2. Start where your readers are.

3. *Avoid jargon.*

4. Use familiar combinations of words.

5. *Use "first-degree" words.*

6. *Stick to the point.*

7. *Be as brief as possible.*

DISCUSSION QUESTIONS

1. Of the guidelines for writing that Thompson gives in his article, which three are the most valuable for you—and why?

2. Do you think that the author's advice can also apply to speaking clearly? Which suggestions in particular could help make you a better speaker?

WRITING ACTIVITIES

1. Write a letter to Edward Thompson telling him what you think of his suggestions and why. Try to follow his suggestions for clear writing in your letter.

2. Thompson recommends that before people write, they should make an outline—a plan for what they are going to put on paper. In what other activities is planning ahead a good idea? Think of one and write about how to plan such a project. You might, for example, write about one of the following: giving a large party, such as a wedding reception or a graduation party; moving into a new home or apartment; taking a family vacation; going on a special date; writing a term paper. Be sure to describe the steps that must be taken in order for the event to succeed. Your topic sentence will be similar to this one: "There are a few steps one should follow when giving a large party."

Check Your Performance   HOW TO WRITE CLEARLY

Skill	Number Right	Points	Total
WORD SKILLS QUESTIONS			
Phonics, Word Parts, Dictionary (5 items)	_____	x 10 =	_____
Vocabulary in Context (5 items)	_____	x 10 =	_____
		SCORE =	_____%
COMPREHENSION QUESTIONS			
Central Point and Main Ideas (3 items)	_____	x 7 =	_____
Supporting Details (4 items)	_____	x 7 =	_____
Transitions (3 items)	_____	x 7 =	_____
Mapping (5 items)	_____	x 6 =	_____
		SCORE =	_____%

FINAL SCORES: **Word Skills** _____%   **Comprehension** _____%

Enter your final scores onto the reading performance chart on the inside back cover.

APPENDIXES

List of Word Pronunciations

Listed below are all the words used in the vocabulary-in-context and words-to-watch activities in the book.

Pronunciation Key

ă pat	ā pay	â care	ä father	ĕ pet	ē bee	ĭ pit
ī pie, by	î pier	ŏ pot	ō toe	ô paw, for		oi noise
ŏŏ took	ōō boot	ou out	th thin	*th* this		ŭ cut
û urge	yōō abuse	zh vision	ə about, item, edible, gallop, circus			

A

abandon (ə-băn′dən)
abrupt (ə-brŭpt′)
abyss (ə-bĭs′)
achieved (ə-chēvd′)
acquire (ə-kwīr′)
acute (ə-kyōōt′)
adequate (ăd′ĭ-kwĭt)
adversity (ăd-vûr′sĭ-tē)
aerial (âr′ē-əl)
alcove (ăl′kōv′)
ancestors (ăn′sĕs′tərz)
anecdotes (ăn′ĭk-dōts)
annotations (ăn′ō-tā′shənz)
antagonist (ăn-tăg′ə-nĭst)
anxiously (ăngk′shəs-lē)
appalled (ə-pôld′)
apparently (ə-păr′ənt-lē)
ardor (är′dər)
armored (är′mərd)
arrogant (ăr′ə-gənt)
artistry (är′tĭ-strē)
ascended (ə-sĕn′dĭd)
aspire (ə-spīr′)
attained (ə-tānd′)

B

barrier (băr′ē-ər)
belabor (bĭ-lā′bər)
biota (bī-ō′tə)
bleakly (blēk′lē)
blue funk (blōō′ fŭngk′)
blurted out (blûr′tĭd out)
bonding (bŏnd′ĭng)
bottled up (bŏt′əld ŭp)
buffer (bŭf′ər)

bunk (bŭngk)
burrowing (bûr′ō-ĭng)

C

campaign (kăm-pān′)
cement (sĭ-měnt′)
certified (sûr′tə-fīd′)
cipher (sī′fər)
civil (sĭv′əl)
clarity (klăr′ĭ-tē)
cocoons (kə-kōōnz′)
collect myself (kə-lĕkt′ mī-sĕlf′)
comprehend (kôm′prĭ-hĕnd′)
condemned (kən-dĕmd)
confirms (kən-fûrmz′)
confronted (kən-frŭn′tĭd)
conveyed (kən-vād′)
core (kôr)
curriculum (kə-rĭk′yə-ləm′)

D

day-in, day-out (dā-ĭn′ dā-out′)
deaden (dĕd′n)
dearly (dîr′lē)
dejected (dĭ-jĕk′tĭd)
delete (dĭ-lēt′)
deliberation (dĭ-lĭb′ə-rā′shən)
demands (dĭ-măndz′)
demise (dĭ-mīz′)
deported (dĭ-pôr′tĭd)
detested (dē-tĕs′tĭd)
detract (dĭ-trăkt′)
devoured (dĭ-vourd′)
disaster (dĭ-zăs′tər)
disbelief (dĭs′bē-lēf′)
disjointed (dĭs-join′tĭd)
dismayed (dĭs-mād′)
displaced (dĭs-plāst′)
disrupt (dĭs-rŭpt′)
dissected (dĭ-sĕk′tĭd)
distribution (dĭs′trĭ-byōō′shən)
diverse (dĭ-vûrs′)
diversifying (dĭ-vûr′sə-fī′ĭng)

E

earnestly (ûr′nĭst-lē)
embellished (ĕm-bĕl′ĭsht)
embraced (ĕm-brāst′)
emerging (ĭ-mûrj′ĭng)
enchanted (ĕn-chănt′ĭd)
endeavoring (ĕn-dĕv′ər-ĭng)
enumeration (ĭ-nōō′mə-rā′shən)
equivalent (ĭ-kwĭv′ə-lənt)
essence (ĕs′əns)
evading (ĭ-vād′ĭng)
evidence (ĕv′ĭ-dəns)
excess (ĕk′sĕs)
excessive (ĭk-sĕs′ĭv)
exorbitant (ĭg-zôr′bĭ-tənt)
expectant (ĭk-spĕk′tənt)
exult (ĭg-zŭlt′)

F

feeble (fē′bəl)
filial (fĭl′ē-əl)
flashy (flăsh′ē)
flaws (flôz)
foothills (fŏŏt′hĭlz)
foresee (fôr-sē′)
formidable (fôr′mĭ-də-bəl)
fragments (frăg′mənts)
fundamental (fŭn′də-mĕn′tl)

G

ghastly (găst′lē)
glazed (glāzd)
good Samaritan (gŏŏd sə-măr′ĭ-tn)
grapple (grăp′əl)
grasp at (grăsp ăt)
grimaced (grĭm′əst)
grisly (grĭz′lē)
groping (grōp′ĭng)

H

halting (hôl′tĭng)
hectic (hĕk′tĭk)
hibernation (hī′bər-nā′shən)

hordes (hôrdz)
horizon (hə-rī′zən)
hostile (hŏs′təl)
hyperactive (hī′pər-ăk′tĭv)

I

illicit (ĭ-lĭs′ĭt)
immersed (ĭ-mûrst′)
immigrants (ĭm′-ĭ-grənts)
immobile (ĭ-mō′bəl)
imprinted (ĭm-prĭnt′ĭd)
incorporating (ĭn-kôr′pə-rāt-ĭng)
infatuated (ĭn-făch′ōō-ā′tĭd)
insight (ĭn-sīt′)
inspiration (ĭn′spə-rā′shən)
intensely (ĭn-tĕns′lē)
intentions (ĭn-tĕn′shəns)
intriguing (ĭn-trēg′ĭng)
intrinsic (ĭn-trĭn′sĭk)
invariably (ĭn-vâr′ē-ə-blē)
ironic (ī-rŏn′ĭk)
ironically (ī-rŏn′ĭ-kəl-lē)
irony (ī′rə-nē)
isolated (ī′sə-lā′tĭd)

L

lackluster (lăk′lŭs′tər)
larvae (lär′vē)
launching pad (lônch′ĭng păd)
ligament (lĭg′ə-mənt)
literally (lĭt′ər-ə-lē)
lurched (lûrchd)

M

maintaining (mān-tān′ĭng)
meager (mē′gər)
mentality (mĕn-tăl′ĭ-tē)
mentors (mĕn′tôrz)
midlife (mĭd′līf′)
migration (mī-grā′shən)
moderation (mŏd′ə-rā′shən)
modify (mŏd′ə-fī)
monsoon rain (mŏn-sōōn′ rān)

mortality (môr-tăl′ĭ-tē)
mute (myōōt)

N

nurture (nûr′chər)

O

objective (əb-jĕk′tĭv)
oblivious to (ə-blĭv′ē-əs tōō)
occurred (ə-kûrd′)
oppressive (ə-prĕs′ĭv)
overcome (ō′vər-kŭm′)

P

painstaking (pānz′tā-kĭng)
pang (păng)
paranoid (păr′ə-noid′)
pathetic (pə-thĕt′ĭk)
peaked (pēkt)
peers (pîrz)
perennial (pə-rĕn′ē-əl)
perilous (pĕr′əl-əs)
persevered (pûr′sə-vîr′)
pervaded (pər-vā′dĭd)
piety (pī′ĭ-tē)
plantation (plăn-tā′shən)
precision (prĭ-sĭzh′ən)
prescribed (prĭ-skrībd′)
pretentious (prĭ-tĕn′shəs)
prime (prīm)
proclaimed (prō-klāmd′)
prodded (prŏd′ĭd)
prosper (prŏs′pər)
protagonist (prō-tăg′ə-nĭst)

Q

quest (kwĕst)
quips (kwĭps)

R

ragged (răg′ĭd)
rapport (ră-pôr′)

reassuring (rē′ə-shŏŏr′ĭng)
reciprocating (rĭ-sĭp′rə-kāt′ĭng)
recruit (rĭ-krōōt′)
reeled (rēld)
relented (rĭ-lĕn′tĭd)
relieved (rĭ-lēvd′)
rendered (rĕn′dərd)
resignation (rĕs′ĭg-nā′shən)
resilience (rĭ-zĭl′yəns)
resolve (rĭ-zŏlv′)
resolved (rĭ-zŏlvd′)
resounding (rĭ-zound′ĭng)
respect (rĭ-spĕkt′)
responsive (rĭ-spŏn′sĭv)
revive (rĭ-vīv′)
revived (rĭ-vīvd′)
rigorous (rĭg′ər-əs)
role models (rōl mŏd′əlz)
roosts (rōōsts)

S

sadistic (sə-dĭs′tĭk)
sanctuary (săngk′chōō-ĕr′ē)
satirized (săt′ə-rīzd′)
seduces (sĭ-dōōs′əz)
seldom (sĕl′dəm)
sentiment (sĕn′tə-mənt)
sequence (sē′kwĕns)
severely (sə-vîr′lē)
sheepishly (shē′pĭsh-lē)
shield (shēld)
shimmered (shĭm′ərd)
showmanship (shō′mən-shĭp)
shrouded (shroud′ĭd)
shuttled (shŭt′ld)
sit-coms (sĭt′kŏmz)
slope (slōp)
snobbish (snŏb′ĭsh)
solely (sōl′lē)
sound (sound)
sound bite (sound bīt)
sparingly (spâr′ĭng-lē)

stammered (stăm′ərd)
steadfast (stĕd′făst′)
struck (strŭk)
subjects (sŭb′jĭkts)
substantial (səb-stăn′shəl)
subversive (sŭb-vûr′sĭv)
succeeding (sək-sēd′ĭng)
summoned (sŭm′ənd)
supplementary (sŭp′lə-mĕn′tə-rē)
surmount (sər-mount′)
surveys (sûr′vāz)

T

tend (tĕnd)
tender (tĕn′dər)
tendon (tĕn′dən)
terse (tûrs)
Tet (tĕt)
to no avail (tōō nō ə-vāl′)
trek (trĕk)

U

upgrading (ŭp′grād-ĭng)
upward mobility (ŭp′wərd
mō-bĭl′ĭ-tē)
ushers (ŭsh′ərz)

V

valedictorian (văl′ĭ-dĭk-tôr′ē-ən)
veered (vîrd)
veiled (vāld)
vendors (vĕn′dərz)
vice (vīs)
vividly (vĭv′ĭd-lē)
voracious (vô-rā′shəs)

W

wafting (wäft′ĭng)
wails (wālz)
wedge (wĕj)
wedlock (wĕd′lŏk′)
word-base (wûrd bās)

Limited Answer Key

An Important Note: To strengthen your reading skills, you must do more than simply find out which of your answers are right and which are wrong. You also need to figure out (with the help of this book, the teacher, or other students) *why* you missed the questions you did. By using each of your wrong answers as a learning opportunity, you will strengthen your understanding of the skills. You will also prepare yourself for the review and mastery tests in Parts I and II and the reading comprehension questions in Part III, for which answers are not given here.

1   Phonics I: Consonants

Practice 1: Sounds of **c**

2.	hard	6.	hard
3.	soft	7.	soft
4.	hard	8.	hard
5.	soft	9.	hard
		10.	soft

Practice 2: Sounds of **g**

2.	hard	6.	hard
3.	soft	7.	soft
4.	hard	8.	soft
5.	soft	9.	hard
		10.	hard

Practice 3: Blends That Begin with **s**

A.
1.	slime	6.	squeal
2.	sweat	7.	describe
3.	stride	8.	crisp
4.	western	9.	splint
5.	masking	10.	unscrew

B.
1.	Spencer	4.	stubborn
2.	Springfield	5.	swore
3.	smoke		

Practice 4: Blends That End in **l**

A.
1.	flick	6.	ablaze
2.	clash	7.	inflate
3.	blame	8.	glass
4.	imply	9.	unclear
5.	bleed	10.	plug

B.
1.	flag	4.	Glory
2.	fly	5.	plenty
3.	black		

Practice 5: Blends That End in **r**

A.
1.	grape	6.	dragon
2.	prevent	7.	abroad
3.	credit	8.	frog
4.	entrance	9.	uncross
5.	jawbreaker	10.	ungrateful

B.
1.	prefers	4.	break
2.	grass	5.	afraid
3.	track		

Practice 6: Blends at the End of a Syllable or Word

A. 1. sa<u>nk</u>
2. ri<u>ft</u>
3. pu<u>mp</u>
4. mi<u>ld</u>
5. wi<u>nd</u>
6. ha<u>nd</u>cuff
7. ti<u>lt</u>
8. li<u>ft</u>off
9. bu<u>mp</u>
10. pri<u>nt</u>er

B. 1. diffi<u>cult</u>
2. ca<u>mp</u>ing
3. ra<u>ft</u>ing
4. co<u>ld</u>er
5. Disneyla<u>nd</u>

Practice 7: Consonant Digraphs

1. mou<u>th</u>
2. <u>Ch</u>inese
3. starfi<u>sh</u>
4. <u>sh</u>op
5. <u>ph</u>rase
6. cra<u>sh</u>ed
7. <u>ch</u>olesterol
8. <u>ph</u>ony
9. rou<u>gh</u>
10. <u>th</u>ick

Practice 8: Silent Consonants

1. knew
2. Wheaties
3. lamb
4. knead
5. check
6. crumbs
7. wholesale
8. write
9. message
10. muggy

2   Phonics II: Vowels

*Practice in the Short **a** Sound*

3. ă
4. ă
5. X
6. X
7. ă
8. X
9. ă
10. X

*Practice in the Short **e** Sound*

3. X
4. ĕ
5. X
6. ĕ
7. X
8. X
9. ĕ
10. ĕ

*Practice in the Short **i** Sound*

3. ĭ
4. X
5. ĭ
6. X
7. ĭ
8. X
9. ĭ
10. X

*Practice in the Short **o** Sound*

3. X
4. X
5. ŏ
6. ŏ
7. X
8. ŏ
9. X
10. ŏ

*Practice in the Short **u** Sound*

3. ŭ
4. X
5. ŭ
6. ŭ
7. X
8. X
9. ŭ
10. X

Practice in the Long Vowel Sounds

A. 2. X
3. ō
4. X
5. ē
6. ā
7. X
8. ī
9. X
10. ū

B. 1. mule
2. Greece
3. day
4. Gold
5. price
6. three
7. sleep
8. erase
9. tiny
10. huge

*Practice in the Silent-**e** Rule*

1. note
2. fuse
3. like
4. unsafe
5. brave

Practice in the Two-Vowels-Together Rule

2. ā
3. ē
4. ē
5. ō
6. ā
7. ā
8. ō
9. ā
10. ē

Practice in the Rule for a Final Single Vowel

1. ✓
2. X
3. ✓
4. X
5. ✓
6. X
7. ✓
8. X
9. ✓
10. X

Practice in Identifying Vowel Sounds

2. ā
3. ă
4. ō
5. ē
6. ī
7. ĕ
8. ĭ
9. ŏ
10. ŭ

*Practice in the Sounds of **y***

4. ē
5. ī
6. ĭ
7. ī
8. ē
9. ē
10. ĭ

Practice with Long and Short Vowel and Vowels Followed by r

4. ¯	8. r
5. r	9. ¯
6. r	10. ˘
7. ¯	11. ¯
	12. ˘
	13. r
	14. r

Practice in Long and Short **oo**

3. o̅o̅	6. ŏŏ
4. ŏŏ	7. ŏŏ
5. o̅o̅	8. o̅o̅
	9. o̅o̅
	10. ŏŏ

3   Phonics III: Syllables

Practice 1: Numbers of Vowels, Vowel Sounds, and Syllables

3.	2	1	1	8.	2	1	1
4.	2	1	1	9.	3	3	3
5.	2	1	1	10.	2	1	1
6.	2	1	1	11.	3	2	2
7.	2	2	2	12.	3	2	2

Practice 2: Dividing Between Two Consonants

2. can-dy   5. trum-pet
3. nap-kin   6. muf-fin
4. har-bor

Practice 3: Dividing Between Three Consonants

2. cen-tral   5. at-tract
3. ad-dress   6. ob-scure
4. com-plete

Practice 4: Dividing Before a Single Consonant

2. bo-nus   5. ma-jor
3. i-tem   6. u-nit
4. fi-nal

Practice 5: Dividing Before a Consonant and **le**

2. i-dle   5. ti-tle
3. rip-ple   6. gar-gle
4. pur-ple

Practice 6: Dividing After Prefixes and Before Suffixes

2. na-tion   5. jump-ing
3. re-call   6. ex-port
4. play-ful

Practice 7: Dividing Between the Words in a Compound Word

2. note-book   5. work-shop
3. rain-coat   6. cut-back
4. pop-corn

4   Word Parts

Practice 1

1–2. b. include
     c. expired
     d. impersonal

3–4. a. precedes
     b. postwar
     c. postpone
     d. preface

5–6. a. subway
     b. supernatural
     c. subtract
     d. supervisor

7–8. a. mistake
     b. monotone
     c. Monogamy
     d. misbehave

9–10. a. repeat
     b. unlikely
     c. unable
     d. return

Practice 2

11–12. a. manageable
     b. imitation
     c. comfortable
     d. reunion

13–14. a. visitor
     b. scientist
     c. waiter
     d. pianist

15–16. a. thankful
     b. grateful
     c. careless
     d. helpless

17–18. a. Catholicism
     b. imprisonment
     c. excitement
     d. vandalism

19–20. a. childish
     b. immediately
     c. boyish
     d. eagerly

Practice 3

21–22. a. portable
       b. beneficial
       c. benevolent
       d. supporting

23–24. a. Biofeedback
       b. convention
       c. inconvenient
       d. biography

25–26. a. manipulate
       b. podium
       c. manual
       d. pedestrians

27–28. a. television
       b. automobile
       c. autobiography
       d. telephone

29–30. a. audio-visual
       b. audition
       c. spectators
       d. spectacles

5   Dictionary Use

Practice 1

1. blush, boat
2. dodo, dogcart
3. lilac, limousine
4. rainwater, ragtime
5. weightlifting, wedding

Practice 2

1. revise
2. kidnap
3. carry
4. giant
5. really
6. schoolteacher
7. please
8. coming
9. believe
10. tunnel

Practice 3

1. hic•cup, 2
2. min•i•mal, 3
3. dis•pos•al, 3
4. in•sen•si•tive, 4
5. com•mu•ni•ca•tion, 5

Practice 4

1. pot
2. pit
3. cut
4. pat
5. pet

Practice 5

1. mag·net — măg′nĭt
2. jan·i·tor — jăn′ĭ-tər
3. en·cour·age — ĕn-kûr′ĭj
4. spec·u·late — spĕk′yə-lāt′
5. trou·ble·mak·er — trŭb′əl-mā′kər

Practice 6

1. verb, noun
2. noun, adverb, preposition
3. adjective, adverb
4. conjunction, adjective, noun
5. adjective, noun, verb

Practice 7

1. hid, hidden *or* hid, hiding
2. one-upped, one-upping
3. skinnier, skinniest
4. worse, worst
5. parties

Practice 8

1. Definition 2
2. Definition 3
3. Definition 2

Practice 9

1. Latin, "act of sowing"
2. Possibly Old French, "bang into"
3. Arabic, "storehouse"

Practice 10

1. capitalize, profit
2. arctic, chilly, cool, frigid, frosty, gelid, glacial, icy
3. conclusion, determination

6   Vocabulary in Context

Practice 1

1. Examples: *a length of 100', a width of 15', a depth of 10'*; c
2. Examples: *actor Tom Cruise, tennis star Steffi Graf, film critics Siskel and Ebert*; b
3. Examples: *snow leopards, koala bears*; a
4. Examples: *Columbo, Jessica Fletcher*; c
5. Examples: *the thumbs-up sign, a shrug of the shoulders*; c

Practice 2

1. *steady customer*
2. *job*
3. *strengthens*
4. *ridiculous*
5. *fair*

Practice 3

1. *simple*; c
2. *famous*; a
3. *unrelated*; b
4. *mild*; b
5. *serious*; c

Practice 4

1. a	4. a
2. b	5. c
3. b	

7   Main Ideas

Practice 1

A.
1.	pet	6.	bedding
2.	shape	7.	greeting
3.	direction	8.	noise
4.	beverage	9.	command
5.	taxi	10.	punishment

B.
11.	a. bird	b.	sparrow
12.	a. furniture	b.	chair
13.	a. vehicle	b.	car
14.	a. weather	b.	cloudy
15.	a. snack	b.	potato chips
16.	a. planet	b.	Venus
17.	a. dance	b.	polka
18.	a. insect	b.	grasshopper
19.	a. cosmetics	b.	eye shadow
20.	a. job	b.	waiter

(Note: Other answers for the specific ideas in Part B are possible.)

Practice 2

1. 1, 3, 2	6. 2, 1, 3
2. 2, 1, 3	7. 1, 3, 2
3. 2, 1, 3	8. 2, 1, 3
4. 3, 1, 2	9. 3, 2, 1
5. 3, 2, 1	10. 3, 1, 2

Practice 3

1. B	2. T	3. T
T	B	N
N	N	B
addicts	headaches	seat belts
cover	include	surveys

Practice 4

1. N	2. T	3. B
B	B	T
T	N	N

Practice 5

1. MI	2. SD	3. SD
SD	T	MI
SD	MI	T
T	SD	SD
sex		
specific		

Practice 6

A. 1. b	B. 3. c	C. 5. b
broad, narrow, work-sharing	4. c	6. a
2. a		
benefits, employees, employers		

8   Supporting Details

Practice 1

List 1
1. Unusual pets
    a. Snakes
    b. Spiders
    c. Rats
2. Traditional pets
    a. Dogs
    b. Birds
    c. Cats

List 2
1. Junk food
    a. Doughnuts
    b. Potato chips
    c. Candy
2. Healthful food
    a. Apples
    b. Carrot sticks
    c. Raisins

Practice 2

A. 1. The delinquent group
    2. The academic subculture
    3. The fun subculture

B. 1. Remedies that keep people from sleeping on their backs
    2. Anti-snoring chin straps
    3. Surgery

Practice 3

A. 1. Switch to a low-tar, low-nicotine brand.
    2. Allow less smoke to enter your lungs.
    3. Put out the cigarette when it's half gone.

B. 1. Prepare slowly and steadily.
    2. Arrive early for a test.
    3. Answer the easier questions first.
    2. Make a brief outline before beginning to write essay questions.

Practice 4

A. 1. c
   2. b
   3. One

B. 6. c
   7. b
   8. medicine should always be stored in its own labeled bottle.

4. floating on air.
5. air-conditioned domes.
9. other drugs the patient is using.
10. c

9   Locations of Main Ideas

Practice 1

1. 2
2. 1
3. 4
4. 1, 7
5. 2

Practice 2

1. c
2. d
3. a
4. c

Practice: Level 1

1. 3
2. 1
3. 5
4. 1
5. 2

Practice: Level 2

1. 3
2. 1
3. 1, 6
4. 2
5. 1

Practice: Level 3

1. 2
2. 1
3. 6
4. 4
5. 1, 7

Practice: Level 4

1. 1, 9
2. 3
3. 4
4. 4
5. 3

10 Transitions

Note: Answers to practices 1–5 will vary. Some answers to practices 6–10 may vary.

Practice 1

1. Furthermore
2. In addition
3. Moreover
4. Also
5. Another

Practice 2

1. then
2. After
3. often
4. While
5. during

Practice 3

1. like
2. Even though
3. In contrast
4. Despite
5. identical

Practice 4

1. To illustrate
2. For example
3. such as
4. including
5. Once

Practice 5

1. cause
2. on account of
3. As a result
4. because
5. Consequently

Practice 6

1. First
2. Second
3. Next
4. Also

Practice 7

1. Before
2. After
3. then
4. later

Practice 8

1. similar
2. alike
3. However
4. differ

Practice 9

1. For instance
2. including
3. such as

Practice 10

1. consequences
2. result in
3. effects
4. So

Practice 11

1. e
2. d
3. b
4. c
5. a

6. d
7. c
8. b
9. a
10. e

Acknowledgments

The American Heritage Dictionary, Third Paperback Edition. Pronunciation key and entries on pages 90, 92, 94–100, 105, 106, 273, 277, and 281. Copyright © 1994 by Houghton Mifflin Company. Reprinted by permission from *The American Heritage Dictionary*, Third Paperback Edition.

Angel, Juan. "The Struggle Continues." Reprinted by permission.

Broderick, Bill. "Life Over Death." Reprinted by permission.

Chan, Vicky. "Friendship and Living Longer." Reprinted by permission.

de Vinck, Christopher. "A Brother's Lesson." Reprinted by permission of *The Wall Street Journal,* copyright © 1985, Dow Jones & Company, Inc.

Isaacs, Maggie. "Dinner Was Reserved for the Family." Reprinted by permission of Maggie Isaacs and *The Philadelphia Inquirer*.

Kellmayer, John. "The Voyage of Tri Lee." Reprinted by permission.

Kugel, Peter. "Why Johnny Can't Think." Copyright © 1988 by The New York Times Company. Reprinted by permission.

Lam, Andrew. "They Shut My Grandmother's Door." Reprinted by permission.

Lopez, Steve. "Room with a New View." From *The Philadelphia Inquirer*, April 9, 1989. Reprinted by permission.

Malcolm X with Alex Haley. "Discovering Words," from *The Autobiography of Malcolm X* by Alex Haley and Malcolm X. Copyright © 1964 by Alex Haley and Malcolm X. Copyright © by Alex Haley and Betty Shabazz. Reprinted by permission of Random House, Inc.

Marjan, Irina. "My Own Two Feet." Reprinted by permission.

Patrick, Edward. "Rosa: A Success Story." Reprinted by permission.

Petricic, Anna-Maria. "Knowledge Is Power." Reprinted by permission.

Piassa, Bernadete. "A Love Affair with Books." Reprinted by permission.

Robinson, Richard McCaffery. "The Lost Teens." Reprinted by permission.

Sanchez, Peter. "The Amazing Monarch Butterfly." Reprinted by permission.

Sifford, Darrell. "Looking Back on Our Youth." From *The Philadelphia Inquirer*, January 25, 1987. Reprinted by permission.

Thompson, Edward T. "How to Write Clearly." Reprinted by permission of the International Paper Company.

Todhunter, Jean Mizer. "Cipher in the Snow." From *Today's Education,* March-April 1975. Reprinted by permission.

White, Clarissa. "Classroom Notetaking." Reprinted by permission.

Index